The
At Home

Heritage Studies 1

HOME TEACHER'S EDITION

Second Edition

BJU PRESS
Greenville, South Carolina

Note:
The fact that materials produced by other publishers may be referred to in this volume does not constitute an endorsement of the content or theological position of materials produced by such publishers. Any references and ancillary materials are listed as an aid to the student or the teacher and in an attempt to maintain the accepted academic standards of the publishing industry.

Home Teacher's Edition for
Heritage Studies 1 Second Edition

A careful effort has been made to trace the ownership of selections included in this teacher's edition in order to secure permission to reprint copyrighted material and to make full acknowledgment of their use. If any error of omission has occurred, it is purely inadvertent and will be corrected in subsequent editions, provided written notification is made to the publisher.

Writers
Dorothy Buckley
Joyce Garland
Debra White

Contributing Writers
Eileen Berry
Peggy J. Davenport
Rosemerry Hedgpeth
Kimberly A. Pascoe
Dawn L. Watkins
Gail H. Yost

Computer Formatting
Peggy Hargis

Project Editors
Student text
Manda Cooper
Home Teacher's Edition
Carolyn Cooper
Rebecca S. Moore

Graphics Coordinator
Mary Ann Lumm

Graphics
Roger Bruckner
Jim Hargis
Brian Johnson
Sam Laterza
Dick Mitchell
John Nolan
Kathy Pflug
John Roberts
Lynda Slattery
Dan Van Leeuwen
Ruth Ann Ventrello
Christine Danaé Visser
Aaron Weaver

Photo Acquisition
Edward Park
Kim Stegall

Greenville, South Carolina 29614

Printed in the United States of America

ISBN 978-1-57924-076-9

15 14 13 12 11 10 9 8 7 6 5

CONTENTS

Photograph Credits

The following agencies and individuals have furnished materials to meet the photographic needs of this textbook. We wish to express our gratitude to them for their important contribution.

Stewart Aitchison
Suzanne R. Altizer
The Boston Athanaeum
Wes Breedlove
George R. Buckley
George R. Collins
Terry M. Davenport
Department of the Army
Eastman Chemicals Division
Sharon Higgs
International Apple Institute
Italian Tourist Agency
Brian Johnson
Library of Congress
Massachusetts Office of Travel and Tourism
National Gallery of Art
National Park Service
John M. Nolan
Edward S. Park
Debbie Parker
Kathy Pflug
Becky J. Smith
Kim Stegall
United States Department of Agriculture (USDA)
Unusual Films
Kay Washer
Dawn L. Watkins
World Bank

Cover/Title Page
Dawn L. Watkins (all)

Chapter 1
Terry Davenport 1; George R. Collins 2 (top); Dawn L. Watkins 2 (bottom); Unusual Films 3, 7, 11, 14

Chapter 2
Brian Johnson 15; Unusual Films 19 (both); Kim Stegall 24

Chapter 3
Terry Davenport 29; Courtesy of Debbie Parker (arrowheads), Sharon Higgs (peace pipe), and Wes Breedlove 33; George R. Collins 35, 39; Brian Johnson 37; Unusual Films 43, 44

Chapter 4
George R. Collins 45; USDA 55; Unusual Films 57 (all)

Chapter 5
Unusual Films 59, 72; George R. Collins 65; Edward S. Park 71

Chapter 6
George R. Collins 73, 74, 79 (inset); Library of Congress 74 (inset); Eastman Chemicals Division 75; George R. Buckley 76; National Park Service 77; Brian Johnson 79; Stewart Aitchinson 80; Unusual Films 86

Chapter 7
The Boston Athanaeum 87; Unusual Films 88, 92, 94, 95, 96, 97 (all), 98 (left, middle), 100; Suzanne R. Altizer 98 (right), 99

Chapter 8
Dawn L. Watkins 101; George R. Collins 102; Unusual Films 103, 111, 112

Chapter 9
George R. Collins 113, 126 (middle left, bottom left, bottom right); Department of the Army 118; Unusual Films 125; Suzanne R. Altizer 126 (top)

Chapter 10
Unusual Films 127, 129, 134 (both), 137; George R. Buckley 128 (top, bottom); World Bank 128 (middle), 138; George R. Collins 128 (left), 132; Italian Tourist Agency 133

Chapter 11
Unusual Films 139, 142 (bottom inset), 144 (top inset), 145 (bottom inset), 148–49, 149 (top inset), 151, 152 (bottom), 154; Kay Washer 141 (top); Becky J. Smith 141 (bottom left); George R. Collins 141 (bottom right), 144–45, 146–47; USDA 142–43; Suzanne R. Altizer 142 (top inset), 143 (top inset), 148 (bottom inset); International Apple Institution 143 (right inset); Terry Davenport 144 (left inset), 146 (top inset), 148–49 (right inset); Kim Stegall 144 (bottom), 149 (bottom inset); Kathy Pflug 145 (top inset); Dawn L. Watkins 146 (bottom), 148 (top inset), 153; Edward S. Park 152 (top)

Chapter 12
Unusual Films 155, 156, 158, 159, 160, 162, 163, 164, 165 (right), 166 (both), 169, 170; Edward S. Park 157 (all); Kim Stegall 161; Terry Davenport 165 (left); National Gallery of Art 167 (top); Brian Johnson 167 (bottom left, bottom right)

Resource Treasury
Massachusetts Office of Travel and Tourism 172 (both), 173 (top); John M. Nolan 173 (bottom); Unusual Films 174 (both)

Note: Page numbers correspond to the reduced copy of the student textbook pages that appear in this teacher's edition.

Heritage Studies 1 for Christian Schools

written especially for a home setting

1 Encourages Christian growth.

What a child learns in Heritage Studies can affect his spiritual growth and ministry. The child should learn discipline in his approach to and his performance of responsibilities. He should be prepared to evaluate and reject false philosophies. He should have a better testimony among unbelievers.

2 Develops good citizenship through the use of history, geography, economics, culture, and government skills.

The Heritage Studies program emphasizes Christian philosophy, character, and attitudes. It gives the child opportunities to use many skills such as making decisions, inferring relationships, and showing respect for his heritage. It also teaches him practical skills such as reading maps and charts, sequencing events, and working with time lines. Thus, the program promotes a balanced approach to social studies instruction.

3 Promotes historic and geographic literacy.

The goal of historic literacy is to emphasize God's plan for the individual, the family, and the nation. Although history is the study of man's actions, it is essentially the record of God's dealing with men. The Christian teacher must be able to distinguish God's leading in historical events and to impress upon the child the significance of the study. Learning history well helps the child more fully appreciate and comprehend his own times. This broad perspective, then, helps him make better decisions and become a responsible Christian citizen.

4 Presents events by incorporating a more traditional emphasis on skills.

The product of Heritage Studies is organized according to a scope and sequence. The scope is *what* knowledge will be covered in the program. There is disagreement among educators about the scope of knowledge that should be presented on the elementary level. Some still hold to the post-1920s experiment in "socializing" the study of history, organizing the material around the child and his environment. Recent research recommends, however, that true historic and geographic understanding rests on the more traditional emphasis on skills, such as working with maps and sequencing events.

5 Organizes knowledge in a spiral pattern and chronological order.

There are many ways to present Heritage Studies knowledge. For example, it can be organized around a unifying framework of themes. Another approach is a spiral pattern in which the same general topics are taken up periodically—every year, or two or three times in a program. Another option, supported by research and experience, is to study history chronologically, exploring eras in order, thereby helping the child see connections between events. This program combines the spiral pattern and chronological approach.

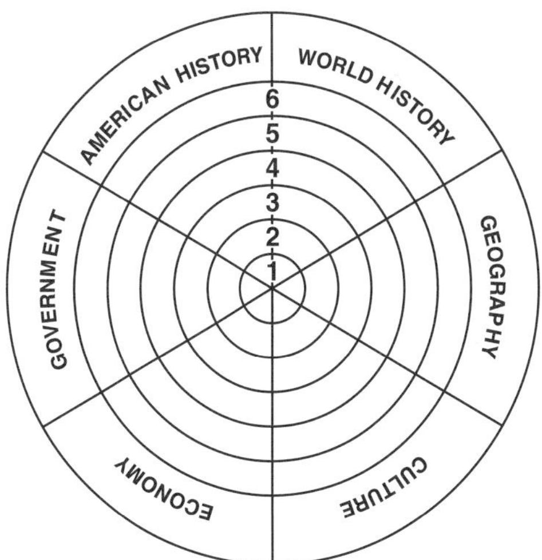

6 Promotes an understanding of and an ability to discern connections among events.

By viewing history in a chronological manner incorporating a time line, the child gains an understanding of and an ability to discern connections among events. He learns about events and people from other countries who influenced his own American heritage and how they relate to each other in history.

7 Strengthens a knowledge of God.

Creation tells us about God (Ps. 19:1; Rom. 1:20). By studying the history of the world and the features of the earth, we can see illustrations of God's wisdom, omnipotence, sovereignty, and benevolence.

TEACHING HERITAGE STUDIES 1

How do I schedule the lessons?

You, the teacher, have a choice in scheduling the teaching of Heritage Studies. Some suggested methods follow.

- You may teach an entire lesson each day, completing the Heritage Studies program in a semester. Science would then be taught the other semester.
- You may teach an entire lesson of Heritage Studies two days a week for the whole year. Science would also be taught two days a week for the whole year.

Day 1

- You may use the scheduling plan provided by the Day symbols in each lesson. By following the numbered days throughout the lesson, you have logical starting and stopping points for discussions and activities. This plan will provide approximately 120 to 130 teaching days.

You will want to arrange the lessons to accommodate your schedule. Many lessons offer several procedures and activities. You may choose to use all of each lesson or only parts of a lesson. You may choose to adapt the material to your own methods. It is recommended that Heritage Studies be taught in twenty- to thirty-minute sessions. The Supplemental lessons are optional.

Where will the needed materials be listed?

You can find lists of the materials you need in order to teach the Heritage Studies program in the following sections of the manual:

Instructional Materials, a section in the introduction to this manual, lists all the essential curriculum items that need to be purchased to teach Heritage Studies 1.

Chapter Overview at the beginning of each chapter contains a list of materials that need to be prepared or purchased ahead of time.

Materials in the Preview of each lesson will list the materials needed to present that particular lesson.

Materials List found in the Supplement of the manual will list all materials needed to teach the entire program.

What pages do I need to copy?

All the pages that you will need to copy for teaching the lessons can be found in the Appendix. The pages in the Supplement may also be copied, though it is not essential. These pages may be viewed by your child directly from the teacher's manual. **Please note:** Although you are permitted to copy pages for your own use, copyright law prohibits the making of copies for any other purpose. Making copies and distributing them in whole or in part to other institutions or individuals is unlawful.

What is in the Student Text?

The student book presents for the child a summary of the more detailed study that the lessons will offer. It reinforces with grade-level text the concepts developed in the teaching time. Although it contains much information, it is only part of the complete package of learning provided by the combination of teacher's edition, TimeLine, student text, and Notebook.

The student book has twelve chapters, each emphasizing one of six categories: American history, world history, geography, government, culture, and economics. To determine the focus of the chapter, look at the color that highlights the chapter number. It corresponds with the color of one of the main category symbols.

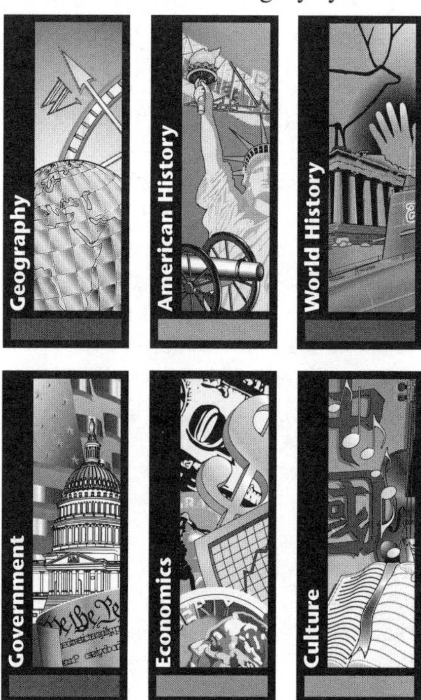

In addition, some chapters have special sections. One such section is *Famous People,* which highlights important or influential people of pre-Colonial America. Another section is *Things People Do,* focusing on common trades, skills, or hobbies of the past and present. The *Learning How* section provides hands-on activities that enliven the lesson and allow your child to experience some flavor of the times as well as learn map skills and develop thinking skills.

What is historic and geographic knowledge?

History and geography can be defined as a body of knowledge. History can also be defined as a way of thinking. The study of these topics, therefore, is a product (body of knowledge) and a process (way of investigating and thinking). The Bob Jones University Press elementary Heritage Studies series continually interweaves the product and process of history and geography.

The products of history and geography are stated in several forms. For example, knowledge can be expressed as a fact. A *fact* is an event that has been observed and recorded by more than one person, the records showing no disagreement among the observers. (This does not mean that a fact cannot be in error.) Knowledge can also be expressed as a *concept,* a mental set of ideas, objects, or events. Finally, knowledge can be expressed as a *principle,* a statement predicting interrelationships among concepts. The Bob Jones University Press elementary Heritage Studies program uses the words *main idea* to include all three forms of knowledge. Note the following examples of each form of knowledge:

- *Fact:* The Separatists founded Plymouth Plantation.
- *Concept:* Religious freedom (The words *religious freedom* encompass the commitment to and struggles for worshiping as one believes proper. To make a mental set of examples that accompany the label, think of people who have sacrificed for their beliefs.)
  - William Tyndale—martyred for translating the Bible into English
  - John Bunyan—imprisoned for preaching
  - The Huguenots—persecuted in France for their beliefs; some fled to America
- *Principle:* The Constitution of the United States guarantees religious freedom. (Notice the interrelationship between the concepts *Constitution* and *religious freedom.*)

How should I teach history and geography skills?

The child should be deriving knowledge through practical experiences that involve action—"hands-on" or "learning-by-doing" activities. Christians can use the inductive method in good conscience, provided they remember that historical recording is fallible and changeable and often disregards many biblical truths. It would be helpful to all Christian teachers to study the principles discussed in *The Christian Teaching of History,* available from Bob Jones University Press.

It is not necessary to follow a certain set of steps, but there are *process skills* employed in this method of teaching. A list of the process skills in the program follows.

- Sequencing events
- Summarizing data
- Making predictions
- Inferring relationships
- Making decisions
- Formulating opinions
- Working with time lines
- Identifying sources of information
- Working with maps and globes
- Using cardinal directions
- Working with tables, graphs, charts, and diagrams
- Identifying key documents
- Valuing the rights of citizenship
- Showing respect for heritage

What attitudes are being developed as I teach?

The dictionary defines *attitude* as "a state of mind or feeling with regard to some matter." Some of the attitudes that you will see develop as your child learns through the Bob Jones University Press Heritage Studies program fall into the following broad categories.

- *Attitudes Toward Schoolwork*
  - Cooperatively share responsibilities and tasks.
  - Demonstrate proper care and handling of maps, globes, and other equipment.
  - Stay with the task in search of comprehension and evaluation of ideas.
- *Attitudes Toward Interests and Careers*
  - Pursue history- or geography-related leisure-time activities.
  - Voluntarily seek additional information about history and related studies.
  - Seek information about careers in research, history, and geography.
- *Attitudes Toward Personal Application of Heritage Studies Principles*
  - Use an objective approach in problem solving.
  - Display a willingness to consider other points of view.
  - Demonstrate divergent thinking in problem solving.
  - Demonstrate curiosity about history, geography, and related subjects.
  - Show an appreciation for his heritage.
  - Uphold foundational principles of his government.
  - Counteract influences detrimental to the perpetuation of his heritage.
  - Reflect a knowledge of history in everyday decision making.
- *Attitudes Toward Oneself*
  - Display confidence in his ability to use geographic skills successfully.
  - Demonstrate a scriptural view of himself through the study of history.
- *Attitudes Toward History and Society*
  - Select cause-and-effect relationships to explain contemporary problems.
  - Identify historical precedent as a way of solving some current problems.
  - Describe historians as persons sensitive to normal human concerns.
  - Demonstrate an awareness of the need for conservation, preservation, and the wise use of natural resources.
  - Demonstrate patriotism.
  - Explain how the study of history and geography can have positive (or, if unbalanced, negative) effects on one's personal life.

Instructional Materials

Student Materials

Text

Heritage Studies 1 for Christian Schools is a four-color text containing a variety of developmental subtopics built around six major topics: American history, world history, geography, culture, economics, and government.

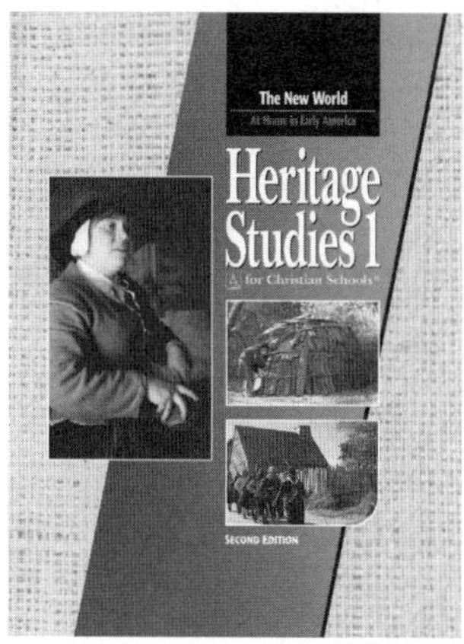

Notebook

The *Heritage Studies 1 Student Notebook* is a consumable companion tool for the text. It contains sixty-six pages that are used primarily for evaluating your child's understanding of the material. The Notebook will also save the teacher time. The pages are designed to be used in a notebook binder.

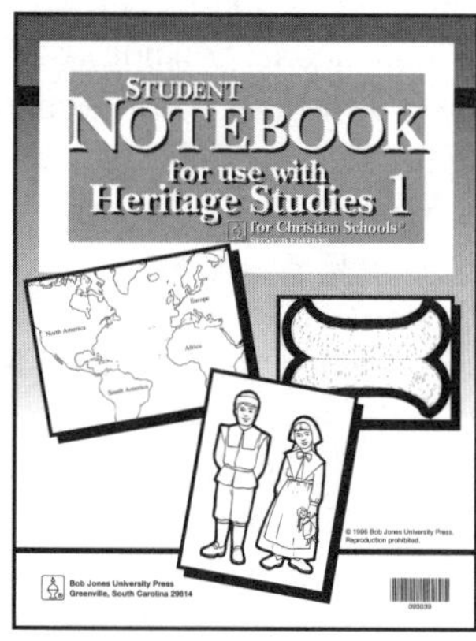

Miscellaneous school supplies

The child will need standard school supplies: crayons or felt-tip pens, pencils, scissors, glue, and so on.

Library trade books

No history program can provide enough information for enthusiastic young readers. A collection of trade books (library books) must be available to your child. Be careful of books that slant the history of certain events. For example, library books about Puritans are generally written by people who do not believe in the God of the Puritans. In these instances, try to find books that present a truthful and objective account of these people.

Teacher Materials

Teacher's edition

The home teacher's edition for *Heritage Studies 1 for Christian Schools* (this volume) is the foundation of the program from which all the activities originate. This volume contains the parts labeled below. Maps and More is a section of colored maps and visuals.

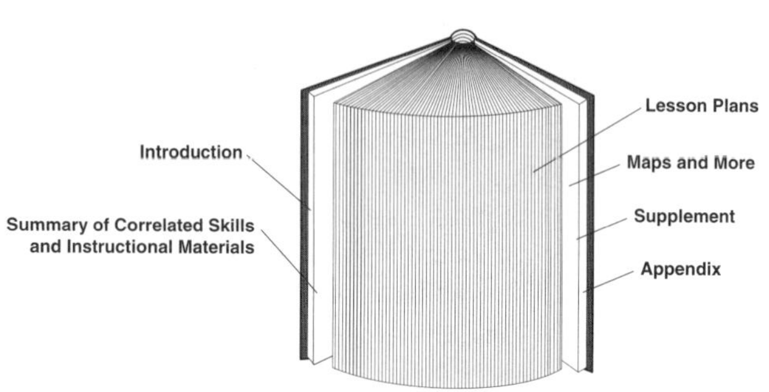

Optional Materials

History TimeLine

The *History TimeLine* is a visual, working chart with figures representing important events or people studied in first grade. It enhances the child's chronology skills.

Heritage Studies Listening Cassette

The cassette tape contains songs and readings that will enhance the child's enjoyment of, understanding of, and participation in the study of history. Cassette A contains selections used in grades 1-3. The first selection on the tape applies directly to the first grade curriculum.

Heritage Studies supplies

Refer to the list in the Supplement of this book.

Tests (optional)

The test packet includes a test for each chapter. The answer key is essential for administering the tests in first grade.

LESSON PLAN FORMAT

Preview

Main Ideas are short statements of historic or geographic knowledge.

Objectives are statements describing the outcome of instruction in terms of student behavior.

Materials is a list of items to be obtained or prepared.

Notes is a section of helpful hints.

Lesson

Introducing the Lesson suggests a way to start the lesson.

Teaching the Lesson suggests a procedure for instruction.

LESSON 50
Things People Need

Text, pages 140-41
Notebook, page 56

Preview

Main Ideas
- Needs are things people must have to live.
- All people have the same basic needs.

Objectives
- Differentiate between things that are needed and things that are not needed
- Distinguish among the four basic needs of people

Materials
- Several camping items (a flashlight, matches, a sleeping bag, and so on)*
- Several miscellaneous items not needed for camping
- A large box in which you place the above items

Notes

In this chapter you have the opportunity to help your child understand the complex question of why God allows Christians to have needs. The most important part of this concept is the fact that God supplies your child's needs. His desire is for His children to trust Him completely with every need and to watch Him work in their lives.

Day 1

Lesson

Introducing the Lesson

Direct a classifying activity. If your child has ever been camping, allow a few moments for him to tell about his trip. Show the box filled with the collected items. Explain that in the box are some things that would be important on a camping trip and some things that would not be important. Ask your child to take out of the box all the items that would be important on a camping trip.

Teaching the Lesson

Direct a text activity on pages 140-41. Remind your child that the people who came to the New World had to choose what to take on the ship with them.

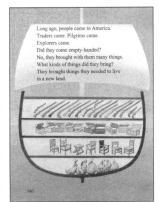

Long ago, people came to America.
Traders came. Pilgrims came.
Explorers came.
Did they come empty-handed?
No, they brought with them many things.
What kinds of things did they bring?
They brought things they needed to live in a new land.

140

Remember that Text Discussion is a guide to help as you read and discuss the text pages. Read in the manner that is comfortable for you and your child. If your child is able to read the text by himself, allow him to do so. If not, allow him to read what he can, or read the text to him.

Text Discussion, page 140

- ➤ How do you think coming by ship instead of coming by wagon would change what the people could take with them?
- ➤ Different ways of traveling mean different ways of getting ready. How would your camping list change if you had to go by bicycle instead of car or truck?
- ➤ Read the first five sentences on page 140. Then read sentence six to find the answer. *(No, they brought some things with them.)*
- ➤ Read the next question. Name a few things the people might have brought to their new homes.
- ➤ Read the last sentence to find the answer. Look at the pictures on the page. What did the settlers bring? *(guns, chairs, chests, bundles)*
- ➤ Why do you think these were important to the settlers? *(Answers will vary; guns—safety and food; chests— clothing; chairs—home.)*

180 Heritage Studies 1 Home TE

Things People Need

People everywhere have needs.
Needs are the things people must have to live.
What things do you need to live?
You need food.
You need a place to live.
You need clothes to wear.
And you need care and love from other people.

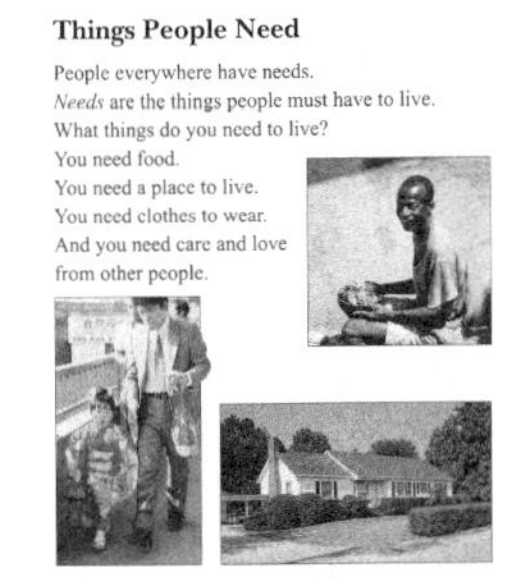

For your heavenly Father knoweth that ye have need of all these things.
Matthew 6:32

141

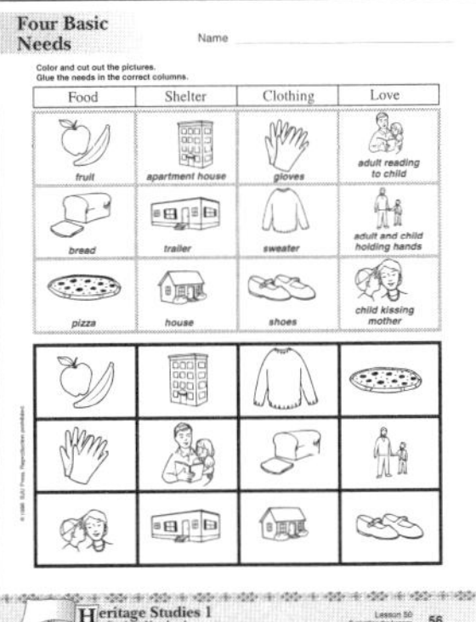

Day 2

Text Discussion, page 141

- ➤ Read the first three sentences. Name some things that you think we need to live today. Read the rest of the page to find out what we truly need in order to live. *(food, clothing, home, and love)*

All people have the same basic **needs**, but the things used to meet those needs may be different.

- ➤ Name some of the things the Indians in the New World needed to live. Do we need these things today? Why do we not need some of the items? *(Answers will vary.)*
- ➤ Why were guns more necessary to the settlers than to us? *(We do not have to hunt for food or stand guard in a fort.)*
- ➤ Who provides your food? *(God provides all food; parents provide for their children from what God has given them.)*

Read the verse on page 141. Ask why God allows us to have needs. Lead your child to the conclusion that God wants us to trust Him. Discuss the ways in which God meets our needs, such as providing us with loving parents or sending rain to help the food grow. Discuss our responsibility to be grateful to God. (BATs: 7c Praise, 8a Faith in God's promises; Bible Promise: H. God as Father)

Evaluating the Lesson

Direct an activity on Notebook page 56. Review the four basic needs as you point to each heading. Explain to your child that he will complete a chart of the four basic needs. Instruct him to color and cut apart the squares of pictures at the bottom of the page. Direct him to glue each picture in the column of the need that it would meet.

Going Beyond

Enrichment

Provide the basic needs story page for your child. (*NOTE:* See the Appendix, page A32.) Allow him to cut a picture from a magazine to complete each square. Instruct him to make up a story using the pictures he has chosen. Allow your child to share his story with the family.

Additional Teacher Information

The modern housewarming party is a variation on a much earlier tradition. When a family finished building a home in pioneer times, they would invite their friends to be with them when they lit the first fire in the fireplace. To be invited to this ceremony bespoke the warmth of the friendship. It was an especially appropriate gathering if the neighbors had helped build the house or clear the land. Today's version is a time for getting to know new neighbors or for inviting old friends to visit a new home.

Chapter 11: Lesson 50 181

Evaluating the Lesson gives ideas to evaluate the child's grasp of the material presented.

Going Beyond

Enrichment includes activities and games. Some of these activities may be done independently.

Additional Teacher Information provides the teacher with extra information to help him expand his knowledge of the related topics. It is not necessary to understand or even to read the information in this section to teach the lesson.

BIBLE ACTION TRUTHS

The quality and consistency of a man's decisions reflect his character. Christian character begins with justification, but it grows throughout the lifelong process of sanctification. God's grace is sufficient for the task, and a major part of God's gracious provision is His Word. The Bible provides the very "words of life" that instruct us in salvation and Christian living. By obeying God's commands and making godly decisions based on His Word, Christians can strengthen their character.

Too often Christians live by only vague guidance—for instance, that we should "do good" to all men. While doing good is desirable, more specific guidance will lead to more consistent decisions.

Consistent decisions are made when man acts on Bible principles—or Bible Action Truths. The thirty-seven Bible Action Truths (listed under eight general principles) provide Christians with specific goals for their actions and attitudes. Study the Scriptures indicated for a fuller understanding of the principles in Bible Action Truths.

Thousands have found this format helpful in identifying and applying principles of behavior. Yet, there is no "magic" in this formula. As you study the Word, you likely will find other truths that speak to you. The key is for you to study the Scriptures, look for Bible Action Truths, and be sensitive to the leading of the Holy Spirit.

1. **Salvation—Separation Principle**
   Salvation results from God's direct action. Although man is unable to work for this "gift of God," the Christian's reaction to salvation should be to separate himself from the world unto God.
   a. **Understanding Jesus Christ** (Matthew 3:17; 16:16; I Corinthians 15:3-4; Philippians 2:9-11) Jesus is the Son of God. He was sent to Earth to die on the cross for our sins. He was buried but rose from the dead after three days.
   b. **Repentance and faith** (Luke 13:3; Isaiah 55:7; Acts 5:30-31; Hebrews 11:6; Acts 16:31) If we believe that Jesus died for our sins, we can accept Him as our Savior. We must be sorry for our sins, turn from them, confess them to God, and believe that He will forgive us.
   c. **Separation from the world** (John 17:6, 11, 14, 18; II Corinthians 6:14-18; I John 2:15-16; James 4:4; Romans 16:17-18; II John 10-11) After we are saved, we should live a different life. We should try to be like Christ and not live like those who are unsaved.
2. **Sonship—Servant Principle**
   Only by an act of God the Father could sinful man become a son of God. As a son of God, however, the Christian must realize that he has been "bought with a price"; he is now Christ's servant.
   a. **Authority** (Romans 13:1-7; I Peter 2:13-19; I Timothy 6:1-5; Hebrews 13:17; Matthew 22:21; I Thessalonians 5:12-13) We should respect, honor, and obey those in authority over us.
   b. **Servanthood** (Philippians 2:7-8; Ephesians 6:5-8) Just as Christ was a humble servant while He was on earth, we should also be humble and obedient.
   c. **Faithfulness** (I Corinthians 4:2; Matthew 25:23; Luke 9:62) We should do our work so that God and others can depend on us.
   d. **Goal setting** (Proverbs 13:12, 19; Philippians 3:13; Colossians 3:2; I Corinthians 9:24) To be faithful servants, we must set goals for our work. We should look forward to finishing a job and going on to something more.
   e. **Work** (Ephesians 4:28; II Thessalonians 3:10-12) God never honors a lazy servant. He wants us to be busy and dependable workers.
   f. **Enthusiasm** (Colossians 3:23; Romans 12:11) We should do *all* tasks with energy and with a happy, willing spirit.
3. **Uniqueness—Unity Principle**
   No one is a mere person; God has created each individual a unique being. But because God has an overall plan for His creation, each unique member must contribute to the unity of the entire body.
   a. **Self-concept** (Psalm 8:3-8; 139; II Corinthians 5:17; Ephesians 2:10; 4:1-3, 11-13; II Peter 1:10) We are special creatures in God's plan. He has given each of us special abilities to use in our lives for Him.
   b. **Mind** (Philippians 2:5; 4:8; II Corinthians 10:5; Proverbs 23:7; Luke 6:45; Proverbs 4:23; Romans 7:23, 25; Daniel 1:8; James 1:8) We should give our hearts and minds to God. What we do and say really begins in our minds. We should try to think of ourselves humbly as Christ did when He lived on Earth.
   c. **Emotional control** (Galatians 5:24; Proverbs 16:32; 25:28; II Timothy 1:7; Acts 20:24) With the help of God and the power of the Holy Spirit, we should have control over our feelings. We must be careful not to act out of anger.
   d. **Body as a temple** (I Corinthians 3:16-17; 6:19-20) We should remember that our bodies are the dwelling place of God's Holy Spirit. We should keep ourselves pure, honest, and dedicated to God's will.
   e. **Unity of Christ and the Church** (John 17:21; Ephesians 2:19-22; 5:23-32; II Thessalonians 3:6, 14-15) Since we are saved, we are now part of God's family and should unite ourselves with others to worship and grow as Christians. Christ

is the head of His Church, which includes all believers. He wants us to work together as His Church in carrying out His plans, but He forbids us to work in fellowship with disobedient brethren.

4. **Holiness—Habit Principle**
   Believers are declared holy as a result of Christ's finished action on the cross. Daily holiness of life, however, comes from forming godly habits. A Christian must consciously establish godly patterns of action; he must develop habits of holiness.
   a. **Sowing and reaping** (Galatians 6:7-8; Hosea 8:7; Matthew 6:1-8) We must remember that we will be rewarded according to the kind of work we have done. If we are faithful, we will be rewarded. If we are unfaithful, we will not be rewarded. We cannot fool God.
   b. **Purity** (I Thessalonians 4:1-7; I Peter 1:22) We should try to live lives that are free from sin. We should keep our minds, words, and deeds clean and pure.
   c. **Honesty** (II Corinthians 8:21; Romans 12:17; Proverbs 16:8; Ephesians 4:25) We should not lie. We should be honest in every way. Even if we could gain more by being dishonest, we should still be honest. God sees all things.
   d. **Victory** (I Corinthians 10:13; Romans 8:37; I John 5:4; John 16:33; I Corinthians 15:57-58) If we constantly try to be pure, honest, and Christlike, with God's help we will be able to overcome temptations.

5. **Love—Life Principle**
   We love God because He first loved us. God's action of manifesting His love to us through His Son demonstrates the truth that love must be exercised. Since God acted in love toward us, believers must act likewise by showing godly love to others.
   a. **Love** (I John 3:11, 16-18; 4:7-21; Ephesians 5:2; I Corinthians 13; John 15:17) God's love to us was the greatest love possible. We should, in turn, show our love for others by our words and actions.
   b. **Giving** (II Corinthians 9:6-8; Proverbs 3:9-10; Luke 6:38) We should give cheerfully to God the first part of all we earn. We should also give to others unselfishly.
   c. **Evangelism and missions** (Psalm 126:5-6; Matthew 28:18-20; Romans 1:16-17; II Corinthians 5:11-21) We should be busy telling others about the love of God and His plan of salvation. We should share in the work of foreign missionaries by our giving and prayers.
   d. **Communication** (Ephesians 4:22-29; Colossians 4:6; James 3:2-13; Isaiah 50:4) We should have control of our tongues so that we will not say things displeasing to God. We should encourage others and be kind and helpful in what we say.
   e. **Friendliness** (Proverbs 18:24; 17:17; Psalm 119:63) We should be friendly to others, and we should be loyal to those who love and serve God.

6. **Communion—Consecration Principle**
   Because sin separates man from God, any communion between man and God must be achieved by God's direct action of removing sin. Once communion is established, the believer's reaction should be to maintain a consciousness of this fellowship by living a consecrated life.
   a. **Bible study** (I Peter 2:2-3; II Timothy 2:15; Psalm 119) To grow as Christians, we must spend time with God daily by reading His Word.
   b. **Prayer** (I Chronicles 16:11; I Thessalonians 5:17; John 15:7, 16; 16:24; Psalm 145:18; Romans 8:26-27) We should bring all our requests to God, trusting Him to answer them in His own way.
   c. **Spirit-filled** (Ephesians 5:18-19; Galatians 5:16, 22-23; Romans 8:13-14; I John 1:7-9) We should let the Holy Spirit rule in our hearts and show us what to say and do. We should not say and do just what we want to do, for those things are often wrong and harmful to others.
   d. **Clear conscience** (I Timothy 1:19; Acts 24:16) To be good Christians, we cannot have wrong acts or thoughts or words bothering our consciences. We must confess them to God and to those people against whom we have sinned. We cannot live lives close to God if we have guilty consciences.
   e. **Forgiveness** (Ephesians 4:30-32; Luke 17:3-4; Colossians 3:13; Matthew 18:15-17; Mark 11:25-26) We must ask forgiveness of God when we have done wrong. Just as God forgives our sins freely, we should forgive others when they do wrong things to us.

7. **Grace—Gratitude Principle**
   Grace is unmerited favor. Man does not deserve God's grace. However, after God bestows His grace, believers should react with an overflow of gratitude.
   a. **Grace** (I Corinthians 15:10; Ephesians 2:8-9) Without God's grace we would be sinners on our way to hell. He loved us when we did not deserve His love and provided for us a way to escape sin's punishment by the death of His Son on the cross.
   b. **Exaltation of Christ** (Colossians 1:12-21; Ephesians 1:17-23; Philippians 2:9-11; Galatians 6:14; Hebrews 1:2-3; John 1:1-4, 14; 5:23) We should realize and remember at all times the power, holiness, majesty, and perfection of Christ, and we should give Him the praise and glory for everything that is accomplished through us.

c. **Praise** (Psalm 107:8; Hebrews 13:15; I Peter 2:9; Ephesians 1:6; I Chronicles 16:23-36; 29:11-13) Remembering God's great love and goodness toward us, we should continually praise His name.

d. **Contentment** (Philippians 4:11; I Timothy 6:6-8; Psalm 77:3; Proverbs 15:16; Hebrews 13:5) Money, houses, cars, and all things on earth will last only for a little while. God has given us just what He meant for us to have. We should be happy and content with what we have, knowing that God will provide for us all that we need. We should also be happy wherever God places us.

e. **Humility** (I Peter 5:5-6; Philippians 2:3-4) We should not be proud and boastful but should be willing to be quiet and in the background. Our reward will come from God on Judgment Day, and men's praise to us here on Earth will not matter at all. Christ was humble when He lived on Earth, and we should be like Him.

8. **Power—Prevailing Principle**
Believers can prevail only as God gives the power. "I can do all things through Christ." God is the source of our power used in fighting the good fight of faith.

a. **Faith in God's promises** (II Peter 1:4; Philippians 4:6; Romans 4:16-21; I Thessalonians 5:18; Romans 8:28; I Peter 5:7; Hebrews 3:18–4:11) God always remains true to His promises. Believing that He will keep all the promises in His Word, we should be determined fighters for Him.

b. **Faith in the power of the Word of God** (Hebrews 4:12; Jeremiah 23:29; Psalm 119; I Peter 1:23-25) God's Word is powerful and endures forever. All other things will pass away, but God's Word shall never pass away because it is written to us from God, and God is eternal.

c. **Fight** (Ephesians 6:11-17; II Timothy 4:7-8; I Timothy 6:12; I Peter 5:8-9) God does not have any use for lazy or cowardly fighters. We must work and fight against sin, using the Word of God as our weapon against the Devil. What we do for God now will determine how much He will reward us in heaven.

d. **Courage** (I Chronicles 28:20; Joshua 1:9; Hebrews 13:6; Ephesians 3:11-12; Acts 4:13, 31) God has promised us that He will not forsake us; therefore, we should not be afraid to speak out against sin. We should remember that we are armed with God's strength.

BIBLE PROMISES

A. **Liberty from Sin—**Born into God's spiritual kingdom, a Christian is enabled to live right and gain victory over sin through faith in Christ. (Romans 8:3-4—"For what the law could not do, in that it was weak through the flesh, God sending his own Son in the likeness of sinful flesh, and for sin, condemned sin in the flesh: that the righteousness of the law might be fulfilled in us, who walk not after the flesh, but after the Spirit.")

B. **Guiltless by the Blood—**Cleansed by the blood of Christ, the Christian is pardoned from the guilt of his sins. He does not have to brood or fret over his past because the Lord has declared him righteous. (Romans 8:33—"Who shall lay any thing to the charge of God's elect? It is God that justifieth." Isaiah 45:24—"Surely, shall one say, in the Lord have I righteousness and strength: even to him shall men come; and all that are incensed against him shall be ashamed.")

C. **Basis for Prayer—**Knowing that his righteousness comes entirely from Christ and not from himself, the Christian is free to plead the blood of Christ and to come before God in prayer at any time. (Romans 5:1-2— "Therefore being justified by faith, we have peace with God through our Lord Jesus Christ: by whom also we have access by faith into this grace wherein we stand, and rejoice in hope of the glory of God.")

D. **Identified in Christ—**The Christian has the assurance that God sees him as a son of God, perfectly united with Christ. He also knows that he has access to the strength and the grace of Christ in his daily living. (Galatians 2:20—"I am crucified with Christ: nevertheless, I live; yet not I, but Christ liveth in me: and the life which I now live in the flesh I live by the faith of the Son of God, who loved me, and gave himself for me." Ephesians 1:3—"Blessed be the God and Father of our Lord Jesus Christ, who hath blessed us with all spiritual blessings in heavenly places in Christ.")

E. **Christ as Sacrifice—**Christ was a willing sacrifice for the sins of the world. His blood covers every sin of the believer and pardons the Christian for eternity. The purpose of His death and resurrection was to redeem a people to Himself. (Isaiah 53:4-5—"Surely he hath borne our griefs, and carried our sorrows: yet we did esteem him stricken, smitten of God, and afflicted. But he was wounded for our transgressions, he was bruised for our iniquities: the chastisement of our peace was upon him; and with his stripes we are healed." John 10:27-28—"My sheep hear my voice, and I know them, and they follow me: and I give unto them eternal life; and they shall never perish, neither shall any man pluck them out of my hand.")

F. **Christ as Intercessor—**Having pardoned them through His blood, Christ performs the office of High Priest in praying for His people. (Hebrews 7:25—"Wherefore he is able also to save them to the uttermost that come unto God by him, seeing he ever liveth to make intercession for them." John 17:20—"Neither pray I for these alone, but for them also which shall believe on me through their word.")

G. **Christ as Friend—**In giving salvation to the believer, Christ enters a personal, loving relationship with the Christian that cannot be ended. This relationship is understood and enjoyed on the believer's part through fellowship with the Lord through Bible reading and prayer. (Isaiah 54:5—"For thy Maker is thine husband; the Lord of hosts is his name; and thy Redeemer the Holy One of Israel; The God of the whole earth shall he be called." Romans 8:38-39—"For I am persuaded, that neither death, nor life, nor angels, nor principalities, nor powers, nor things present, nor things to come, nor height, nor depth, nor any other creature, shall be able to separate us from the love of God, which is in Christ Jesus our Lord.")

H. **God as Father—**God has appointed Himself to be responsible for the well-being of the Christian. He both protects and nourishes the believer, and it was from Him that salvation originated. (Isaiah 54:17—"No weapon that is formed against thee shall prosper; and every tongue that shall rise against thee in judgment thou shalt condemn. This is the heritage of the servants of the Lord, and their righteousness is of me, saith the Lord." Psalm 103:13—"Like as a father pitieth his children, so the Lord pitieth them that fear him.")

I. **God as Master—**God is sovereign over all creation. He orders the lives of His people for His glory and their good. (Romans 8:28—"And we know that all things work together for good to them that love God, to them who are the called according to his purpose.")

SUMMARY OF CORRELATED SKILLS AND INSTRUCTIONAL MATERIALS

	Chapters and Lessons	Suggested teaching days	Lesson pages	Text pages	Notebook pages
	WATER AND LAND				
	1 **Earth and Seas**	3	2-5	1-5	1
	2 **Maps and Directions**	2	6-9	6-9	2
1	3 **Mapmakers and Travelers**	3	10-14	10-11, 13	3
	4 **Making Maps**	2	14-16	12, 14	4
	Aztecs (Supplemental)		17-18		
	COLUMBUS AND HIS SHIPS				
	5 **Maps from Today and Long Ago**	3	20-23	16-17	5-7
	6 **Christopher Columbus**	3	23-26	18-19	8
2	7 **Columbus Makes a Plan**	3	27-30	20-22	9
	8 **The Ships and Crew**	2	31-34	23-24	10-11
	9 **The New World**	2	35-38	25-28	12-13
	Columbus Day (Supplemental)		39-40	175	

Bible Action Truths; Bible Promises	Heritage Studies skills
Bible Promises: H. God as Father, I. God as Master	summarizing data, making predictions, inferring relationships, making decisions, formulating opinions, working with maps and globes
BAT: 1b Repentance and faith; Bible Promise: I. God as Master	summarizing data, making predictions, inferring relationships, making decisions, formulating opinions, identifying sources of information, working with maps, using cardinal directions, working with diagrams
BATs: 5c Evangelism and missions, 7d Contentment	sequencing events, summarizing data, inferring relationships, making decisions, formulating opinions, working with time lines, working with maps, using cardinal directions, showing respect for heritage
BAT: 6a Bible study	summarizing data, inferring relationships, making decisions, formulating opinions, working with maps, using cardinal directions, showing respect for heritage
BATs: 1a Understanding Jesus Christ, 2a Authority, 5c Evangelism and missions	inferring relationships, making decisions, formulating opinions, working with maps
BAT: 6a Bible study; Bible Promise: I. God as Master	inferring relationships, working with time lines, identifying sources of information, working with maps and globes
BAT: 2d Goal setting	making predictions, inferring relationships, making decisions, working with time lines, working with maps
BATs: 2a Authority, 7d Contentment	sequencing events, making predictions, making decisions, working with maps and globes, using cardinal directions
BATs: 2c Faithfulness, 2e Work	sequencing events, making decisions, identifying sources of information, working with graphs
BATs: 2a Authority, 8a Faith in God's promises	formulating opinions, working with time lines, working with maps, using cardinal directions, working with charts, showing respect for heritage
	formulating opinions, working with maps, working with diagrams, showing respect for heritage

	Chapters and Lessons	Suggested teaching days	Lesson pages	Text pages	Notebook pages
	PEOPLE OF THE NEW WORLD				
	10 People of the New World 10/1	2	42-44	30-31, 184	14
	11 The Woodland Indians 10/6	3	45-48	32-35	15
3	**12 The Plains Indians** 10/8	3	49-52	36-38	16-17
	13 Indians of the North and Northwest 10/13	2	53-56	39-41, 178	18-19
	14 The Southwest Indians 10/15	2	57-59	42-44	
	Things the Indians Gave Us (Supplemental) Test 10/17		60-61	176-77, 182-83	
	NEW HOMES IN THE NEW WORLD				
	15 First Settlements 10/20	2	64-66	46-47	20
	16 Sir Walter Raleigh 10/22	1	67-68	48	21
	17 On to Jamestown 10/27	2	69-71	49-50	
4	**18 John Smith Leads the Way** 10/29	2	71-75	51-54	22-23
	19 Growing Crops 11/3	2	76-78	55, 57	24
	20 The Settlement Grows 11/5 Test 11/7	2	78-80	56, 58, 180-81	25

Bible Action Truths; Bible Promises	**Heritage Studies skills**
BAT: 1a Understanding Jesus Christ	inferring relationships, making decisions, formulating opinions, working with maps, valuing the rights of citizenship
BATs: 5c Evangelism and missions, 7c Praise; Bible Promises: H. God as Father, I. God as Master	inferring relationships, making decisions, identifying sources of information, working with maps
BATs: 2c Faithfulness, 2e Work, 2f Enthusiasm	inferring relationships, making decisions, formulating opinions, showing respect for heritage
BATs: 3a Self-concept, 5c Evangelism and missions	sequencing events, working with time lines, working with maps, using cardinal directions, identifying sources of information
BAT: 2e Work; Bible Promise: I. God as Master	summarizing data, formulating opinions, working with time lines, showing respect for heritage
	summarizing data, working with maps, working with charts, showing respect for heritage
BATs: 2c Faithfulness, 2d Goal setting, 2e Work	inferring relationships, making decisions, formulating opinions, working with maps, showing respect for heritage
BATs: 3a Self-concept, 7b Exaltation of Christ	summarizing data, inferring relationships, making decisions, formulating opinions
BATs: 2e Work, 7d Contentment	summarizing data, making predictions, making decisions, formulating opinions
BATs: 2c Faithfulness, 2d Goal setting, 2e Work, 3a Self-concept, 4a Sowing and reaping, 7b Exaltation of Christ, 7d Contentment	sequencing events, summarizing data, making predictions, inferring relationships, making decisions, formulating opinions
BAT: 3d Body as a temple; Bible Promise: I. God as Master	sequencing events, summarizing data, making predictions, formulating opinions
BATs: 5a Love, 7d Contentment; Bible Promises: H. God as Father, I. God as Master	sequencing events, summarizing data, making decisions, formulating opinions, working with time lines, working with maps

Chapter	Chapters and Lessons	Suggested teaching days	Lesson pages	Text pages	Notebook pages
5	**God's Laws and Man's Laws**				
	21 Obeying God	2	82-84	60-61, 174	
	22 Sailing to the New World	3	84-87	62-63, 173	26
	23 Choosing New Laws and Leaders	3	88-91	64-66, 179	
	24 Living in the New World	2	91-95	67-69, 172, 177	27-28
	25 Giving Thanks	2	96-98	70-72, 176	
6	**Maps of Old Places**				
	26 Making Towns and Cities	3	100-102	74-75	29
	27 Indian Towns	2	102-5	76-79	30
	28 Finding Old Towns	3	106-9	80-82, 184	31
	29 Old Plymouth	1	109-11	83-84	32
	30 Planning a Town	2	112-14	85-86	33

Bible Action Truths; Bible Promises	Heritage Studies skills
BAT: 1c Separation from the world	sequencing events, making predictions, inferring relationships, making decisions, formulating opinions, working with maps
BATs: 3c Emotional control, 5c Evangelism and missions, 6b Prayer, 7a Grace, 7b Exaltation of Christ, 7c Praise, 7d Contentment, 8a Faith in God's promises, 8c Fight, 8d Courage; Bible Promise: H. God as Father	formulating opinions, working with maps, using cardinal directions, working with diagrams
BATs: 2a Authority, 4c Honesty, 7d Contentment, 8d Courage	summarizing data, identifying sources of information, working with charts, identifying key documents, valuing the rights of citizenship, showing respect for heritage
BATs: 1c Separation from the world, 6b Prayer, 6c Spirit-filled, 7c Praise, 8a Faith in God's promises, 8d Courage; Bible Promises: H. God as Father, I. God as Master	sequencing events, inferring relationships, making decisions, working with maps
BATs: 1a Understanding Jesus Christ, 2c Faithfulness, 2e Work, 7b Exaltation of Christ, 7c Praise	sequencing events, summarizing data, making decisions, formulating opinions, working with time lines, valuing the rights of citizenship, showing respect for heritage
BATs: 6c Spirit-filled, 7d Contentment	summarizing data, inferring relationships, making decisions, formulating opinions, identifying sources of information, working with graphs and charts, showing respect for heritage
BATs: 5c Evangelism and missions, 7a Grace, 8b Faith in the power of the Word of God	sequencing events, inferring relationships, making decisions, formulating opinions, identifying sources of information, working with maps
BAT: 2a Authority	sequencing events, summarizing data, making predictions, inferring relationships, making decisions, formulating opinions, identifying sources of information, working with maps, showing respect for heritage
BAT: 8a Faith in God's promises	summarizing data, making predictions, inferring relationships, making decisions, formulating opinions, identifying sources of information, working with maps
BAT: 6b Prayer	sequencing events, summarizing data, inferring relationships, making decisions, formulating opinions, working with time lines, identifying sources of information, working with maps, using cardinal directions, valuing the rights of citizenship, showing respect for heritage

	Chapters and Lessons	Suggested teaching days	Lesson pages	Text pages	Notebook pages
	Schools Then and Now				
	31 Schools in America	1	116-17	88-89	34
	32 Learning to Read	1	118-20	90-91	35-36
7	**33 The Hornbook**	2	121-24	92-95	37-38
	34 Schools Today	2	125-27	96-97	39
	35 Rules About Schools	2	127-30	98-100	40
	Trading with the Indians				
	36 Early Trading	2	132-34	102-4	41
	37 Animal Furs	2	134-36	105-6	42
8	**38 Captured but Not Conquered**	2	137-40	107	43-44
	39 Trading	1	141-42	108-9	45
	40 Wampum	2	142-45	110-12	

Bible Action Truths; Bible Promises	Heritage Studies skills
BATs: 3a Self-concept, 5a Love, 6a Bible study, 8b Faith in the power of the Word of God	summarizing data, inferring relationships, making decisions, formulating opinions
BAT: 6a Bible study	making predictions, inferring relationships, making decisions, formulating opinions, identifying sources of information, working with maps, using cardinal directions, identifying key documents, valuing the rights of citizenship, showing respect for heritage
BATs: 2a Authority, 2c Faithfulness, 2e Work, 6a Bible study	making predictions, inferring relationships, making decisions, formulating opinions, valuing the rights of citizenship, showing respect for heritage
BATs: 2a Authority, 6a Bible study, 7c Praise, 7d Contentment	sequencing events, inferring relationships, formulating opinions, working with charts, valuing the rights of citizenship, showing respect for heritage
BATs: 1c Separation from the world, 2a Authority, 2b Servanthood	summarizing data, making decisions, formulating opinions, identifying sources of information, working with graphs, valuing the rights of citizenship, showing respect for heritage
BAT: 5e Friendliness	summarizing data, making predictions, inferring relationships, making decisions, formulating opinions, working with charts
Bible Promises: H. God as Father, I. God as Master	sequencing events, summarizing data, making predictions, inferring relationships, making decisions, formulating opinions, working with maps, using cardinal directions
BATs: 1b Repentance and faith, 1c Separation from the world, 3a Self-concept, 5a Love, 5b Giving	making predictions, inferring relationships, making decisions, formulating opinions, working with time lines, working with maps, showing respect for heritage
BATs: 3a Self-concept, 4c Honesty, 7d Contentment	inferring relationships, making decisions, formulating opinions, working with diagrams
BATs: 4c Honesty, 7c Praise, 7d Contentment	making predictions, inferring relationships, making decisions, formulating opinions

	Chapters and Lessons	Suggested teaching days	Lesson pages	Text pages	Notebook pages
9	**ADVENTURERS**				
	41 Goods from the New World	2	148-50	114-15	46
	42 Young Robert La Salle	2	150-52	116-18	47
	43 The Sun King	3	153-56	118-20	48
	44 La Salle's Dream Come True	3	156-60	121-23	49
	45 How Places Get Their Names	2	161-63	124-26	50
10	**THE ONE TRUE GOD**				
	46 Other Gods in the New World	2	166-69	128-30, 178	51
	47 Religions in the New World	1	169-71	131-32	
	48 The Puritans	2	171-74	133-34	52-53
	49 A Separatist Sunday	2	175-78	135-38	54

Bible Action Truths; Bible Promises	Heritage Studies skills
BAT: 3d Body as a temple	sequencing events, making decisions, working with time lines, working with charts
BATs: 2c Faithfulness, 2e Work	making predictions, inferring relationships, formulating opinions, working with maps, using cardinal directions
BATs: 3c Emotional control, 5a Love, 5d Communication	sequencing events, formulating opinions, valuing the rights of citizenship
BATs: 2c Faithfulness, 4c Honesty	sequencing events, summarizing data, inferring relationships, working with time lines, working with maps, using cardinal directions
BATs: 1c Separation from the world, 3d Body as a temple; Bible Promise: D. Identified in Christ	inferring relationships, making decisions, formulating opinions, working with maps
BATs: 1a Understanding Jesus Christ, 1b Repentance and faith, 5a Love, 5c Evangelism and missions, 6b Prayer, 7a Grace, 7c Praise; Bible Promises: A. Liberty from Sin, B. Guiltless by the Blood, C. Basis for Prayer, D. Identified in Christ, F. Christ as Intercessor, H. God as Father, I. God as Master	formulating opinions, showing respect for heritage
BATs: 1b Repentance and faith, 5c Evangelism and missions, 8a Faith in God's promises, 8b Faith in the power of the Word of God; Bible Promises: A. Liberty from Sin, I. God as Master	inferring relationships, making decisions, formulating opinions
BATs: 1a Understanding Jesus Christ, 1b Repentance and faith, 7c Praise	sequencing events, making predictions, inferring relationships, making decisions, formulating opinions, working with time lines, working with maps, using cardinal directions
BATs: 1b Repentance and faith, 3e Unity of Christ and the church, 6b Prayer, 7c Praise, 7d Contentment, 8a Faith in God's promises; Bible Promises: H. God as Father, I. God as Master	inferring relationships, formulating opinions, identifying sources of information

	Chapters and Lessons	Suggested teaching days	Lesson pages	Text pages	Notebook pages
	People Have Needs and Wants				
	50 Things People Need 3/11	2	180-82	140-41	55-56
	51 People Need Food and Shelter 3/16	2	182-85	142-45	57-58
11	**52 People Need Clothes and Love** 3/18	2	186-89	146-49	59
	53 Things People Want 3/23	2	189-91	150-51	
	54 Saving and Spending Money 3/25 Test 3/27	2	192-94	152-54	60
	Families Together				
	55 You Are Special 3/30	2	196-98	156-58	61-62
	56 A Family Is Special 4/1	2	199-201	159-61	63
	57 A Family Has Rules 4/6	2	202-4	162-64	64
12	**58 A Family Works and Plays Together** 4/8	3	205-7	165-66	65
	59 A Family Has a History 4/13	2	208-10	167-68	66
	60 You Have a History 4/15 Test 4/17	2	210-12	169-70	

Bible Action Truths; Bible Promises	Heritage Studies skills
BATs: 5a Love, 7c Praise, 7d Contentment, 8a Faith in God's promises; Bible Promise: H. God as Father	sequencing events, summarizing data, making decisions, formulating opinions, working with graphs and charts, valuing the rights of citizenship, showing respect for heritage
BATs: 6a Bible study, 8a Faith in God's promises; Bible Promise: H. God as Father	sequencing events, summarizing data, inferring relationships, making decisions, working with time lines, identifying sources of information, working with charts, valuing the rights of citizenship, showing respect for heritage
BATs: 1c Separation from the world, 4b Purity, 5a Love, 6a Bible study, 7c Praise, 7d Contentment, 7e Humility, 8a Faith in God's promises; Bible Promises: E. Christ as Sacrifice, H. God as Father	sequencing events, making predictions, inferring relationships, making decisions, formulating opinions, showing respect for heritage
BATs: 5a Love, 7d Contentment, 8a Faith in God's promises; Bible Promise: H. God as Father	inferring relationships, making decisions, formulating opinions, identifying sources of information, working with charts, valuing the rights of citizenship, showing respect for heritage
BATs: 4a Sowing and reaping, 5b Giving, 5c Evangelism and missions, 7d Contentment, 8a Faith in God's promises; Bible Promise: H. God as Father	sequencing events, summarizing data, inferring relationships, making decisions, formulating opinions, working with tables and charts, valuing the rights of citizenship
BAT: 3a Self-concept; Bible Promise: H. God as Father	making decisions, identifying sources of information, working with charts, showing respect for heritage
BAT: 3a Self-concept; Bible Promise: I. God as Master	inferring relationships, working with time lines, identifying sources of information, working with graphs, showing respect for heritage
BAT: 2a Authority; Bible Promise: H. God as Father	inferring relationships, making decisions, formulating opinions, working with tables, valuing the rights of citizenship
BATs: 2e Work, 2f Enthusiasm, 3e Unity of Christ and the church, 5a Love, 6a Bible study, 6b Prayer, 7c Praise	inferring relationships, working with charts, showing respect for heritage
BAT: 3a Self-concept	inferring relationships, working with time lines, identifying sources of information, working with diagrams, showing respect for heritage
BATs: 1c Separation from the world, 2e Work, 4c Honesty, 5a Love, 6c Spirit-filled	sequencing events, summarizing data, inferring relationships, working with time lines, identifying sources of information, showing respect for heritage

LESSON PLANS

1 LESSONS 1-4

Water and Land

This chapter takes a general look at geography—different sizes of land and bodies of water. Then it introduces the four cardinal directions: north, east, south, and west. There is a brief discussion of past and current mapmakers. Your child will learn how to read the keys of simple maps, interpret picture maps, and distinguish left from right.

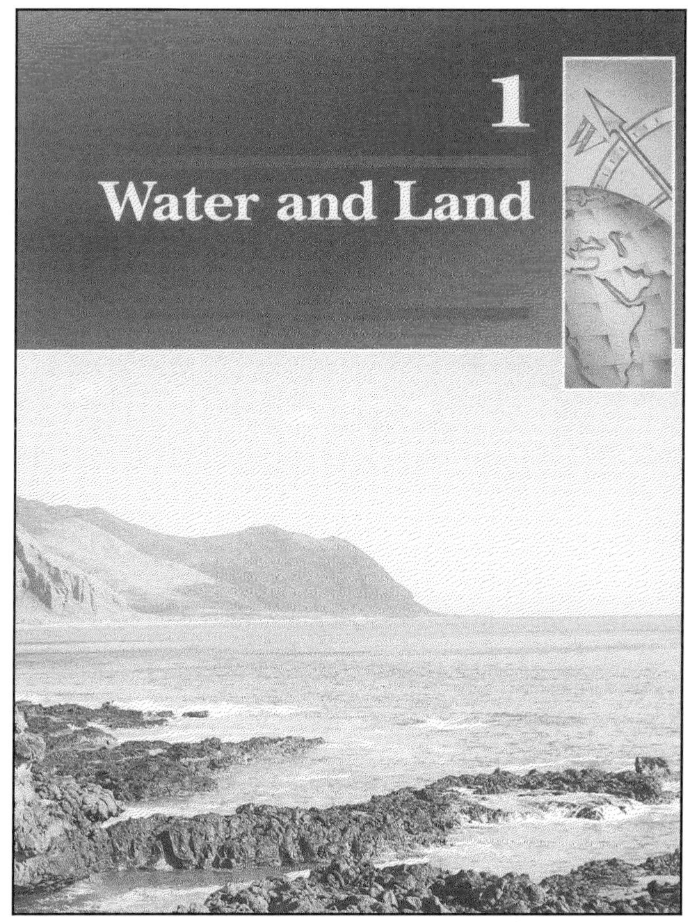

Materials

The following materials must be obtained or prepared before the presentation of the lesson. These items are labeled with an asterisk (*) in each lesson and in the Materials List in the Supplement. For further information see the individual lessons.

- *Heritage Studies 1 Student Textbook*
- *Heritage Studies 1 Student Notebook*
- A globe (Lesson 1) (*NOTE:* A globe will be used in many lessons throughout the curriculum.)
- Appendix, pages A2-A5 (Lesson 1)
- A directional compass (Lesson 2) (optional)
- Appendix, page A6 (Lesson 2)
- A yellow circle (Lesson 2)
- The History TimeLine Packet (Lesson 3) (*NOTE:* The History TimeLine Packet will be used in many lessons throughout the curriculum.)
- Appendix, page A6 (Lesson 3)
- 10 cardboard tubes (Supplemental Lesson)

Maps, charts, games, and other black-and-white visuals can be found in two places in your teacher's edition—the Supplement and the Appendix. All the pages that need to be copied for use in the lessons can be found in the Appendix. Those found in the Supplement can be used directly from your manual and do not need to be copied, though they may be copied if you so desire. *NOTE:* Maps and More, the group of color visuals that follow the lessons, is not a part of the Appendix or Supplement and may not be copied.

LESSON 1
Earth and Seas

Text, pages 1-5
Notebook, page 1

Preview

Main Ideas

- Large and small bodies of water are held in low places in the earth.
- Oceans and continents are the largest bodies of water and masses of land on Earth.

Objectives

- Identify on the map the continent on which you live
- Assemble map puzzles

Materials

School supplies such as crayons, glue, scissors, and pencils that you would have in your teaching area are not listed in the Materials list of each lesson.

- A pitcher of water
- A rock
- 5 letter envelopes for continent puzzle pieces
- A globe*
- *Heritage Studies 1 Student Notebook**
- *Heritage Studies 1 Student Textbook**
- Appendix, pages A2-A5: each continent shape cut apart into puzzle pieces*

Some reproducible pages in the Appendix have gray shaded areas. The shading does not always copy. Use a crayon to shade your copy an appropriate color.

As you read the lesson, you will notice that there is a variety of types or styles of print. Questions and information to be given directly to your child are in the regular print. *(The answers to questions are shown in italics within parentheses.)* *Instructions and information directed to you as the teacher are given in a different italicized print.* *(NOTE*s give information to the teacher also.) **Terms** that you will want your child to become familiar with are in bold print.

You may choose to teach this lesson or other lessons in one day. If you would like to spread the lesson over more than one day, the suggested teaching days are marked for you.

Day 1

Lesson

Introducing the Lesson

Direct a demonstration about lakes. Allow your child to tell about large bodies of water he has seen. *(ponds, lakes, oceans)* Take your child and a pitcher of water outside to conduct the following demonstration.

When your child is asked to give his opinion (a "what-do-you think" question), an answer may not be listed. Accept any answer and, if needed, guide your child by asking further questions to reach a better answer.

Demonstration Discussion

➤ Why do you think ponds, lakes, and oceans are where they are?

➤ Where do you think would be a good place for us to pour water to make a "lake"? Pour the water. *If your child chooses a poor site—one that is level or humped—pour a little water there and then repeat the question about a good place.*

➤ Why did the water stay in a "lake"? *(Because the place was lower than the land around it, the water could not run off.)*

➤ Look around for other places to make little "lakes." What can you say about the land where any "lake" is? *(It is lower than the land around it.)*

A lake can be in a mountain. If there is a low place in the mountain, such as a volcanic crater surrounded by higher ground, a lake may form.

➤ Place the rock in the lake. On how many sides does the rock have water? If your rock does not have water on all sides, make a larger lake.

➤ Do you know what we call land that has water on all sides? *(Answers will vary; an island.)*

And God called the dry land Earth; and the gathering together of the waters called he Seas: and God saw that it was good.

Genesis 1:10

When do you see puddles?
A puddle is some water in a low place.
Why are some puddles bigger than others?

Here is a puddle in the parking lot.

2

Have you ever seen a pond?
A pond is like a huge puddle.
It is a lot of water in a low place.

What do you think a lake is?

3

Teaching the Lesson

Direct a text activity on pages 1-5. Ask your child to describe what he sees on page 1. Then ask him to compare that picture to the demonstration he saw outside.

The Text Discussion is a guide to help as you read and discuss the text pages. When instructions say to read the text, read in the manner that is comfortable for you and your child. If your child is able to read the text by himself, allow him to do so. If not, allow him to read what he can, or read the text to him. As the year progresses, your child may find it easier to read on his own.

Text Discussion, page 2

- How do puddles form? *(Water collects in low places.)*
- Why are some puddles bigger than others? *(Some low places are bigger than others.)* (*NOTE*: Not all low places will fill with water. Sandy soil allows water to drain away almost immediately.)
- Name activities that are done in or on ponds, lakes, and oceans. *(Answers may include boating, swimming, fishing, and sightseeing.)*
- Why can these activities be done in or on those bodies of water and not in a puddle? *(They are large enough.)*

Text Discussion, page 3

- Read the first two lines. How is a pond like a puddle? *(Both are low places where water collects.)*
- How is a lake like a puddle? *(A lake is water that has collected in an even larger low place.)*

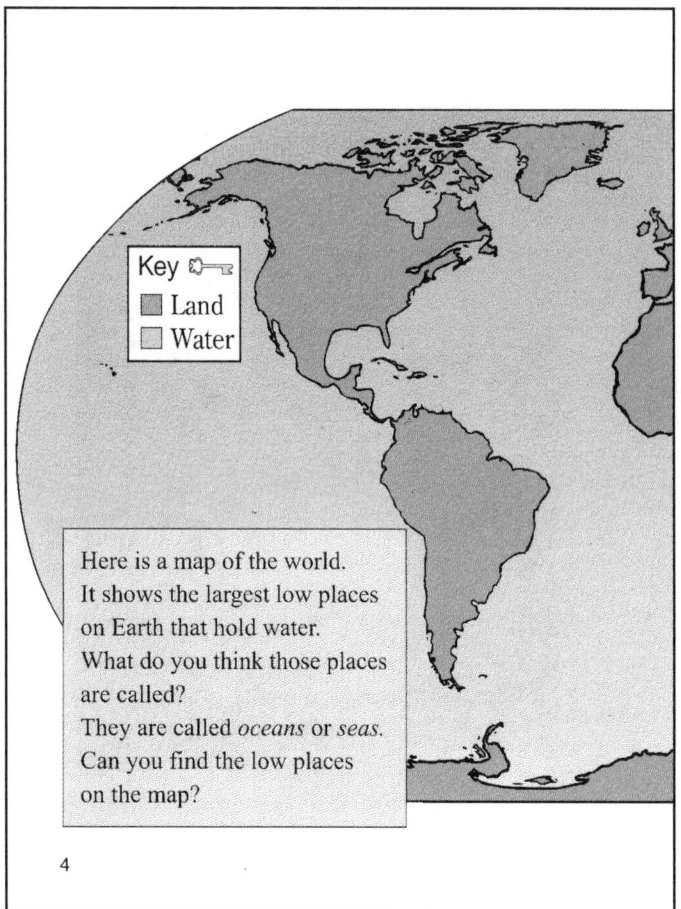

Key
Land
Water
Here is a map of the world.
It shows the largest low places
on Earth that hold water.
What do you think those places
are called?
They are called *oceans* or *seas*.
Can you find the low places
on the map?
4

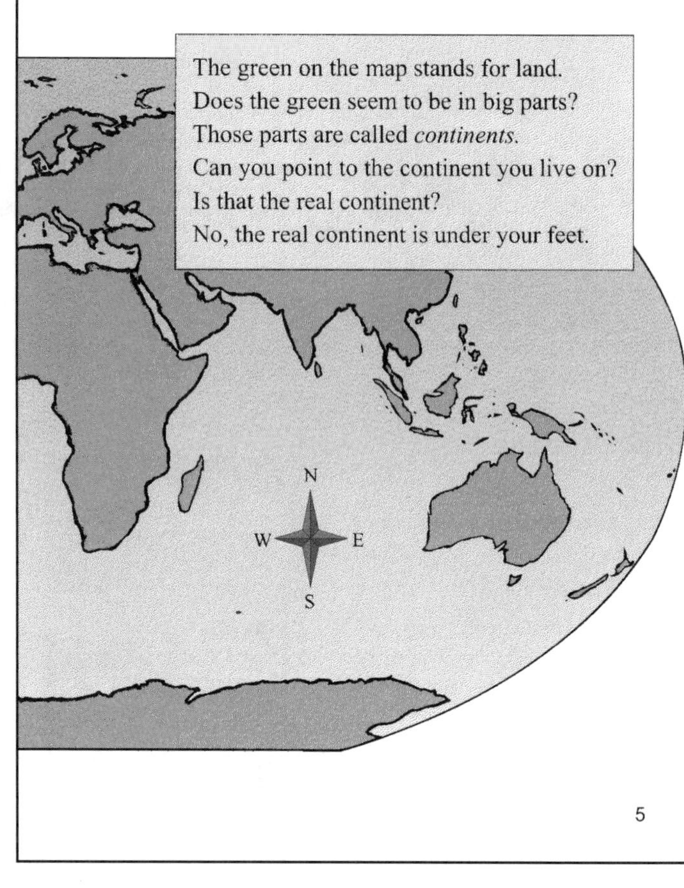

The green on the map stands for land.
Does the green seem to be in big parts?
Those parts are called *continents*.
Can you point to the continent you live on?
Is that the real continent?
No, the real continent is under your feet.
N
W
E
S
5

Day 2

Text Discussion, pages 4-5

- ➤ What do you think the different colors represent on the map? *(Blue is for lower places that hold water; green is for higher places, dry land.)*
- ➤ Look at the small box on page 4. What do you think the box on the map is called? *(a key)*
- ➤ Why do you think the chart is called a key? *(Accept all answers; then show your child how it "unlocks" the meaning of the map.)*
- ➤ Look at the word *Water* beside the blue box. All the blue on the map stands for low places on Earth that hold water. Where are the low places on the map? *(under the blue on the map)*
- ➤ What are the largest bodies of water called? *(oceans, seas)*

Mapmakers use colors to represent elevations: blue represents a lower elevation than green does; green represents a lower elevation than does yellow or brown. Try not to let your child assume that green means vegetation is present.

- ➤ What is an island? *(a small piece of land surrounded by water)*

The **oceans** and **seas** surround big and small pieces of land. *Point to the Hawaiian Islands on the map.* These islands are the tops of mountains in the ocean that stick out of the water just as the rock stuck out of our puddle.

If you need help finding the islands, use a labeled map for yourself.

- ➤ What do the large green parts on the map represent? *(continents)*

The **continents** are the biggest pieces of land that are surrounded by oceans. *If the word* continent *is unfamiliar, ask your child to say it with you once or twice.*

- ➤ Are the blue and green areas on pages 4-5 the real islands, oceans, and continents? *(no)*

Maps are drawings of real places. The real continent or island we live on is under our feet, under the building, under the town or city.

- ➤ Why do we have maps? *(Answers will vary; draw your child to the conclusion that because we cannot see a whole ocean or continent from where we are, we have to make smaller representations.)*

Use a globe to demonstrate that the earth is round like a ball. Maps on paper take the maps from globes and make them flat. Since the earth is like a ball, globes are more nearly correct in copying what real land and water look like.

➤ Why do people make flat maps? *(easier to use; easier to carry)*

A long, long time ago, people did not know that the world is round. They thought it was flat like a map.

➤ What may people have thought happened to ships that got near the edge of the flat world? *(Answers will vary. Almost everyone believed that ships "fell off" the earth near the edge.)*

Explain that the Bible has always said that the earth is round. Read Isaiah 40:22a: "It is he that sitteth upon the circle of the earth."

Day 3

➤ Look at the map on pages 4-5. Point to the continent or island you live on. *Give guidance as needed.* What is the name of the continent or island?

➤ How did the continents and oceans get here? *(God created them.)*

Turn to page 2 and read the verse. Ask your child to tell about other things God created. (Bible Promises: H. God as Father, I. God as Master)

Evaluating the Lesson

Direct a puzzle activity on Notebook page 1. Explain to your child that the Notebook page shows the same map as is given in the text on pages 4-5.

Puzzle Activity

➤ Look at the colors used in the key in the text.

➤ Look at the key on the Notebook page. Find the words *Land* and *Water.* There is one more item on this chart. It says "Where I live." Choose a color other than blue or green to use for that item. Color in the chart and then color the map.

Australia is the smallest continent, but it is included with many Pacific Islands in a division of the earth's land called *Oceania.* To avoid confusion, the map puzzles do not include any islands—only continents. If you live on an island, help your child draw in a representation.

➤ Here is an envelope with a map puzzle in it. Put the puzzle together. Once the puzzle is together, try to find the landmass on your Notebook page map. Repeat with the other envelopes and puzzle pieces.

The puzzle work not only evaluates the learning but also expands the teaching.

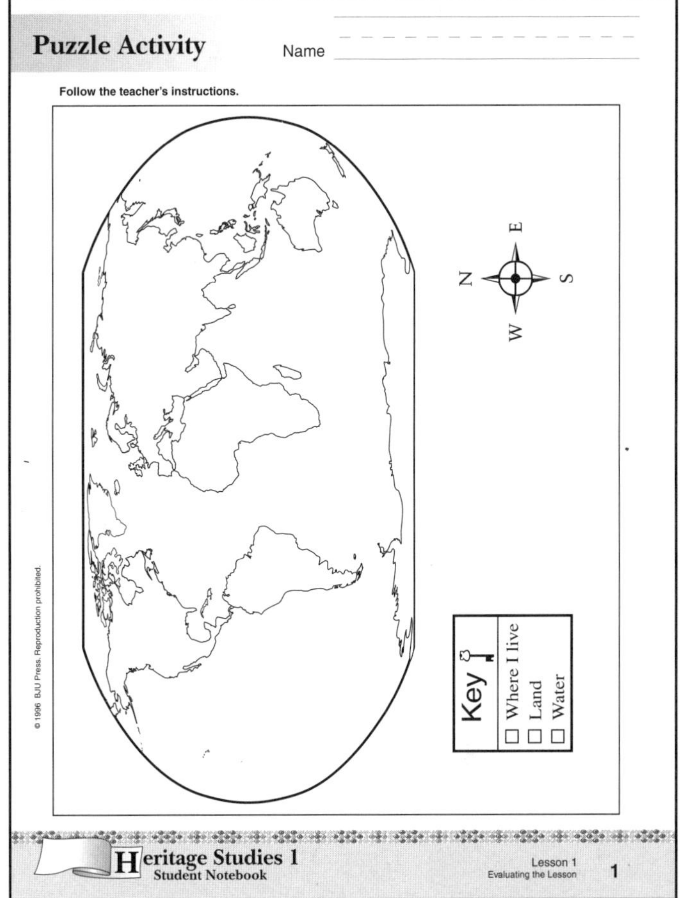

Puzzle Activity Name

Follow the teacher's instructions.

Heritage Studies 1 Student Notebook Lesson 1 Evaluating the Lesson 1

Going Beyond

Enrichment

Make copies of the continent outlines on stiff paper and cut them out. (*NOTE:* See the Appendix, pages A2-A5.) Allow your child to use these continent "stencils" to trace the continents onto paper and to color and label them.

Additional Teacher Information

Flat maps of the world are called *projections,* based on the method of using light to project markings from a globe onto the paper. Light shining inside a globe throws the images on the globe onto paper beside it.

Flat maps distort the earth's curved surface in some manner. The Mercator projections, for example, show the lines of longitude running parallel. This arrangement expands the land near the poles so that Greenland appears larger than South America. In reality, South America is eight times larger than Greenland.

Flat maps, despite their distortions, are useful. In fact, they are called *developable maps* for their great usefulness. The Mercator maps show accurate wind directions. Sailors find them useful in plotting a straight-line course between two points.

LESSON 2
Maps and Directions

Text, pages 6-9, 180-81
Notebook, page 2

Preview

Main Ideas

- There are four cardinal directions: north, east, south, and west.
- People use directions to help them travel.

Objectives

- Find the direction north
- Indicate directions on a map

Materials

- A small sticker
- Maps and More 1, page M1

Maps and More is a collection of colored maps, visuals, charts, and graphs found at the end of Lesson 60. Display the charts from your teacher's edition for use in the lessons. These visuals may not be copied.

- A directional compass (optional)*
- A Bible
- A red construction-paper *N*
- Appendix, page A6: pattern for the *N**
- A yellow circle to represent the sun, hung on the west wall*

You will need to find north in order to put up the *N* in your room. You may use a compass if you have one. Let the compass rest on a nonmetallic surface. When the arrow settles, turn the compass until the *N* is under the point of the arrow. Then put the paper *N* on the wall or window that faces north. You may want to put up all the directions in the room and leave them up all year. Then put the yellow circle on the west wall. If you do not have a compass, use the rising or setting sun to determine the direction. Follow the *Learning How* instructions on text page 7.

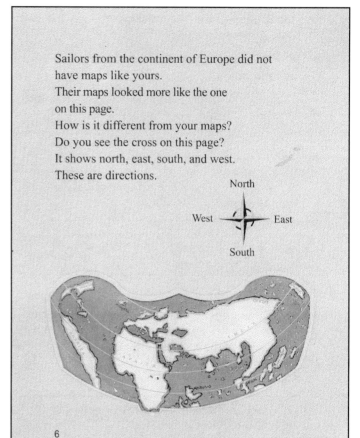

Sailors from the continent of Europe did not
have maps like yours.
Their maps looked more like the one
on this page.
How is it different from your maps?
Do you see the cross on this page?
It shows north, east, south, and west.
These are directions.

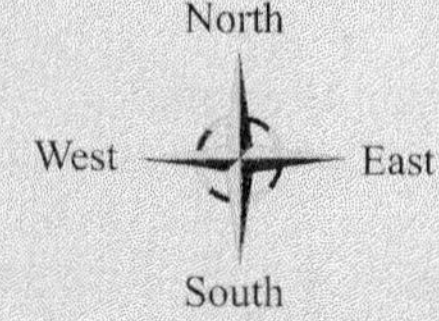

6

Day 1

Lesson

Introducing the Lesson

If your child has already mastered left and right, this activity can be used as a review or not at all.

Direct a left and right exercise. Give your child a sticker for the back of his right hand. Then do a little practice by instructing him to raise his right hand.

Introduce the exercise. Ask your child to stand. Tell him to stretch his right hand as far to the right as he can. Use directions such as touch the floor with your right hand, wave your left hand, and touch your head with your left hand. As you exercise with your child, be sure to face the same direction.

Teaching the Lesson

Direct activities on text pages 6-9. Ask your child to look at the maps on page 6 and on Maps and More 1.

Map Discussion, page 6

➤ How are the two maps different? *(Answers will vary but should include the inaccurate shapes of the Americas on the page 6 map.)*

➤ Where can you find the directions on the map on page 6? *(Your child should point to the compass.)*

A design like this appears on many maps. It is called a **compass rose.** It shows the directions north, east, south, and west. The design is called a rose because when it is fancy, it looks like a flower.

➤ Find the compass rose on pages 180-81. Run your finger up the arrow that points to the top of the map. Your finger is moving north on the map.

➤ Look at the *N* in the room. The *N* stands for the direction north. Name some things that are north of where you are. *(Accept all reasonable answers. Your child will probably name objects that are between him and the letter. Or, he may name things that are not in the room, such as the swing set or the sandbox.)*

➤ Where does the sun set? *(in the west)* Can you remember seeing the sun set?

> You will direct attention to a *Learning How* activity for the first time this year. One of your purposes in teaching these sections will be to teach your child to follow the directions for gathering materials, doing the activity, and considering the results of the activity.

◆ LEARNING HOW ◆

To Find Directions

1. Go outside just before sunset. Look for the sun.
2. Hold your left arm straight out from your side. Hold your left palm up toward the sun, as though you were an officer stopping traffic. Now you are facing north.

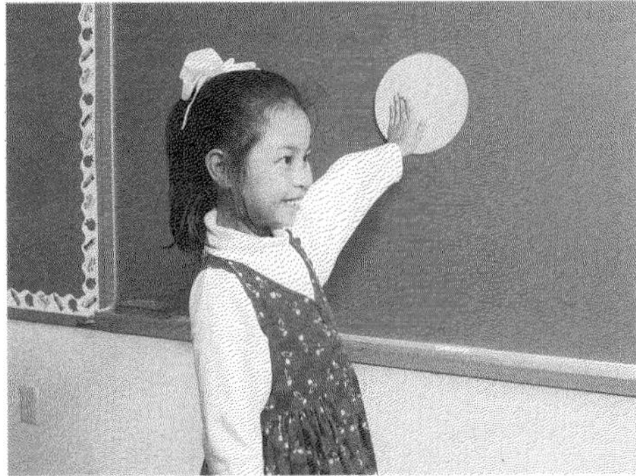

3. What direction is behind you? What direction is on your right?

7

Learning How Activity, page 7

➤ *You may want to substitute the following for the first step on page 7.* Pretend that it is late afternoon and that the sun is going down. Stand and look at the yellow sun on the wall. The sun is going down in the west.

➤ Follow the other steps as listed in the text.

> You may want to try this with the real sun later. Warn your child *not* to look at the sun directly.

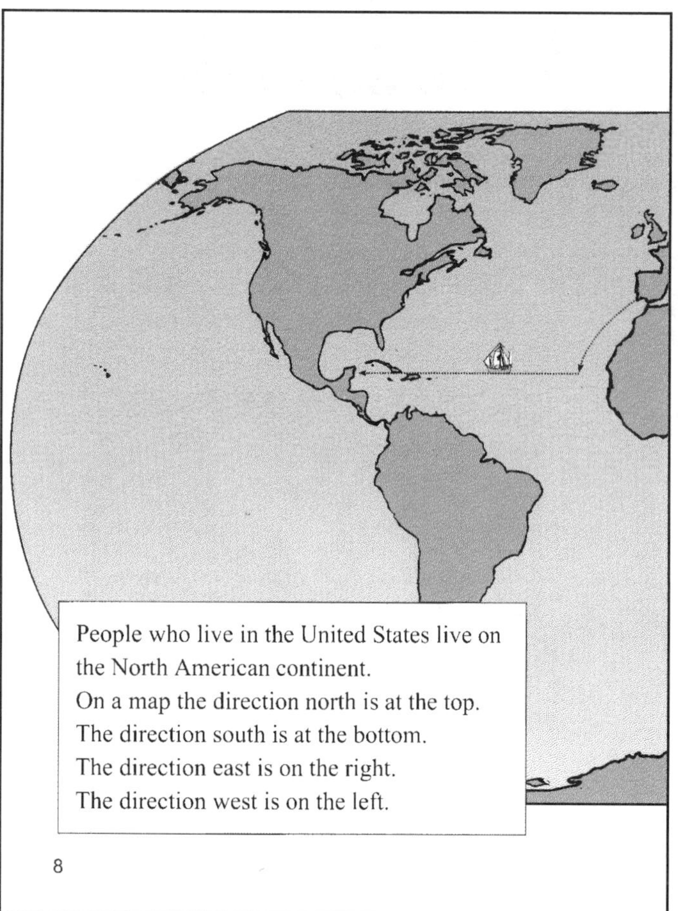

People who live in the United States live on the North American continent.
On a map the direction north is at the top.
The direction south is at the bottom.
The direction east is on the right.
The direction west is on the left.
8

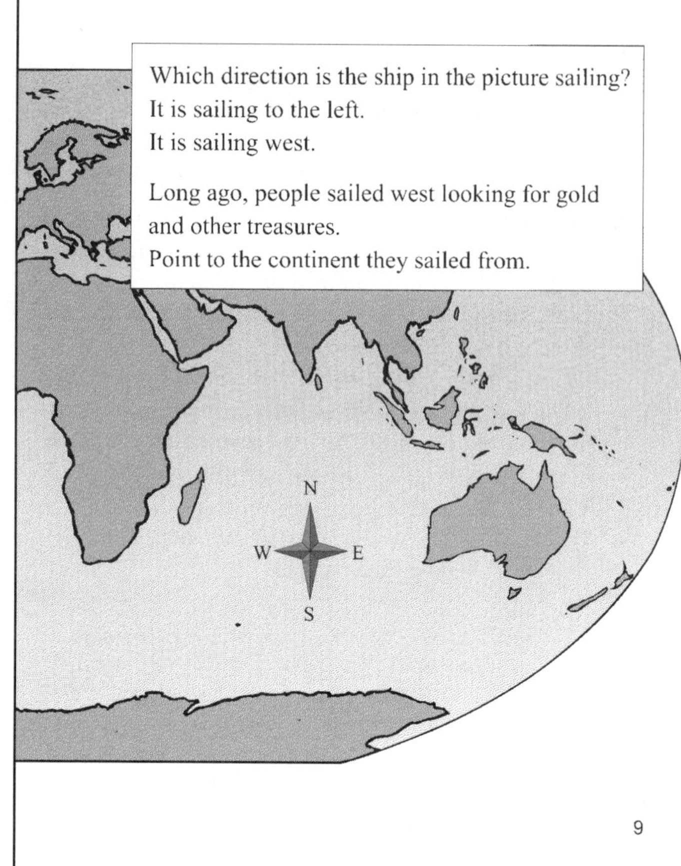

Which direction is the ship in the picture sailing?
It is sailing to the left.
It is sailing west.
Long ago, people sailed west looking for gold and other treasures.
Point to the continent they sailed from.
N
W
E
S
9

Day 2

Text Discussion, pages 8-9

- Find the compass rose on the map. Find north. On maps, north is toward the top and south is toward the bottom.
- Which side is east on? *(right)* Which side is west on? *(left)*
- Look at the ship on the map. Which direction is the ship sailing? *(It is headed to the left of the map; therefore, it is sailing west.)*
- Why do you think a ship from long ago would be going west?

Many people were looking for gold and other treasures. They thought the lands to the west had much gold, and they wanted to find the fastest way to get there.

- Point to the continent that the ship sailed from. This is Europe.
- Point to the continent the ship sailed to. Can you find the same continent on Maps and More 1? This is North America. The United States is on the North American continent.
- Turn your book so that the arrow pointing north points toward the *N* on the wall. Imagine that the ship on the page could sail off the book. Where would the ship sail?

Read Psalm 89:12a: "The north and the south thou hast created them." God created our whole earth and all that is in it. He also made the rules by which everything in the world exists. The directions that we use on maps are not ideas we made up ourselves but rules God set in place for us. We only decided that we would use the top of maps to represent north. (Bible Promise: I. God as Master)

Read Psalm 103:12: "As far as the east is from the west, so far hath he removed our transgressions from us." Ask your child what transgressions are. *(sins)* Ask how far the east is from the west. After your child answers, explain that the phrase means that God takes our sins so far in the other direction that we never see them again. (BAT: 1b Repentance and faith)

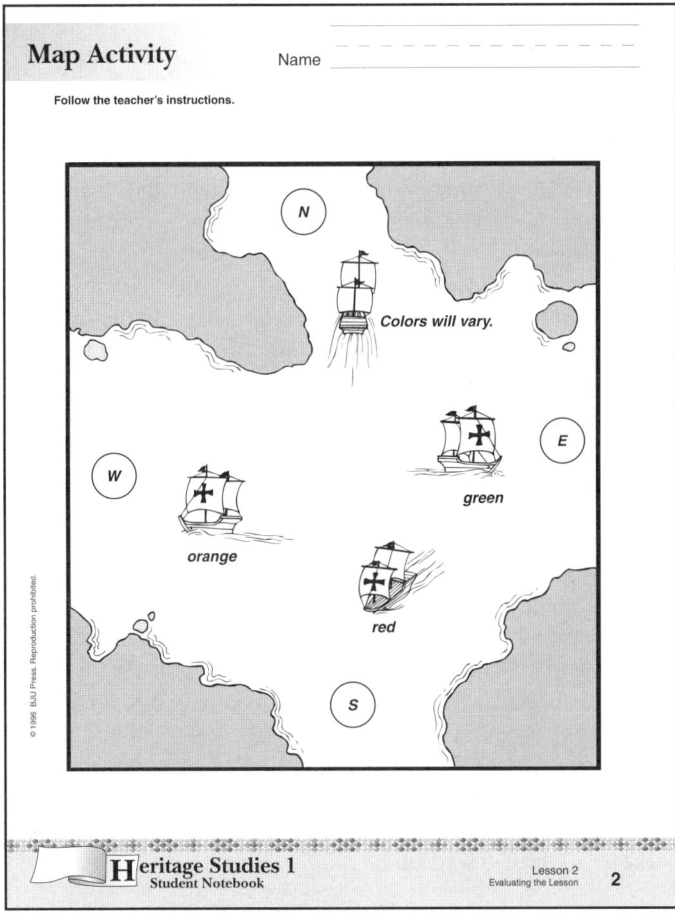

Evaluating the Lesson

Direct a map activity on Notebook page 2. Direct your child's attention to the blank circles at the top, sides, and bottom of the page.

Map Activity

- Fill in the *N* for north where it should go on the map. Do the same with *E, W,* and *S.*
- Look at the ships in the picture. Decide which ship is headed west and color that ship orange.
- Which ship is going south? Color that ship red.
- Which ship is headed east? Color that ship green.
- Choose any other color you like for the last ship. Which way is the last ship headed? *(north)*

Going Beyond

Enrichment

Allow your child to look at a directional compass. Explain that at one time the sun and stars were the only means people had to tell directions. A compass helps people find directions now. Show him that the needle will point toward the north by itself and that you must turn the face of the compass until the *N* is under the needle.

Additional Teacher Information

The oldest maps in existence are from ancient Babylonia. They are city maps on clay tablets. The mapmaker worked on damp clay with a stylus and then baked the map to rock hardness. The material and methods the Babylonians used explain the endurance of their work.

LESSON 3
Mapmakers and Travelers

Text, pages 10-11, 13
Notebook, page 3

Preview

Main Ideas

- People travel from place to place for different reasons.
- Maps of Earth have improved over the years.

Objectives

- Name modes of transportation
- Trace a route on a map

Materials

- A long piece of cardboard with a curved or jagged edge

The cardboard is to represent the edge of a continent. Place the cardboard on a shelf in a cabinet or closet that your child can reach up to but not see over. In order to help your child understand how difficult it was for people to make maps without the help of aerial or space photographs, he will be asked to draw the edge of the cardboard after having only felt it.

- A piece of blank paper
- A current calendar
- Maps and More 1, page M1
- The History TimeLine from the History Timeline Packet*
- The figure of the Indian groups (about 950) from the History TimeLine Packet*
- The figure of the Viking ship (1000) from the History TimeLine Packet*
- Appendix, page A6: Viking ship*
- Appendix, page A7: World map*

Notes

If you have purchased the History TimeLine Packet, you will refer to it for the first time in this lesson. A time line is a simple way to organize the important events in history. It can easily be used to establish a sequence of events and illustrate relationships between the events pictured. You will want to post the TimeLine before beginning this lesson. Figures from the History TimeLine Packet for Grade 1 will be added to the TimeLine throughout the year. You may also choose to add pictures of your own to the TimeLine as opportunities arise.

You may have difficulty displaying the whole TimeLine in your home. Consider hanging it along a hallway or even in the garage. You may hang it in layers, leaving room between the layers for the pictures. If you do not have wall space, you may tape the pipeline together in a way similar to a hinge. This will enable you to fan fold it and display it each time you need it.

If you have not purchased the History TimeLine, you will want to make one of your own. The pipeline itself may be made from a number of different items, such as string, ribbon, cash register tape, and bulletin board edging. Your time line should begin in the year 950 and go through 1685. You will need to find pictures to place along the time line. These may be found in magazines, coloring books, and computer resources. Your child may prefer to draw the pictures.

Day 1

Lesson

Introducing the Lesson

Direct a mystery activity. Tell your child that he is going to be like a sailor and mapmaker of long ago. Explain that on the shelf inside the closet door you have put a piece of cardboard that is like a little continent. Tell him that you want him to feel the edge of the "continent." Give him a blank sheet of paper and ask him to draw a map of the edge of the continent as best as he can remember.

Mystery Activity

➤ What do you think about your map?

Long ago, people had to make maps of the world by sailing ships around the edges of islands and continents. These people could not see all at once the edge they were drawing on their maps.

➤ Does your map look exactly like the map you felt? *(no)* What would help you make your map better?

➤ *Show the cardboard to your child.* Could you draw a better map now that you can see the "continent" you were exploring? *(yes)*

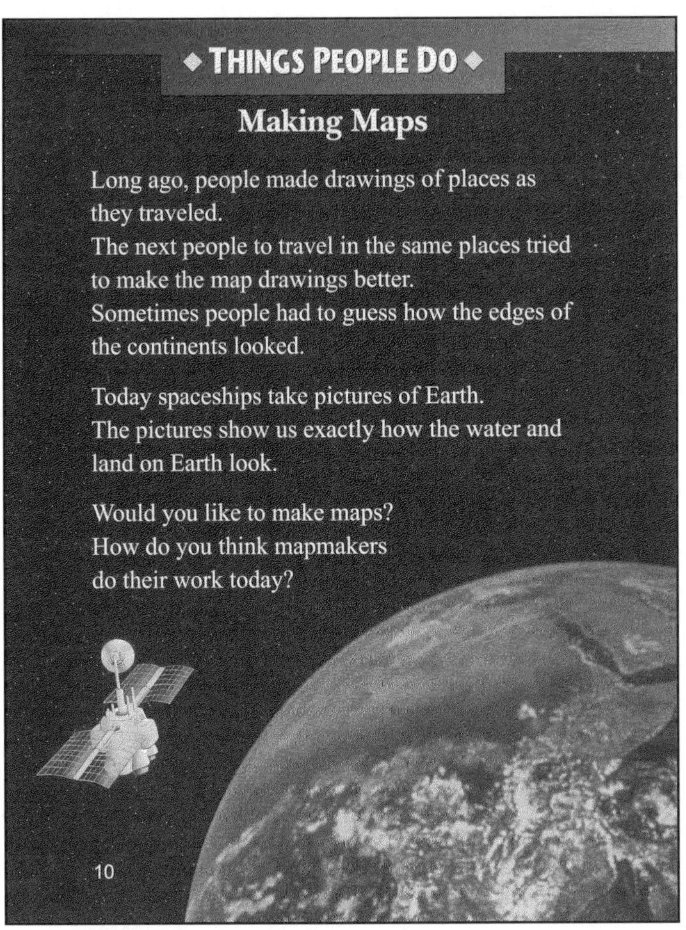

◆ THINGS PEOPLE DO ◆

Making Maps

Long ago, people made drawings of places as they traveled.
The next people to travel in the same places tried to make the map drawings better.
Sometimes people had to guess how the edges of the continents looked.

Today spaceships take pictures of Earth.
The pictures show us exactly how the water and land on Earth look.

Would you like to make maps?
How do you think mapmakers do their work today?

10

People use the oceans to travel from place to place.
How else can people get from place to place?
Why do you think people want to go from one place to another?
Sometimes people want a warmer place to live.
Sometimes they want to do different kinds of work.

11

Teaching the Lesson

Direct a text activity on pages 10-11 and 13. Ask your child to turn back to the old map on page 6. Remind him that at one time people thought the world looked like this. Then direct him to turn to page 10.

Text Discussion, page 10

- ➤ What does the photograph show? *(part of the earth from space)*
- ➤ How do you think a photograph taken from space helps a mapmaker? It lets him see the whole place he is drawing; it shows exactly how the water and land look.
- ➤ What are some of the reasons that people make maps? The most important reason for maps is to help people get from one place to another without getting lost.

Text Discussion, page 11

- ➤ Name all the ways you can think of that people travel. I will write them down.
- ➤ Draw lines through each kind of travel that could not have been used a long time ago. *(all air travel, any travel using gasoline engines or steam power, and any modes relying on power other than water, wind, or human or animal energy)*

Long ago, people could not travel as fast as they do today. For them, the fastest travel for long distances was by ship.

- ➤ Look at the picture on the page and tell me what is happening. Read page 11.
- ➤ Why do people move to different places?

People move to a new place sometimes because they think the place where they live is too hot, too cold, too wet, or too dry. Some people move because the work they do makes them travel. A builder has to go where houses are needed, and a person who takes photographs must travel to many places. Missionaries also need to travel to different places. (BAT: 5c Evangelism and missions)

◆ FAMOUS PEOPLE ◆

Leif Ericson

Leif Ericson's father was a Viking sailor. Leif sailed on his father's ship. He learned to find his direction by the stars and sun. When Leif grew up, he sailed his own ship. He explored North America hundreds of years ago.

13

Day 2

Text Discussion, page 13

- ➤ Long ago, people moved to America on the famous ship the *Mayflower*. How long do you think it took the *Mayflower* to sail across the ocean? It took about sixty-three days. *Show your child on a calendar what date is sixty-three days from today. On Maps and More 1, show him with your finger a route from England to the northeastern United States.*
- ➤ How long do you think it takes to fly the same distance today in an airplane? It takes about six hours.
- ➤ Look at the Viking ship on page 13. A ship like this one may have been the first to come to the Americas. The Vikings were sailing on the oceans more than a thousand years ago. *You may want to allow your child to color the Viking ship.*
- ➤ How big do you think the real Viking ship was?

A Viking ship was about as long as a double tractor-trailer truck. It was the fastest ship in the world at that time. In good weather it could go 100 miles in a day. The Vikings liked to travel. They lived in Norway. *Show your child where Norway is on the World map.*

- ➤ Look at the picture on page 13. What kind of clothing is the boy wearing? The boy is a Viking boy.
- ➤ Read the page. Do you think Leif Ericson was a good sailor?

Leif became the most famous of the Viking sailors. *Show on the World map where Leif Ericson may have sailed. Use the World map to trace the journey.*

- ➤ Color each segment of the path with a different-colored crayon.
- ➤ Which way is the ship moving? *(The first and second legs go west; the third leg goes south; the fourth goes north; the fifth, west; the sixth, south.)*
- ➤ Leif did not have a map to follow. How did he know which way to steer his ship? *(by the sun and stars)*
- ➤ Do you remember how to find the direction *west* by using the sun?

Day 3

Add figures to the History TimeLine. Tell your child that the Viking ships sailed to many places. At that time, no ships were better than the Viking ships. Even today with all the modern tools, no one can make a Viking ship any better than the Vikings did. Place the figure on the TimeLine at the year A.D. 1000. Ask your child whether he thinks people were already living in the lands that Leif sailed to. *(yes)* Place the figure of the Indian people (about 950) on the TimeLine. Then read the story about Leif's travels. This story is based on the few facts that are known about Leif's life. The dialogue and some of the events are imagined.

Leif Ericson's father, Eric the Red, had a fine long ship. It had many sets of oars and a carved wooden snake's head on the front. It had sailed for many years on the open sea. It had taken many men to places far away from Norway. On this day, Eric the Red gave the ship to his son.

"I have traveled all I will travel," said Eric the Red. "You must now take the ship and discover new lands. I must stay here."

Leif shook his father's hand. "I wish we still traveled together, but I respect your word. I will take the ship and find places no one has seen before and come back and tell you of them."

And then taking loyal and able sailors with him, Leif Ericson sailed off. By day he watched the sun, and by night he followed the stars. He sailed past the lands his father had discovered long before.

One day he saw land that had tall trees on it. His sailors said, "This is not any place we have ever been before. Who has ever seen such tall trees?"

Leif ordered the ship to go toward the land. When it got near, he got into a smaller boat and rowed to the shore. He stepped off on the continent of North America. He may have been the first person from Europe to do that.

He and his men stayed there a while. They built small houses; they hunted and fished. One of the men found a huge field of wild grapes. When he showed them to Leif, Leif said, "I'm going to call this place Vinland because of all the vines growing here."

The longer they stayed, the better the men liked the place.

Leif said, "This place is so much better than the other places we have lived. The days and nights are nearly the same length—not like home where the nights are sometimes short and sometimes long. It is not as cold here as it is at home either. And the fields are easy to farm, and the animals are plentiful. I think we should go back and tell the others what a fine land we have found."

And so they did. The Vikings made settlements in many places on the way to Vinland. Leif did not go back because when his father died, he became the Viking ruler.

Discussion

- ➤ Can you think of some reasons that the Vikings liked Vinland? *(The lengths of the nights and of the days were the same; the weather was warmer; the land had animals, fish, and grapes; the fields were easy to farm.)*
- ➤ Why do you think many people went to the new lands that Leif had found? They wanted a better place to farm and build houses; perhaps some of them thought they could do a different kind of work there.
- ➤ Why did more people settle in places where the land is good and the animals and fish are plentiful? *(Life was easier in such places.)*

Remind your child that Christians move from place to place as they feel the Lord leads them. He should be willing to go where God directs and to be happy there. (BAT: 7d Contentment)

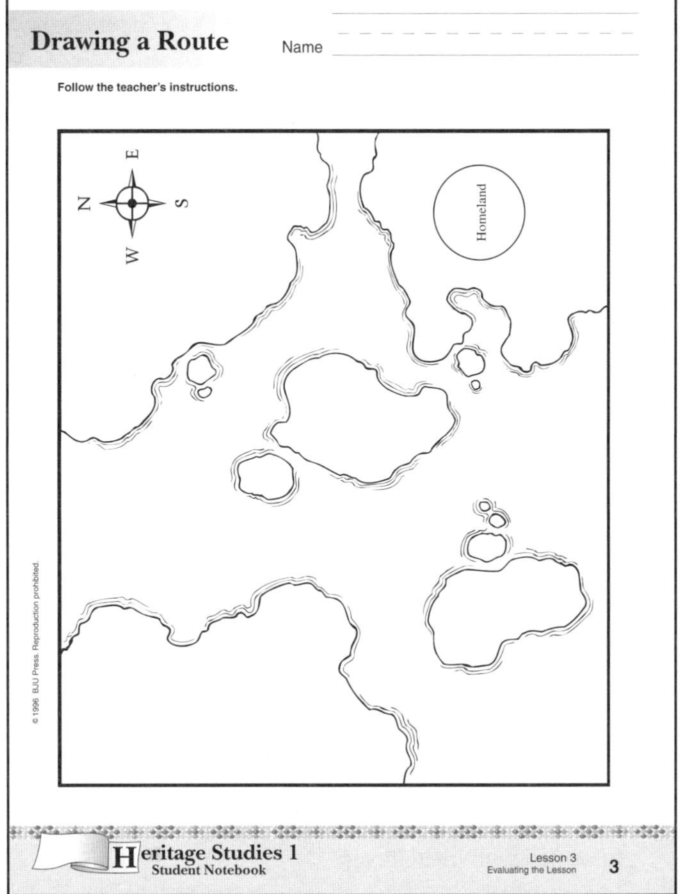

Evaluating the Lesson

Direct a map and discussion activity on Notebook page 3. Tell your child to imagine that he lives inside the circle on the map. He should choose another place on the map to sail to. When he has chosen the place, he should draw on the map the route that he will take. Remind him to look at Leif Ericson's route. He did not make the whole trip without stopping. Your child may want to follow Leif's example, stopping along the way to rest and get food and fresh water.

When your child has mapped out where he is going and the route he is taking, allow him to tell you about his choices. You may want to ask your child questions, such as "Which direction did you travel first?" and "Why did you choose the place you did?"

Going Beyond

Enrichment

Give your child building blocks, construction paper, crayons, scissors, and blank paper. Allow him to build small Viking settlements, using the blocks for houses and the construction paper to represent water and land. After he has completed a settlement, he can draw a map of it.

Additional Teacher Information

Eric Thorvaldsson, known as Eric the Red because he had shoulder-length red hair, was banished from Iceland for killing two men in a quarrel. Having heard there was an island west of Iceland, he decided to look for it.

What he found was the largest island in the world. He named it Greenland, hoping to entice others to settle there. The name was somewhat misleading, for although the climate today is rather like Maine's, the place was inhospitable for eight months of the year during Eric's time. It was from Greenland that Leif set sail and made his discoveries.

Other Vikings out of Scandinavia had been on the move since the end of the eighth century. One group, a tribe called *Rus,* settled in what is now Kiev. The word *Russia* was derived from the clan name. Some others settled in what is now Normandy, France—named for the Norsemen who lived there.

LESSON 4
Making Maps

Text, pages 12, 14
Notebook, page 4

Preview

Main Ideas

- People use directions to find places.
- Maps help people get to other places.

Objective

- Answer questions by reading a map

Materials

- Maps and More 3, page M2
- A ruler
- Supplement, page S2: State map
- Supplement, page S3: Geographical map
- Supplement, page S4: Combined map

Maps and More, found at the end of Lesson 60 in this teacher's edition, is a group of reduced charts and visuals from the classroom visual packet. Not all of the pages from the classroom visual packet are found in this volume. Some charts are not needed in the home school. Please remember that these pages cannot be copied.

Day 1

Lesson

Introducing the Lesson

Direct a map activity. Ask your child to point out on Maps and More 3 where he thinks he lives. Show him where the spot is, as nearly as you can on such a general map.

Teaching the Lesson

Direct a map discussion. Show your child the Geographical map of the United States. Long ago, before there was a United States, a map of the land looked like this.

Map Discussion

➤ What do you think the markings on the map show? The markings show mountains, lakes, and rivers. *Point out the different geographical features and let your child name them—mountains, lakes, and so on.*

People use the directions north, east, south, and west to find their way from place to place. Look at the map on this page.

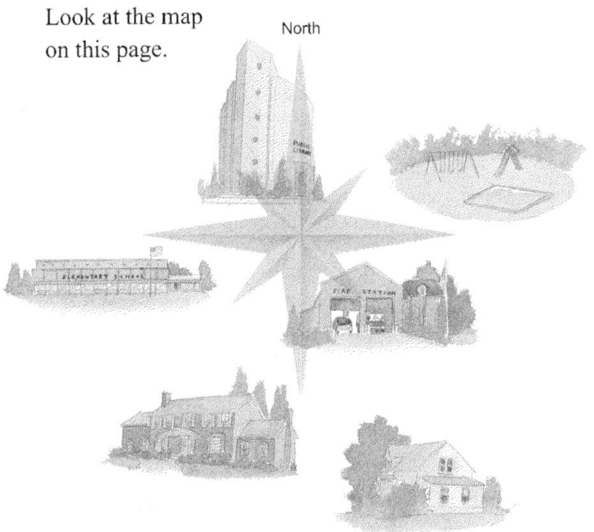

Which way would you tell someone to go who wanted to go from the school to the playground? Should the person go east, west, north, or south?

12

- ➤ Although the land of the United States still looks the same (has the same mountains, rivers, and lakes), some maps now also show the way the states divide the land, as the State map does.
- ➤ Do you know how many states there are? There are fifty. *If you live on the continental United States, point to your state.*

Two of the states are not on this map. The states of Hawaii and Alaska do not touch the other states. They are farther away. Alaska is north of these states, and Hawaii is west of them.

- ➤ Some maps show both how the land looks and how the states are divided. *Show your child the Combined map.* What do you think a **boundary** is? It is an edge of a country or land. The United States has two oceans for boundaries.
- ➤ Which sides of the country have oceans? *(east and west)*

Text Discussion, page 12

- ➤ Read page 12.
- ➤ Which direction is labeled? *(north)*
- ➤ In which direction are the houses? *(south)*
- ➤ Which direction would you go from the school to get to the playground? *(east)*

Map Discussion, Maps and More 3

- ➤ Look at Maps and More 3 and find the letters that stand for the directions north, east, south, and west.
- ➤ Find the school. How did you know which place is the school? *(He may be able to read the word on the map; he may have chosen by the clues, such as the bus beside the school.)*
- ➤ Find the playground. Which direction would you travel from the school to get to the playground? *(east)*
- ➤ Find the hospital. Find the school again. Which direction should you go to get to the school from the hospital? *(south)*

It is not necessary in this lesson to ask for combinations such as *southeast.* This concept will be presented in Lesson 32.

- ➤ Point to the school. Which direction would you go to get from the school to the fire station? *(east)*

People use directions to get from place to place. You are able now to "read" a map. "Reading" a map is not the same as reading a book. Reading a map means being able to find places on it.

Draw a parallel between reading a map to get somewhere and reading the Bible to get "directions" for living. Explain that God gave us His Word to tell us how to get to heaven and how to live right on Earth. (BAT: 6a Bible study)

◆ LEARNING HOW ◆

To Read a Map

1. Take out your Notebook, some colored pencils, and a ruler.
2. Take out the Notebook page your teacher tells you to.
3. Answer the questions your teacher asks by looking at the map. Use the pencils to color the map as your teacher tells you.

14

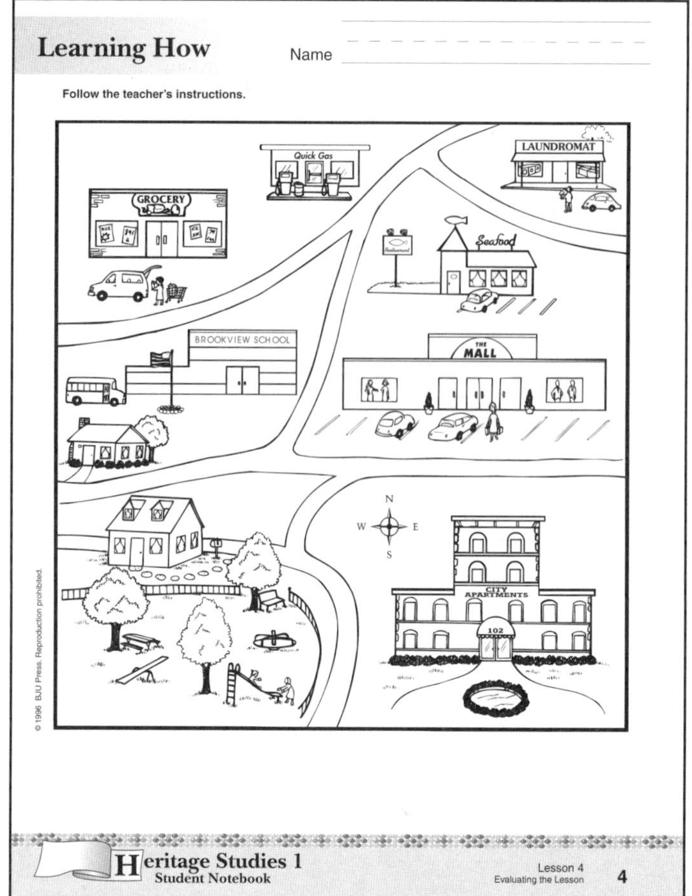
Learning How Name

Follow the teacher's instructions.

Heritage Studies 1 Student Notebook — Lesson 4 Evaluating the Lesson — 4

Day 2

Evaluating the Lesson

Direct a *Learning How* activity on text page 14 and Notebook page 4. Read the steps to your child.

Learning How Activity

- Find the park and playground on your map. Color the park area.
- Lay your ruler on the page north to south, putting the ruler on top of the park. What would you come to if you went north from the park as far as you could? *(the gas station)* Color the gas station.
- What is east of the gas station? *(Laundromat)* Color the Laundromat.
- What is the next place south of the Laundromat? *(the restaurant)* Color the restaurant.
- Lay the ruler east to west under the restaurant. Find the place west of the restaurant. *(the grocery store)* Color the grocery store.
- Lay your ruler north to south again over the grocery store. What is the next place south of the grocery store? *(the school)* Color the school.
- Choose one of the houses or the apartment building to live in. Color the place you choose.
- Name some places on the map that are north of the house that you chose.

Going Beyond

Enrichment

Provide a United States map puzzle for your child to put together. You may purchase one or make a map puzzle of your own. Allow your child to use a complete map, such as the State map in the Supplement, as a guide. Give help as needed.

Additional Teacher Information

There are many kinds of maps. A *product* map uses symbols to represent all the items made or grown in a certain area. An *economic* map shows the natural resources of a place. *Climate* or *weather* maps are used to show changing or recorded atmospheric conditions. *Navigation* maps plot currents and conditions of bodies of water. A *blueprint* is a map of a building. The map with the geographical features used in the lesson is called a *physical* map. The map of the states is a *political* map.

Supplemental Lesson
Aztecs

Preview

Main Ideas

- There were civilizations present in the New World before Columbus arrived.
- The Aztec nation had a cultural hierarchy, culminating in the First Speaker.
- The Aztec people were master builders and engineers.

Objective

- Name some improvements the Aztec leaders ordered

Materials

- Maps and More 4 and 5, page M3
- 10 cardboard tubes from rolls of paper towels*
- A marble
- A globe (optional)
- Supplement, page S5: the Aztec cities and causeways
- Supplement, page S6: the picture map, showing the pipeline and the water fountain

Lesson

Introducing the Lesson

Direct an inferring activity. Ask your child to guess what the people are doing in the picture on Maps and More 4. *(Answers will vary; they are buying and selling food in a market.)*

Activity Questions

➤ Do the people live where it is warm or cold? *(warm)*

➤ What makes you think the climate is warm? We can tell the climate is warm because of palm trees, open houses, and light clothing in the picture. The people in the picture lived a long time ago. They lived in Mexico.

> You may want to show Mexico on a globe and then point out the United States.

Teaching the Lesson

Direct a listening activity. Show Maps and More 5 and read the following information.

> Many people lived in the New World before travelers like the Vikings came. Some of the people lived in forests. Somc lived on plains. Some lived near the ocean. Some lived in great cities with large temples and markets on the streets. The cities had rules and leaders. Many of these people lived in what are now the states of Colorado and Arizona.
>
> Other people lived in Mexico. One group of people who built beautiful cities was the Aztec people. They built wide streets and large buildings. Thousands of people lived in some cities.

Listening Discussion

➤ Have you ever heard of the Aztecs?

Aztec markets were held in a large, open square in the center of the city. Farmers, noblemen, potters, basket weavers, and many other people came there to trade. Hundreds of goods were available in the market: canoes, fruits, flowers, animals, silver jewelry, vegetables, turkeys, eggs, sandals, cloaks, and copper knives, for example. The market was set up in sections: fruits in one place, baskets in one place, clothes in another. On market day, hundreds of people crowded into the plaza looking for things they wanted.

➤ The market had strict rules. Why do you think inspectors and judges were necessary?

Official inspectors checked the weights and the scales in every stall. No one was allowed to have an unfair scale. A special group of judges sat in a certain place in the market to settle quarrels over prices and trades.

➤ Why do you think groups of people need leaders?

In order to live together, people must have rules, and they must follow them. To have rules, people need leaders to help them make the rules and to see that they are obeyed. Name some rules you have. (BAT: 2a Authority)

➤ Who do you think the man on Maps and More 5 might be? Describe him.

The Aztec ruler was called First Speaker. He was a mighty king with gold and silver treasures. He talked about the laws with old and wealthy men. When he decided on a law, the people obeyed him. First Speakers thought of ways to help their people.

➤ What titles might we give the First Speaker today? *(king, ruler, leader, etc.)*

➤ What do you think the title *First Speaker* tells about his power? *(His word was most important.)*

Picture Map Activity

- ➤ Look at this map showing the Aztec cities and **causeways** (raised roads). The odd shapes represent Aztec cities. Some cities were built on land; others were built on **islands** (small pieces of land surrounded by water). The cities in the middle of the water were not always connected by bridges to the land.
- ➤ How could the people get from the island to the land if there was no bridge? *(by canoe or boat)*

One First Speaker had an idea to help his people. The Aztecs tied hundreds of canoes together and put boards over them. After the canoes were all in place, the Aztecs replaced the canoes with dirt and stones. Then the bridges became roads that were sturdy and permanent.

- ➤ Trace with your finger the causeways or roads leading out of the largest island city.

Direct a demonstration. Explain that the main Aztec city on land was far from good drinking water in the forest. People had to carry water five miles every day.

Select an area in the room that will represent a fountain in the Aztec market. The area should be far enough from the door of the room that it will take several cardboard tubes in a row to reach from the door to the area. Place a chair by the door. When putting the paper towel tubes together, be sure that the squeezed portion of the tubes is on the upper side, to prevent the marble from getting caught.

Demonstration Discussion

- ➤ Can you think of a faster way to get water to the city?
- ➤ I will be the First Speaker. Pretend you are a member of the council. Let's go to the "fountain." What problems are the townspeople having getting water? *(too far to walk, too heavy to carry, etc.)* What do you think should be done?
- ➤ As First Speaker, I will solve this problem. We will build a pipe to carry water from the forest to the city. All the potters will make a part of the pipe.

Pretend that these paper towel tubes are pieces of pipe. Let's go to the "forest" (the door). Squeeze the lower end of the first tube into the upper end of the second tube. Continue with all the tubes, fitting the end of the last tube into the top of the next tube. Place the first tube on the back of the chair. The last three or four tubes should rest on the floor.

- ➤ Do you think the potters did as the First Speaker said? *(yes)*
- ➤ What do you think of the First Speaker's solution to the water problem? Test the new pipe. Put the marble in the end by the door and let it go. It should roll out the other end.
- ➤ Do you think the Aztec people were glad that they had listened to their leader?

The Aztecs believed that one of their gods was a giant snake with feathers. Ask your child why he thinks the Aztecs had such strange beliefs. *(because they did not know about the true God)* Remind him that Christians should tell people about the Savior. (BATs: 1a Understanding Jesus Christ, 5c Evangelism and missions)

Evaluating the Lesson

Direct a listing activity. Invite your child to list the ways the First Speakers helped their people. *(Answers may include solving the water problem, making good roads, and talking about laws.)*

Direct a map activity. Show your child the map with the pipeline and the water fountain. Instruct him to point out the items on the map that show how the Aztecs lived. *(Water fountain and pipeline made water easy to get; roads led from one part of the city to another; bridges made travel over water easier; fields were cleared for planting, etc.)*

Going Beyond

Additional Teacher Information

First Speakers were always members of the royal family. That is, the current leader was the son, grandson, nephew, or brother of the past leader. But family connection was not enough to insure the position. A man had to prove himself brave in battle and wise in decision making to be elected by the council.

Montezuma II was the last leader of the Aztecs. He was the nephew of the previous First Speaker and the grandson of Montezuma I. Montezuma I (also called Montezuma the Wrathy) had conquered lands from southern Mexico to Guatemala. Montezuma II had proved himself a brave warrior, and he was well educated. It appears that he was an unassuming man. When the Council of Four sent to tell him that he had been elected First Speaker, he was found dressed in common clothes sweeping the steps of the temple.

2 Lessons 5-9

Columbus and His Ships

In Chapter 2 your child will learn about Christopher Columbus, his boyhood, and his later years. He will discuss Columbus's goal of reaching Asia and the reasons he set such a goal. Lesson 6 features a mapmaking activity, and Lesson 8 introduces a simple picture graph. The chapter ends with a supplemental, or optional, lesson about Columbus Day.

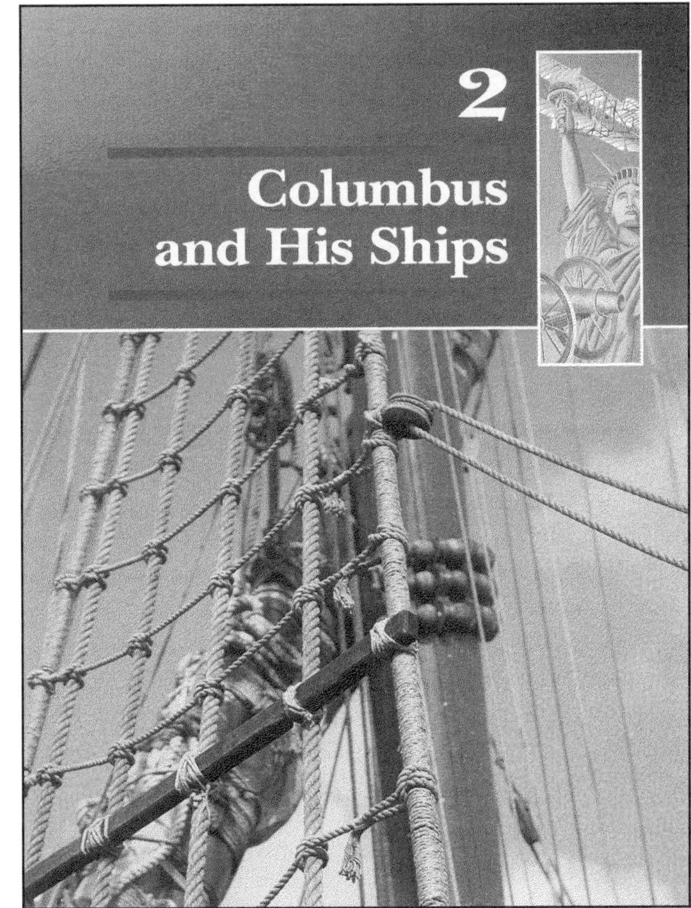

Materials

The following materials must be obtained or prepared before the presentation of the lesson. These items are labeled with an asterisk (*) in each lesson and in the Materials List in the Supplement. For further information see the individual lessons.

- A sturdy stepladder or alternative (Lesson 5)
- Colored-paper shapes (Lesson 6)
- Appendix, page A8 (Lessons 6, 7, and 9)
- A small piece of silk (Lessons 7 and 9)
- A porcelain object (Lessons 7 and 9) (optional)
- Spices (Lessons 7 and 9)
- Appendix, page A9 (Lesson 7)
- Dolls, toys, or stick puppets (Lesson 7)
- Pictures or objects—wagon, ship, plane (Lesson 8)
- An hourglass or egg timer (Lesson 8)
- Items or pictures—corn, sweet potato, parrot, gold trinkets (Lesson 9)

LESSON 5
Maps from Today and Long Ago

Text, pages 16-17
Notebook, pages 5-7

Preview

Main Ideas

- Long ago, men did not know about all the continents on the earth.
- The maps men made showed the land they had seen.
- Today we use maps that show all the land of the earth.

Objectives

- Distinguish between maps used long ago and maps used today
- Construct a map mobile

Materials

- A sturdy stepladder or alternative*
- A medium-sized cardboard box
- 2 to 3 items to place in the box, such as a toaster, a shoe, a lamp, or a plant
- Maps and More 1 and 6, pages M1 and M4
- A globe
- Several objects of various shapes: oval, cube, cone, and sphere
- A wire hanger
- A hole punch
- String

Set up the stepladder with the cardboard box beneath or beside it. Place the two or three items in the box so that your child can see only the top of each item.

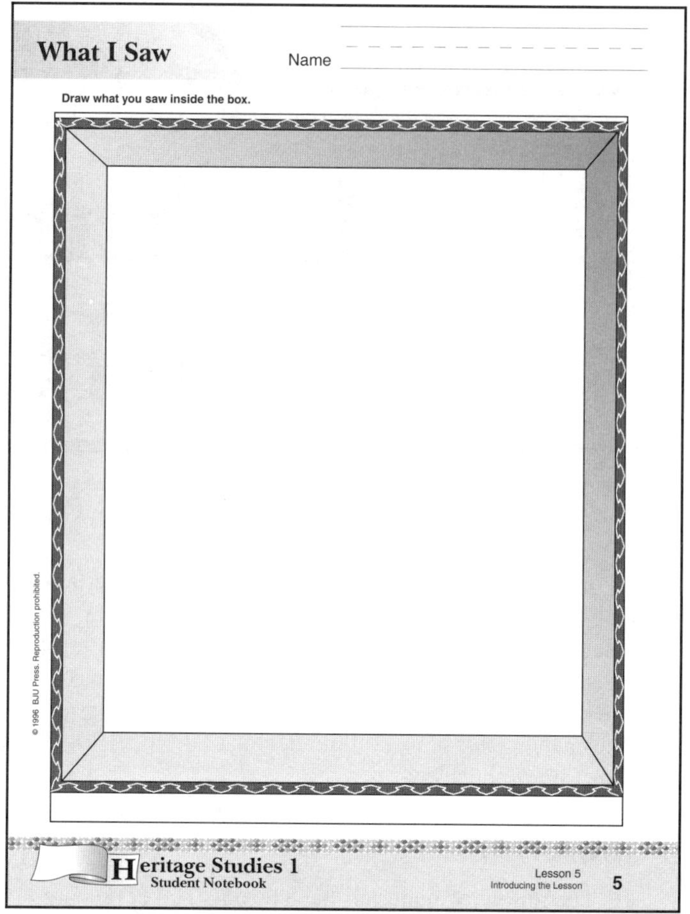

What I Saw
Name
Draw what you saw inside the box.
© 1996 BJU Press. Reproduction prohibited.
Heritage Studies 1
Student Notebook
Lesson 5
Introducing the Lesson
5

Day 1

Lesson

Introducing the Lesson

Direct an observing activity using Notebook page 5. Instruct your child to climb up onto the stepladder and look down into the box. Ask him to describe exactly what he sees. Elicit that he is viewing only the tops of objects.

Direct your child to draw on the Notebook page the top of each item as he saw it. Display the items from the box. Ask whether his drawings look just like the objects. *(no)* Point out that his drawings are different because they show only the top view.

Teaching the Lesson

Direct a comparing activity. If your child has ridden in an airplane, allow him to describe how things on the ground looked from high in the air. Encourage him to describe fields, trees, roads, buildings, and bodies of water. Ask whether these things look the same from an airplane as they do from the ground. *(no)* Help him to conclude that all a person can see from an airplane is the top of the things on the ground below.

Discussion, Maps and More 6

➤ Look at the two pictures on Maps and More 6. They represent different views of the same thing. What landmarks are shown? *(mountains, volcano, river, lake, roads, houses)*

Many, many years ago men did not have maps like we have today.
Their maps showed only the land they had seen.
How many continents can you find on this map?
It shows Europe, Africa, and Asia.

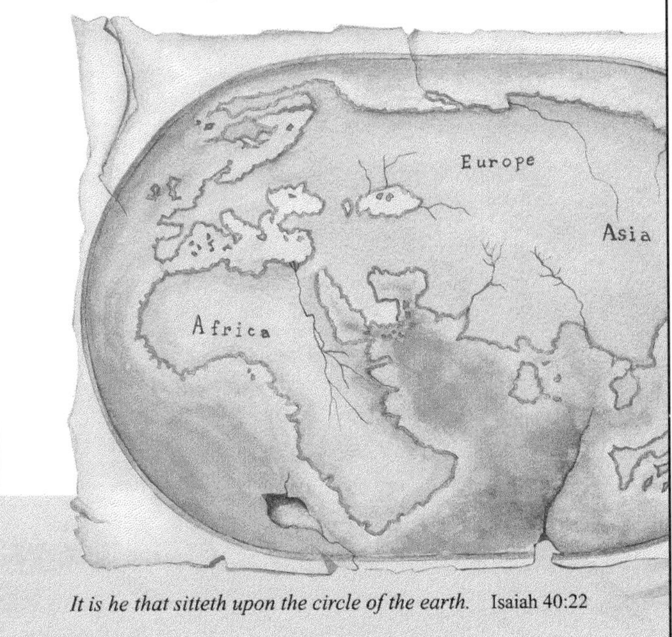

It is he that sitteth upon the circle of the earth. Isaiah 40:22

What special kind of map do we use to show the whole world?
We use a globe. Many years ago, people did not use globes.

Some people even thought the world was flat, not round like a globe. Why do you think they might have thought this?

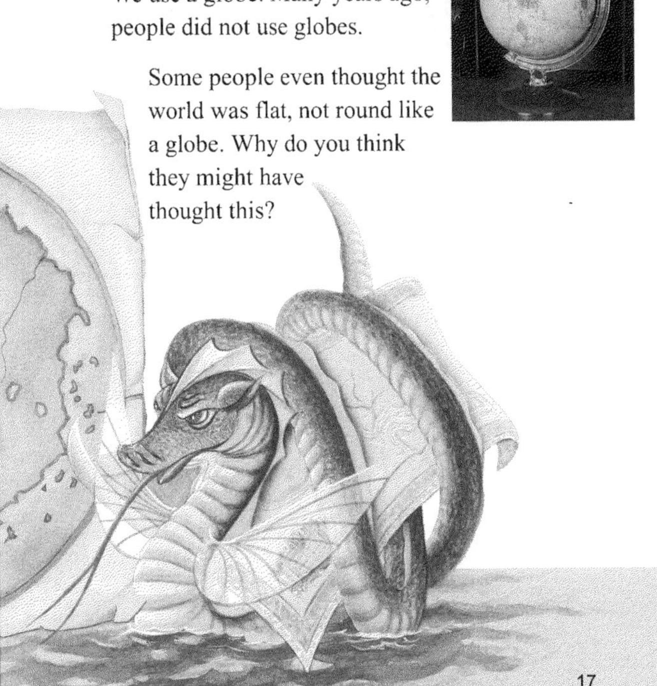

17

- How are the two pictures different? *(Answers will vary.)*
- Which picture shows how a river looks from the ground? *(the top one)*
- What view of a river does the bottom picture show? *(how a river looks from above)*

The bottom picture resembles a map. A map is simply a representation, or picture, of a part of the earth. It gives a "bird's-eye view"—a view from above—of land and water.

Day 2

Direct a text activity on pages 16-17. Direct your child to study the maps on pages 16-17 and on Maps and More 1.

Text Discussion, page 16

- Does the map on pages 16-17 look like the maps we use today? *(no)* Compare the odd shapes of the continents with the shapes on Maps and More 1.
- Many years ago, could people go up in an airplane to see what the land looked like? *(no)* Read page 16.

Mapmakers did the best they could by visiting other places and sailing along the coasts of the continents, but even then their work was not always exactly right. Some continents were missing.

- Why do you think North America, South America, and Australia are not shown? *(Answers will vary but should include that the mapmakers had not seen those lands.)* Maps today are made from pictures taken from the air and are therefore much more accurate than maps of long ago.

Text Discussion, page 17

- Look at the globe. Today we know not only the correct shape of the continents but also the correct shape of the whole earth.
- Describe the shape of the earth. *(round, ball-shaped, etc.)*
- Look at the objects I have collected. Pick out the ones that are shaped like the earth.
- Read the first two sentences on page 17. A globe is the best kind of map. Since it is shaped just like the earth, the continents are most like the real continents.
- Why do we not always use a globe to learn about the world? *(too difficult to carry around, too small to find some places, could not find our town or street on the globe, etc.)*
- Read the rest of page 17.

Many, many years ago some people actually thought the earth was flat. Some other people had even stranger ideas. They thought that the earth was carried on the back of a giant turtle or maybe a spider. Some even thought that a giant man held the earth on his back.

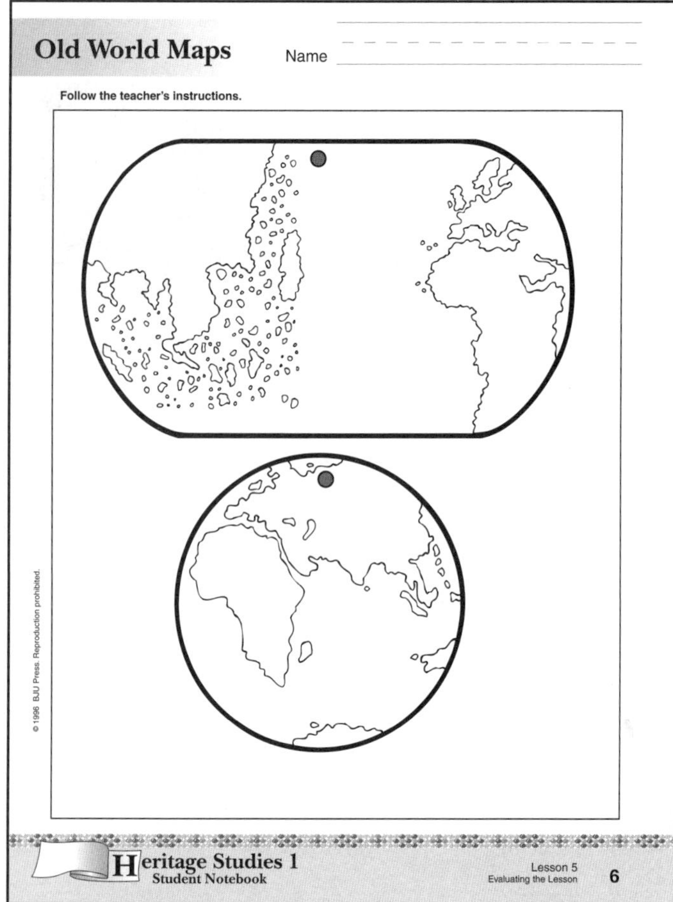

Old World Maps
Our World
Name
Assemble as the teacher instructs.
Follow the teacher's instructions.
© 1996 BJU Press. Reproduction prohibited.
Heritage Studies 1
Student Notebook
Lesson 5
Evaluating the Lesson
6

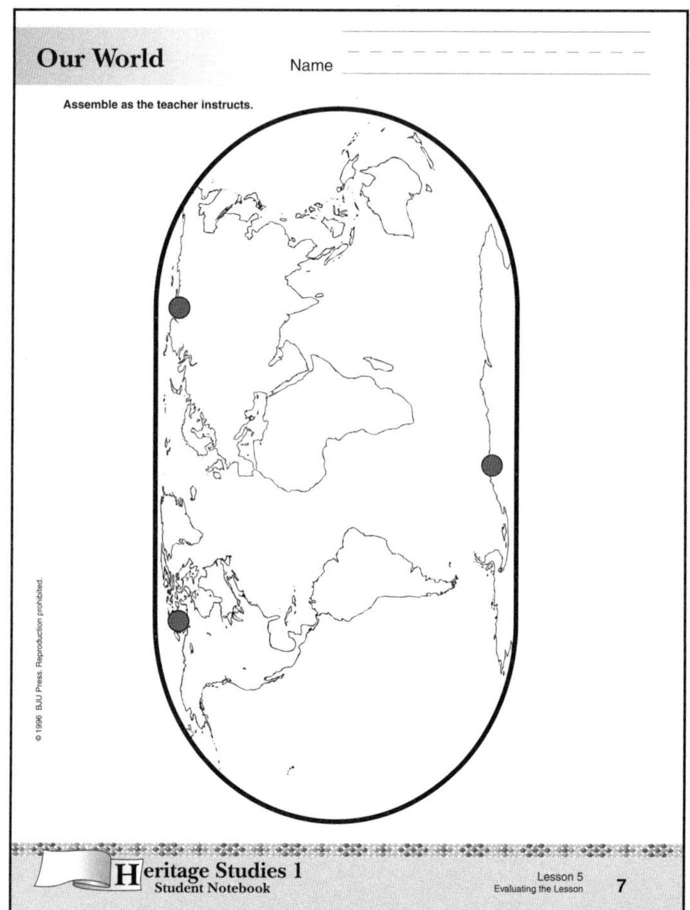

➤ Why do you suppose people long ago thought these things? *(They could see only the land stretching out flat around them; they thought the earth had to be sitting on something.)*

Many people who lived long ago were not able to read and study the Bible. Copies of the Bible were hard to get, and most people could not read anyway. Read aloud again Isaiah 40:22 from page 16. The Bible tells us the shape of the earth. If the people who lived long ago had read and believed the Bible, they would have known that God created the earth round. God's Word tells us many important things about His creation. (BAT: 6a Bible study; Bible Promise: I. God as Master)

Day 3

Evaluating the Lesson

Direct a mobile-making activity on Notebook pages 6-7. Explain that some of these maps show what people who lived long ago thought the earth looked like. One of the maps shows what we know the earth looks like today.

Mobile-making Instructions

- ➤ Color the water on the maps blue and the land green or brown.
- ➤ Cut three equal lengths of string.
- ➤ Punch holes in the designated spots on each map.
- ➤ Thread a piece of string through each hole at the top of the modern map and tie the map onto the coat hanger.
- ➤ Choose one of the old world maps to tie to the bottom of the modern map.
- ➤ Hang the completed mobile in the room.

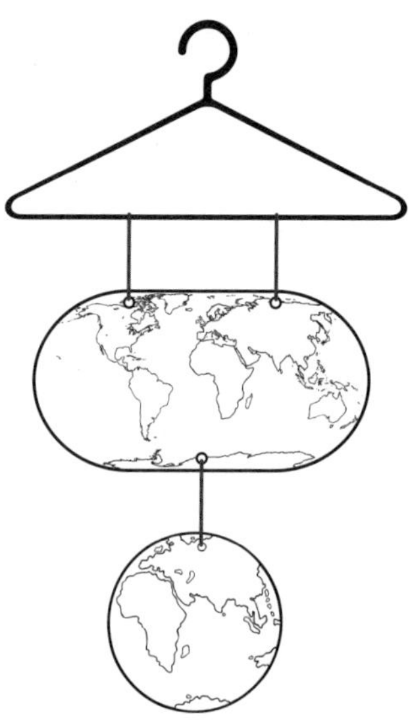

Going Beyond

Enrichment

Give your child the globe. Tell him that you will name a continent. He is to find the continent on the globe and place his finger on it. Explain that he will receive ten points for each continent he can correctly locate. Challenge him to see how many points he can gain. Name the continents with which your child may be familiar.

Additional Teacher Information

Geography is often considered one of the oldest academic disciplines. Its beginnings can be traced back to ancient Greece, about the sixth century B.C. Even the word *geography* has roots in Greece; it is derived from the Greek word meaning "earth description." Many of these Greek geographers' early writings described their physical surroundings.

The Greeks also made observations about the whole earth. Aristotle is most often given credit for concluding that the earth is a sphere. He used philosophical reasoning and astronomical observations to reach his conclusion; later Greek geographers agreed with him.

After the collapse of the Roman Empire, many of the ideas of the early geographers were lost to the inhabitants of Europe. But the ideas of Aristotle, Herodotus, and Ptolemy were preserved in the Arab world. Not until the age of exploration in the late fifteenth century was European interest again raised.

LESSON 6
Christopher Columbus

Text, pages 18-19
Notebook, page 8

Preview

Main Ideas

- When he was young, Christopher Columbus wanted to sail on a ship.
- Columbus became a mapmaker.
- Educated men knew that the earth was round.

Objectives

- Copy and complete a map and a map key
- Locate the desk on a room map

Materials

- A piece of drawing paper
- Colored-paper shapes to represent furniture*
- A large piece of plain paper for a room map
- Colored pencils
- A ruler or yardstick
- Appendix, page A8: The New World map

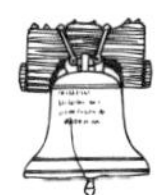

Cut the colored paper into various shapes and sizes that could represent pieces of furniture in your room (e.g., red circles for tables, yellow rectangles for the desk and bookcases, black squares for chairs). To make the mapmaking activity easier, you may want to lightly pencil in the desk, chairs, bookcases, tables, or other large items you want to include on the map. Do not be concerned with *exact* scale, but do try to approximate it. During the lesson, use the colored pencils and the ruler to "draw" and color in the shapes on the map and the key.

Day 1

Lesson

Introducing the Lesson

Read a poem to your child. Read the following poem by Marchette Chute. Instruct your child to listen carefully to learn about the poet's plan.

My Plan

When I'm a little older
I plan to buy a boat,
And up and down the river
The two of us will float.

I'll have a little cabin
All painted white and red
With shutters for the window
And curtains for the bed.

I'll have a little cookstove
On which to fry my fishes,
And all the Hudson River
In which to wash my dishes.

Poem Discussion

- What does the poet plan to do? *(buy a boat, live in the boat on the river)*
- When does the poet plan to do this? *(when she is a little older)*
- What would you like to do when you get older?

Guide a writing and drawing activity. Write the following poem starter on a sheet of paper.

When I'm a little older,
I plan to

Instruct your child to complete the poem, telling something he would like to do when he gets older. Ask him to draw pictures to illustrate the poem.

Do not be concerned with rhyme and meter during this writing activity. The purpose of this exercise is to encourage thinking and putting ideas down on paper. A few words will be sufficient.

Christopher Columbus

Christopher Columbus lived in a big city.
He liked to watch the ships sail in and out
of the harbor.
He wanted to be the captain of a big ship.
When he grew up, Christopher made maps.
He sailed many places. He read many books.
The writers of the books said the world
was round.
"I believe the world is round too,"
thought Christopher.

18

Day 2

Teaching the Lesson

Direct a text activity on page 18. Direct your child to look at the picture on page 18.

Text Discussion, page 18

- How old do you think the boy is?
- Point out the things in the picture that indicate that this boy lived a long time ago.
- Read the first three sentences.
- What did Christopher Columbus plan to become some day? *(the captain of a big ship)*
- *Point to Genoa on The New World map.* This town on the coast of Italy was Columbus's home.
- Listen as I read about the beginning of Christopher Columbus's adventures.

"Christopher! Where is that boy?" Domenico Columbus looked at his wife. "As soon as he finishes his work, he's off to the docks. What is it about those ships that he likes so much?"

Christopher's parents knew that their oldest son would not be happy staying at home. Christopher was just fourteen years old when he waved good-bye to his family and sailed away the first time. At first he worked as a cabin boy, helping the sailors and the captain of the ship. But soon he was a sailor himself.

He sailed from town to town to town on little ships. But Christopher wanted more adventure. He went to work on a bigger ship. This ship sailed to places far

Going Beyond

Enrichment

Give your child the globe. Tell him that you will name a continent. He is to find the continent on the globe and place his finger on it. Explain that he will receive ten points for each continent he can correctly locate. Challenge him to see how many points he can gain. Name the continents with which your child may be familiar.

Additional Teacher Information

Geography is often considered one of the oldest academic disciplines. Its beginnings can be traced back to ancient Greece, about the sixth century B.C. Even the word *geography* has roots in Greece; it is derived from the Greek word meaning "earth description." Many of these Greek geographers' early writings described their physical surroundings.

The Greeks also made observations about the whole earth. Aristotle is most often given credit for concluding that the earth is a sphere. He used philosophical reasoning and astronomical observations to reach his conclusion; later Greek geographers agreed with him.

After the collapse of the Roman Empire, many of the ideas of the early geographers were lost to the inhabitants of Europe. But the ideas of Aristotle, Herodotus, and Ptolemy were preserved in the Arab world. Not until the age of exploration in the late fifteenth century was European interest again raised.

LESSON 6
Christopher Columbus

Text, pages 18-19
Notebook, page 8

Preview

Main Ideas

- When he was young, Christopher Columbus wanted to sail on a ship.
- Columbus became a mapmaker.
- Educated men knew that the earth was round.

Objectives

- Copy and complete a map and a map key
- Locate the desk on a room map

Materials

- A piece of drawing paper
- Colored-paper shapes to represent furniture*
- A large piece of plain paper for a room map
- Colored pencils
- A ruler or yardstick
- Appendix, page A8: The New World map

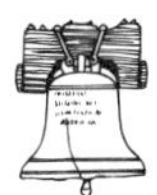

Cut the colored paper into various shapes and sizes that could represent pieces of furniture in your room (e.g., red circles for tables, yellow rectangles for the desk and bookcases, black squares for chairs). To make the mapmaking activity easier, you may want to lightly pencil in the desk, chairs, bookcases, tables, or other large items you want to include on the map. Do not be concerned with *exact* scale, but do try to approximate it. During the lesson, use the colored pencils and the ruler to "draw" and color in the shapes on the map and the key.

Day 1

Lesson

Introducing the Lesson

Read a poem to your child. Read the following poem by Marchette Chute. Instruct your child to listen carefully to learn about the poet's plan.

My Plan

When I'm a little older
I plan to buy a boat,
And up and down the river
The two of us will float.

I'll have a little cabin
All painted white and red
With shutters for the window
And curtains for the bed.

I'll have a little cookstove
On which to fry my fishes,
And all the Hudson River
In which to wash my dishes.

Poem Discussion

- What does the poet plan to do? *(buy a boat, live in the boat on the river)*
- When does the poet plan to do this? *(when she is a little older)*
- What would you like to do when you get older?

Guide a writing and drawing activity. Write the following poem starter on a sheet of paper.

When I'm a little older,
I plan to

Instruct your child to complete the poem, telling something he would like to do when he gets older. Ask him to draw pictures to illustrate the poem.

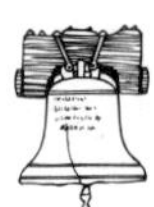

> Do not be concerned with rhyme and meter during this writing activity. The purpose of this exercise is to encourage thinking and putting ideas down on paper. A few words will be sufficient.

Christopher Columbus

Christopher Columbus lived in a big city.
He liked to watch the ships sail in and out of the harbor.
He wanted to be the captain of a big ship.
When he grew up, Christopher made maps.
He sailed many places. He read many books.
The writers of the books said the world was round.
"I believe the world is round too," thought Christopher.

18

Day 2

Teaching the Lesson

Direct a text activity on page 18. Direct your child to look at the picture on page 18.

Text Discussion, page 18

- How old do you think the boy is?
- Point out the things in the picture that indicate that this boy lived a long time ago.
- Read the first three sentences.
- What did Christopher Columbus plan to become some day? *(the captain of a big ship)*
- *Point to Genoa on The New World map.* This town on the coast of Italy was Columbus's home.
- Listen as I read about the beginning of Christopher Columbus's adventures.

"Christopher! Where is that boy?" Domenico Columbus looked at his wife. "As soon as he finishes his work, he's off to the docks. What is it about those ships that he likes so much?"

Christopher's parents knew that their oldest son would not be happy staying at home. Christopher was just fourteen years old when he waved good-bye to his family and sailed away the first time. At first he worked as a cabin boy, helping the sailors and the captain of the ship. But soon he was a sailor himself.

He sailed from town to town to town on little ships. But Christopher wanted more adventure. He went to work on a bigger ship. This ship sailed to places far away. But this time the ship didn't sail very far before an enemy ship saw it. The enemy ship attacked, and the ship Christopher was on sank.

Christopher clung to part of the ship. He kicked and paddled his way many miles to the shore. The shore Christopher reached was not part of his own country. Since he was hurt in the fight with the enemy ship, it took many days for Christopher to get well enough to travel again.

When he began to feel better, Christopher thought about what he should do. "My brother Bartholomew lives near here," Christopher remembered. Christopher went to live with his brother. He worked in Bartholomew's mapmaking shop. He learned to speak the language of this new country. He even learned to read this new language.

➤ Would you want to get on a ship again after being on a sinking ship?
➤ Do you think Christopher ever went back to sea?
➤ Read the rest of page 18 to find out what Christopher did.
➤ Did Christopher plan to be a mapmaker? *(No, he wanted to be the captain of a ship.)*
➤ Do you think Christopher had given up his dream to be captain of a ship?

Being a ship's captain was hard work; a person needed to know about many different things before he could do that job. Christopher Columbus wanted to learn everything he could before he had a ship of his own.

➤ How did Christopher learn the things he needed to know? *(read books, sailed on others' ships)*

Direct a map-reading activity. Explain that some of the maps Christopher made may have looked like the one on textbook pages 16 and 17. Ask your child whether he would like to be a mapmaker like Christopher was. Explain that even though he has not sailed to as many places, seen as many things, or read as many books as Columbus had, he can make a map of something he knows very well—his own schoolroom.

◆ **LEARNING HOW** ◆

To Make a Map

1. Gather some colored pencils, a ruler, and a large piece of paper.
2. Make a map showing where things are in your classroom. Use symbols to show where desks, bookcases, and other things are.
3. How is your map like the maps Columbus made? How is it different?

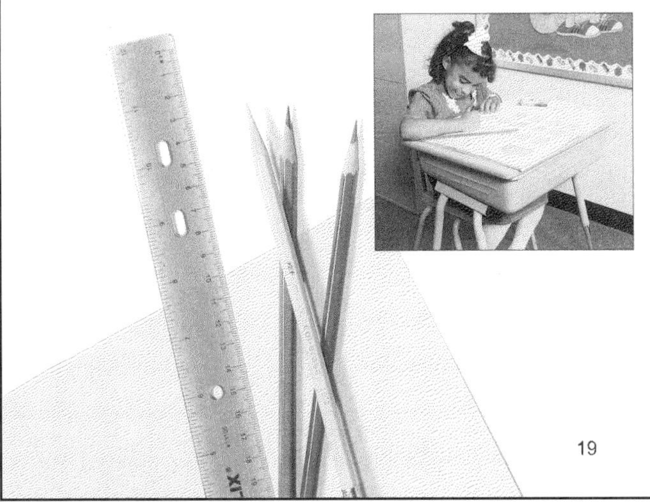

19

Day 3

Learning How Activity, page 19

➤ Read the steps on page 19. Imagine that you are floating on the ceiling.
➤ What things that you are looking down upon would you put on a map of the room? *Write the suggestions. Then show the paper shapes.*
➤ Determine which shapes would best show each object named. Remember that the shape is a picture of how the object looks from above.
➤ *Place on the table the large sheet of paper representing the room.*
➤ Make a map of the room by placing each of the furniture items on the paper where it belongs. Remember that the map will look like a picture of the floor of the room, as seen from the ceiling. *The items may be glued in place when they are correctly positioned.*
➤ Create a map key using the colored pencils and ruler.
➤ Look again at the map on pages 16-17. What are some ways that the map you made is like the maps Christopher Columbus might have made? *(It shows a picture of what something looks like from above. It shows where things are. It uses different colors to mean different things.)*
➤ Tell how the maps are different. *(Our map shows a much smaller area. It has a map key.)*
➤ Do you think making maps was good training for Christopher Columbus?

Discuss some of the things your child will have to do and learn before he can do the things he wrote about at the beginning of the lesson. (BAT: 2d Goal setting)

Classroom Map
Name
Draw a map of your classroom.
Make a key for your map.
Mark your desk on the map.
© 1996 BJU Press. Reproduction prohibited.
Heritage Studies 1
Student Notebook
Lesson 6
Evaluating the Lesson
8

Evaluating the Lesson

Direct an activity on Notebook page 8. Instruct your child to copy the map of the room onto his Notebook page. Encourage him to add any other items to the map that he would like, such as the wastebasket or a lamp. Remind him to make a map key, adding to the key the things he added to the map.

Going Beyond

Enrichment

Provide additional mapmaking materials. Encourage your child to make another map of a place he knows, such as the back yard, his bedroom, the park, and so on. Display the completed map in a special place.

Additional Teacher Information

Not much is known about Christopher Columbus's early life. He was born in Genoa, Italy, in 1451. His name was Christoforo Colombo in Italian, and it would seem likely that this is the name his parents gave him. But later in his life, Christopher Columbus called himself *Cristóbal Colón,* the Spanish version of his name. All of Columbus's known letters and writings are in Spanish. Some historians believe that Christopher's grandfather may have been a Spanish Jew who fled from Spain during the early years of the Spanish Inquisition.

Christopher's father was a weaver who probably assumed that his son would follow him in this trade, as was the custom. But Christopher had other ideas. Genoa was a wealthy seaport, and Christopher probably spent much of his time talking with the captains whose ships were docked there. When he was about fourteen, Columbus was hired as a cabin boy on one of these ships. He made several journeys during his teenage years and as a young adult before settling in Lisbon, Portugal, in 1476.

While living in Lisbon, Columbus met and married Felipa, a Portuguese noblewoman. She died not long after their son, Diego, was born. It was about this time that Columbus began his search for funds for a voyage to the Indies.

LESSON 7
Columbus Makes a Plan

Text, pages 20-22
Notebook, page 9

Preview

Main Ideas

- Columbus wanted to find a faster and easier way to the Asian countries of India, Japan, and China.
- Columbus needed help to raise money to pay for his journey.
- Most people did not think Columbus's plan would work, but the king and queen of Spain finally agreed to help him.

Objectives

- Perform a short dramatization
- Predict the outcome of Columbus's visit to the king and queen of Spain

Materials

- A small piece of silk*
- Something made of gold
- Something made of porcelain (optional)*
- A variety of spices originating in Asia, such as pepper, ginger, nutmeg, cloves, and cinnamon*
- A wooden tongue depressor or craft stick*
- A globe
- Appendix, page A8: The New World map*
- Appendix, page A9: the Columbus ship, cut out and glued to a tongue depressor*
- Dolls, toy people, or stick puppets of your own creation*

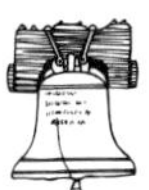

Save the silk, porcelain, gold, and spices for use in Lesson 9.

Day 1

Lesson

Introducing the Lesson

Direct a listening activity using Notebook page 9. Read aloud the names of the make-believe lands pictured on Notebook page 9. Ask your child to speculate about what these places may be like. Encourage him to find on the map each land you mention as you read the make-believe story.

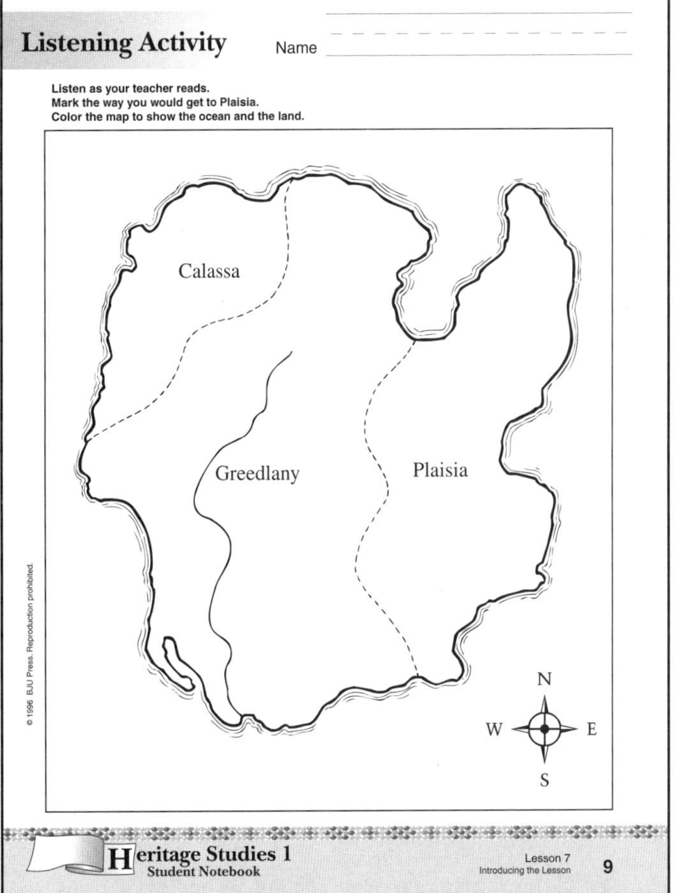
Listening Activity
Name
Listen as your teacher reads.
Mark the way you would get to Plaisia.
Color the map to show the ocean and the land.
Calassa
Greedlany
Plaisia
N
W
E
S
© 1996 BJU Press. Reproduction prohibited.
Heritage Studies 1
Student Notebook
Lesson 7
Introducing the Lesson
9

Far away to the east is a land where the most wonderful things grow in big flat fields, on round bushes, and even in trees. Now, I don't mean things like strawberries and blackberries and pineapples and bananas. Those things are wonderful. But the things that grow in this country are unusual too.

In the country of Plaisia, the farmers grow toys. Have you ever seen a toy plant? Pretty, talking baby dolls and trucks that you can sit in and that really work grow there. And the farmers of Plaisia have something you can't find anywhere else: robots that can do anything you want them to—even clean up your room. If I told you about all the toys that grow there, it would take all day and half the night. In Plaisia you can buy ten wonderful toys for just fifty cents. Do you have fifty cents to spend?

Until just yesterday we could walk east from our country of Calassa through Greedlany and right into Plaisia. We had to pay a few pennies to use the Greedlany roads. But a few pennies is not too much to spend to reach a land where such wonderful toys grow. But the Greedlaners got greedy. They watched the toys from Plaisia cross their country in our wagons and cars. And they thought, "We should be making money too. Those Calassians use our roads. If we make the people from Calassa pay more, we could get rich."

Now the Greedlaners have a new rule. They will buy the toys from Plaisia. And if we still want the toys, we have to buy from them. We cannot walk across their country and into Plaisia anymore. We cannot go into their country at all. And the worst part is the prices they want us to pay for the toys. Those greedy Greedlaners want more than one hundred dollars for each toy. Can you pay that much money?

Discussion and Notebook Activity, page 9

- Why did the Greedlaners make this new rule? *(They got greedy. They wanted more money than they had. They did not like the Calassians.)*
- Would God be pleased with the Greedlaners? *(no)*

God is not pleased when Christians are greedy or want more than He has allowed them to have. He wants Christians to be happy with the things they have. (BAT: 7d Contentment)

- Do you agree that the only way to get to Plaisia is to travel through Greedlany?
- Could there be another way to reach Plaisia?

Help your child discover that if he had a boat, he could sail around Greedlany and get to Plaisia. Talk about different routes of travel, using the four directions he has learned.

- Color the map appropriate colors and draw lines to indicate the way you would travel to Plaisia.
- When Christopher Columbus was a young man, something very much like this story happened. *Point to Italy on The New World map.* Remember that this was Columbus's homeland.
- *Point to Asia on The New World map.* This Far Eastern land had wonderful things to sell. But the people who lived in the land between Asia and Columbus's home did things much like the Greedlaners did.

Day 2

Teaching the Lesson

Direct a sensory activity. Review the problem Columbus had in getting from Italy to Asia. Discuss what Columbus's people should do. *(Discussion should include building ships and sailing to Asia.)*

Sensory Activity

- Feel the silk. Describe how it feels. Silk is a very expensive kind of cloth that was made only in Asia.
- Look at the porcelain. What would happen if you dropped it? *(It would break.)* It would break because it is delicate. Porcelain is sometimes called *china* because it was first made in a part of Asia called China.
- Smell each one of the spices. You may taste them also.

In those days men were trying to find a way to reach Asia by ship.
They tried to sail down the coast of Africa and around it.
But Christopher said, "There is another way to Asia. I want to sail across the great ocean."
He thought he knew a shorter way to bring back beautiful things from that faraway land.

20

- Why do you think the spices would be important to people long ago?

In those days, people did not have refrigerators, freezers, or tin cans to keep foods fresh. Their meat and other foods "went bad" very quickly. The phrase *went bad* means that it rotted or became unfit to eat. The strong spices like pepper and cinnamon covered the bad, or rotten, taste of the foods.

- Can you name something that is made of gold?
- Feel the gold item. The men who wanted to find another way to Asia hoped they would find gold there too.
- Which thing from Asia seems most valuable to you: silk, porcelain, gold, or spices? *(Answers will vary.)*
- Read page 20. How did Columbus think he could reach Asia and the beautiful and delicious things there? *(He could sail across the great ocean.)*

Demonstration and Discussion

- What does this globe represent? *(the earth)*

Most people in Columbus's day believed that the earth was round. They thought that if a ship sailed far enough to the west, it could reach the lands in the east.

- Hold the Columbus ship against the globe and move it toward the west, beginning at Europe and ending at Asia.

Before the King and Queen

Christopher Columbus needed money to make his trip.
What might he need money for?

Columbus went to see the king of the country where he lived.
He asked the king to give him money for ships.
He told the king, "I will find a shorter way to Asia for you."

The king laughed.
"The distance to Asia is greater than you think.
And you ask for too much money. I will not help you."

Do you think Columbus gave up?
No. Columbus thought, "I will not let him stop me."
He went to see the king and queen of another country.
He asked them to help.

22

People had not tried to sail this way for many reasons. Some sailors were afraid to sail where they could not see the land. They thought they might not be able to get back to the land if they could not see it. They also thought there might be terrible monsters in the ocean water. Those people wanted to sail down the coast of Africa and around it.

➤ Move the ship to show sailing around Africa.

Some people thought the ocean was very, very wide. They believed it would take months, maybe even years to sail across it. No ship could carry enough food and water to last for such a long trip. Then the sailors would have nothing to eat or drink.

➤ Do you think these reasons made Columbus change his mind about sailing across the great ocean? *(no)*

Direct a text activity on pages 21-22. Read the first two sentences on page 21.

Text Discussion, page 21

➤ Why would Christopher Columbus need money to make the trip across the great ocean? *(Answers will vary.)*

He would need to pay for the ships, food, and gear such as ropes. He would also need to pay the men who sailed with him.

➤ Do you think he would need a lot of money or a little bit of money? *Discuss possible ways for Columbus to get the money he needed.*

➤ Read the rest of the page to find out what Columbus did to get money.

A few other people may have had enough money to pay for Columbus's voyage, but Columbus needed the king's permission to make such an important trip. *Ask your child to share times when he has needed permission to do something. (BAT: 2a Authority)*

Text Discussion, page 22

➤ Do you think the king agreed to help Columbus? Read the first section on page 22.

➤ What reasons did the king give for not helping Columbus? *(The distance is too great; you want too much money.)* Many people agreed with the king.

➤ Read the first sentence of the next section and answer the question. Then read the rest of the page.

➤ Do you think this king and queen will help Columbus?

Evaluating the Lesson

Direct a role-playing activity. Explain to your child that he will be using the pretend people to present a miniplay telling about Columbus's visit with the king of his country. Guide him in developing a story line to follow. Think about the following questions as you plan the drama:

- Where did Columbus want to go?
- Why did he want to go there?
- Why did the first king not want to help Columbus?
- Do you think the other king and queen agreed to help Columbus?

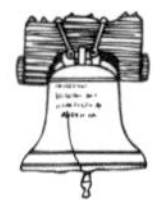

You may wish to present this dramatization to the whole family later in the day. You may also want to involve other members of the family rather than using the pretend characters.

Going Beyond

Enrichment

Provide a children's cookbook and labeled containers of two or three spices that could be bought in Asia. Encourage your child to find recipes that list one or more of these spices as ingredients. Allow him to choose one recipe for you to make together for your family to enjoy.

Additional Teacher Information

Columbus gained much of his inspiration from reading about the adventures of Marco Polo. Marco was just a young man when he traveled with his father and uncle, Venetian merchants. The three left Venice in 1271 and reached the Far East in 1275.

Kublai Khan was the grandson of Genghis Khan of Mongolia. Having conquered and united all the Mongol tribes, Genghis Khan had turned first to northern Cathay (China) and then westward. Genghis Khan pushed his empire into Persia and southern Russia. It was not until the reign of Kublai, the Grand Khan, that all of Cathay fell under Mongol control.

Marco Polo quickly became a favorite of the Grand Khan. By the age of twenty-three, Marco was serving as an advisor to Kublai Khan. During the seventeen years Marco spent in Cathay, he traveled throughout the huge Mongol empire. Although reluctant to allow them to leave, the khan finally granted permission for Marco and his father and uncle to return home in 1292.

Not long after returning to Venice, Marco was captured during a naval battle. While held in the Genoese prison, he talked to a fellow prisoner about his travels. Upon being released from prison, Rustichello, the fellow prisoner and a famous writer, published *The Book of Sir Marco Polo Concerning the Kingdoms and Marvels of the East.* The book soon was exciting readers with detailed descriptions of gold, spices, and other riches.

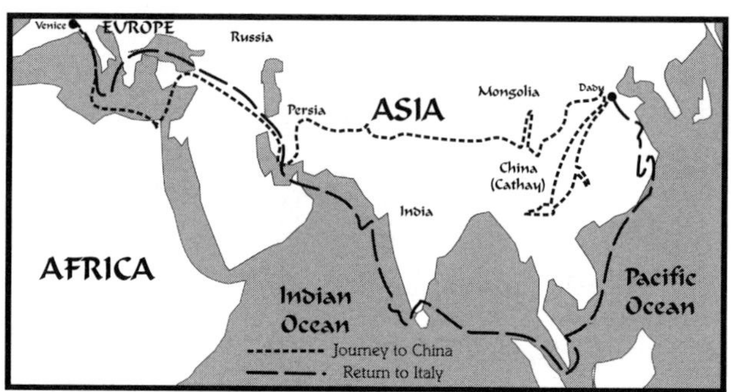

LESSON 8
The Ships and Crew

Text, pages 23-24
Notebook, pages 10-11

Preview

Main Ideas

- People use many different ways to travel.
- Ferdinand and Isabella provided three ships for Columbus's journey.
- The tiny ships were made of wood.
- Eighty-nine men sailed with Columbus on the three ships.

Objectives

- Read a picture graph
- Sequence events from the life of Christopher Columbus

Materials

- Pictures or toys: wagon, airplane, ship*
- An hourglass or egg timer*

Notes

The board game Setting Sail is introduced in the Enrichment section. (*NOTE:* See the Appendix, pages A10-A13.) If you choose to use the game, take the following steps to prepare the game pieces.

First, to assemble the **game board,** make one copy of each game board sheet and affix the copies to the inside of a manila file folder. (*NOTE:* You may need to trim the inside edge of one page to make it line up to the game board blocks on the adjoining page.) You may want to add color with colored pencils or felt-tip pens. To add durability to the game, you may also want to laminate the board and the pieces or cover them with Con-Tact paper.

Next, make five copies of the sheet of **game cards** and affix each copy to a stiff backing such as poster board. After laminating, cut the cards apart.

Finally, make one copy of the **spinner and picture key** sheet. Affix the copy to a stiff backing. After laminating, cut out the numbered square, the arrow, and the picture key. To assemble the spinner, place the rounded end of the arrow over the center of the numbered square. You may want to add reinforcement to the arrow for extra durability around the hole. Then push the brad through to assemble the spinner. To let the arrow spin freely, bend the prongs of the brad approximately $\frac{1}{8}$" from the head. Tape the prongs to the back of the square to keep the brad from spinning with the arrow. For additional spinning ease, bend the square slightly away from the arrow. The square will curve slightly downward, and the arrow will spin freely.

Put the spinner, the picture key, the game cards, and several items to be used as game markers (checkers, bottle caps, or large buttons) in a resealable plastic bag or an envelope. Attach the bag or envelope to the back of the game board folder.

Day 1

Lesson

Introducing the Lesson

Read some riddles. Place the pictures or toys on the table. Tell your child that you will read some riddles about transportation, or ways to travel. Ask him to choose the object which would best fit the riddle.

Bump, bump, rumble.
Along the path,
Down the hill,
My rickety wooden wheels follow.
Behind a team
Of brown mares—
They must pull me wherever I go.
Bump, bump,
Rumble, bump.
What am I?
(a wagon)

Up in the air, in the bright blue sky,
You can't see me at all—
Just my whispy white tail.
Later like a great steel whale,
Along the ground I crawl.
Do you wonder how I can fly?
What am I?
(an airplane)

Like a graceful swan,
I spread my square snowy wings
Into the wind.
The blue tossing waves
Carry me away and then
I sail home again.
What am I?
(a ship)

Ask which riddle describes the type of transportation Columbus needed to make his voyage. *(the last one; a ship)* Discuss the reasons the other types of transportation would not work. Point out that the airplane had not yet been invented.

King Ferdinand and Queen Isabella thought about what Columbus said.
They talked with their helpers.
The king and queen took eight years to decide.
Finally they told Columbus, "Yes, we will help you."

What do you think Columbus did next?
He found three ships that could make a long trip.
He found eighty-nine men who were not afraid to sail with him.

23

Pictograph

Name ______________

Answer questions about the pictograph.

The Crew of the *Pinta*

captain	
ship owners	
special workers	
able seamen	
apprentice seamen	

The Pinta had more (able seamen) / ship owners than special workers.

The Pinta had only one (captain) / apprentice seaman.

The largest group of men was the (able seamen) / apprentice seamen.

Heritage Studies 1 Student Notebook — Lesson 8 Teaching the Lesson 10

Teaching the Lesson

Direct a text activity on page 23. Review the things learned about Christopher Columbus thus far, emphasizing especially his plan for sailing to Asia. Remind your child that Columbus asked the king of the country where he lived for money. Ask what the king told Columbus. *(no)* Discuss what Columbus decided to do then.

Text Discussion, page 23

➤ Read the first section on page 23.

Columbus visited King Ferdinand and Queen Isabella many times. They wanted to hear about his plan. They wanted their helpers to hear about the plan. King Ferdinand and Queen Isabella did not give Columbus an answer right away.

➤ How would you feel if you were called to come before a king or queen?

➤ How would you feel if you had to wait eight years for an answer to something? Columbus had to wait for an answer longer than most first graders have been alive.

➤ Read the rest of page 23. Look at the pictures of Columbus's ships and compare them. Notice especially the difference in the sizes of the ships.

➤ Which ship do you think Columbus planned to sail on? Columbus sailed on the largest of the three ships, the *Santa María.*

➤ How many men did Christopher Columbus find to sail with him? *(eighty-nine)*

It was not easy for Columbus to find men who wanted to go with him. Some men thought he was crazy. Some did not trust him because he was from another country. And some were afraid.

Notebook Activity, page 10

➤ Look at the picture on text page 23. Can you tell how many men are on each ship or what their jobs were? *(no)*

➤ Look at the chart on Notebook page 10.

There were twenty-six men who sailed on the ship named the *Pinta.* This chart shows special information about their jobs. This kind of chart is called a **picture graph,** or pictograph. Each man on the picture graph stands for one man who sailed on the *Pinta.* The words on the left of the graph tell the jobs of the men on the ship. *Read each title in order and discuss how many men held that job.* (*NOTE:* The special workers group included physicians, carpenters, coopers [barrel makers], tailors, and stewards.)

➤ Read each sentence at the bottom of the page. *Allow your child time to study the graph and circle his choice before going on to the next one.*

◆ THINGS PEOPLE DO ◆

Building Ships

Long ago, men made ships from wood.
They cut and shaped the wood.
They nailed the pieces together to make the ship.
Then they rolled the ship to the water on a cart.

Today, most ships are not made of wood.
They are made from steel.
Many hundreds of people work to build each ship.

24

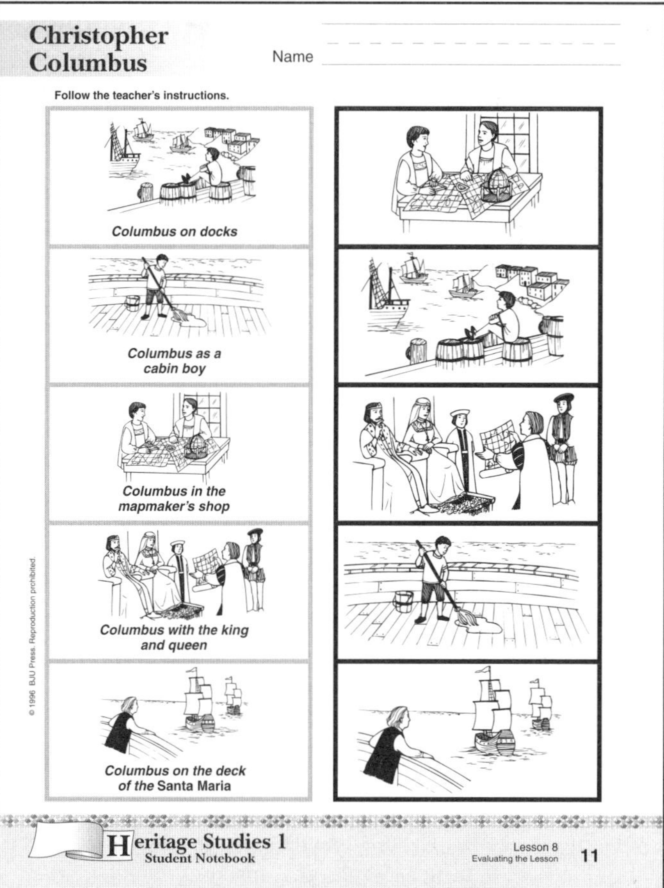
Christopher Columbus

Name

Follow the teacher's instructions.

Columbus on docks

Columbus as a cabin boy

Columbus in the mapmaker's shop

Columbus with the king and queen

Columbus on the deck of the Santa Maria

© 1996 BJU Press. Reproduction prohibited.

Heritage Studies 1
Student Notebook

Lesson 8
Evaluating the Lesson

11

Day 2

- ➤ Pretend you are a sailor on one of Columbus's ships. It is your job to watch the hourglass. When the sand runs out, you must turn it over immediately. Keep track of the number of times you turn it as we continue the lesson.
- ➤ Each of the three ships had men who did the jobs shown on the picture graph on Notebook page 10. Which job would you have wanted if you had sailed with Columbus?
- ➤ Point to the apprentice group on the picture graph.

Most of the men on the ships began as apprentice seamen, or beginning sailors. Often the apprentice seamen were quite young—sometimes only nine or ten years old. The experienced sailors had a special name for these young apprentices. They called them **grumetes.** The youngest grumetes, or the ship's boys, had a very important job. They kept track of time on the ship. They used big hourglasses that worked in much the same way as this little one works.

- ➤ Why would the grumetes' job be so important? *(It was the only way the sailors would know the time. It let the sailors know when they had to work and when they could rest.)*
- ➤ What would happen if the boy forgot to do his job? *(Answers will vary; no one would know the time; everyone would get confused, etc.)* The rest of the crew counted on the grumete to do his job well just as they counted on the captain to do his job well.

> The Lord wants Christians to do their work so that other people can depend on them. (BATs: 2c Faithfulness, 2e Work)

- ➤ How many times have you turned the glass? *Discuss how much time that actually is.*

Direct a text activity on page 24. Read the first section on page 24. Ask whether this wooden ship was very big compared to today's ships. *(no)* Then read the second section, calling attention to the modern shipyard. Discuss the similarities and differences in the two pictures.

Evaluating the Lesson

Direct an activity on Notebook page 11. Discuss with your child what is happening to Christopher Columbus in each picture. Allow him to color the pictures and to cut them out along the solid lines. Instruct him to put the pictures in the order in which they happened and to glue them in order in the gray squares.

Going Beyond

Enrichment

Introduce the Setting Sail game. Explain that the game board shows some scenes from the town of Palos, Spain, where Columbus went to get things ready for his trip. Explain each of the larger pictures on the game board: Columbus choosing ships, recruiting sailors, and purchasing and loading supplies such as food and water.

The players in this game will be gathering things for a trip to sea just as Columbus did. Describe each of the pictures along the path, using the picture key as a guide. Trace the path with your finger, beginning at the palace and going to the finish mark. Point out the two possible shortcuts, noting the arrow on the space before each shortcut that indicates whether the player should take the shortcut or the long way.

Sort the game cards into three stacks, matching the symbols drawn on them. Point out that these symbols match those on the game board. Place the stacks on the table faceup along with the game markers.

Give directions for playing the game. Explain that the object is get to the *Finish* square with the most game cards. All players begin with their game markers at the *Start* square. Each player spins once to determine who begins the game. The player with the highest number goes first. Then, in turn, each player spins, moving his marker ahead as many spaces as the spinner indicates. If he lands on the drawing of a ship or the sailors or the supplies, he takes and keeps a card of the same symbol. If he lands on a *Free* space, he may draw one card of his choice. If he lands on the drawing of the sinking ship or the spoiled supplies or the returning sailor, he must return a card with the corresponding symbol if he has one. If he lands on any of the four "special instruction" spaces, he should follow the directions given there. Play continues until all players reach the *Finish* square. (The exact number on the spinner is NOT required.) The first player to reach the *Finish* square may choose two cards of his choice. The rest of the players receive no extra cards. The player with the most game cards wins.

Additional Teacher Information

Juan de la Cosa, owner and master of the *Santa María,* traveled with Columbus on both his first and second voyages. On the second voyage he sailed as a cartographer, or mapmaker. Just six years later, in 1500, he became famous for his rendering of a map of the world. Between the years 1498 and 1506, he made three more voyages to the newly discovered lands, exploring and mapping parts of the South American coast. He went to Hispaniola to live in 1509 and one year later was killed during an ambush while exploring the Isthmus of Panama.

Martín Alonso Pinzón, of Palos, Spain, was the captain of the *Pinta.* He was a well-known and able seaman, and his popularity in the town of Palos prompted many men to sign on with Columbus's crew. Columbus distrusted him; he believed that Pinzón wanted to steal the glory of his achievement as well as any riches that could be found. Columbus recorded several incidents in his journal as evidence to his suspicions but never confronted Pinzón because of the man's popularity with the crew. Martín Pinzón reached Spain in the *Pinta* before Columbus and the crew of the *Niña.* But Ferdinand and Isabella refused to give Pinzón audience without Columbus. Pinzón returned to his home in Palos, where he died a few days later.

Vincente Yañez Pinzón, brother to Martín, captained the *Niña.* He remained loyal to Columbus throughout the voyage and later returned to explore the newly discovered lands.

LESSON 9
The New World

Text, pages 25-28
Notebook, pages 12-13

Preview

Main Ideas

- Columbus and his men sailed for many days without seeing land.
- Columbus thought he had reached a part of Asia.
- Columbus called the people he met Indians.
- America is named for Amerigo Vespucci, one of the first men to realize that this land was not part of Asia.

Objective

- Distinguish between things Columbus was looking for and the things he found

Materials

- A calendar (optional)
- Examples of items Columbus found in the New World: corn, a sweet potato, a parrot (or picture of a parrot), small gold trinkets*
- The items collected for Lesson 7: porcelain, silk, spices, and gold
- The figure of Christopher Columbus (1492) from the History TimeLine Packet
- Maps and More 16, page M9
- Supplement, page S7: a rhyme
- Appendix, page A8: The New World map

Day 1

Lesson

Introducing the Lesson

Teach an old playground rhyme. Discuss any songs or chants for skipping rope or playing games that you know. Show your child the rhyme about Columbus, explaining that it is quite old. Read it in a sing-song fashion. Encourage your child to repeat the rhyme several times with you. Then tell him that for many days the deep blue sea was the only thing Columbus and his men could see.

Teaching the Lesson

Direct a text activity on pages 25-28. Talk about any experiences you have had on a ship or boat. Discuss whether you have ever sailed so far away from land that you could not see it anymore.

The New World

The sailors were afraid.
The ships had been sailing for more than one month.
Many men grumbled and complained.
"We should have reached Asia by now," they said.
"Maybe the world *is* flat."
They wanted to turn back.

25

Map and Text Discussion, pages 25-26

- ➤ Read page 25 and the first section on page 26.
- ➤ On the calendar, count backwards the number of days that the sailors did not see land (a little more than a month). *Talk about something that your family did that long ago and compare it to the amount of time the men were sailing.*
- ➤ How would you feel if you were in a boat for so many days without seeing land? *(frightened, nervous, angry, etc.)* Even though they were afraid, the sailors should not have grumbled and complained.

God wants Christians to trust Him to protect them when they are scared. And He wants them to always obey the people who have authority over them. *(parents, pastor, etc.)* (BATs: 2a Authority, 8a Faith in God's promises)

- ➤ Point to Asia on The New World map, using your right hand, and to Columbus's three ships, using your left hand.
- ➤ What direction did Columbus sail? *(west)*
- ➤ Run your left hand across the map to the west. Could Columbus really reach Asia by sailing west? *(Actually yes, but not by sailing almost due west as he did. Accept either answer.)* We know something that Columbus did not know—two other continents blocked his way.

Columbus did not listen to the men.
He said, "I will punish anyone who grumbles."
Then he told them the king and queen had promised to reward the first man to see land.

The next day someone did see land.
It happened very early in the morning.
The sun was not up yet.
The other men were still sleeping.
"Land!" he yelled. "Land!"

26

Christopher Columbus had seen land. He thought he had come to a part of Asia called *India.*
He called the people he met *Indians.*
But those people did not call themselves Indians.

Columbus made three more ocean trips.
Each time he looked for the spices and soft cloth.
He never understood that he had not found a new way to India.
Now we remember Columbus on *Columbus Day.*

One hundred years later, Spanish people built towns far from where Columbus had been.
They were on the other side of the New World.
The Spanish called their place New Mexico.
Some of that land is still called New Mexico.

27

Text Activity, pages 26-27

- Columbus finally did see something more than the deep blue sea. Read the last section on page 26.
- Have you ever been up so early in the morning that the sun was not up yet? On the ship, someone had to be awake all the time.
- Read the first section on page 27.
- Why do you think Columbus was sure he had found a part of Asia? *(That is what he was looking for. He did not know about the continents that stood in his way. He wanted to believe he had accomplished his goal.)*

Comparing Activity

- *Place in a group on the table the items that represent what Columbus found in the New World*
- Have you seen items like these before? *(yes)* Except for the gold trinkets, Columbus and his men had never seen such things.
- Do you remember what things Columbus wanted to find in Asia? *(silk, porcelain, gold, spices) Place the set of items collected for Lesson 7 in a group on the table.*
- Compare the two sets of items. What one item can be found in both sets? *(the gold jewelry)*
- Do you think Columbus realized he was not in Asia when he did not find any silk, porcelain, or spices? Read the second section on page 27.
- Point to the West Indies on The New World map. This is the place where Columbus came.
- Read the last section on page 27.
- Where did the Spanish people build homes? *(in New Mexico)*
- *Point to the area on The New World map where New Mexico is located, noting how far it is from the West Indies. Then point out New Mexico on Maps and More 16.*

The homes built by the Spanish looked like buildings in Spain. The speech and customs of the people were Spanish as well. Share experiences you may have had in New Mexico or other Spanish locales.

Day 2

TimeLine and Text Activity, page 28

- Read page 28. Amerigo Vespucci sailed to the New World three or four years after Columbus did. Many years later a mapmaker read Amerigo's book. He thought Amerigo had discovered the lands he wrote about. So the mapmaker named the lands after Amerigo. He wrote a book and put the name *America* on the continents.

Later, the mapmaker found out that he had made a mistake. Amerigo Vespucci did not discover the lands. He only wrote a book about them. Christopher Columbus had discovered the two continents. The

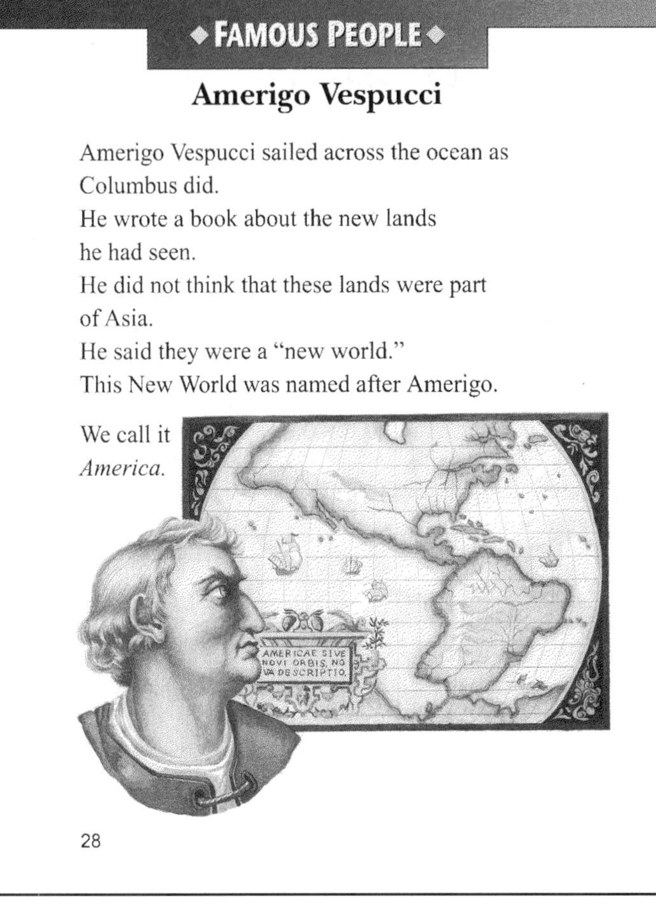

◆ FAMOUS PEOPLE ◆
Amerigo Vespucci
Amerigo Vespucci sailed across the ocean as Columbus did.
He wrote a book about the new lands he had seen.
He did not think that these lands were part of Asia.
He said they were a "new world."
This New World was named after Amerigo.
We call it *America.*
AMERICAE SIVE NOVI ORBIS, NO VA DESCRIPTIO.
28

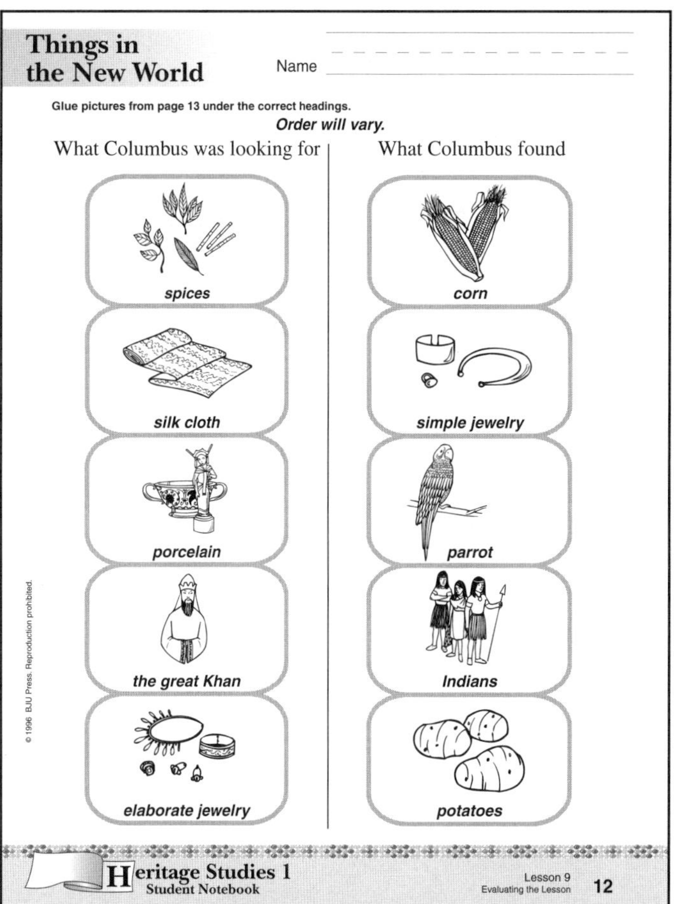

Things in the New World
Name
Glue pictures from page 13 under the correct headings.
Order will vary.
What Columbus was looking for
What Columbus found
spices
corn
silk cloth
simple jewelry
porcelain
parrot
the great Khan
Indians
elaborate jewelry
potatoes
© 1996 BJU Press. Reproduction prohibited.
Heritage Studies 1
Student Notebook
Lesson 9
Evaluating the Lesson
12

mapmaker tried to fix his mistake. He wanted everyone to call the continents *Columbia* instead. But it was too late. By then, everyone was calling the New World **America.**

- Columbus's journey changed the whole world. It affected people in the New World and people in the Old World. *Review briefly the important aspects of Columbus's story.*
- Put the figure of Columbus on the TimeLine at the year A.D. 1492.

Evaluating the Lesson

Direct an activity on Notebook pages 12-13. Review the things that Columbus was looking for and the things he found. *(spices, gold, silk, porcelain; sweet potatoes, corn, parrots, small gold trinkets, Indians)*

Notebook Activity

- Read the titles at the top of each column on page 12.
- Color and cut out the items on page 13.
- Place the cutouts under the correct heading on the chart on page 12, gluing them in place.

Going Beyond

Enrichment

Provide materials for a ship-building activity. You will need construction paper, clay, toothpicks, and glue. Also have available walnut shells, Styrofoam balls, or egg cartons. (*NOTE:* If you use egg cartons, you will want to cut the carton into individual sections.) You may wish to prepare one ship to use as a guide. Encourage your child to make several ships and to decorate each one differently with construction paper or crayons.

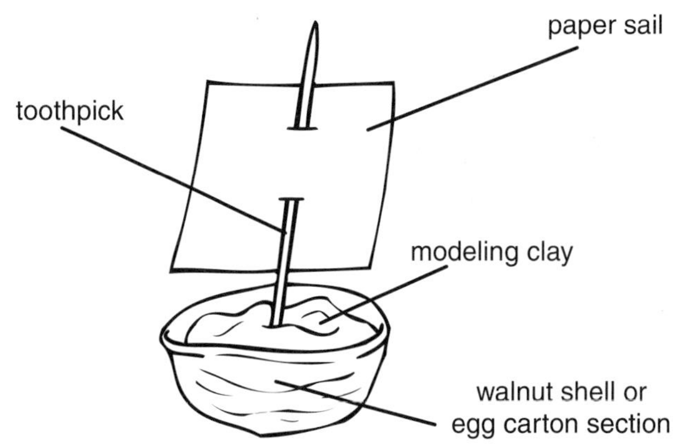

paper sail
toothpick
modeling clay
walnut shell or
egg carton section

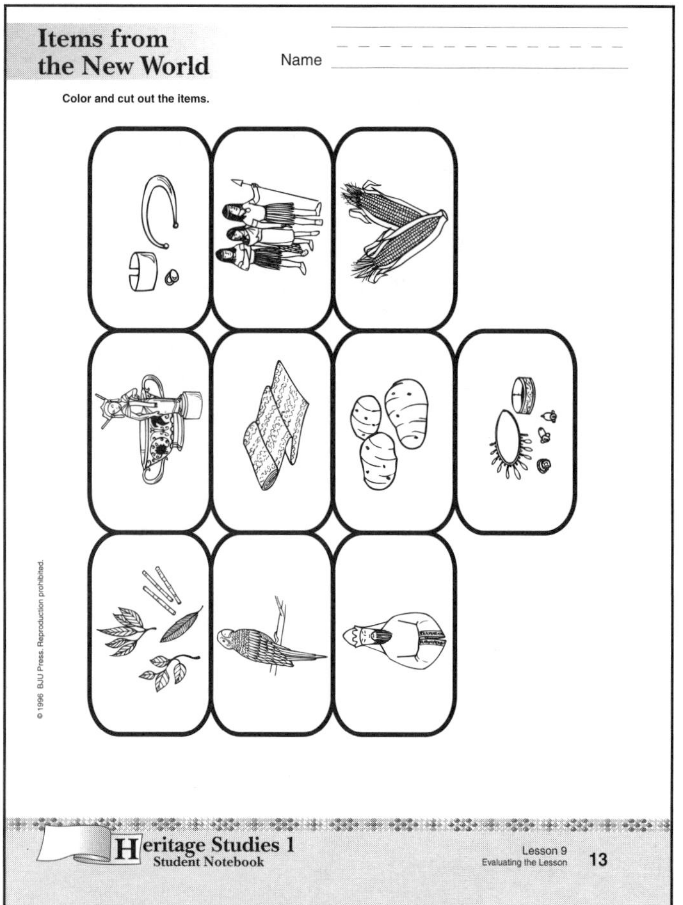
Items from the New World

Name

Color and cut out the items.

Heritage Studies 1 Student Notebook

Lesson 9 Evaluating the Lesson 13

Additional Teacher Information

Columbus had less trouble securing ships and sailors for his second voyage. Ferdinand and Isabella provided seventeen ships and provisions to help start a colony. The fleet sailed in the fall of 1493, exploring islands along the way to Hispaniola. Bad news awaited Columbus at the fort of La Navidad. The fort had been built from the wreckage of the *Santa María* and had been manned by about forty sailors from the first voyage. Upon reaching the fort, which was to have been the sight of the new colony, Columbus found total destruction. The men he had left there had treated the native people badly; the natives had killed everyone and burned the fort. Columbus then chose another part of the island on which to build his settlement, Isabella.

But Isabella proved to be a poor location, swampy and mosquito-filled. The site was abandoned and another settlement begun just before Columbus returned to Spain in the spring of 1496.

It was a full two years before Columbus was able to return to Hispaniola. On this voyage he discovered still more of the Caribbean islands. He also reached the mainland of South America, which he believed to be the Garden of Eden. When he reached Hispaniola, the colonists were ready to revolt. They were tired of the weather and the native foods. And they had not found the gold they had hoped to find. The colonists blamed their troubles on Columbus, and he was sent back to Spain in chains.

After much persuasion and a wait of fourteen months, Columbus was granted permission to make one final journey. Ferdinand and Isabella forbade him to return to the settlements he had started. He was desperate to find proof that the lands he had reached were the East Indies. But the old ships he had been given began to leak, and he and his men were marooned on the island of Jamaica for more than a year.

Columbus returned to Spain in 1504. He spent the last year and a half of his life petitioning the king and queen to restore to him his "rights and privileges." Ferdinand and Isabella ignored his requests, and Columbus died on May 20, 1506. Only family and a few friends attended his funeral.

SUPPLEMENTAL LESSON

Columbus Day

Text, page 175

Preview

Main Ideas

- Holidays help us to remember important things from long ago.
- We celebrate Columbus's discovery on October 12.

Objective

- Make a banner for use in a Columbus Day celebration

Materials

- Decorations for a variety of familiar holidays
- Maps and More 8, page M5
- A piece of art paper

Notes

This is an optional lesson. If you choose to use this lesson, you may want it to follow the last lesson in Chapter 2. You may instead prefer to use the lesson on the holiday it details: Columbus Day, October 12.

Lesson

Introducing the Lesson

Direct a discussion. Display the holiday items you have collected. Allow your child to tell what each item makes him think of. Write the names of the special days. Explain that the name for all these special days is **holidays.** Discuss the reasons we celebrate each holiday. Emphasize that celebrating holidays helps us remember important things that happened in the past. We have a special day to help us remember the day Columbus reached America. Ask your child whether he knows what that day is called. *(It is called Columbus Day.)*

Teaching the Lesson

Direct a text activity on page 175. Read the information on page 175. Discuss the various parts of the ship shown in this diagram of one of Columbus's ships.

Columbus Day

The first Columbus Day was October 12, 1492. One of Columbus's men saw land on that day. Columbus and his men had been sailing for more than thirty days.

Would you like to take a trip on a ship like Columbus's?

Text Discussion, page 175

- ➤ Where do you think the sailors slept? *(Answers will vary; on the rough boards of the deck.)* Read the last sentence on page 175 again.
- ➤ Tell why you would or would not like to sail on a ship like this.
- ➤ Look at Maps and More 8. Point to the land Columbus found.
- ➤ Read the first sentence on page 175 again. Do you think that this first Columbus Day was a little while ago or long ago? *(long ago)*
- ➤ Tell why you think that. *(Possible answers are the appearance of the ship or the clothes the sailors are wearing. Some children may understand that the date 1492 indicates "long ago," but an understanding of the date is not necessary.)*

For three hundred years, people did not think much about Columbus's journey. They did not think what he did was important. But people began coming to this "new" land. After many, many years, a few people began celebrating Columbus Day each October 12. Some cities celebrated with parades.

- ➤ Discuss any parades you have seen, especially Columbus Day parades.

The United States made Columbus Day a **national holiday** in 1971. That means that everyone in the United States celebrates Columbus Day. (*NOTE:* You may want to explain that the national holiday is not always celebrated on October 12. The U.S. Congress decided that Columbus Day would be celebrated on the second Monday in October.)

➤ Why do you think Columbus Day is an important holiday?

Evaluating the Lesson

Direct an art activity. Encourage your child to make a banner that might be used in a Columbus Day parade. He might include on the banner some of the things he has learned about Christopher Columbus. He may like to dress up as Columbus, a sailor on one of his ships, a Native American, or even as King Ferdinand or Queen Isabella. Allow him to show his banner to other family members or friends in the neighborhood.

3 | LESSONS 10-14

People of the New World

This chapter presents to your child the people who lived in the New World before Columbus arrived in 1492. Indians from five different geographic areas are discussed. Activities, demonstrations, stories, and artwork aid your child's understanding of the kind of life these native peoples lived. The chapter ends with a supplemental, or optional, lesson on things we received from the Native Americans.

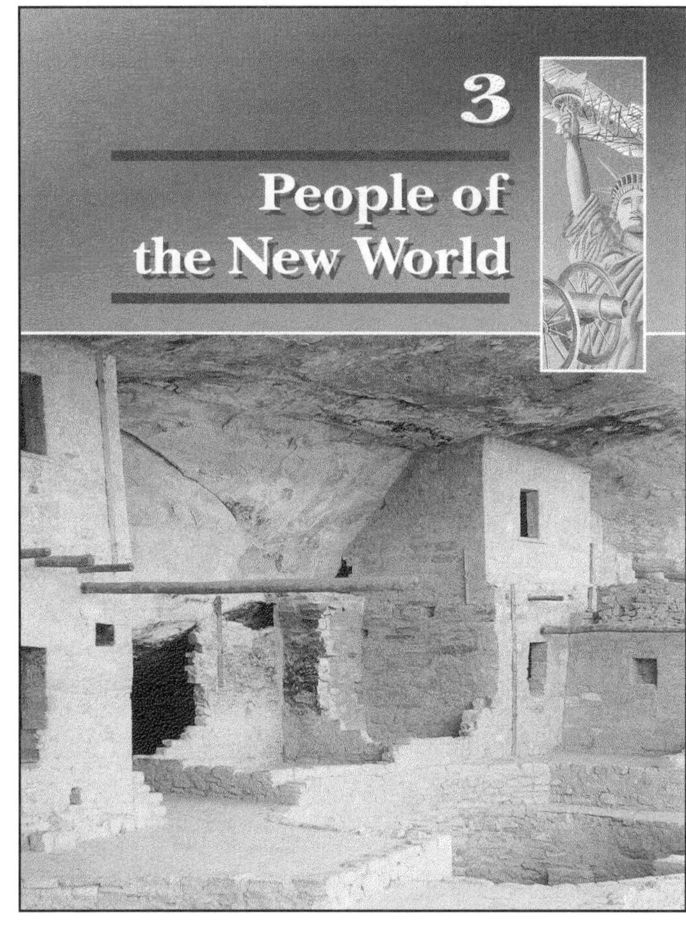

Materials

The following materials must be obtained or prepared before the presentation of the lesson. These items are labeled with an asterisk (*) in each lesson and in the Materials List in the Supplement. For further information see the individual lessons.

- Several modern tools (Lesson 11)
- Some dried meat (Lesson 12)
- 12 to 15 twigs or dowels about 12" long (Lesson 12)
- String (Lesson 12)
- 3 or more toothpicks (Lesson 12)
- A completed Indian weaving (Lesson 14)
- Two colors of construction paper (Lesson 14)
- A cotton boll or a piece of cotton wool (Lesson 14) (optional)
- Several pieces of cotton fabric (Lesson 14)

LESSON 10
People of the New World

Text, pages 30-31, 184
Notebook, page 14

Preview

Main Ideas

- Many groups of people lived in the New World before Columbus arrived.
- The Indians called themselves by other names.
- American Indians had settled in each region of what is now North America.

Objective

- Answer questions about a picture map

Materials

- Maps and More 9, page M6
- The figures of the Indians (about 1200 and about 1400) from the History TimeLine Packet
- A sheet of paper

Notes

Although only six groups of Indians are shown on the map on the textbook pages, there were more than a hundred different groups living in North America in 1492. Each group of Indians lived off the things that they could find around them, but most of them were not "savages" as the Spanish explorers and the English settlers thought. The aim of this chapter is to present the different Indian groups as separate civilizations that, even though they did not worship Him, God in His mercy provided for.

Day 1

Lesson

Introducing the Lesson

A demonstration about names. Tell your child that one person can have many names.

Demonstration Discussion

➤ What different names do you know for me? *(Mother or Father, Mr. or Mrs. ____, your first name, Christian, American, etc.)*

➤ What is another name for you? *(given name, full name, nickname, daughter or son, etc.)*

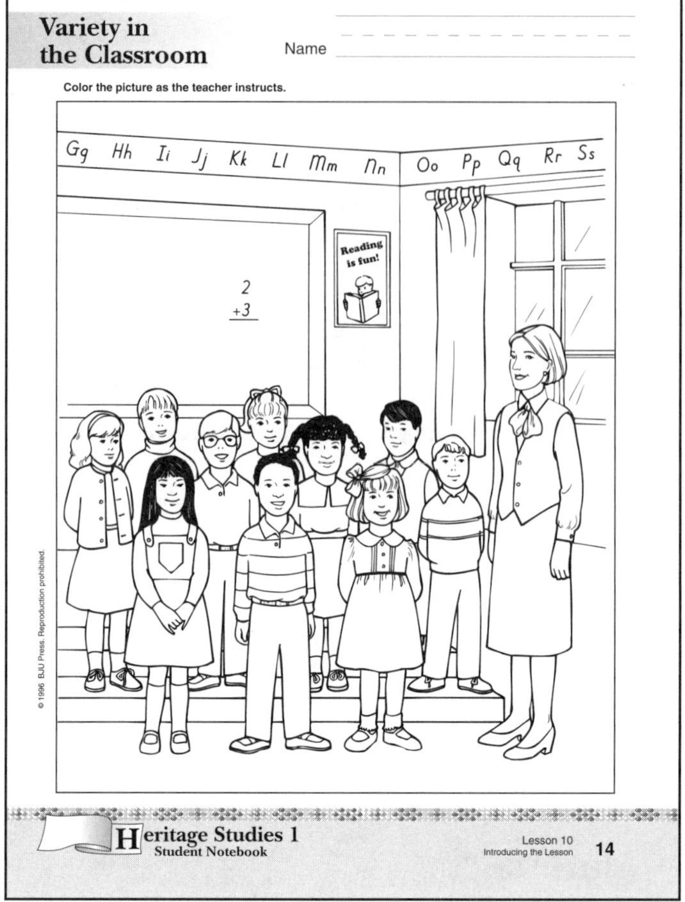

➤ Jesus has many names too. What names do you know for Jesus? *(Lord, Christ, the Good Shepherd, the Rock, Emmanuel, etc.)*

Discuss the meaning of some of these names. (BAT: 1a Understanding Jesus Christ)

➤ Do you think a group of people (such as a team) can also be known by more than one name?

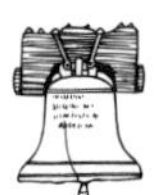

You may want to allow your child to choose an Indian name to use during this chapter. See the Enrichment section.

Direct an activity on Notebook page 14. Instruct your child to look at the drawing of the group of children on the Notebook page. Write the headings *We can call everybody* and *We can call some* on a sheet of paper.

Notebook Discussion

➤ What could we call the entire group pictured? *(students, class, children, first graders, Americans, etc.)* *Write the names on the paper under the first heading.*

➤ Could we place the children in any smaller groups? *(yes)*

➤ What names could we give to the smaller groups? *(boys, girls, light haired, dark haired, etc.)* *Write the suggestions on the paper under the second heading.*

Columbus called the people he met
in the New World *Indians.*
Why did he give them this name?
Before Columbus came, the people he
met called themselves by another name.
They called themselves *Arawaks.*
Only the Arawaks and one other group of
people lived on the tiny islands Columbus saw.
30

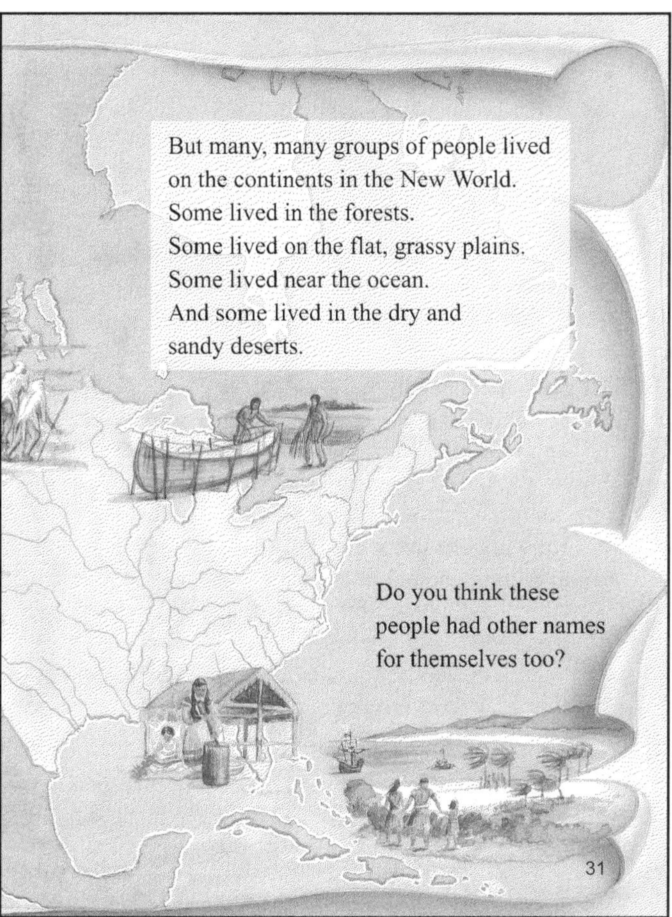

But many, many groups of people lived
on the continents in the New World.
Some lived in the forests.
Some lived on the flat, grassy plains.
Some lived near the ocean.
And some lived in the dry and
sandy deserts.
Do you think these
people had other names
for themselves too?
31

(*NOTE:* Choose a convenient time for your child to color the picture on the Notebook page if he wishes to do so.)

➤ This chapter is about several groups of people that have at least two names: the name we know them by and the name they called themselves.

Day 2

Teaching the Lesson

Direct a text activity on pages 30-31. Read page 30.

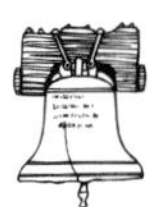

Remember that the Text Discussion is a guide to help as you read and discuss the text pages. When instructions say to read the text, read in the manner that is comfortable for you and your child. If your child is able to read the text by himself, allow him to do so. If not, allow him to read what he can, or read the text to him. As the year progresses, your child may find it easier to read on his own.

Text Discussion, page 30

➤ What two names were given to the people that Columbus met in the New World? *(Indians, Arawaks [ar´ə wäks])*

➤ Why did Columbus call the people **Indians?** *(He thought he had reached India. The people there are called Indians.)*

Today the term *Indian* is not as acceptable as **Native American.** In discussing early history we have chosen to refer to native people as Indians when speaking generally of several nations at once or when the specific names are not known.

➤ Point to the **Awaraks** on their island in the lower right corner of page 31.

➤ How many other groups of Indians lived on these islands? *(one)*

Text Discussion, page 31

➤ Read page 31.

➤ Look at Maps and More 9. Where did other Indians live? *(on the continents, in the forests and deserts, on the plains, and near the ocean)*

The Resource Treasury in the back of the student text contains additional information about various topics. During your discussion of Native American tribes, you may want to refer to page 184 to point out the geographic features of the area where each tribe lived.

➤ When Columbus arrived, were there already people living in many places throughout the land he found? *(yes)*
➤ By what name do we know these people? *(Indians)* *Discuss each group of Indians, pointing out its location on Maps and More 9. Guide your child in learning to pronounce each name. Encourage him to describe the things he notices about each group.*
➤ How do you think the Indians felt when Columbus and his men, and later many more people, came to their land? *(Answers will vary but may include frightened, angry, excited.)*
➤ What do we sometimes call the land Columbus found? If you are not sure, you may look again at the title of the chapter. *(the New World)*

This land was not really "new"; the people Columbus met had been living here for many hundreds, even thousands, of years.

Add figures to the TimeLine. Display the TimeLine and the pictures of Indians.

TimeLine Discussion

➤ Since Indians were here when Columbus came, where do you think we should put one group of Indian figures on the TimeLine? *(before Columbus, at 1400)*
➤ Look at the Leif Ericson figure on the TimeLine. Leif Ericson lived many years before Christopher Columbus lived.
➤ Did Indians live in the land before Leif Ericson came? *(yes)* Did Indians also live there after Leif Ericson came? *(yes)*
➤ Put another group of Indians at 1200 on the TimeLine.

Evaluating the Lesson

Direct a map-reading activity. Allow your child to use the Maps and More 9. Review which is his right hand and which is his left hand. Instruct him to raise his right hand if the answer is *true* and his left hand if the answer is *false.* Use statements such as the following:

- All the people living in the New World called themselves by the name Indian. *(false)*
- Some Indians lived on islands. *(true)*
- Some Indians lived in the desert. *(true)*
- No Indians lived in the cold north. *(false)*
- All Indians lived in the same kind of house. *(false)*

Going Beyond

Enrichment

Tell your child that Indian names may sound different to us but that each name tells us something about that person. Discuss with your child some translations of Indian names: Sings Like a Bird, Crazy Horse, Swift Arrow, and so on. Discuss the possible meanings of these names.

Encourage your child to pick an Indian name for himself that tells something special about him. Give him a name tag to write the name on. Allow him to wear his name throughout the study of this chapter. You may want to give each member of your family an Indian name.

At a later time you may want to explain that an Indian girl kept the same name throughout her whole life. A boy's name, however, was changed often several times during his life, whenever he performed some brave deed or reached a new level of maturity or ability. You may want to allow the males in your family to change their names as appropriate situations arise during the study of this chapter.

Additional Teacher Information

The first Native Americans Columbus met were the Arawaks. These people lived on the islands of the Greater Antilles and the Bahamas. They were peaceful farmers and fishermen living in large villages.

Thinking Columbus a god, the Arawaks provided him and his men with food and water. They continued their kindnesses to the white men until the white men began to take advantage of them. Because Arawaks were not hunters or warriors, they had few weapons with which to fight the white men. Due to the harsh treatment they received and to the diseases brought by the Spanish explorers, all of the estimated sixty thousand Arawaks died within a short time.

The second group of Native Americans encountered by Columbus were the Caribs. The Caribs lived in small villages on the islands of the Lesser Antilles. Unlike the Arawaks, the Caribs were very warlike. They were known to kill and eat their prisoners. The word *cannibal* comes from *Caribales,* a word the Spanish used to describe the Caribs. The Caribbean Sea is named for these people, who were also excellent sailors.

Lesson 11
The Woodland Indians

Text, pages 32-35
Notebook, page 15

Preview

Main Ideas

- Some Indians lived in the forests.
- Some Indians were farmers and hunters.
- Indians made the tools they needed from the things around them.
- Indians made their homes and clothing from the things around them.

Objective

- Identify things Woodland Indians used for food and for making tools, clothing, and homes

Materials

- Maps and More 9 and 10, pages M6-M7
- Several modern tools like those the Indians would have needed: an ax, needles, a shovel, a pocketknife, and so on *

Day 1

Introducing the Lesson

Direct a listening activity. Show your child Maps and More 10. Allow him to describe each picture.

Listening Activity

➤ Point to each photograph, describing the color of the trees and the season which each represents.

➤ Listen while I read about how one group of Indians explained why the seasons change.

The Trees That Promise Spring's Return

Long, long ago, all the trees had voices. They talked and talked, for there was no one to stop them, and they had much to talk about. What might trees have to talk about, you ask? They talked of their love for the kind Sun and of his good friends Zephyr and Spring. And they talked, in hushed voices, about the wicked monsters.

The most wicked of the monsters were Winter's warriors: Storm Wind and Frost. The trees feared these two more than any other, for they slashed and tore at the trees. The monsters ripped their beautiful leaves and broke their strong arms. Winter commanded his warriors to do these things because the trees loved the Sun and his friends, the Spring chiefs.

Warrior Storm Wind brought to the trees Winter's first command. "Drop your leaves! We want nothing flowery and green to remind us of Spring." The trees did not want to obey, and the Winter warriors knew this. So Warrior Frost sent his servant Autumn to paint the leaves with beautiful colors. This made the trees want to keep their leaves even more. They would not drop their leaves! Then Storm Wind came and pulled every leaf off every tree.

Then Winter's laughter shook the earth. "Ha, Ha! Spring is gone from the earth. Spring and the Sun have no friends left here. The world will obey me now. Ho, Ho!"

A quiet but determined voice said, "I am friend to Spring." It was White Pine.

"We shall see," thundered Winter. "You still hold your long green leaves, but when I give my command, your leaves will be gone like all the others!"

No, thought White Pine, I will not turn my back on my friend Spring. So he called a great council of his tribe.

"I will not obey Winter's evil commands," shouted White Pine. "Who will challenge Winter and his warriors with me? Who will be faithful to Spring?"

"I am faithful," said Red Pine, Juniper, and Hemlock.

"I am faithful," said Balsam, Cypress, and Cedar.

All the brave trees in the tribe promised to stand with White Pine. All, that is, except Tamarack. He had not heard White Pine's speech, for he was struggling with Oak for the good place on the high hill.

"Tamarack, will you stand with us against Winter?" White Pine asked when the trees found Tamarack on the hill.

"I must finish my struggle with Oak first. Then I will stand against Winter," promised Tamarack.

Now Oak had heard what White Pine said. Oak was not part of White Pine's tribe, but he was a friend of Spring. "Honorable White Pine, I belong to the broad-leaf tribe. My leaves are not beautiful and slender like yours. But I am a friend of the Sun and of Spring. If I may join with you, I will stand on this high hill and shake my leaves at Winter."

"Ha," said Tamarack. "Oak is not one of us. He will not be able to keep his pitiful leaves when Storm Wind blows his fiercest. No, and he will not keep his place on this hill. I will."

"On high hill or flat land, I promise to keep my leaves until Spring and the Sun return to warm the land," said the sturdy voice of Oak.

All the trees knew how Winter hated the sound of dry leaves rattling. "It is a good plan," said White Pine.

Soon Autumn arrived to paint the broad-leaf tribe with his lovely colors. Then came Frost and Storm Wind with chill and rain. "Drop your leaves!" commanded Winter as his warriors whipped and struck and screamed.

The tribe of White Pine stood strong. They held their beautiful long green leaves while Autumn painted and Frost and Storm Wind fought. Oak stood strong. He held his leaves, first painted flaming red and then blown cracked and dry by Storm Wind's blasts. He shook the dry leaves in Winter's face while Winter howled.

Only Tamarack gave in. Too busy in his struggle with Oak, he forgot to drink from the well of his tribe. The water kept the other trees' leaves green and in place, but Tamarack's long leaves began to fall. Soon he stood like the broad-leaf trees, stripped of his leaves, while Frost danced his war dance around the trees and across the water.

White Pine saw Tamarack's shame. To the rest of the tribe and to Oak he said, "Stand strong. Tamarack has given in to Winter, but we must not."

Though Winter ruled long and hard, White Pine and the others kept their promise. They raised their voices, saying, "We are the friends of Spring. Be strong and brave. Spring will return."

And Spring did return. He brought with him his friend the Sun, who warmed the land and water and air with his smiling face. Zephyr, the fresh breeze, warmed the cold trees with his gentle breath. He rustled the dry leaves of Oak as Spring brought new growth to all the trees.

White Pine looked at Tamarack's little budding leaves. "Tamarack, you did not keep your promise. You listened to the commands of Winter. You gave in to Frost and Storm Wind. You are a coward and a braggart. You cannot live on the high hill. Oak, the friend of Spring and of our brave tribe, may have the hill forever."

Tamarack begged for White Pine's mercy. But he would not hear. The other trees would not hear. They sent him away to live in the swamps.

Since that long ago time, the tribe of White Pine hold up their green leaves in the face of Winter. They remind all who see them that Spring will return.

- Do you think this story is true? *(no)* Why?
- Why did Indians tell stories, or **legends,** such as this one?

The Indians did not have God's Word; they did not know the one true God. They tried to explain the things that happened around them, like the changing of the trees, by making up names for gods and telling stories about them.

- Do you think people today might do this same thing? *(yes)*
- How can we help these people to learn about the one true God? *(tell others about Him, send them Bibles, pray for missionaries, etc.)* (BAT: 5c Evangelism and missions)

Woodland Peoples

Woodland people lived in the forest.
Most Woodland people were farmers.
They cut down some of the trees.
Then they planted vegetables.

Woodland people made canoes from trees.
Woodland people hunted for animals
in the forest.
What do you think the people did with the
animals they killed?
They ate the meat and used the skins to make
clothes and shoes.

Every moving thing that liveth shall be meat for you; even as the green herb have I given you all things.
Genesis 9:3

32

Day 2

Teaching the Lesson

Direct a text activity on pages 32-35. Tell your child that one of the Indian groups you have discussed made up the story he just heard. Explain that trees and forests were very important to this group of Indians.

Text Discussion, page 32

- Point to the tribe of Indians on Maps and More 9 that you think told the story I read. *(Iroquois)*
- Read page 32 to find out what made the forest important to these Indians. *(They lived in the forest, hunted in the forest, and made canoes from trees.)* (*NOTE:* The Bible verse will be discussed later in the lesson.)
- How did most **Woodland Indians** get food to eat? *(They were farmers; they grew it themselves.)*

The Woodland Indians' farms were not big like farms of today; they were more like our gardens.

- What are some things the Indians might have grown? *(Answers will vary.)*
- How did the Woodland Indians get meat to eat? *(by hunting)*
- The Indians did not have guns to hunt with before Columbus came. What do you think the Indians used to hunt with instead of guns? *(Answers may include bow and arrows.)*

◆ THINGS PEOPLE DO ◆

Making Tools

The people made everything they needed before Columbus came.
They made *tools* from wood and stone or animal bone.
Tools are things people use to help them do work.
What tools do you use?

They made axes and knives from stone and bits of bone.
They used the axes to cut down trees and to make canoes.
They used stone or bone to make needles for sewing.
They made arrows from stone or bone too.
What did they use the arrows for?

33

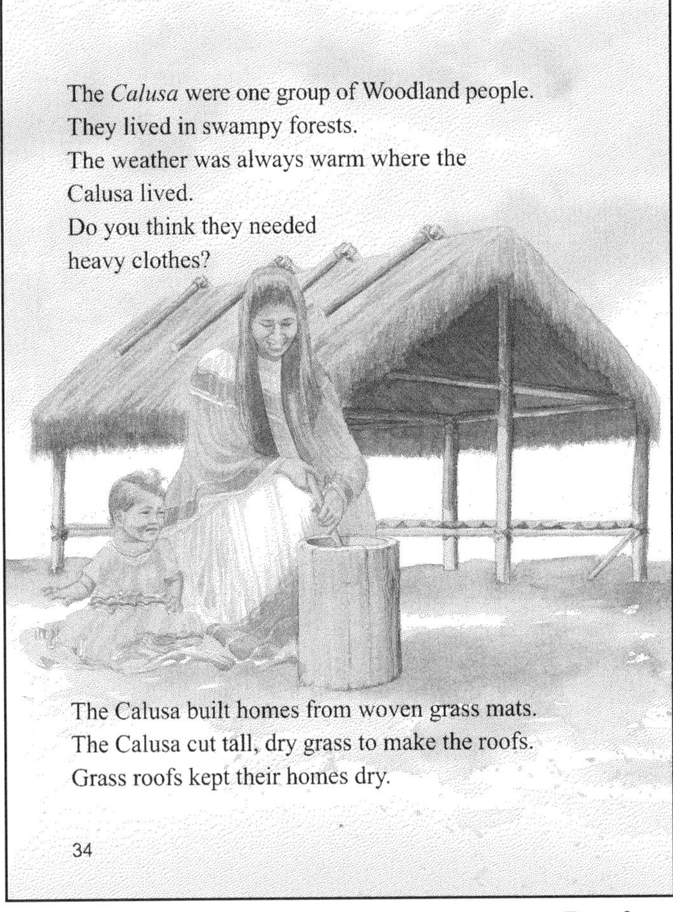

The *Calusa* were one group of Woodland people.
They lived in swampy forests.
The weather was always warm where the Calusa lived.
Do you think they needed heavy clothes?

The Calusa built homes from woven grass mats.
The Calusa cut tall, dry grass to make the roofs.
Grass roofs kept their homes dry.

34

➤ *Display the tools you have gathered. Allow your child to demonstrate or discuss the use of each tool.* The Indians needed **tools** like these, but their tools would not have looked exactly like modern tools.

Text Discussion, page 33

➤ Read page 33.

➤ How were the Indians' tools different from our tools? *(Answers will vary but should include that they were made of stone and bits of bone instead of metal or plastic.)*

➤ What other tools might the Indians have made? *(Answers will vary.)*

Read the Bible verse on page 32. Tell your child that the Lord promised Noah and all his children that the animals and plants would be their food. This promise was for everyone, even the Indians who did not believe in God. Ask your child why he thinks God provided food and other things for people who did not know Him. *(He is loving and merciful.)* (Bible Promise: H. God as Father, I. God as Master) Point out that, even today, the food we eat comes from animals and plants. Remind your child that we should be thankful for the things that God provides for us. (BAT: 7c Praise)

Day 3

Text Discussion, pages 34-35

➤ *Point out the two groups of Woodland Indians, the Iroquois (ĭr´ ə-kwoi) and the Seminoles (sĕm´ə-nōls), on Maps and More 9.* Read pages 34 and 35. (*NOTE:* The Seminoles included many smaller tribes. The **Calusa** tribe was one of the smaller Woodland tribes that were part of the Seminole group.)

➤ Why did these two groups make different kinds of homes and wear different kinds of clothes? *(They lived in different places.)* Each group used things they found near them to make clothes, to build homes, and to provide food.

The *Iroquois* were another group of
Woodland people.
The Iroquois were really five small groups made
into one very large group.
They called themselves
"People of the Long House."
Why do you think they called
themselves by that name?
The Iroquois built very long houses from
wooden poles and bark.
Many families lived in each house.

35

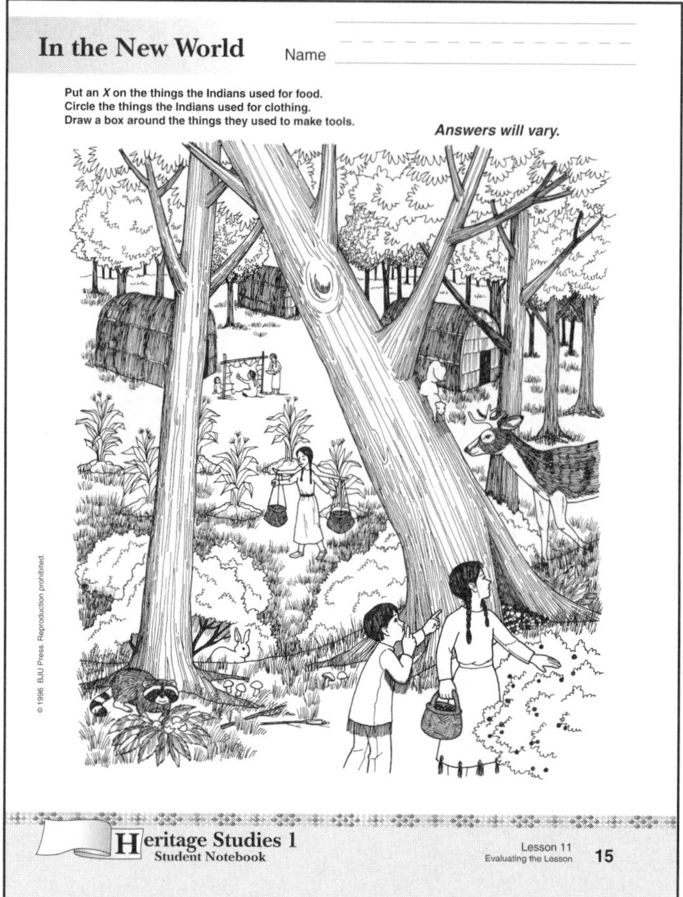

In the New World Name

Put an *X* on the things the Indians used for food.
Circle the things the Indians used for clothing.
Draw a box around the things they used to make tools.

Answers will vary.

Heritage Studies 1
Student Notebook

Lesson 11
Evaluating the Lesson 15

Evaluating the Lesson

Direct an activity on Notebook page 15. Allow time for your child to study the picture on the Notebook page. Ask what kind of Indians would live in a place like this. *(Woodland Indians, Calusa [Seminole], or Iroquois)* Read the directions to your child. Remind him that some things may be marked more than one way.

Going Beyond

Enrichment

Each Indian tribe had its own language and/or dialect. They communicated with Indians of other tribes when necessary through sign language. You may want to find some books about sign language. Encourage your child to learn some of the simpler signs.

Additional Teacher Information

The people we now know as Iroquois called themselves *Hodenosaunee,* which means "The People of the Longhouse." The name Iroquois is the French adaptation of the Algonquian word *Irinakoiw,* or "real adders." Often a group or tribe would have one name for itself; this name usually meant "The People" or something similar. The neighboring Native American groups knew these same people by other names—ones which meant things like "Enemy" or "Snake" in their language.

The Iroquois Confederation consisted of five nations, or tribes, who lived in what is now New York State. The white men knew this group of united people as the League of Five Nations. The Iroquois also called themselves the Extended Lodge, or the Great Peace. (*NOTE:* Later, a sixth tribe joined the confederation, making it the League of Six Nations.)

Experts are unsure when this league was formed, but it had been in existence for many years—perhaps as many as two hundred—before these people came in contact with white men. The Iroquois took as their symbol the pine tree, the Tree of the Great Long Leaves. Their symbol tree had four white roots stretching to the north, south, east, and west. An eagle perched at the top of the tree warned of approaching danger.

The American War for Independence caused a division among the League of Six Nations. The Oneida and the Tuscarora decided to fight with the Americans during the war, while the remaining four tribes voted to fight with the British. This division brought about a civil war among the Iroquois people. The end of the war brought the end of the Iroquois league when the council chiefs voted to put out the council fires.

LESSON 12
The Plains Indians

Text, pages 36-38
Notebook, pages 16-17

Preview

Main Ideas

- Some Indian groups lived on the flat plains.
- Plains Indians hunted buffalo to meet many of their needs.
- Each person in an Indian family had a job to do.

Objective

- Illustrate some of the activities from the life of a Plains Indian

Materials

- Some dried meat*
- 12 to 15 relatively straight twigs about 12" long*
- String*
- A sheet of paper
- 3 or more toothpicks*
- Maps and More 9, page M6

Notes

The Sioux (also known as the Dakota) were not actually living on the Great Plains when Columbus arrived in the New World. At that time they were living in the woodlands at the edge of the plains. As the white men pushed the Indians of the east coast westward, the Sioux were, in turn, pushed onto the plains. They are included here because they embody much of what we think of when we hear the name *Indian.*

Day 1

Lesson

Introducing the Lesson

Direct a tasting activity. Give your child a small piece of dried meat. Encourage him to use his senses to help him describe the meat. Ask the following questions:

- How does the meat look?
- How does it smell?
- How does it feel?
- How does it taste?

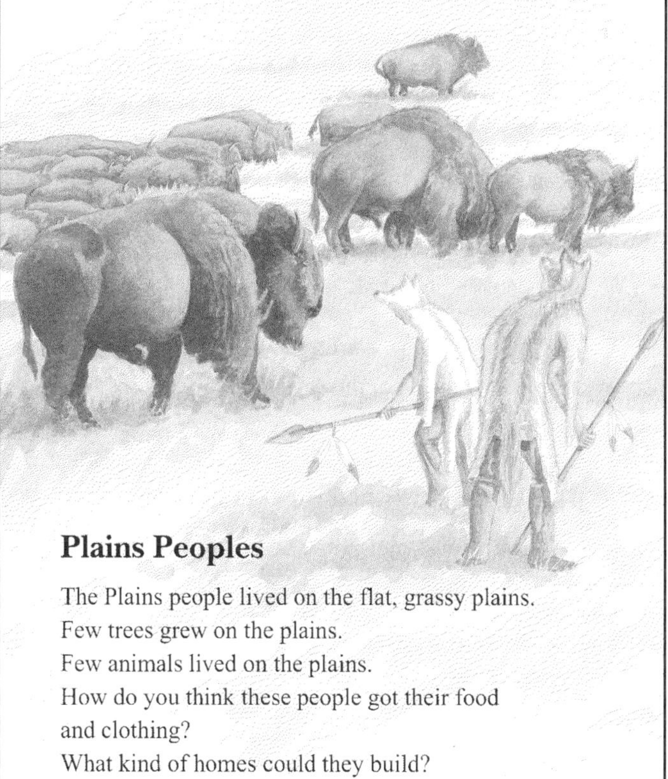

Plains Peoples

The Plains people lived on the flat, grassy plains.
Few trees grew on the plains.
Few animals lived on the plains.
How do you think these people got their food and clothing?
What kind of homes could they build?

36

Ask your child whether he would like to eat meat like this every day. Explain that the group of Indians he will hear about today prepared and ate meat much like this.

Teaching the Lesson

Direct a text activity on pages 36-38. Tell your child to look at the **Sioux** (soo͞) on Maps and More 9.

Text Discussion, page 36

- ➤ Woodland Indians got things such as food and materials to build their homes from the forest. Where do you think the **Plains Indians** such as the Sioux might find food, a place to live, and clothes to wear in a place without lots of trees?
- ➤ Read page 36.
- ➤ Point to the **bison** in the picture. This one animal provided most of the things that the Plains Indians needed. What is another name for this animal? *(a buffalo or American bison)*
- ➤ Whose job do you think it was to hunt the buffalo? *(the men's)* The **buffalo** lived in herds, or very large groups. They traveled together across the flat plain.

Text Discussion, page 37

- ➤ Read page 37.
- ➤ The Sioux did not have guns. How do you think the Indians hunted these buffalo?
- ➤ As I read the following information, I want you to act out each way the Indians hunted.

The *Sioux* were one group of Plains people.
They hunted buffalo.
Hunting buffalo gave them the things they needed.
They ate the buffalo meat.
They made tools from the buffalo's bones.
They used the buffalo's skin to make clothes and shoes.
They even made their homes from these skins.
Do you know what this kind of home is called?
It is called a *tipi.*

37

Pause after each paragraph to give your child the opportunity to act out the hunting technique.

During the summer when the grass on the plain grew tall, the Sioux men would sneak up on the buffalo herd. The tall grass would hide the hunters. If the hunters were very quiet, the buffalo would not be frightened away until many of them had been killed with the flying arrows.

During the winter the grass that the Sioux used to hide in died. Then the hunters covered themselves with wolves' skins. They crawled on the ground, pretending to be wolves. Healthy buffalo were not afraid of wolves, so the Sioux men could get very close to the buffalo. Again they could kill many buffalo before the others ran away.

In some parts of the plains there were tall cliffs. When a herd of buffalo was close to a cliff, the Sioux men would sneak up behind them. When the men were close to the animals, they would jump up, yelling and waving blankets. The frightened buffalo would run away from the men and over the edge of the cliff. More men waited at the bottom of the cliff to kill any buffalo that did not die in the fall. The Sioux could kill a whole herd this way. A whole herd of buffalo could give enough meat and skins to last through a long and cold winter.

- What other things do you think the Sioux men might have used their bows and arrows for? *(Answers will vary but should include protecting their families or fighting other Indians.)*

The Sioux men had one way of showing everyone their brave deeds. They wore big feathered headdresses.

- How do you think a headdress would show a person's bravery?

Each feather a Sioux man wore in his hair had a special meaning. A dot on a feather meant the brave had killed an enemy. A split feather meant that he had suffered many battle wounds.

- Why did mostly old men and chiefs wear the very large headdresses? *(Answers will vary. It would take many years for a man to earn enough feathers to make a large headdress.)*
- Which two sentences on page 37 tell other things that the Indian men did with the buffalo? *(They ate the buffalo meat. They made tools from the buffalo's bones.)*
- Who do you think did jobs like cooking the buffalo meat, preparing the buffalo skins, and making clothes and shoes? *(the women in the tribe)*
- Do you think the women or the men had harder jobs?

Each job was important. Some jobs were easy and some were difficult, but each job helped to keep the Plains Indians' families well and safe.

- What might happen if one person did not do his job? *(The family might not have anything to eat. They might not have clothes to wear or a place to sleep. An enemy tribe might attack the camp and hurt them.)*
- What might happen if we do not do our jobs? (BATs: 2c Faithfulness, 2e Work, 2f Enthusiasm)

Direct a demonstration. Call attention to the picture of the **tipi** *(*tē′ pē) on page 37. Give your child the sticks and string. (*NOTE:* Small dowels may be used if twigs are not available.)

Demonstration Discussion

- What were the tipis made from? *(buffalo skins)*

A frame of sticks or poles held the buffalo skins up. Each tipi frame had about twelve poles. After horses became available to the Plains Indians, tipis were much larger. Some of the largest tipis had frames of more than thirty poles.

- Use the twigs and string to try to build a tipi.
- What shape is the tipi? *(a cone shape)*

The actual sticks were about twenty feet long. Two Sioux women could set up a tipi in less than fifteen minutes.

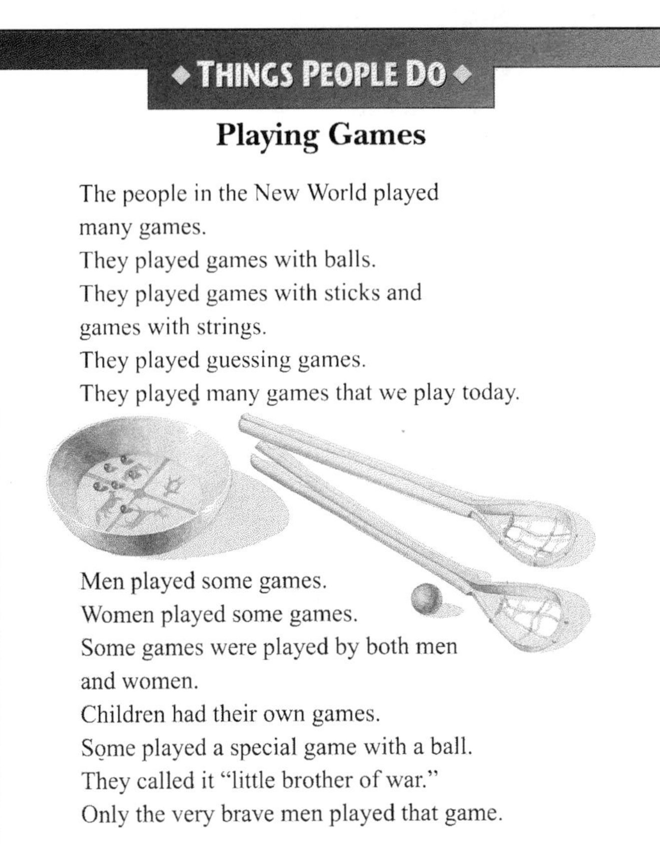

◆ THINGS PEOPLE DO ◆

Playing Games

The people in the New World played many games.
They played games with balls.
They played games with sticks and games with strings.
They played guessing games.
They played many games that we play today.

Men played some games.
Women played some games.
Some games were played by both men and women.
Children had their own games.
Some played a special game with a ball.
They called it "little brother of war."
Only the very brave men played that game.

38

Symbols Name

Follow the teacher's instructions.

Draw some symbols of your own.

© 1996 BJU Press. Reproduction prohibited.

Heritage Studies 1
Student Notebook

Lesson 12
Evaluating the Lesson 16

Day 3

Text Discussion, page 38

- ➤ The Sioux worked hard, but they wanted to have fun too. Read the first section on page 38.
- ➤ What things do you do when you want to have fun?
- ➤ *Write the headings* Ball games, Stick games, String games, *and* Guessing games *on a sheet of paper.* Read the headings.
- ➤ Name some games you play that fall into each category, and I will write the names under the correct headings.
- ➤ Do you think the Indians might have played any of these games?
- ➤ Read the rest of page 38. Are there some games today that only boys or only girls play?
- ➤ How do you think the "little brother of war" game might have been played?

Evaluating the Lesson

Direct an activity on Notebook pages 16-17. Remind your child that the Sioux used buffalo skins to make their tipis. Often they decorated the skins to show important happenings in their families or brave things they had done.

- ➤ Look at each of the pictures on Notebook page 16.
- ➤ What meaning do you think the Sioux may have given to each picture or symbol?
- ➤ Cut out the tipi from page 17 and decorate it with some of the symbols from Notebook page 16.
- ➤ Pretend you are a Sioux warrior and that the symbols you choose "tell a story" about your life as an Indian brave. You may want to think up some symbols of your own to illustrate other important events in the life of a Sioux warrior. You can put these symbols in the empty spaces on Notebook page 16 and on the tipi.
- ➤ Roll the finished tipi into a cone and glue the edges together. Glue toothpicks at the top of the tipi to make it look like the sticks used for the tipi frame.

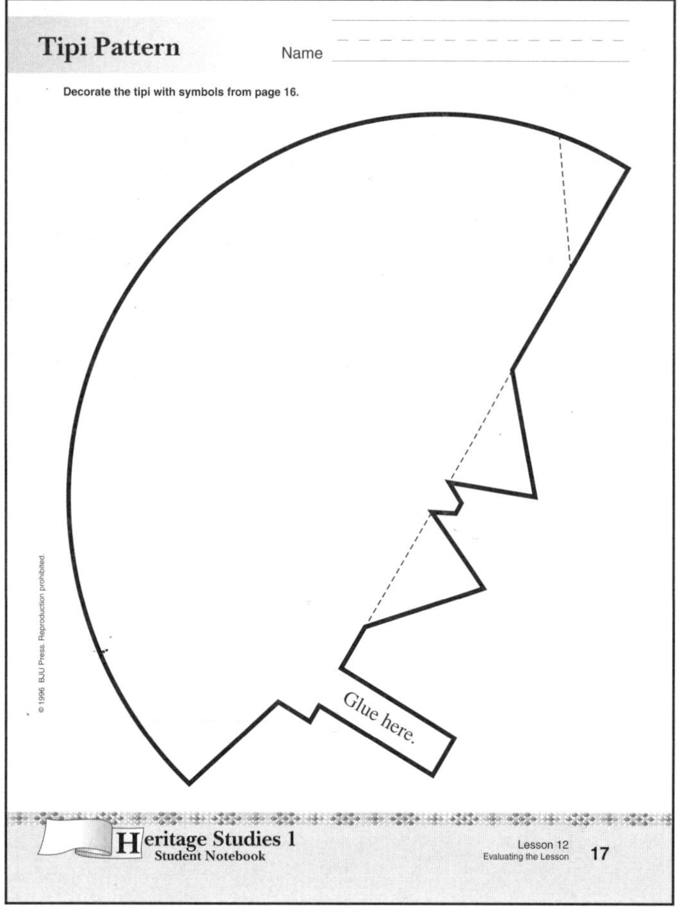

Tipi Pattern Name

Decorate the tipi with symbols from page 16.

Heritage Studies 1 Student Notebook — Lesson 12 Evaluating the Lesson 17

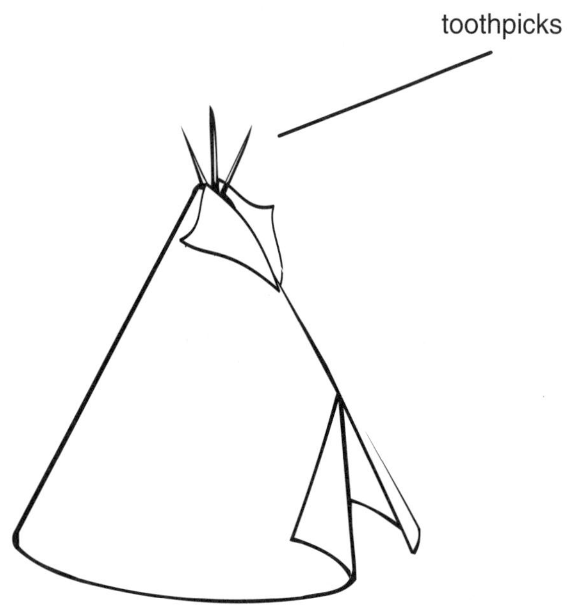

Going Beyond

Enrichment

Show the copy of the Sioux honor feathers, in the Supplement, page S8. Allow your child to cut similar feathers from construction paper to make a feathered headdress. Encourage him to think of other markings to put on the feathers to indicate the bravery or good deeds of the wearer. (*NOTE:* You may want to point out that of the groups studied in this chapter, only the Sioux wore feathered headdresses.)

All Native Americans played guessing games. The following stone game is a simple form of a guessing game.

Find two small stones that are approximately the same size. Paint a red dot on one of the stones. Cut out 70-80 construction-paper counters. Play the game in groups of four or more players. Each person should take ten counters; these will be used to keep track of the number of correct guesses he makes. The participants should sit in a circle. One person should take the stones and, without letting the other players see them, pass one stone to the person on his right. The person to the left of the first person should then guess which stone was passed. If he guesses correctly, he takes both stones, places one counter in front of himself, and then passes one stone. If he guesses incorrectly, the first person should take both stones back and pass one again, letting someone else guess this time. The game continues as long as all the participants want to play. The person who guesses correctly the most times wins.

Additional Teacher Information

Native Americans did not play games exclusively for enjoyment. Children's games and toys were often used to teach the skills they would need as they grew older. Often with older Native Americans, games were used for gambling. Special items, possessions, clothes, homes, and in some cases even wives and children were wagered.

Games were often associated with the customs and culture of a particular tribe. Salmon and fishing were important in the games of the Northwest Coast Indians, while the weather and corn were important in the games of the Southwest Indians.

Native Americans did not cheat at their games. They believed that their gods loved games and were always watching as they played. Some games were associated with the ceremonies of the tribe. Such games could be played only at certain times of the year.

LESSON 13

Indians of the North and Northwest

Text, pages 39-41, 178
Notebook, pages 18-19

Preview

Main Ideas

- Some Indians lived in the cold northern lands.
- Some Indians fished and hunted for whales in the ocean.
- Indians did not worship the true God.

Objective

- Distinguish between items made and used by different Indian groups

Materials

- Maps and More 9 and 12, pages M4 and M6

Notes

There is some debate concerning whether to include Eskimos with the ethnic group Indians or to place them instead in the group of Mongoloid, or Oriental, peoples. We have included them with the Indians because of their pre-Columbian presence in America, making them Native Americans.

Day 1

Lesson

Introducing the Lesson

Direct a map-reading activity. Call attention to Maps and More 9. Remind your child that the Indians pictured on the map lived in America before Christopher Columbus came.

Map-reading Activity

➤ Point to the compass rose. The compass rose shows directions. What are the four directions on this compass rose? *(north, south, east, west)*

➤ Point to the home of the Hopi on the map. Which direction would they go to get to the home of the Sioux? *(north)*

➤ *Continue to review directions in this way using the other Indian groups discussed to this point.*

Arctic Peoples

The *Inuit* lived in the north lands. They fished in the cold water. They hunted for bears and seals and whales.

During the winter, the Inuit lived in homes of ice and snow.
During the summer, they built homes from mud and sticks.
They called their homes *igloos.*
The Inuit were once called *Eskimos.*

39

➤ Find the two Indian groups that lived farthest north. *(Inuit, Nootka)* Today we will learn about these two groups.

Teaching the Lesson

Direct a text activity on pages 39-41. Point to the northernmost group of Indians, the **Inuit** (ĭn´yo͞o-ĭt). Tell your child that these people lived very near the North Pole.

Text Discussion, page 39

➤ What do you know about the North Pole? *(It is very cold; snow covers the ground; etc.)*

➤ Read the first section on page 39. Look at Maps and More 12. Name the animals shown. *(polar bear, whale, seal, caribou or deer)*

These animals are very different from the animals that the Plains Indians or the Woodland Indians hunted. Buffalo, deer, and wild turkey did not live in the icy northland. The Inuit hunted the animals that lived near them.

➤ Read the rest of the page. Look at the picture of the home. Is it an Inuit summer home or winter home? *(summer)*

If the hunting season was good, the Inuit used skins to build their summer homes. If not, then mud and sticks could be found.

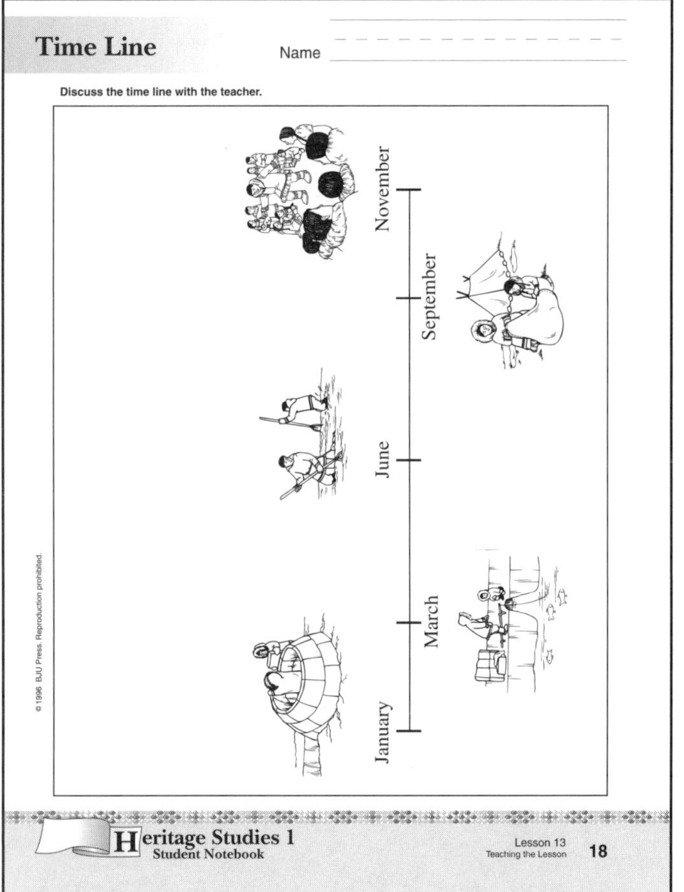
Time Line
Name

Discuss the time line with the teacher.

January
March
June
September
November

© 1996 BJU Press. Reproduction prohibited.

Heritage Studies 1
Student Notebook
Lesson 13
Teaching the Lesson
18

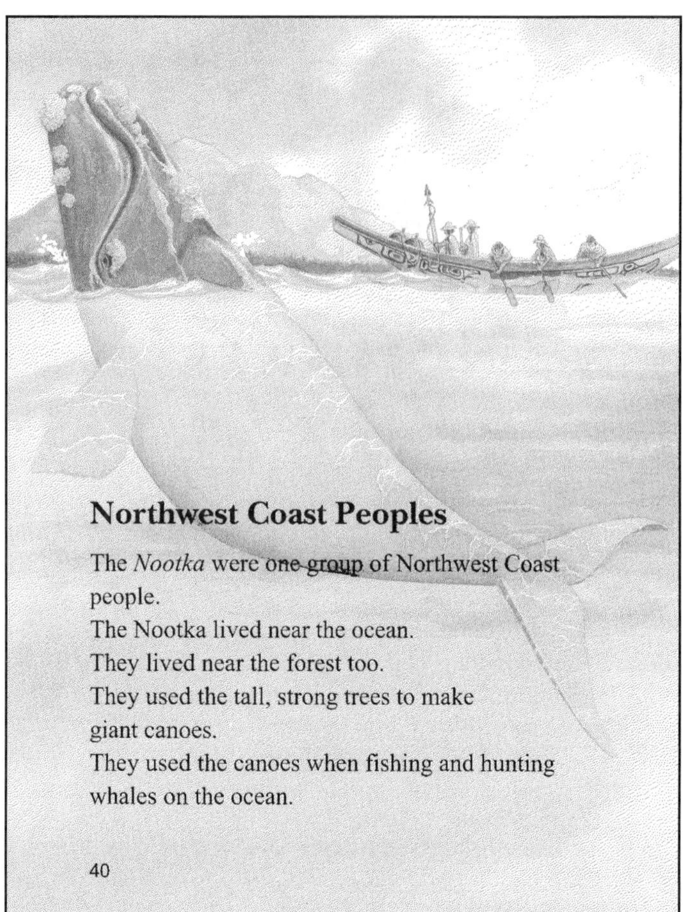
Northwest Coast Peoples

The *Nootka* were one group of Northwest Coast people.
The Nootka lived near the ocean.
They lived near the forest too.
They used the tall, strong trees to make giant canoes.
They used the canoes when fishing and hunting whales on the ocean.

40

➤ Why would they have different homes in the different seasons? *(During the winter, the home of skins or sticks and mud would be too cold. During the summer, the home of snow and ice would melt.)*

Direct an activity on Notebook page 18. Call attention to the History TimeLine. Remind your child that we use a time line to tell the order in which things happened. Ask whether the things shown on the TimeLine happened during one year or over a period of many years. *(many years)*

Notebook Activity

➤ Look at page 18 of your Notebook. Does the time line pictured show many years? *(no)*

Time lines can show just one year, or they might show even less time.

➤ When does the time line on page 18 begin? *(in January)*
➤ At what time of year was there a gathering for celebration? *(November)*
➤ Look at the picture for June. The men are hunting for seals. Did the tribe have the great celebration before or after the hunt? *(after)*
➤ Why would they have a big celebration after the hunt? *(Answers will vary but may include that they were thankful for the food and skins from the hunt.)*
➤ Do you think that June was the only time the family went hunting?
➤ What makes you think that?
➤ If you were making a similar time line for your life, what would you put on it?

Events might include the beginning of school, favorite holidays, birthdays, the last day of school, family vacation, visits from grandparents, and so on. Each person's time line would be different from the others'.

> As God directs Christians' lives, He allows different things to happen to each of them. Those things help to make each Christian the person God wants him to be. (BAT: 3a Self-concept)

Day 2

Text Discussion, pages 40-41 and 178

➤ Read page 40. Point to the **Nootka** (no͞ot´kə) on Maps and More 9.

Other groups of Indians lived in the north as well, but it was not so cold and icy where these Indians were. This group of people lived on the coast, or near the ocean. The warm ocean breezes helped to make their homeland much warmer than the Inuit homeland was.

The Nootka also used the tall, strong trees to make warm homes.
The Nootka homes were long.
What other Indian group built long homes?

The Nootka made a special object for their long homes.
Tall posts stood at each corner.
They cut the posts to look like different animals.
Each home had different animals cut in its posts.
The giant post in the center of one side had a hole in it.
What do you think the hole was for?

41

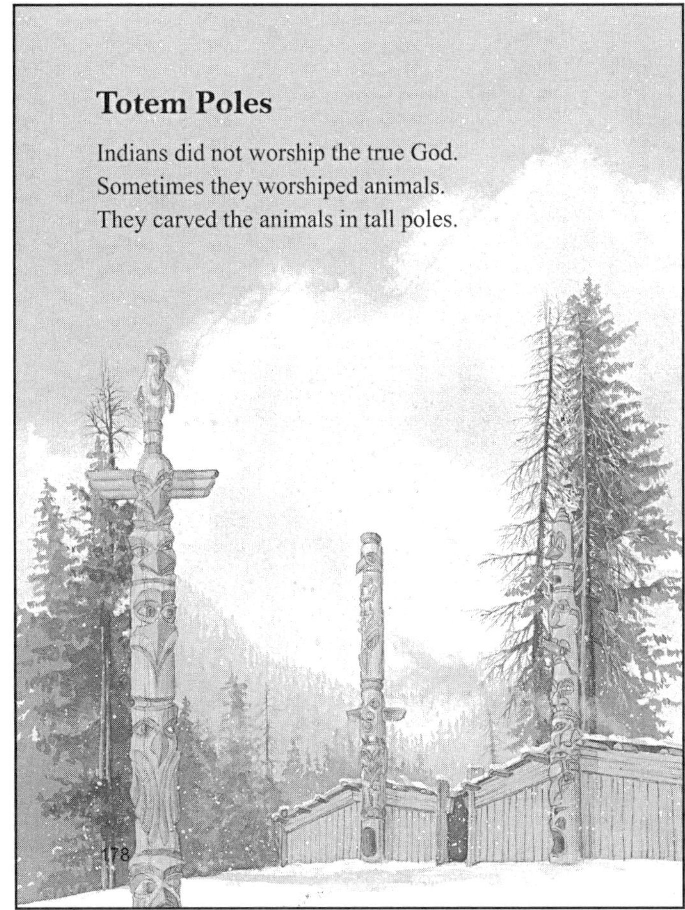

Totem Poles

Indians did not worship the true God.
Sometimes they worshiped animals.
They carved the animals in tall poles.

178

➤ Point to the men in the canoe on page 40.

Since they lived near the ocean, the Nootka made boats. The men would choose a large tree for making a boat. They would cut the tree and then carefully burn and cut out the inside. When it was just right, the men would fill the boat with water and very hot rocks.

➤ Why do you think the men put the hot rocks and water into the boat?

The hot rocks heated the water. The hot water made the wood easy to bend. The men would bend the sides of the boat outward. Then they would empty the boat and let the wood dry. This kind of boat would hold many men on a whale-hunting trip.

➤ Would you like to hunt whales in such a boat?
➤ Read the first section on page 41. Look at page 35. Compare the longhouses of the Iroquois with the Nootka longhouses.
➤ Which house would you rather live in?
➤ Do you see the unusual poles on the Nootka longhouse? Read the rest of the page to find out about these strange poles.
➤ Can you find the doors to the longhouses? *(the hole in the center pole)*

The Northwest Coast Indians were the only Indians to make such unusual doorways and corner posts for their houses.

➤ Read page 178 to find out more about these strange poles.
➤ Can you name some of the animals pictured on the poles? *(Accept any answer)*

By identifying the animals on a pole, the Nootka could tell what family lived in that longhouse. The animals stood for special family stories or special things that happened to the family.

Remind your child that people who do not know about Christ need to hear about Him. (BAT: 5c Evangelism and missions)

➤ Look at the paintings on the boat in the picture on page 40.

A Nootka could tell to whom a canoe belonged by the paintings on it; the canoes were usually decorated with the same animals as the family's pole.

The Nootka and the Inuit
Name
Draw lines to match each Indian with the things he would know how to use.
Nootka
Inuit
© 1996 BJU Press. Reproduction prohibited.
Heritage Studies 1
Student Notebook
Lesson 13
Evaluating the Lesson
19

Evaluating the Lesson

Direct an activity on Notebook page 19. Call attention to the two Indians in the center of the page. Read the group name under each picture. Point out the other items pictured on the page. Tell your child that each item was important to one of these two groups of Indians. Instruct him to decide with which group the item belongs and to draw a line to connect the item with the correct Indian.

Going Beyond

Enrichment

The Northwest Coast Indians held huge feasts called **potlatches** to celebrate special events. At the birth of a child, the completion of a house, or the erecting of a totem pole, a tribe member would invite relatives from other villages to come to a potlatch. The celebration would last several days; on the last day the host would give gifts to his guests.

Perhaps your family would like to have a potlatch. The food need not be Indian food. Invite another family to join you in your potlatch. Help your child to choose one thing that he would like to give to your guests (for example, a picture, a paper hat, a pencil, or a small toy).

Additional Teacher Information

All the Native American tribes of the Northwest Coast held potlatches. *Potlatch* is a Chinook word meaning "to give." These ceremonies often lasted many weeks; they could take place only after the host chief or village had accumulated great wealth and much food.

The original purpose of any potlatch was celebration of a special occasion, but there was an underlying purpose as well. To an outsider, the host appeared to be very generous. To the members of the tribe, the potlatch was a way to show off one's great wealth and, in the process, shame the invited guests. The goal was a higher social standing in the tribe.

Gifts included huge whaling canoes, clothing, jewelry, and blankets. A host would often give away everything he had at one potlatch. His one consolation was this: each guest was obligated to return the invitation at a later date. This future host would most assuredly provide gifts even more beautiful and extravagant in the hopes of attaining an even higher social rank.

LESSON 14
The Southwest Indians

Text, pages 42-44

Preview

Main Ideas

- Southwest Indians lived in the hot, dry desert.
- The Hopi built their homes from dried mud and placed them one on top of the other.
- The Indians were the first Americans.

Objectives

- Weave a "blanket" from construction paper
- Write sentences and draw a picture describing an interesting aspect of life in one Indian group

Materials

- A completed Indian weaving*
- Two 12" square pieces of construction paper of different colors*
- Supplement, page S9: picture of the cotton boll
- A cotton boll or a piece of cotton wool (optional)*
- Several small pieces of cotton fabric*
- Maps and More 9, page M6
- A sheet of paper
- A piece of drawing paper

Day 1

Lesson

Introducing the Lesson

Direct a *Learning How* activity on text page 43. Read the directions with your child. Follow the steps listed in the text. (See the figures at right.) Help your child use a small amount of glue to fasten each woven strip in place.

◆ LEARNING HOW ◆

To Make an Indian Weaving

1. Gather two or more colors of construction paper, a pair of scissors, a ruler, a pencil, and some glue or tape.
2. Use the ruler to draw straight, thick lines on the pieces of construction paper.
3. Fold one piece of paper in half. Cut along the straight lines from the folded edge. Stop cutting each line before you reach the edge of the paper. Unfold the paper.
4. Cut the other pieces of paper into long strips along the straight lines. Weave these strips over and under the strips on the unfolded piece of paper. Decorate the weaving with Indian designs.

a.

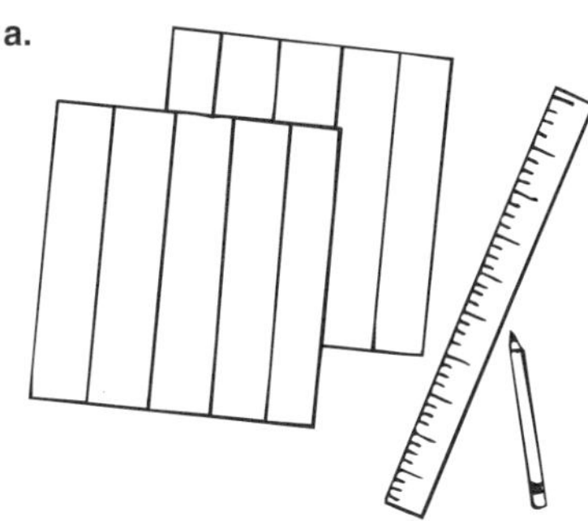

b.

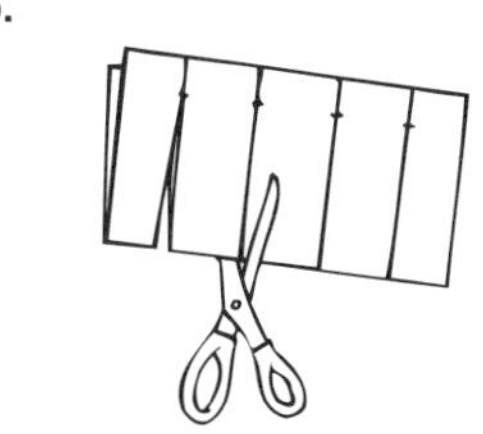

c.

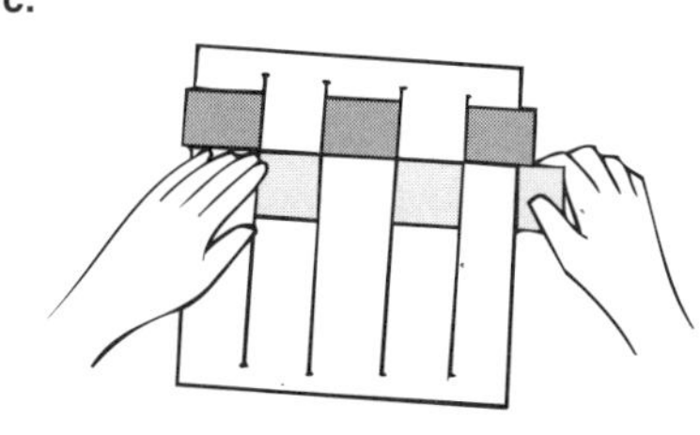

Southwest Peoples

The Southwest people lived in the hot, dry desert.
They were farmers.
They ate the vegetables that they grew.
They made beautiful things from the plants.

The *Hopi* built homes from dried mud.
They built their homes on top of one another.
What do their homes look like to you?

42

Day 2

Teaching the Lesson

Direct a discussion. Review the ways the Indian groups provided food and clothing. *(mostly by hunting animals)* Not all Indian groups provided food and clothing in this way; some Indians were farmers.

Discussion

- ➤ What are some things that a group of farming Indians might eat? *(Answers should include fruits and vegetables.)*
- ➤ What do you think these farming Indians would use for clothing?
- ➤ Look at the picture of the cotton boll. Many Indians grew this plant.
- ➤ Feel the cotton boll or piece of cotton wool and then describe it. (*NOTE:* If you were unable to find a cotton boll, use the cotton fabric.)

The people used the fluffy inside part to make thread. Then they used the thread to make cloth, much as you used construction paper to weave your "blanket." The threads were much smaller than the construction-paper strips; it took much longer for the Indians to weave a piece of cloth large enough for making clothing. Cotton is still used today to make clothes.

- ➤ Feel the scraps of cotton fabric. Have you ever seen similar fabric?

Direct a text activity on pages 42 and 44. Point to the man weaving cloth on page 42. Read the page. Encourage your child to answer the question at the bottom of the page. *(Answers will vary but should include apartment buildings.)*

Text Discussion, page 42

- ➤ What did the **Hopi** (hō´pē) use to build their homes? *(dried mud)*
- ➤ Why didn't the Hopi use buffalo skins or wood to build their homes? *(Those things could not be found in the desert.)*
- ➤ Describe a desert. *(dry, sandy, hot, not much growing or living there)* Do you think it was easy for the Hopi to grow food and cotton in the desert? *(no)*
- ➤ Even in the dry desert there are some small lakes and rivers. How did the Hopi get the water from these lakes and rivers to their plants? *(Answers will vary but may include that they dug ditches for the water to flow through.)*

The Hopi tried to plant their food near a river or lake, but often they had to dig very long ditches for the water to reach their plants. The Hopi, like the other Indian groups, used the things around them to make homes, to make clothes, and to provide food.

> Remind your child that God has provided these important things for all people, no matter where they live on the earth. (BAT: 2e Work; Bible Promise: I. God as Master)

- ➤ Look at the homes on pages 29 and 42. Do you see something unusual about the doors on these houses? *(There are no doors at ground level, and there are ladders beside most houses.)*

To protect themselves from other Indians, the Hopi put doors on the tops of their houses. When an enemy came, a Hopi climbed up his ladder and pulled it up after him. He went into his house and was safe from his enemy. Sometimes a house was built over the doorway for the house below. Then the family living in the bottom level had to climb all the way to the top house on the outside and then all the way down again on the inside to reach their home. There were sometimes as many as five levels of houses built one on top of the other.

- ➤ Would you like to live in a house like the ones the Hopi people made?

Today, some groups live
just as people lived
long ago.
But most do not.
They do not make things
from wood and stone.
They do not build homes
from bark or buffalo skin.

But we remember things the early people did.
We remember things they taught the people who
came to the New World.
And we remember that they were
the first Americans.

Text Discussion, page 44

➤ Look at Maps and More 9. Point to the Hopi. Tell some interesting things about these Indians. Give information you remember about each group of Indians.

➤ Do you think Indians today live as the Indians did before Columbus came to America? *(Answers will vary.)* Read the first section on page 44.

Most Native Americans today live in houses similar to the ones we live in. They go to school and they play many of the same games that we enjoy. They even speak the same language. Some Native American groups do teach their young children about the old ways. Their children learn to speak a Native American language; they hear the old stories and learn to play the Native American games.

➤ Why do you think the older Native Americans want their children to know about these things? *(Answers will vary; they are part of the Native American heritage or history.)*

Some things the Indians of long ago did or made or said are part of our country's history as well.

➤ Read the last section on the page.

Evaluating the Lesson

Direct an art and writing activity. Review the six different groups of Indians your child has learned about during the chapter. Ask your child to tell some of the ways the groups are alike and some ways they are different. Then write one or both of the following sentence starters on the sheet of paper:

I like the ____ best because

I wish I were a(n) ____ because

Give your child a piece of drawing paper. Instruct him to complete the sentence and to draw a picture illustrating his completed sentence.

Going Beyond

Enrichment

Provide construction paper, light brown paint, paintbrushes, newspapers, medium-sized boxes such as shoe boxes or cardboard milk cartons, and craft sticks.

Tell your child that he will be constructing a Hopi pueblo, or village. Direct him to paint his boxes and to use the construction paper and craft sticks to add details such as doors and support beams. Refer to the pictures on pages 29 and 42 of the text.

When the individual boxes are completed, ask your child to construct the village. Encourage him to decide which boxes to place on the lower levels and which to place above. Tell your child that some pueblos were five houses high. He may want to construct his village to this height.

Additional Teacher Information

Less than half of today's Native American population lives on reservations. Reservations are pieces of land belonging to these native people. The term originated in the 1800s after the Native American people were forced into small sections of land "reserved" for their use. In exchange for large sections of their homelands, the Indians were given schools, medical care, and other services.

Today there are approximately three hundred reservations in the United States; almost two-thirds are in the western states. Many of these reservations are shared by more than one tribe. The reservations range in size from sixteen million acres at the Navajo Reservation in Arizona, New Mexico, and Utah, to one-quarter acre at the Golden Hill Reservation in Connecticut.

SUPPLEMENTAL
LESSON
Things the Indians Gave Us

Text, pages 176-77, 182-83

Preview

Main Ideas
- Many places in America have Indian names.
- Many of the foods eaten by Americans today were first grown by the Indians.

Objective
- Name one thing Americans have today as a result of contact with the Indians

Materials
- Pictures or examples of any of the following: a hammock, moccasins, a canoe, cotton cloth*
- Maps and More 16, page M9
- A sheet of paper

Notes
The map on pages 182-83 of the text shows just thirty-three of the more than one hundred Native American tribes found in North America at the time of Columbus. The approximate locations of the homelands and hunting grounds of these tribes are shown.

Lesson

Introducing the Lesson
Direct a map-reading activity. Call attention to the map on pages 182-83. Explain that the map shows some of the groups of Indians that lived in the land when Columbus came. Each color shows where a different group lived and hunted long ago.

Map Discussion
➤ Point to the area where you live. Which group lived in the area where we live today? (*NOTE:* If you do not live in the United States, choose an area that you or your child is interested in.)

➤ Are there other areas where the same group of Indians lived and hunted long ago?

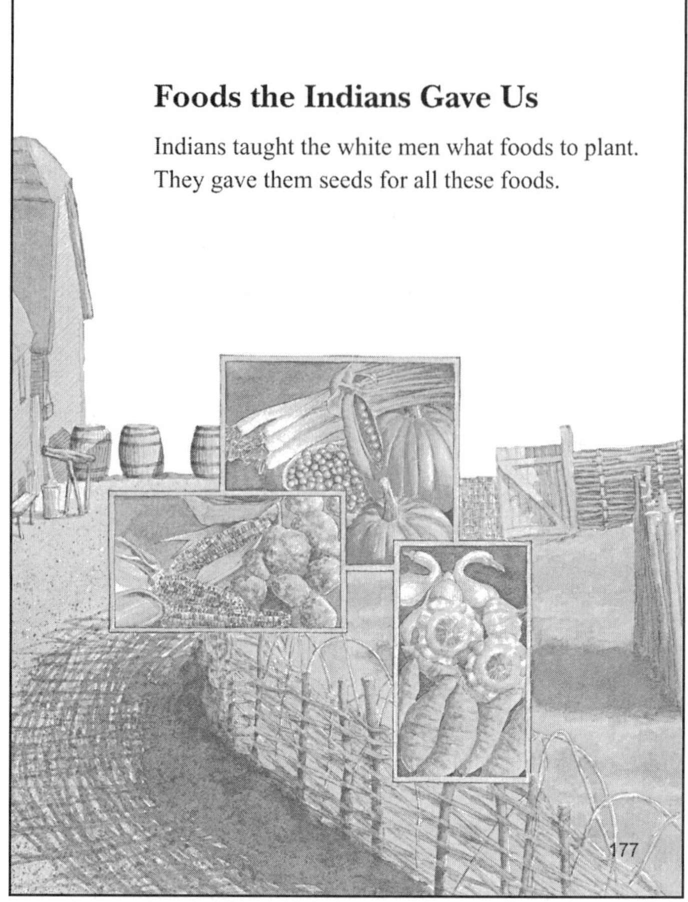

Foods the Indians Gave Us
Indians taught the white men what foods to plant. They gave them seeds for all these foods.
177

Teaching the Lesson
Direct a text activity on page 177. Read the information on page 177. Encourage your child to name as many of the foods as he can. Identify the foods for him that he does not know. *(corn, potatoes, onions, peas, pumpkins, squash, sweet potatoes)*

Text Discussion, pages 176-77
➤ Which of these foods do you like best?

➤ What are some ways that we prepare the foods that Indians gave us?

Columbus and his men had never seen these foods before. Only the Indians knew how to grow these foods. We might not have some of our favorite foods if the Indians had not shared their food with the people who came to their land.

➤ Food was not the only thing the Indians shared with us. *Point to each item or picture of an item that you collected.* How do you think the Indians used this item?

➤ What are some ways we might use some of these items?

➤ *Write these words on a sheet of paper:* toboggan, jaguar, raccoon, yucca, Niagara. Read these words. These are some Indian words that have become part of our language. Do you know the meaning of any of these words? *Explain to your child the words with which he is not familiar.*

Direct a map-reading activity. Show Maps and More 16. Many places in America have names that were first Indian words. If your home is located in the United States, point out your state on the map, asking your child whether he knows the name of your state. Use the following list to share the origin and meaning of the name of your state. If your state is not one of the twenty-six states having Indian names, share the name of a neighboring state. You may also want to tell about cities, parks, or other places in your area that have Indian names.

Alabama (Alibamu) I clear the thicket

Alaska (Aleut or Inuit) great lands

Arizona (Papago and Pima) little spring place

Arkansas (French version of Sioux) from *Kansas,* southwind people

Connecticut (Mohegan) river whose waters are driven in waves by tides or winds

Idaho (Shoshone) salmon eaters

Illinois (French version of Algonquian) from *Illini,* man

Iowa (Sioux tribal name) sleepy ones

Kansas (Sioux) south wind

Kentucky (Wyandot-Iroquois) meadowland

Massachusetts (Algonquian) large hill place

Michigan (Chippewa) big lake

Minnesota (Sioux) milky or clouded water

Mississippi (Chippewa or Choctaw) big river

Missouri (Missouri) canoe carrier

Nebraska (Omaha) broad water

New Mexico (Aztec) taken from the Aztec god, Mexitli

North and South Dakota (Sioux) friend

Ohio (Iroquois) beautiful river

Oklahoma (Choctaw) red people

Tennessee (Cherokee) traveling waters

Texas (Spanish version of Caddo) friend

Utah (Apache) one that is higher up, referring to the Ute Indians living in the mountain country

Wisconsin (Chippewa) grassy place

Wyoming (Lenni Lenape) large prairie place

(*NOTE: Indiana* is not an Indian word, but this state's name was influenced by the Indians nevertheless. It means "land of the Indians.")

Evaluating the Lesson

Play a word game. Tell your child that you would like him to think of things that the Indians shared with the men who came to this land. Read aloud the following phrase. Help your child add foods, place names, inventions, or other Indian words to complete the sentence.

The Indians gave us many things. We can thank them for ____.

4 | **LESSONS 15-20**

New Homes in the New World

This chapter discusses the first settlements in the New World, focusing mainly on Jamestown, the first permanent English settlement. Two important leaders, Sir Walter Raleigh and Captain John Smith, are highlighted. The chapter involves your child in the planting of crops.

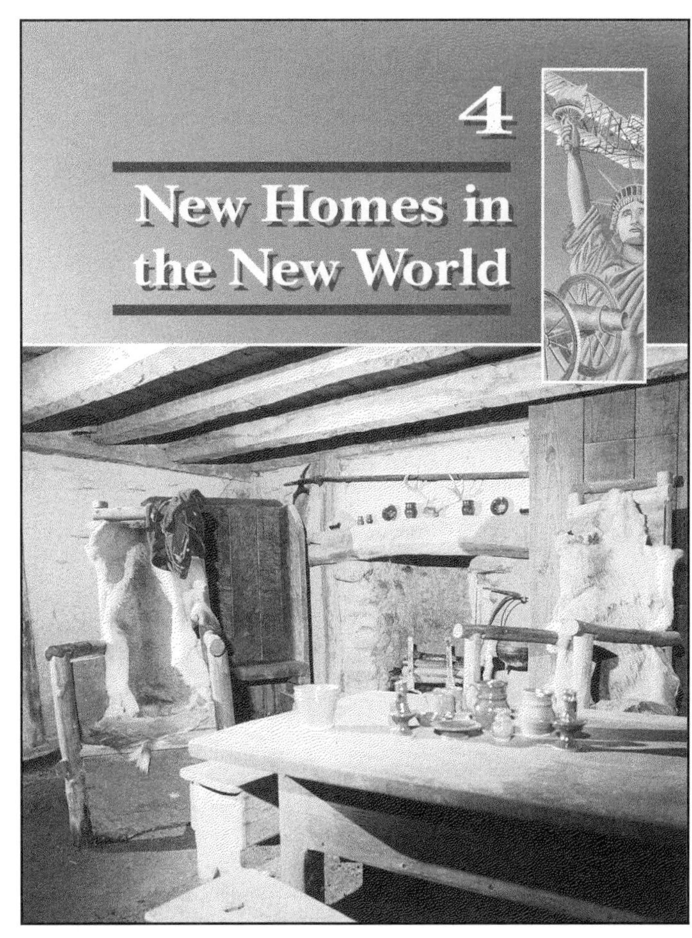

Materials

The following materials must be obtained or prepared before the presentation of the lesson. These items are labeled with an asterisk (*) in each lesson and in the Materials List in the Supplement. For further information see the individual lessons.

- A welcome sign (Lesson 15)
- A toy sword (Lesson 16)
- A toy tiara or paper crown (Lesson 16)
- A picture of the current president of the United States (Lesson 17)
- An ear of corn or a picture of one (Lessons 18 and 19)
- Squash or a picture of squash (Lesson 19)
- Beans or a picture of beans (Lesson 19)
- Plastic cups or egg carton sections (Lesson 19)
- Some seeds (Lesson 19)
- Two prepared index cards (Lesson 20)

LESSON 15
First Settlements

Text, pages 46-47
Notebook, page 20

Preview

Main Ideas

- A settlement is a group of people living in a new place.
- The Indians built the first settlements in the New World.
- People from other countries came to the New World for many reasons.
- The northern part of the New World is called North America.
- Rules help people live and work together.

Objectives

- Identify the blue areas on a map as water
- Locate England on a map
- Locate North America on a map
- Draw routes that ships may have taken to journey from England to the New World
- Locate on a map the place where your family lives

Materials

- A piece of cardboard or poster board
- A wooden stake or stick
- A felt-tip pen
- Maps and More 1 and 14, pages M1 and M8
- A welcome sign prepared by writing *Welcome to* on the cardboard and attaching it to the top of the wooden stake

Notes

The first English settlement, Roanoke Island, was a small, flat, sandy land about twelve miles long and three miles wide. It was originally part of Virginia but is now in an area of North Carolina known as the Outer Banks. This settlement, which disappeared, is often called the Lost Colony. To emphasize the meaning and use of the term *settlement,* we have referred to it here as the Lost Settlement.

What is a *settlement?*
A settlement is a group of people living in a new place. The group of people make up a town or a city.

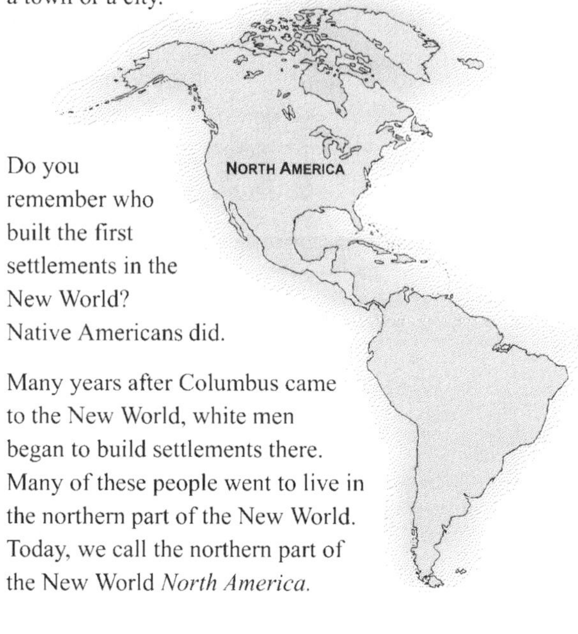

Do you remember who built the first settlements in the New World?
Native Americans did.

Many years after Columbus came to the New World, white men began to build settlements there. Many of these people went to live in the northern part of the New World. Today, we call the northern part of the New World *North America.*

46

Day 1

Introducing the Lesson

Direct a role-playing activity. Tell your child that he is going to take a walk to a "new town" and pretend he is a settler. Go with him to an open area near your home, taking the welcome sign and the felt-tip pen with you.

Role-playing Activity

- ➤ Do you think this would be a good place to build a new town? *(Accept reasons both for and against settling here.)*
- ➤ What would be a good name for the new town? *Help your child write the name on the sign.* Place the sign in the ground.
- ➤ What jobs need to be done to make this area like a town?
- ➤ Why do you think we will need laws and leaders for the new town?

Teaching the Lesson

Direct a text activity on pages 46-47. Read the first section on page 46 to your child.

Text Discussion, page 46

- ➤ What is another word for ***settlement?*** *(town)*
- ➤ Who built the first settlements in the New World? *(the Indians)*

➤ How do we know that the Indians built the first settlements in the New World? *(because the Indians were there when Columbus arrived)*

➤ Read the rest of page 46. Since this new land was unknown to the settlers, they often called it the New World. What was new about this place to these early settlers? *(land, homes, friends, and many experiences)*

➤ Why do you think white men went to the New World to build settlements? *(They wanted adventure; they wanted to own land; they wanted to worship as they pleased; they wanted to live with fairer laws.)*

Map-reading Activity

➤ Look at the map on page 46. This is the **New World.**

➤ Look at the tan section named **North America.** This is where some of the early settlers went to live. Do you live in North America?

> If you live on a continent other than North America, point out the location of your continent on Maps and More 1 and ask your child to name the continent and the country in which you live.

➤ Point to the section of North America where you live. What is the country that you live in called? *(your country's name)*

➤ What do you think the blue parts of the map represent? *(water—specifically oceans, seas, lakes, rivers)*

➤ Look at the green continent below North America. Do you know what the name of this continent is? It is **South America.**

Day 2

Text Discussion, page 47

➤ Read the first sentence. Point to North America (the New World) on Maps and More 1. Where do you think the **Old World** was?

➤ Point to England on the map. Many of the early settlers came from England, so it was the Old World to them.

➤ What is between the Old World and the New World? *(water, specifically the Atlantic Ocean)*

➤ How did the settlers get from the Old World to the New World? *(by ship)* How could people today make this trip? *(by ship or by airplane)*

➤ Do you think the journey made by the settlers from England to the New World took a few hours, a few days, or a long time? *(a long time)*

➤ How do you think the early settlers felt leaving their homeland and sailing for a long time aboard ships to a land that they had never seen?

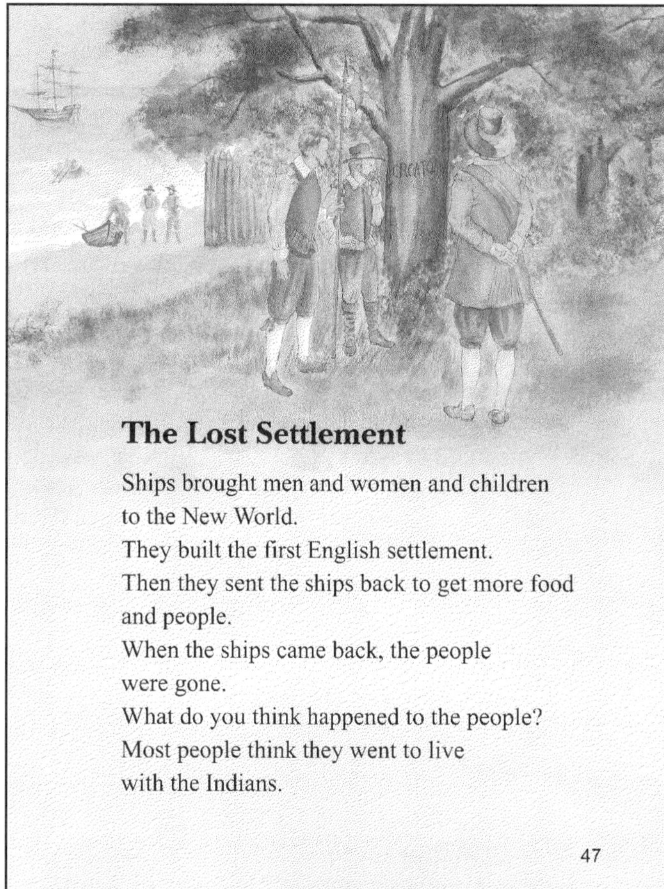

The Lost Settlement

Ships brought men and women and children
to the New World.
They built the first English settlement.
Then they sent the ships back to get more food
and people.
When the ships came back, the people
were gone.
What do you think happened to the people?
Most people think they went to live
with the Indians.

47

This early group of settlers included ninety-one men, seventeen women, and nine boys in addition to sailors. They sailed in three ships in the summer of 1587; it took about two and one-half months to reach the New World.

➤ Read the second sentence. What do you think the settlers needed to do to build their new settlement? *(build houses, a church, and a fort to protect themselves against Indians; plant crops; set up some rules and some leaders of the settlement, etc.)*

➤ Look at Maps and More 14. A coat of arms was a symbol of the settlement just as the American flag is a symbol of our country.

Look at the red cross on a silver background. Notice deer in the top section. The motto, or saying, for the new settlement was "By Harmony Small Things Grow." This motto means that when all the people work and live together in peace, the settlement will grow strong.

➤ Was this motto a good goal for the early settlers?

➤ Do you think the settlements had leaders and rules? How do you think these leaders and rules were chosen?

Building a new settlement was hard work for everyone. (BATs: 2c Faithfulness, 2d Goal setting, 2e Work) (*NOTE:* Democracy was a foreign idea for these settlers. The rules of the new settlements were probably decided upon by only a few leaders or maybe even by a prominent ruling family.)

- ➤ Read the third sentence on page 47. Why do you think the settlers needed more food? *(Their supply was running out, and the new crops had just been planted and were not ready to eat.)*
- ➤ What do you think the settlers ate until some of their crops grew? *(Possible answers include berries, animals from the forest, and fish from the stream.)*
- ➤ Do you think the settlers got discouraged or sick or wished that they had not come to the New World?
- ➤ Read the next two sentences. What do you think happened to the people? Read the last sentence.
- ➤ Look at the picture. What do you see? How would you have felt coming to the New World and seeing this empty settlement?

Evaluating the Lesson

Direct an activity on Notebook page 20. Instruct your child to color blue the areas that represent water.

Notebook Activity Instructions

- ➤ Look at the *X* on the right. This is England. Draw a line from England in the Old World to the picture of the crown.
- ➤ Shade in North America with your green crayon.
- ➤ Draw a line from the picture of the settler's house to the *X* in the New World.
- ➤ Make a path of arrows, showing how the ships may have journeyed from the Old World to the New World. *(Arrows should go across the Atlantic Ocean, from England to North America.)*
- ➤ Draw a line from the star to the place on the map that shows about where your home is. (*NOTE:* If your homeland is not shown, ask your child to draw a line to a place where his ancestors lived.)

Going Beyond

Enrichment

Display Maps and More 14. Your child will need a piece of construction paper with an outline of a shield on it and the examples of some common symbols for coats of arms. (See Appendix, pages A14-A15.) Red, blue, black, green, purple, yellow, and white are the colors generally used in heraldry. You may wish to provide these colors of construction paper. Tell your child to think about the "new town" that he pretended to settle. Direct him to use any combination of the symbols to design a coat of arms to represent his settlement. Tell him to write at the bottom of the paper a motto, or saying, that would be a good goal for people in a new town.

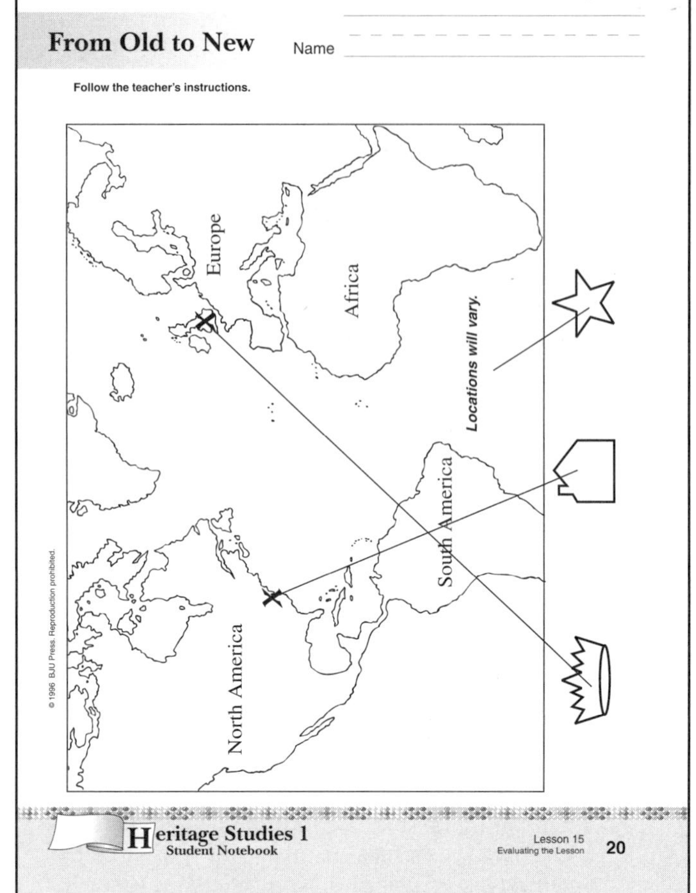

Additional Teacher Information

In 1584, Sir Walter Raleigh sent an expedition to the New World. The men selected Roanoke Island as the best place to establish the first English settlement. The newly discovered land was named Virginia after Queen Elizabeth, the Virgin Queen.

In 1585, seven ships sailed from England to Roanoke Island with 108 men. They built homes and a fort, but before the year was out, the men were near starvation; all but fifteen returned to England for supplies and food.

In July 1587, Governor John White and more settlers arrived at Roanoke Island but found no sign of their fellow Englishmen. The settlers decided to rebuild the settlement. A few days after their arrival, Governor White's granddaughter, Virginia, was born to Eleanor and Ananias Dare. Soon Governor White returned to England for more supplies.

Governor White did not return to the settlement until August 1590. On the island, he saw a large tree with *CRO* cut into its bark. The settlement lay empty and in ruin. Near the fort was another carving, *CROATOAN*. Governor White suspected that the people had gone to this nearby village of Native Americans for help, but he was never to have his questions answered. Some people believe that the settlers were killed by members of another tribe; others think that they drowned trying to reach England; still others believe that the settlers intermarried with the native people.

LESSON 16
Sir Walter Raleigh

Text, page 48
Notebook, page 21

Preview

Main Ideas

- Every nation has a leader.
- Nations try to gain more territory in different ways.
- People follow rules for their benefit and for the benefit of others.
- Sir Walter Raleigh, with the aid of Queen Elizabeth, sent the first English settlers to live in the New World.

Objective

- Identify characteristics and accomplishments of Sir Walter Raleigh

Materials

- Maps and More 15, page M8
- A toy sword*
- A toy tiara or paper crown*

Notes

From 1581, Sir Walter Raleigh spelled his name *Ralegh,* as did his son and grandson until the end of the seventeenth century. The modern version *Raleigh* is most often used in historical writing and is, hence, used here.

Day 1

Lesson

Introducing the Lesson

Direct a role-playing activity. Show your child Maps and More 15. Explain that because Queen Elizabeth was so pleased with the success of Walter Raleigh's explorations, she honored him by making him a knight in 1585. From then on, he was called Sir Walter Raleigh. He was given many lands, great wealth, and much power. Take turns with your child using the crown and sword to role-play being knighted.

For the remainder of this lesson, you may want to address your child as Queen (her name) or as Sir (his name).

◆ FAMOUS PEOPLE ◆

Sir Walter Raleigh

Sir Walter Raleigh was a soldier and a seaman.
He wanted to take settlers to the New World.
Queen Elizabeth of England would not let
Sir Walter go.
But she did let him send the first settlers.
And she helped him pay for the ships and food.

The settlement that Sir Walter paid for was lost.
No one knows what happened to the settlers.

48

Teaching the Lesson

Direct a text activity on page 48. Read the first section.

Text Discussion, page 48

➤ Why do you think Raleigh wanted Englishmen to go to live in the New World?

➤ What good things might England gain if Englishmen went to the New World? *(riches, new land for England, etc.)*

➤ Listen as I read the sentences that let us know that Raleigh liked adventure. "Sir Walter Raleigh was a soldier and a seaman. He wanted to take settlers to the New World."

➤ Read the rest of the page. Why do you think Queen Elizabeth did not let Sir Walter Raleigh go to the New World?

➤ What happened to the settlers that were sent by Sir Walter Raleigh? *(They disappeared.)*

The settlement at Roanoke Island came to be called the Lost Settlement. The buildings were empty, and all of the people were gone.

➤ How do you think Raleigh felt when he heard the news about the Roanoke Settlement?

Although this settlement was lost, Sir Raleigh had made it easier for others to go to the New World later. (BATs: 3a Self-concept, 7b Exaltation of Christ)

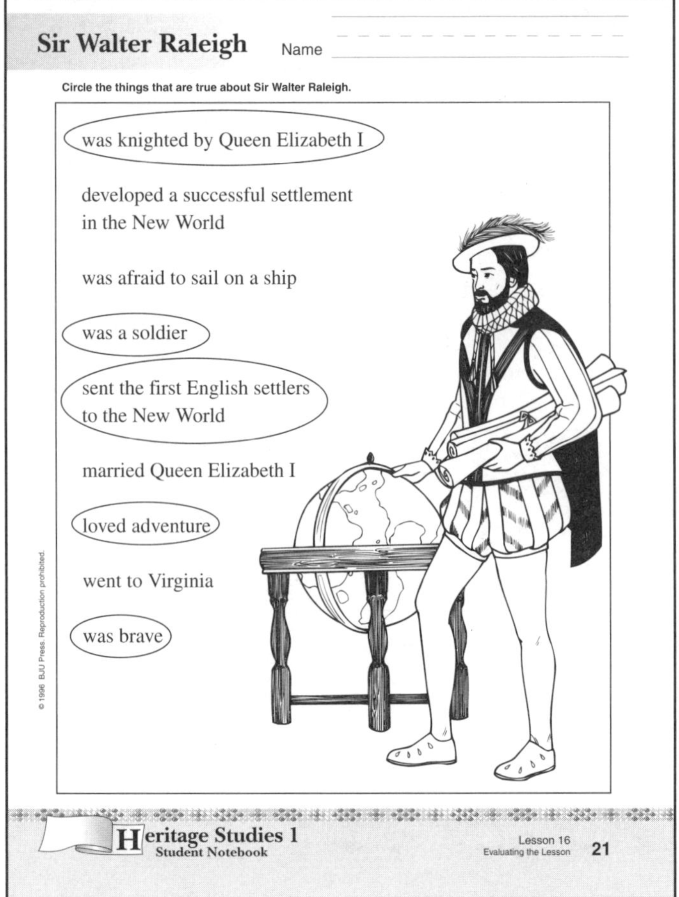

Sir Walter Raleigh
Name
Circle the things that are true about Sir Walter Raleigh.
was knighted by Queen Elizabeth I
developed a successful settlement in the New World
was afraid to sail on a ship
was a soldier
sent the first English settlers to the New World
married Queen Elizabeth I
loved adventure
went to Virginia
was brave
© 1996 BJU Press. Reproduction prohibited.
Heritage Studies 1
Student Notebook
Lesson 16
Evaluating the Lesson
21

➤ Look at the picture of Sir Raleigh. How is he dressed? What does he have in his hat? *(a feather)*

Evaluating the Lesson

Direct an activity on Notebook page 21. Read aloud the phrases listed, instructing your child to circle only the phrases that are true about Sir Walter Raleigh.

Going Beyond

Enrichment

Your child may want to try to write some poetry. Print the following first line on a sheet of paper:

I went sailing on the sea.

Encourage him to write one additional line to complete the couplet and then to draw and color a picture to illustrate the poem.

Additional Teacher Information

Queen Elizabeth I was the daughter of King Henry VIII and his second wife, Anne Boleyn, whom the king had beheaded in 1536 on charges of adultery and treason. As a castaway, young Elizabeth Tudor was raised by a governess in a country house 150 miles from the court. Though she was denied material things from King Henry, she was given a fine education. She mastered several languages, history, mathematics, and even architecture. It was King Henry's sixth wife, Catherine Parr, who requested that Elizabeth be brought back to the royal household. At the death of King Henry VIII, Elizabeth was third in line for the throne, after her half-brother, Edward, and her half-sister, Mary (whose rule of five years gave her the name *Bloody Mary* because of the hundreds of Protestants that she had burned at the stake in the name of the Catholic Church). At the death of Mary in 1588, Elizabeth came to rule England, bringing with her a refreshing change for the country and a devotion for the people. Queen Elizabeth—proud, courageous, shrewd, and intelligent—restored peace and order to her country. By the end of her reign, she had made England the wealthiest, most powerful nation in the western world. Never married, this *Virgin Queen* ruled England well for forty-five years, was loved by all of England, and was respected by the world. This period in English history is known as the Elizabethan Age, after the ruler who made England great.

Sir Walter Raleigh was born around 1552 at his family's estate in Devonshire, England. In 1580, he distinguished himself as the captain of the army in Ireland. Then in the following year, he became a member of Queen Elizabeth's court. It is said that at his first meeting with the queen, Raleigh placed his coat over a mud puddle for the queen to walk upon. Though this story is probably not true, it is certain that Raleigh was one of the queen's favorites. She granted him ships and money to send an expedition to the New World but denied his going. The queen gave Raleigh an estate of twelve thousand acres in Ireland, where he successfully raised potatoes, which had been introduced from the New World. He took part in England's victory over the Spanish Armada in 1588 and led many expeditions against Spanish possessions.

Raleigh lost favor with the queen when he married one of her maids of honor. Then upon the death of Queen Elizabeth, the new king, James I, charged Raleigh with treason and had him imprisoned in the Tower of London, where he remained for twelve years with his family and servants. Upon his release in 1616, Sir Walter Raleigh led another expedition to South America, searching for gold. He invaded Spanish territory against the king's orders and was sentenced to death. It is said that he joked with his executioner and even gave the signal for the ax to fall.

LESSON 17
On to Jamestown

Text, pages 49-50

Preview

Main Ideas

- People came to the New World for many reasons.
- Jamestown was established in 1607 by Englishmen seeking gold.
- Some names of places honor rulers.

Objective

- Answer questions about the founding of Jamestown

Materials

- The figure of Jamestown (1607) from the History TimeLine Packet
- A picture of the current president of the United States*
- A clean rag or sponge
- Cleanser
- A special treat of your choice

Day 1

Lesson

Introducing the Lesson

You may replace the desk cleaning in the following activity with another appropriate job, if you so desire. It does not need to be a difficult job or one that takes a long time.

Direct a decision-making activity. Tell your child that you have a special treat for him but that he will need to earn it. Explain that he may either scrub his desk inside and out or "hunt for gold." Emphasize that he will receive his treat if he finds "gold" or if he earns it by working. If he chooses to hunt for gold but does not find any, he will then need to scrub his desk before receiving his treat. If your child chooses to hunt for gold, allow time for him to hunt in a designated room or area, being sure there is nothing made of gold there. Point out after he searches eagerly for gold without finding any that he ended up having to work anyway. Give the special treat. Explain that this activity was similar to what happened when the first Englishmen came to the New World. Most of them were gold hunters, not workers. But no gold was found, so they either had to work or had to return to England.

Jamestown

Three small ships sailed up a river
on a warm day in May 1607.
Why do you think those ships were there?
The ships carried one hundred five men
from England.
These men had come to live in North America.
They came to hunt for gold.
They wanted to become rich.

49

Teaching the Lesson

Direct a text activity on pages 49-50. Direct your child's attention to the illustration on page 49.

Text Discussion, page 49

- ➤ Do the men in the picture look as though they are dressed in their work clothes? *(no)* These men in fancy clothes were among the first Englishmen to come to live in the New World.
- ➤ Read page 49. What was the most important thing for these new settlers—adventure, gold, or land? *(gold)*
- ➤ Do you think that these Englishmen knew how to hunt for gold? *(probably not)*
- ➤ Do you think these men found gold?

The men named the river the James River, after their king.
They called the place they landed *Jamestown.*
Why do you think they gave it that name?
Do you think it had another name first?
Most of the men in Jamestown came from rich families.
They did not know how to work hard.
They thought they would find gold in the new land.
They hoped it would be easy to find.
They would go back to England when they had found lots of gold.
Do you think they found gold?

50

Day 2

Text Discussion, page 50

➤ Look at the picture of the president of the United States. Do you know what this president's name is?
➤ Do you think it would be an honor, a good thing, for a town to be named after the president of the United States? *(yes)*
➤ Do you know of any places that are named after presidents of the United States?

There are many towns named after the following presidents: Washington, Jefferson, Madison, Monroe, Quincy [for John Quincy Adams], Jackson, Van Buren, Harrison, Tyler, Polk, Taylor, Fillmore, Pierce, Buchanan, Lincoln, Johnson, Grant, Hayes, Garfield, Arthur, Cleveland, McKinley, Roosevelt, Taft, Wilson, Harding, and Coolidge.

➤ Even long ago people honored their rulers by naming places after them. Read the first four sentences on page 50.
➤ Why did the settlers name their new colony **Jamestown** and the river the James? *(They named them to honor King James.)*
➤ Look at the picture of King James. Describe what he is wearing.
➤ Read the rest of the page. Why do you think rich men would be interested in finding more gold in North America?
➤ Do you think that these men were planning to live in North America for a long time? *(probably not)*
➤ Let me read the sentence that shows this. "They would go back to England when they had found lots of gold."
➤ Do you think that these men came to North America for the right reasons? (BATs: 2e Work, 7d Contentment)

History TimeLine Activity

➤ What country did King James rule? *(England)*
➤ Can you remember the name of the person who ruled England and helped Sir Walter Raleigh organize expeditions to the New World? *(Queen Elizabeth)*
➤ At the death of Queen Elizabeth I, James I became the next ruler of England. Look at the figure of Jamestown. Put it on the History TimeLine at 1607.

Evaluating the Lesson

Direct an oral evaluation. Explain that you will read aloud some statements. Tell your child that if the statement is true, he should move his hands in a wavelike motion to symbolize the motion of a sailing ship; if the statement is false, he should place his hands in his lap. Use the following statements.

- Jamestown was named after James I. *(true)*
- James I was king of Spain. *(false)*
- Jamestown was started in 1607. *(true)*
- The settlers sailed in ships from England to the New World. *(true)*
- The settlers sailed across the Pacific Ocean to get to the New World. *(false)*
- The settlers sailed for one year before reaching Jamestown. *(false)*
- One hundred men, women, and children sailed on three ships to reach Jamestown. *(false)*
- Most of the men who sailed were rich. *(true)*
- Jamestown is in Virginia. *(true)*

Going Beyond

Enrichment

Give your child scraps of fabric, felt, glue, chenille wires, felt-tip pens, and old-fashioned, round-tipped, wooden clothespins. Encourage him to use the materials to "dress" a clothespin to resemble either an early settler or an Indian. You might want to display a settler and an Indian that you have prepared. Stand the completed dolls in a box of sand to represent their presence in the colony.

Additional Teacher Information

The voyage in 1607 of the group that came to be known as the *Virginia Venturers* was sponsored by the London Company. For five months the 105 men endured a long and dangerous trip, fighting bad weather, overcrowding, disease, and malnourishment. About half of the men who sailed were gentlemen—rich men whose hands had never been blistered by gripping an ax handle all day, whose backs had never ached from a hard day of planting corn, whose bodies had never grown weary from any sort of manual labor. There were a few laborers, but not nearly enough to work hard to establish a new colony in the New World. By the end of the year, fewer than one-third of these first men of Jamestown were alive.

Native Americans taught the settlers how to grow beans, corn, and squash; how to hunt deer and wild turkey; and how to catch fish. If the settlers had listened to this practical advice, they could have avoided the Starving Time of 1608-10. Instead, the settlers put their time and energy on another crop that had been introduced by the Indians—tobacco.

LESSON 18
John Smith Leads the Way

Text, pages 51-54
Notebook, pages 22-23

Preview

Main Ideas

- All societies have leaders and some kind of government.
- Captain John Smith was a wise leader in Jamestown.
- Rules help people live and work together.
- People follow rules for their benefit and for the benefit of others.
- The Indians taught the settlers about planting and preparing corn.

Objective

- Sequence pictures depicting events in early Jamestown

Materials

- An ear of corn*
- A Bible
- A scrap of paper

Notes

The houses of the Jamestown settlers were mostly half-timbered structures. The frames were solid but of crude wood that had been hacked out with an ax. The spaces between the frames and the braces were filled with wattle and daub. Wattle was a kind of woven wood, with upright sticks to form the "warp" and flexible twigs intertwined between them to form the "weft." Daub was a clay-and-straw mixture plastered over this primitive type of support. A thatched roof of straw and a chimney of logs lined with clay completed each house, which often was barely six feet high and twelve feet wide.

Day 1

Lesson

Introducing the Lesson

Direct a listening activity. Read the following story about a boy who dreamed of adventure.

Mrs. Smith gently nudged her sleeping son. "John! John! Wake up! It's time to get ready. Remember, Father promised to take you fishing today."

Usually young John Smith was a hard one to get up in the morning, but not today. He leaped out of bed and seemed to jump right into his clothes. Today was different! Today he had to hurry! Today he wanted to hurry because he was going to the sea with Father!

The conversation at breakfast was hurried and full of excitement.

"Why does the sea have to be so far away? How long will it take us, Father? Couldn't we take some carrots to make old Dobbin go faster?" John fired the questions, his voice getting louder and more excited with each one. That's the way it always was for John Smith.

"Now, now, John, have patience. We'll get there in due time. Dobbin is a fine horse, steady and dependable. You'll have plenty of time to do your dreaming by the sea," Mr. Smith assured him with a smile. "Come on! Let's get going!"

John sprang into place next to Father, waved good-bye to Mother, and headed out toward the sea—the wonderful sea. Dobbin with the two-wheeled cart seemed to crawl along the dusty lane. John knew they had a long way to go. He dared not pester Father about it right now. He would just try to imagine what adventures lay ahead. John Smith loved adventure! If he couldn't find any adventure, he would make some of his own! That's the way it always was for John Smith.

The crisp air changed slowly to fog—great, gray, suffocating fog, surrounding them on all sides. As they approached the marshland, the fog became so thick that they could scarcely see. John loved this kind of mood. It was great for imagining and thinking about adventure! Yes, that's the way it always was for John Smith.

"Father," John whispered, "do you think we might get lost? Do you suppose robbers might be hiding? What will we do if they attack us? We have nothing but your gun and Mother's breakfast rolls to offer them! Do you think that will be enough? Do you think we'll be all right?"

Mr. Smith smiled at his son and patted his shoulder. He was used to questions like this from John. "We'll be okay, Son," Mr. Smith said, "just as long as they don't take Mother's breakfast rolls away from us!"

John laughed with his father, all the while his eyes darting this way and that, looking for the slightest stir in the bushes and leaves.

Captain John Smith was one of the leaders
in Jamestown.
He worked with the men to build houses
and a church.
How were these houses different from the house
you live in?
The men covered twigs and planks with mud
to make the walls.
They made the roofs of straw or grass.

51

After an hour or so, the fog began to disappear. The sun was peeking its smiling face through the clouds. Everything seemed to dance with excitement. Even the flowers fluttered their greeting to John Smith and his father. Flocks of birds pointed the way to the sea—John's sea.

"We're getting closer, aren't we, Father? Are we almost there?" John asked wide-eyed. "I can hardly wait to see the water! It makes me want to get on a ship and go exploring."

Mr. Smith nodded and smiled, for he knew that that's the way it always was for John. "Yes, Son, the sea is full of great mystery. It's okay to dream of adventure, just as long as you know they're just dreams. Here we are; just around the bend is where we'll stop."

When they reached the fishing village, John jumped from the cart before Mr. Smith could get Dobbin to a full stop. His excitement had grown bigger and bigger all morning long, and now he couldn't keep it in. He had finally reached the sea! John Smith rushed to the shore and stood looking silently out over the endless stretch of water.

"Where does it go?" John asked aloud to no one in particular. "What's it like on the other side? Oh, how I wish I could go exploring right now. Someday, someday . . ." John promised himself, "someday, I'll sail on this great sea. Someday I'll find some *real* adventure." And that's the way it always was for John Smith!

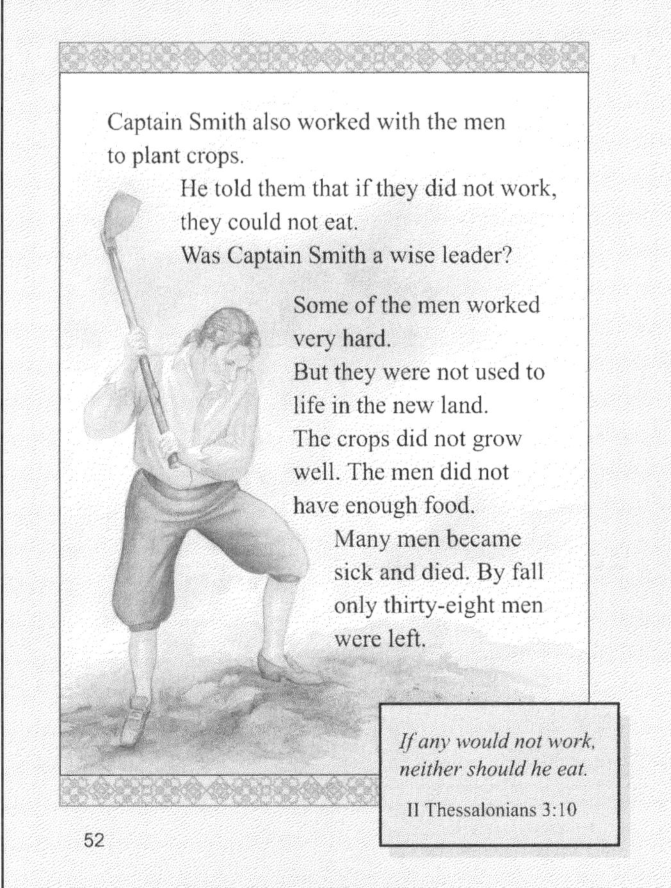
Captain Smith also worked with the men
to plant crops.
He told them that if they did not work,
they could not eat.
Was Captain Smith a wise leader?

Some of the men worked
very hard.
But they were not used to
life in the new land.
The crops did not grow
well. The men did not
have enough food.
Many men became
sick and died. By fall
only thirty-eight men
were left.

If any would not work,
neither should he eat.

II Thessalonians 3:10

52

What do you think Captain Smith did then?
He went to the Indians for help.
He got corn and other food from the Indians.
Soon more men came from England.
They brought more food.
With help from the Indians and from England,
the men lived through the winter.

53

Teaching the Lesson

Direct a text activity on pages 51-54. Explain that this lesson tells some of the adventures of the grown-up John Smith. Read page 51.

Text Discussion, page 51

- ➤ Did John Smith ever sail the sea? *(yes)*
- ➤ What sea did he sail to reach Jamestown? *(the Atlantic Ocean)*
- ➤ Do you think that John Smith's dream for adventure came true?
- ➤ Describe the houses in the picture. Do you know anyone who lives in a house like this?
- ➤ Do you think this kind of house would be warm in the winter and comfortable in the summer?
- ➤ What kinds of hazards might there be with a straw or grass roof on the house? *(fire, possible leaks from heavy rains)*
- ➤ Were most of the Jamestown settlers rich or poor? *(rich)*
- ➤ Were these men used to hard work? *(no)*

Text Discussion, page 52

- ➤ Read page 52. What rule did John Smith give to the men of the settlement? *(If you do not work, you cannot eat.)*
- ➤ Do you think that this is a good rule? Why?

Explain that God gave this rule in the Bible. Read II Thessalonians 3:10. (BATs: 2c Faithfulness, 2d Goal setting, 2e Work, 4a Sowing and reaping)

- ➤ *Write 105−67=38 on a scrap of paper.* There were 105 men who first came to Jamestown. Sixty-seven men died the first few months, leaving only 38 to do the work of the settlement and to make it successful.
- ➤ Do you think that those 38 men could survive and make Jamestown successful? (BATs: 2c Faithfulness, 2d Goal setting, 2e Work, 3a Self-concept)

Day 2

Text Discussion, pages 53-54

- ➤ *Show an ear of corn.* This crop was the answer to many of the problems at Jamestown. Read pages 53-54.
- ➤ Who told the settlers about corn and how to grow it? *(the Indians)*
- ➤ Do you think that the Indians were always helpful to the men at Jamestown?
- ➤ What help came from England? *(Possible answers include more food, tools, clothes, and workers.)*
- ➤ What help do you think the ladies offered for the new settlement at Jamestown?
- ➤ Do you think that the men were disappointed that they were not getting rich? (BATs: 3a Self-concept, 4a Sowing and reaping, 7b Exaltation of Christ, 7d Contentment)

Still more men came from England in the spring.
Soon many men lived in Jamestown.
Even two ladies came with one group
from England.
The men were not getting rich.
But the settlement grew.

54

Jamestown Name ______

Color and cut out each picture. Arrange the pictures in order.
Write the number order in each circle.

© 1996 BJU Press. Reproduction prohibited.

Heritage Studies 1 Student Notebook — Lesson 18 Evaluating the Lesson 22

Evaluating the Lesson

Direct an activity on Notebook pages 22-23. Explain that each of the pictures on page 22 represents an event in early Jamestown. Instruct your child to color each picture and cut it out. Encourage him to arrange the pictures in the order that they happened before he glues the pictures onto page 23.

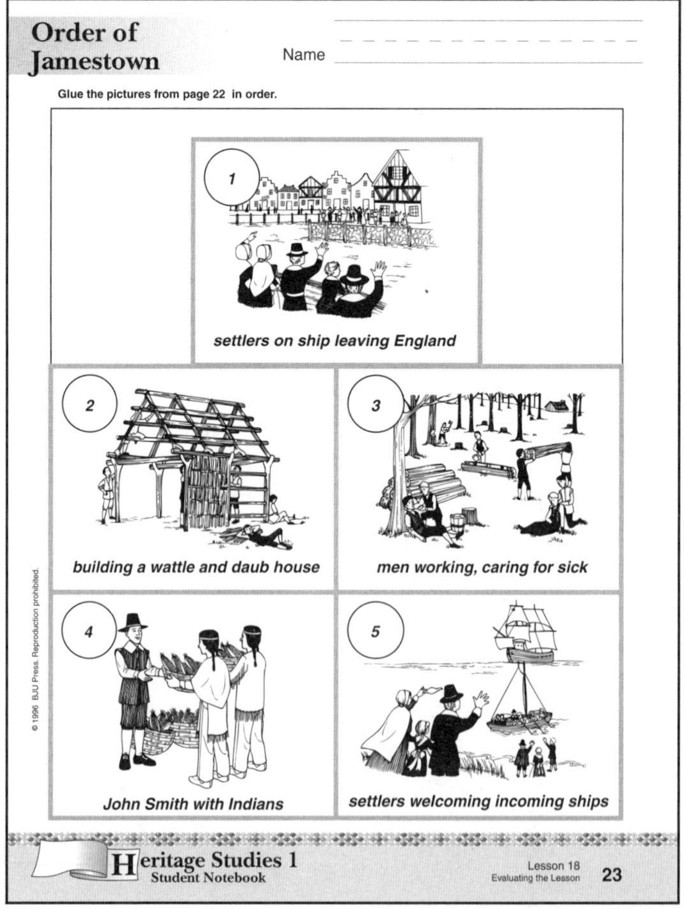

Order of Jamestown Name ______

Glue the pictures from page 22 in order.

1 *settlers on ship leaving England*

2 *building a wattle and daub house*

3 *men working, caring for sick*

4 *John Smith with Indians*

5 *settlers welcoming incoming ships*

© 1996 BJU Press. Reproduction prohibited.

Heritage Studies 1 Student Notebook — Lesson 18 Evaluating the Lesson 23

Going Beyond

Enrichment

Give your child small twigs, straw, and modeling clay that he can use to build his own wattle and daub houses. (*NOTE:* The recipe below makes enough clay for two small houses.) Tell him to refer to the pictures on text page 51. You may want to display the completed houses in the box of sand described in the Enrichment of Lesson 17.

Modeling Clay

2 cups flour
1 cup salt
2 cups water
4 teaspoons cream of tartar
2 tablespoons cooking oil

Combine all the ingredients in a saucepan and cook over low heat for about three minutes, stirring frequently. When the mixture forms a ball, remove from heat. After the mixture has cooled, store in an airtight container. Do not refrigerate. This mixture will keep for a month or more.

Additional Teacher Information

Captain John Smith was a man of many adventures. From the age of sixteen, he roamed the world as a soldier, serving in many armies. He was only five feet tall; was energetic, forceful, and intelligent; and had a red beard and a boastful manner. But John Smith was a true leader. According to a story told by John Smith himself, he was captured in 1608 by Chief Powhatan and sentenced to die for killing two warriors. John Smith said that he was forced to kneel with his head on a stone, ready to be beaten by clubs, when the chief's youngest daughter, Pocahontas, rushed to his rescue. Smith said that Pocahontas put his head in her lap and begged her father to spare his life. Captain John Smith was set free, and peaceful relations between the settlers and the Native Americans were restored for a long time. This adventurous man never married, but near the end of his life, when a stranger asked him whether he had any children, John Smith replied, "Virginia and New England are my children."

Chief Powhatan's youngest daughter was actually named Matoaka, but because she was so lighthearted and lively, she became better known by her nickname *Frolicsome,* or *Pocahontas,* as it was in her native tongue. Captured and sold to an English captain in 1611 for the price of a copper kettle, Pocahontas lived among the settlers, learned English, and was taught the ways of Christianity. She was soon baptized and given the Christian name of Rebecca. Later she met and fell in love with an English tobacco planter, John Rolfe. The two were married in April 1614. Pocahontas remained a devoted friend of John Smith.

It was during this exciting period of history that the beautiful King James Version of the Bible was developed (1604-11). Forty-seven learned men worked on the translation that took seven years.

LESSON 19
Growing Crops

Text, pages 55, 57
Notebook, page 24

Preview

Main Ideas

- People often choose to live in areas that provide resources for meeting their needs.
- The Indians taught the people of Jamestown how to grow food to eat.
- Farmers of today care for the crops that they plant and grow.

Objectives

- Plant some seeds and care for them as they grow
- Illustrate the step-by-step process of growing crops

Materials

- Squash, such as yellow, acorn, or zucchini, or a picture of one of these*
- Beans, such as kidney, lima, navy, or string beans, or a picture of one of these*
- An ear of corn or a picture of corn*
- Plastic cups or egg carton sections*
- Enough soil to fill the cups or egg carton sections
- Some seeds* (*NOTE:* Lima beans or navy beans are probably the easiest and quickest crops to grow.)
- A piece of paper
- A piece of cotton clothing

Day 1

Lesson

Introducing the Lesson

Read some riddles. Place the squash, corn, and beans in front of your child. Read the riddles. After each riddle, allow your child to guess what vegetable the riddle is describing.

Hidden in silk
With ears yellow or white,
This tasty cob
Is good to the last bite!
What am I? *(corn)*

Smooth or bumpy,
Bulb-shaped or long,
With this kin to the pumpkin,
Your meal can't go wrong.
What am I? *(squash)*

◆ THINGS PEOPLE DO ◆

Growing Crops

The people in Jamestown
had to grow food to eat.
The Indians helped.
They gave the men seeds
to plant.
The men learned to plant crops
that would give food.
They learned to plant
crops that could be
sold for money.

Today, people still
need to grow food
to eat. They still
grow crops that can
be sold for money.
What do we call the
people who grow
crops?
We call them *farmers.*

55

Red, brown, or green,
For your salad, soup, or pie,
Baked, boiled, or steamed,
These plump veggies rate high.
What am I? *(beans)*

The Indians taught the settlers of early Jamestown how to plant and grow these important vegetables.

Teaching the Lesson

Direct a text activity on page 55. Read the first section. Show the seeds.

Text Discussion, page 55

- ➤ How can such a tiny seed grow to be a mature plant bearing vegetables? *(Answers will vary.)* (Bible Promise: I. God as Master)
- ➤ There is a new word in the paragraph that means "plants that are grown for man's use." Can you find the word that is being described? *(crop)*
- ➤ Corn, squash, and beans are food **crops** that people eat or that they feed to their animals. Can you name other food crops? *(Answers will vary.)*
- ➤ Can food crops be sold for money? *(yes)*
- ➤ Do you think the Jamestown settlers sold their food crops for money? *(probably not, because they needed the food for themselves)*

◆ LEARNING HOW ◆

To Plant a Crop

1. Gather some plastic cups or egg cartons, some soil, water, and some seeds.
2. Fill each cup or egg carton section with soil. Plant one seed in each cup or section.Pour a little water over the soil.
3. Observe your crops every day. Add a little water every few days.
4. How long does it take for the crops to grow? How long do you think it will be before the crops are ready to eat? Would you like to care for a whole field of your crop? What would you have to do differently?

57

From Seed to Plant Name ______________

Draw a picture to match each step, showing how your seed grew.

1.	2.
3.	4.

© 1996 BJU Press. Reproduction prohibited.

Heritage Studies 1 Student Notebook — Lesson 19 Evaluating the Lesson 24

➤ Not all crops are food crops. Look at this piece of paper. What crop do you think produces paper? *(trees)*

➤ Name some other ways that the Indians and the settlers used the trees. *(Possible answers include to build houses and canoes and to make dishes and tools.)*

➤ *Show a piece of cotton clothing.* What crop produces the fibers to make this kind of cloth for clothing? *(cotton)*

➤ Can cotton crops be sold for money? *(yes)*

The Indians taught the Jamestown settlers about another crop—a crop that they could not eat, or wear, or use to build their settlement. This crop was harmful long ago and is still harmful today. (BAT: 3d Body as a temple) The crop that the Jamestown settlers grew was tobacco, a plant that the people smoked.

➤ Can the tobacco crop be sold for money? *(yes)*

➤ Read the remainder of page 55.

You may want to do the *Learning How* activity outdoors or on a desk or table covered with newspaper.

Day 2

Evaluating the Lesson

Direct a *Learning How* activity on text page 57. Read the steps of the activity. Then reread each step, allowing time for your child to accomplish that task before going on to the next step. Ask each question from Step 4. *(Answers will vary.)* Encourage your child to observe and water his crop each day for the next several weeks until the seeds germinate and grow.

Direct a follow-up activity on Notebook page 24. After your child has had a couple of weeks to care for his crop and to see it grow, tell him to draw the step-by-step process, illustrating how his seed grew to be a plant. Encourage him to write a sentence or to dictate a sentence for you to write for him about each step.

It may be easier for your child to draw the plant as he views it. He could draw the first step now and then the others at appropriate intervals.

Going Beyond

Enrichment

Staple several sheets of construction paper together for two booklets. Entitle one booklet "Food Crops" and the other booklet "Other Crops." Encourage your child to find and cut out pictures of crops from magazines and to glue the pictures in the appropriate booklets.

Additional Teacher Information

In the spring of 1608, John Smith persuaded two captive Native Americans to teach the settlers how to plant corn. Thus, forty acres of corn were planted with the Indians supervising and giving instructions to the settlers. It was not until the settlers of Jamestown were established agriculturally that the future of Jamestown was secure.

When John Rolfe came to Jamestown in 1611, he experimented with growing tobacco seeds. The crop grew well in the Virginia soil, and in 1613 John Smith sent his first boatload of tobacco to England, making it the first successful export of the settlement. The tobacco crop grew so well in Virginia that it saved the people from bankruptcy.

Interestingly, James I, the monarch for whom Jamestown was named, was vehemently opposed to tobacco. He proclaimed what science has only recently concluded, that tobacco is harmful to the brain and the lungs.

LESSON 20
The Settlement Grows

Text, pages 56, 58, 180-81
Notebook, page 25

Preview

Main Ideas

- Many different people and groups contributed to American culture.
- Each region has a unique history of exploration, settlement, and growth.
- Jamestown was the first lasting English settlement in the New World.

Objectives

- Decide which items to take on an imaginary journey to the New World
- Determine whether statements refer to Jamestown or England

Materials

- Maps and More 16, page M9
- Two index cards with a *J* on one card and an *E* on the other card*
- A sheet of paper

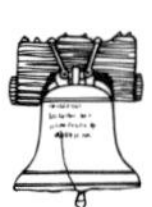

The game Journey to Jamestown is introduced in the Enrichment section. (*NOTE:* See Appendix pages A16-A19.) If you use this game, prepare the game pieces as you did for the game in Lesson 8, making just one copy of each sheet of game cards.

Day 1

Lesson

Introducing the Lesson

You may want to have other family members participate in this activity.

Direct an activity on Notebook page 25. Tell your child to pretend that he is in the next group of people to sail to the New World. Tell him that the ship is small and that there is not much room, but the crew will be allowed to select seven things to take with them.

What to Take?

Name ______________________

Look at the list below. In the space called *Your Choices*, write the seven things that you want to take. After your crew has agreed upon the seven things to take, write the things in the space called *Your Crew's Choices.*

Your Choices

1. ______________________
2. ______________________
3. ______________________
4. ______________________
5. ______________________
6. ______________________
7. ______________________

Your Crew's Choices

1. ______________________
2. ______________________
3. ______________________
4. ______________________
5. ______________________
6. ______________________
7. ______________________

folding cot   fishing pole   hunting knife   candles
party dress   ax   vegetable and grain seeds   schoolbooks
musket and powder   iron pot   table and chair   shovel
Bible   sled   dog   flower seeds   sewing kits   canteen
wool blankets   dishes   medicine kit   warm clothes

Each year more and more people came
to Jamestown.
Most of these people were white men.
But one ship brought ninety young ladies to live
in the settlement.
And another ship brought twenty black men.
What do you think happened to these men?
They were sold to white men in Jamestown.
They had to work hard for those men.

Read the suggested list of items on the Notebook page. Allow time for your child to select seven items and to write these items under the topic *Your Choices.* You will also need to make a list of your seven choices.

Allow your child to be the captain of the crew. Compare the lists each of you made and agree upon an appropriate list of items to take to the New World. Instruct your child to list the seven items decided upon by his crew under the heading *Your Crew's Choices.* Explain that all travelers to the New World probably had to make similar choices. (BAT: 7d Contentment; Bible Promises: H. God as Father, I. God as Master)

Day 2

Teaching the Lesson

Direct a text activity on pages 56 and 58 and pages 180-81. Read page 56.

Text Discussion, page 56

- Do you think girls would have wanted to go to Jamestown? Why or why not?
- Was it right for the white men to buy black men to work for them? *(no)* (BAT: 5a Love)

Text Discussion, pages 58, 180-81

- Read page 58. What name was given to the area where the new settlements were built? *(Virginia)*

The name *Virginia* was chosen in honor of Queen Elizabeth I. The people referred to her as their **Virgin Queen** because she had never been married. (*NOTE:* See Additional Teacher Information in Lesson 16.)

- Find the state of Virginia on the map on pages 180-81.
- Can you find Virginia on Maps and More 16? *If you live in the United States, point out where your location is in relation to Virginia. If your child has been to Virginia, you may want to allow a few minutes for him to recall his experiences in Virginia—where he went, how he got there, what he saw, whom he visited.*

TimeLine Discussion

- Look at the time line on page 58 and then at the History TimeLine displayed in the room. What group of people were in the New World first? *(the Indians)*
- Did the ships of Columbus or the ships of the Vikings come next? *(the ships of the Vikings)*
- Which came first—the establishment of Jamestown or the coming of Columbus to the New World? *(the coming of Columbus to the New World)*

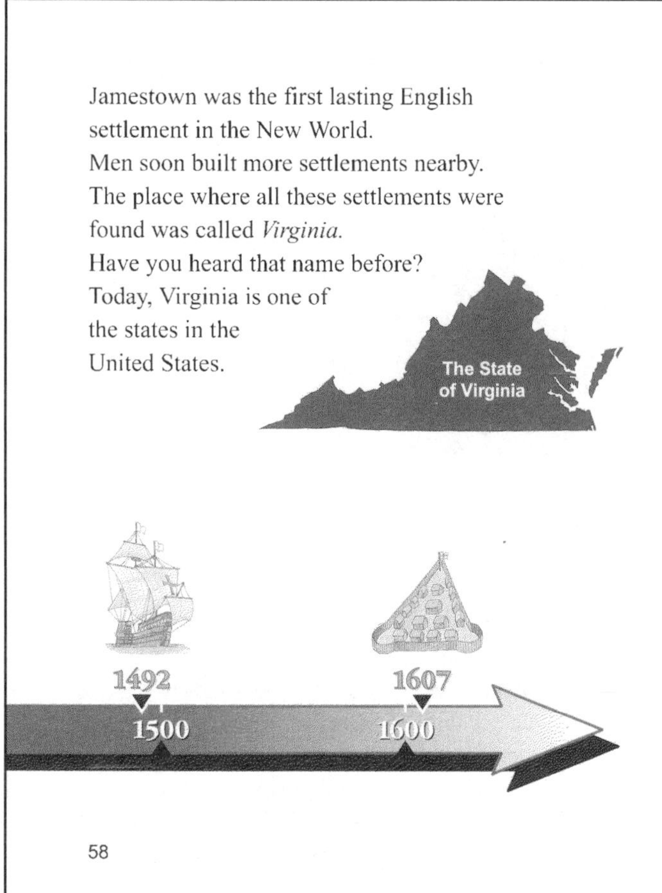
Jamestown was the first lasting English settlement in the New World.
Men soon built more settlements nearby.
The place where all these settlements were found was called *Virginia.*
Have you heard that name before?
Today, Virginia is one of the states in the United States.

58

Evaluating the Lesson

Direct a comparison of Jamestown and England. Give your child the two cards with the letters on them. Explain that you will read several statements. If the statement is about Jamestown, he should hold up his *J* card for Jamestown; if the statement is about England, he should hold up his *E* card for England. For two statements, both answers are correct. Use the following statements.

- This is part of Virginia. *(J)*
- This was ruled by King James I. *(E and J)*
- This was in the New World. *(J)*
- Men thought that they would find gold here. *(J)*
- Captain John Smith was born here. *(E)*
- People lived in houses made of sticks and mud with grass or straw roofs. *(J and E)*
- Black men were sold to white men to work for them as slaves. *(J)*
- They sent ships to the New World. *(E)*
- Kings and queens ruled this place for years and years. *(E)*
- Captain John Smith was a wise leader here. *(J)*
- Indians helped the settlers here. *(J)*

Going Beyond

Enrichment

Introduce the Journey to Jamestown game. This game reviews ideas from Lessons 17-20. Explain each game piece. The game board is a simple map showing a path from England to Jamestown. The starting point is in England. Each player may choose which route to travel as he crosses the Atlantic Ocean to Jamestown. On the return trip to England to get more supplies, he must use the other route.

Take turns selecting the game cards and moving the game pieces the number of spaces forward or backward as indicated on the cards. Place each used card facedown on the bottom of the pile. The game continues until a player reaches England on his return trip. That player is the winner.

Additional Teacher Information

In 1619 the first black men arrived in America. Some of these black men were put to work on the governor's land near Jamestown, and others were sent to outside settlements. At first these men worked as indentured servants, just as white men did, and after about seven years they were free to make a living for themselves. It was not long, however, before black men faced a lifetime of servitude. Forty years later slavery became lawful in Virginia. In the years to come, many more people were captured in Africa and traded as slaves in America. By the end of the seventeenth century, most of the workers on the settlement were enslaved Africans. Any servants or slaves, white or black, not sold within a reasonable time were sold to a *soul-driver,* a man who would drive them through the country until he had sold each one for a profit.

Also in 1619, one hundred boys and girls arrived from England to become apprentices and learn trades. Some who could not afford passage came as indentured servants, agreeing to serve their masters for seven years before being freed to live on their own.

Women came too—ninety "young, handsome and honestly educated maids." Some married quickly; others chose to remain single.

The Virginia Company charter was rewritten twice, and in 1612 the boundaries of Virginia Colony included a vast area that today covers forty-two of the fifty states, part of southern Canada, and the island of Bermuda. The charter remained in effect until 1624, after which the crown took over the government of the colony. During that time, 6,040 of the 7,289 immigrants that came to Jamestown died. Most died of famine, but others died of disease or war.

5 | LESSONS 21-25

God's Laws and Man's Laws

In these lessons your child will use role-playing, maps, and demonstrations to learn about the history and influence of early Plymouth, Massachusetts. The unit concludes with descriptions of the first Thanksgiving and a view of contemporary celebrations.

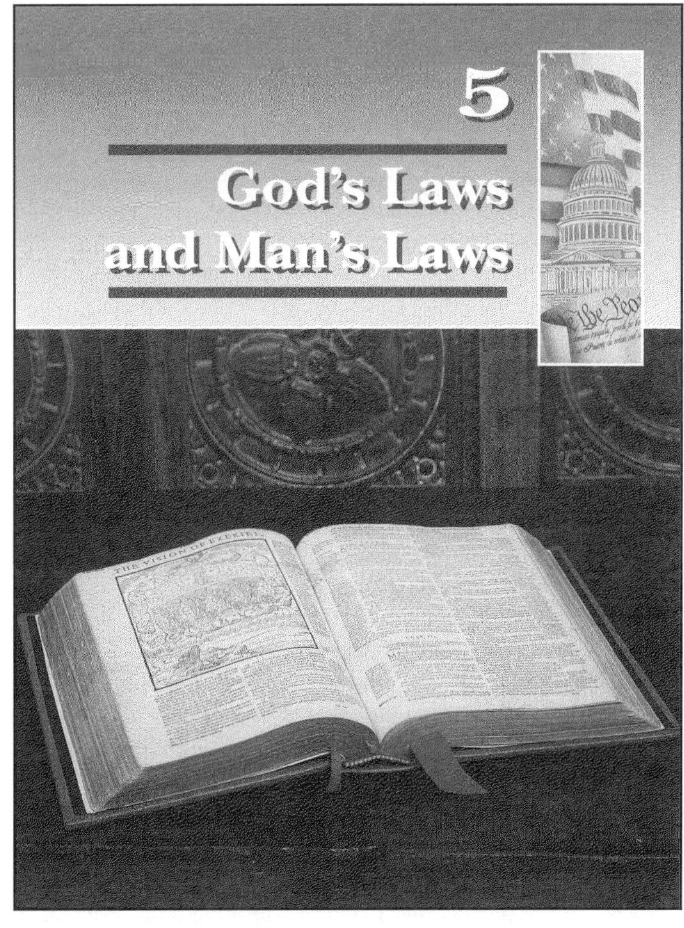

Materials

The following materials must be obtained or prepared before the presentation of the lesson. These items are labeled with an asterisk (*) in each lesson and in the Materials List in the Supplement. For further information see the individual lessons.

- 5 dolls or play people (Lesson 21)
- Appendix, page A20 (Lesson 21)
- Appendix, page A21 (Lesson 22)
- 8 craft sticks or tongue depressors (Lesson 22)
- Selected area about 90' x 26' (Lesson 22)
- 9 grains of dried corn (Lesson 24)
- Ingredients for Indian Pudding (Lesson 25)

LESSON 21
Obeying God

Text, pages 60-61, 174

Preview

Main Ideas

- The Separatists chose to obey God.
- The Separatists had to leave their homeland in order to obey God.

Objectives

- Indicate on a map where the Separatists started their journey
- Act out a scene that depicts the Separatists deciding to leave England

Materials

- A newspaper
- 5 dolls or play people*
- Appendix, page A20: map of England and the New World*

Would you like the president of the United States
to tell you which church to go to?
The king of England told his people that
everyone had to belong to the king's church.

Some English people did not go to
the king's church.
These people said, "We must obey God
in our worship."
They "separated" from the king's church.
They called themselves *Separatists.*

Wherefore come out from among them, and be ye separate.
II Corinthians 6:17

60

Day 1

Lesson

Introducing the Lesson

Direct a discussion. Hold up a newspaper. Explain that you are going to read a make-believe article.

President Declares All People Will Go to His Church

Yesterday the president of the United States said that beginning next Sunday, all people in the United States will go to the same kind of church. The president will be the head of the church. No one will read his own Bible anymore. The Bible will be read only at church.

- ➤ What would our family do if the article were true?
- ➤ What would our pastor do?
- ➤ In the days of the Pilgrims, the king and queen of England made such rules. Do you think everyone in England obeyed those rules?

Teaching the Lesson

Direct a text activity on page 60. Read the Scripture verse on page 60. Explain that ***separate*** means "apart from, different from." Assemble five dolls or play people in one place. Then move one "person" to a far corner of the room. Explain that the person you moved is now "separate" from the group.

Text Discussion, page 60

- ➤ Read the first section on page 60. The people of England had to decide what to do about the king's rules.
- ➤ Read the last section on the page. Some of the people chose to leave England so that they could worship God in the way they believed was right.
- ➤ Why do you think the people who left were called **Separatists?** *(because they separated from, or left, the group)*
- ➤ Use your play people to act out what the Separatists did.
- ➤ Do you think leaving their friends was hard for the Separatists? (BAT: 1c Separation from the world)
- ➤ Talk about ways that you are like the Separatists. *(Answers may include ways that Christians set themselves apart from the world, such as by being honest, by wearing modest clothes, and by not drinking.)*

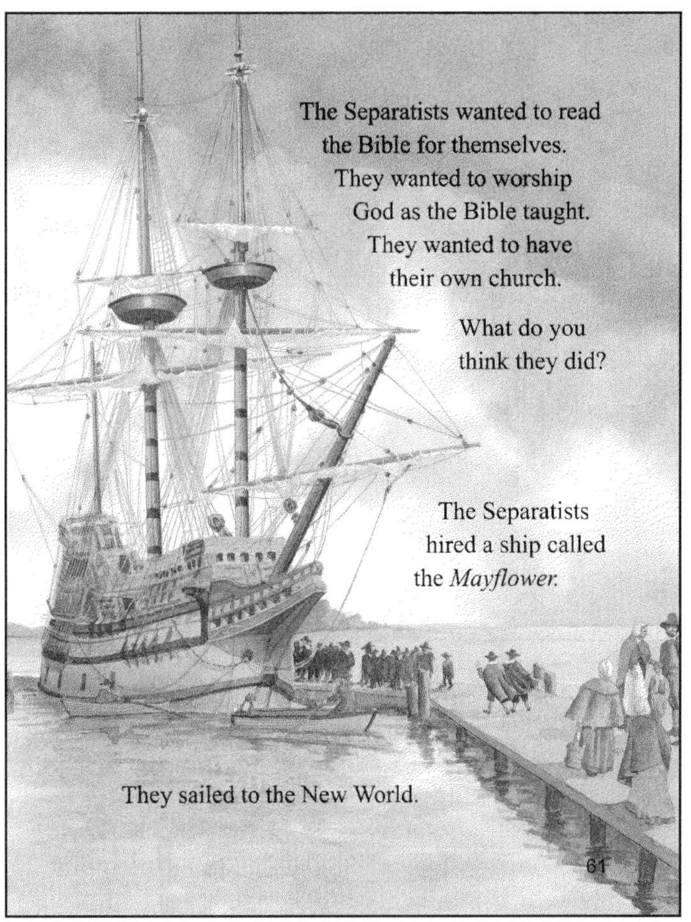

The Separatists wanted to read
the Bible for themselves.
They wanted to worship
God as the Bible taught.
They wanted to have
their own church.
What do you
think they did?
The Separatists
hired a ship called
the *Mayflower.*
They sailed to the New World.
61

The Bible of Plymouth Plantation

This is a Geneva Bible.

This is the kind of Bible that the Separatists brought to New England.

It was the first Bible in English to have the verses numbered.

The print in this Bible was easy to read.

Many English families owned a Bible like this.

174

Day 2

Text Discussion, pages 61 and 174

- Listen to the "news" article again. Think about what would be the worst thing if this announcement were true. *(Answers will vary, but help your child to see that not being able to read the Bible on his own would be the worst.)*
- Read page 174. Look carefully at the Geneva Bible and compare it to your own Bible.
- Read page 61. *Discuss the page.*
- How would you feel if you had to leave your country and go somewhere else to live?

Map Activity

- On the map of England and the New World put a red *X* on England.
- Why did the Separatists leave their homes in England and come to America? *(to worship God as they believed they should)*
- Some people who came to America were not Separatists. What reasons might these other people have had for coming to America? *(Answers may include making money, looking for gold, and getting away from trouble.)* All these people brought important ideas to the New World.

Evaluating the Lesson

To perform this role-playing activity, you will need to enlist the involvement of other family members or some of your child's friends. If that is not possible, you will play the parts of the king and the people who stayed behind in England. Your child will play the part of the Separatists.

Direct a role-playing scene. The characters include the king of England, the people who stayed in England, and the people who chose to leave England to worship in freedom (the Separatists). Begin with an arrangement of chairs to simulate pews in the church. The king is making his announcement to the members of the church. Read the narration and demonstrate the actions as appropriate.

> The people of England were surprised to hear the news. *(Show surprise.)* The king had commanded them to go only to his church. He told them that he was in charge of the church. He said everyone had to obey. *(King stands before the others and motions as rules are read.)*

The people talked among themselves. *(Nod and pretend to talk together.)* Some of them argued with each other. *(Someone stands and pretends to argue.)* They prayed together. *(Kneel to pray.)* Some people wanted to stay in England and try to obey the king. Others said they had to leave and go where they could obey God as they thought they should.

So some people packed a few things. *(Make motions of packing things in trunks.)* They said good-bye to their old friends. *(Shake hands or embrace.)* Some of the people who left and some who stayed cried at the parting. *(Wipe eyes.)*

The Separatists got on the ship. *(Walk away from the others. Pretend to carry trunks or bundles. Pantomime getting on a ship, stepping up and handing bundles to those already aboard.)* They waved once more. *(The Separatists wave and continue to wave during the last line.)* They set off for a new life in a new place.

Going Beyond

Additional Teacher Information

Pilgrims is an encompassing name for all travelers to the New World at the time. Some think that *Puritan* is a more accurate term for the *Mayflower* group, but even that is slightly misleading. Puritans were those people who wanted to stay in the Church of England to "purify" it, to rid it of the Roman Catholic trappings and methods. The Separatists, however, felt that the Church of England could not be salvaged and that the best answer was to leave altogether. Thus the settlers at Plymouth were Separatists and others who came for nonreligious reasons. Ten years later, Puritans came to the New World and settled the Massachusetts Bay Colony, headed by John Winthrop. (*NOTE:* See the Additional Teacher Information at the end of Lesson 30 for more about this colony.)

The Separatists did not set off directly for the New World. They lived eleven years in Holland before conditions became unbearable. In 1620, they finally concluded that the only way to have freedom of worship was to sail to the uncharted New World.

LESSON 22

Sailing to the New World

Text, pages 62-63, 173
Notebook, page 26

Preview

Main Ideas

- The passage to the New World was difficult and crowded.
- The Separatists were persecuted even aboard ship.
- There was no place to live when they arrived.

Objectives

- Fill in a diagram of the *Mayflower*
- Identify on a map where the ship landed

Materials

- Appendix, page A20: map of England and the New World*
- Appendix, page A21: a diagram of the ship*
- 8 craft sticks or tongue depressors*
- Selected area about 90' x 26'*

Choose an area near your home to illustrate the size of the *Mayflower.* If it is a large open area, you may want to mark the corners. A simple way to estimate the length and width is to step it off. An average adult stride is about three feet. If you are near a football field or baseball field, you might use the markings given to help designate your area. The bases on a baseball field are ninety feet apart.

Day 1

Lesson

Introducing the Lesson

Direct a demonstration and text activity on page 173. Take your child outside and stand in the area which you have previously selected. Explain that this area is approximately the size of the *Mayflower.*

Mayflower

This is an exact copy of the ship the Separatists sailed on.

Would you like to sail to England on this *Mayflower?*

How does it look compared to a modern ship?

173

The *Mayflower* was small.
It was about as long as eight average cars lined up.
It was about as wide as four cars side by side.

There were 102 passengers on the *Mayflower.*
Many were children.
Joseph Mullins was six years old.
So was the girl Remember Allerton.
A baby was born on the ship.
The captain had more than twenty men in his crew.
How do you think all these people got along on the small boat?

The crew made fun of the Separatists for praying and singing hymns.
Do you think the people stopped praying and singing?
No, they did not.

62

Demonstration

- *Within this area, mark a smaller area about two feet square.* This is about how much room was available for each person. Would you like to have only this much room to live in for two months?
- Imagine what each person brought with him. Remember how little space there was.
- What do you think the Separatists did on their long, crowded trip across the ocean?
- Think of the purpose for the trip.
- Do you think that the Separatists read the Bible and sang hymns? The Separatists prayed and sang many times on their journey. (BATs: 6b Prayer, 7c Praise)
- Let's pretend we are Separatists and sing a hymn or chorus.

Text Discussion, page 173

- Compare the two ships in the pictures.

The first ship is a replica or copy of the *Mayflower,* the ship that brought the Separatists here. It is actually much smaller than a modern ship. Dozens of *Mayflowers* would fit on similar modern ships.

Day 2

Teaching the Lesson

Direct a text activity on pages 62-63. Read the first two sections on page 62, reviewing information about the *Mayflower.*

Text Discussion, page 62

- Were there any children your age? *(at least two)*
- How do you think the children felt as they left on the *Mayflower?*

> You may want to reflect on the Christian's duty to resist fear and anger and to have faith. (BATs: 3c Emotional control, 8a Faith in God's promises, 8d Courage)

- Read the rest of the page. Why do you think the crew made fun of the Separatists?

> Sometimes when a Christian does the right thing, other people who are not doing right feel guilty. Instead of repenting, they will often make fun of the one doing right. The Separatists did not stop singing and praying. They were faithful to God. They wanted to be a witness to the sailors. (BATs: 5c Evangelism and missions, 7b Exaltation of Christ, 8c Fight)

Read a story. Tell your child to pretend that he is in a small boat that is rocking, rocking on the waves. He can see no land in any direction.

"Here," said a woman, "eat some dried fish. And here, don't you want a little bread?"

Remember Allerton tried to bite the bread. It was hard as wood. A bit of the crust flaked off in her mouth. She looked at the fish in her hand, but she did not try to eat it.

A sailor went by with a rope in his hand. "Well," he said, "if you don't want that, Missy, I'll take it."

"Ah," said another sailor, "leave her alone."

"Bah," said the first. "You and your 'be nice.' I for one will be very glad when they die of not eating and we can throw them all overboard. The good-for-nothings."

Remember stared at the sailor with wide eyes. He looked down and laughed at her. When he went away, her mother came to her.

"The Lord hears him," she said. "So never mind him. I think he will soon see we mean him no harm."

Remember snuggled in close until the cloak her mother wore fell over her. For the first time that day, she was not cold.

The days went by and all the days looked the same. Gray water was all around and gray clouds above. It was hard to imagine that the boat had moved at all, though a cold wind was always pushing them.

"Oh no," said Joseph Mullins, "lemon juice again!" He squinted his eyes and shook his head. "It tastes awful."

"But it keeps away the sickness," said his father. "Take it, now, like a good lad."

Joseph took a spoonful and swallowed it. He coughed and sputtered until he saw Remember laughing at him.

Remember's father came striding toward Joseph's father. "A sailor is sick," he said. "We should pray for him."

"Who is it?"

"The one who is always hoping to throw us overboard."

Before anyone else could say a word, the captain appeared. "My man has died," he said.

The other sailors wrapped the man up and threw his body into the sea.

"He died so quickly," said Remember's mother.

The sailors and the captain went back to sailing the ship. But they never made fun of their passengers again.

- Why might the sailors have stopped making fun of the Separatists?
- Why were the Separatists willing to pray for a man who had been mean to them? *(They knew that the man needed God to save him.)* (BAT: 7a Grace)

The Separatists landed in the New World.
The settlers called the place *Plymouth Plantation.*

The captain of the *Mayflower* kept saying,
"Hurry up! Find a place to stay."
He wanted to sail back to England.
At last the Separatists found a good place
to build houses.

63

Text Discussion, page 63

- When a sailor spotted land, he would often yell "Land ho!" Imagine how the Separatists felt when they heard this yell from one of the sailors on the *Mayflower.*
- Read the first section on page 63.
- Do you think there were any hotels or houses for the new settlers? *(no)*

After weeks at sea in the cold and the damp, the Separatists came to a land deep with snow. There were no houses and no friends to welcome them. What the Separatists saw was a hard winter shore with dark woods. But the people prayed and thanked God for a safe arrival. (BAT: 7d Contentment)

Day 3

- Look at the red *X* on the map of England and the New World. Remember that this is where the Separatists began their journey.
- Draw a blue arrow from England to Plymouth and place an *X* over Plymouth. Now trace the route from England to Plymouth with your finger.
- Name the ocean that the ship traveled over. *(Atlantic)*

Some of the men got off the ship to look for a place to stay. The women and children lived on the ship for a while. Some of the women took clothes to the cold streams to wash them.

- ➤ Read the rest of the page to find out whether the captain helped the Separatists look for a place to build homes. *(No, he just wanted them to hurry.)*
- ➤ What important things would the men look for in a place that is good to settle? *(Answers will vary but should include fresh water, a way to get food, and shelter or at least something to build shelter from.)*

The men found a place and began to build a shelter. They called their new home **Plymouth Plantation,** after the city in England.

The names of cities and towns often have meanings. Many place names in America come from Indian words. (*NOTE:* Review Indian names from Chapter 3.)

- ➤ At first the settlers built just one shelter. How do you think it must have been for all the settlers to live in one shelter for a while?

Until the first shelter was ready, the people had to live on the *Mayflower.* As soon as the men could, they began to build houses. People like to live with their own families in their own houses. The Separatists trusted God to take care of them. (Bible Promise: H. God as Father)

- ➤ Tell about times you have had to trust God to help you and your family.

Evaluating the Lesson

Direct an activity with Notebook page 26. Tell your child to color the figures, cut them out, and then to glue each one to a craft stick or tongue depressor. Direct him to tell about each figure and show where it would fit in the diagram of the ship. Review the events that led to the Separatists' having to leave their homes. *(The king made laws they could not live with.)*

As an alternative, you may ask your child to draw pictures in the sections of the ship, using the picture on text page 175 as a guide.

Going Beyond

Enrichment

Ask a member of your family to supervise the drawing of a large diagram of the *Mayflower.* Allow your child to draw the equipment, passengers, cargo, and so on for the ship. Encourage him to represent the children on the ship as well as the adults. Your child may prefer to use the characters from Notebook page 26 to put on this large ship.

Ready for the Mayflower
Name
Color and cut out the figures.
© 1996 BJU Press. Reproduction prohibited.
Heritage Studies 1
Student Notebook
Lesson 22
Evaluating the Lesson
26

Additional Teacher Information

The *Mayflower* had been used for wine transport before the Separatists hired it. As a result, it was much cleaner and sweeter-smelling than most other vessels of the day.

The *Speedwell* had begun the journey with the *Mayflower* but had leaked twice and was finally abandoned. The *Mayflower* sailed alone from Plymouth, England, in September 1620 under Captain Christopher Jones. A baby was born onboard on the trip, and one Separatist died, probably from scurvy since he had refused his daily doses of lemon juice.

Aboard the *Mayflower,* the Separatists, devout Christians, were often made fun of by the rough crewmen. Dedicated to their faith, the Separatists continued with prayer and the reading of the Scriptures. It is reported that even when stopping leaks and making repairs to the ship, the people "committed themselves to the will of God and resolved to proceed." Upon the sighting of land, it is reported that the Separatists knelt on the deck, thanked God, and sang "Old Hundredth" (the doxology), giving all praise to God.

A replica of the ship, the *Mayflower II,* was built in England and sailed from Plymouth, England, on April 20, 1957. After fifty-three days at sea, it put to shore at Provincetown. The ship now rests in the harbor of Plymouth, Massachusetts.

LESSON 23
Choosing New Laws and Leaders

Text, pages 64-66, 179

Preview

Main Ideas

- The Separatists provided for self-government.
- The early leaders were elected officials.
- The people wrote down their laws and kept records of daily life.

Objective

- Make up a schoolroom law

Materials

- A sheet of parchment or similar paper

Day 1

Lesson

Introducing the Lesson

Direct a discussion. Ask your child whether he has ever made a promise to someone. Ask how important he thinks it is to keep a promise once he has made it. Remind him that to break a promise is dishonest. (BAT: 4c Honesty) Discuss why it is hard to keep a promise sometimes.

The Separatists made a promise to each other before they got off the *Mayflower.* Ask your child what he thinks the promise was about.

Teaching the Lesson

Direct a text activity on pages 64 and 66. Read the first two sentences on page 64.

Text Discussion, page 64

➤ Why do you think people need laws, or rules, to go by?

➤ Read the next two sentences. Name any laws you can think of for the place in which we live. Think of a reason that we need each law.

Before the Separatists got off their ship,
they made some laws.
Why do you think people need laws?
Laws help people live together without trouble.
What laws do you know of in your town?

The Separatists signed their names to the laws.
They called their laws the *Mayflower Compact.*
A *compact* is an agreement, a promise.

64

Rules and laws are necessary. They help people get along together. In the United States, laws are meant to help each person, not just certain groups. (BAT: 2a Authority)

➤ Think of ways that people show they plan to keep a promise. *(Answers may include shaking hands or signing a paper.)*

➤ Read the last section on the page.

➤ What did the Separatists call their promise? *(a compact)*

➤ Why do you think the men signed their names to the **compact?** *(to show they promised to keep the laws)*

The promise the men made to each other was the first law for the Separatists in the New World. Although the people were far away from their home in England, they were still Englishmen. The land they settled would belong to England. They brought their English ideas about laws to their new home in the New World. Many of our ideas about law today come from these settlers' laws.

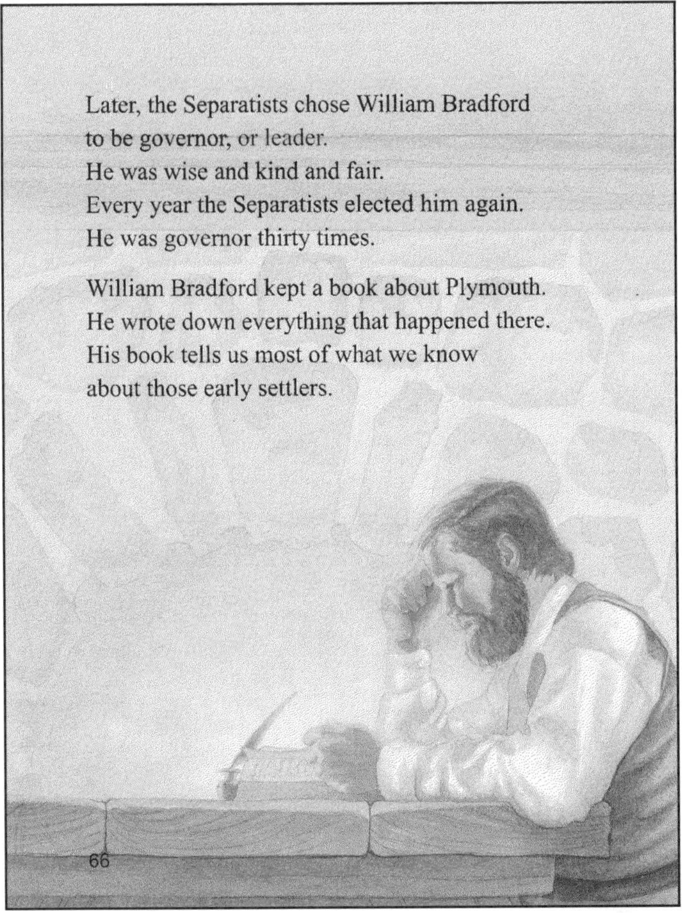

Later, the Separatists chose William Bradford
to be governor, or leader.
He was wise and kind and fair.
Every year the Separatists elected him again.
He was governor thirty times.

William Bradford kept a book about Plymouth.
He wrote down everything that happened there.
His book tells us most of what we know
about those early settlers.

66

Day 2

Text Discussion, page 66

Your child may not know the answers to the first four questions. You will find out exactly how much he does know by asking the questions. He may have learned some of the information by listening to your discussions.

- ➤ Do you know what we call the leader of our country? *(the president)* Tell his name.
- ➤ Do you know how often the people of the United States elect or choose a president? *(every four years)*
- ➤ Do you know what we call the leader of our state? *(the governor)* Tell his name.
- ➤ Do you know how often the people of our state elect a governor? *(every four years or every two years, depending on where you live)*
- ➤ Read the first section of page 66 to find out who an early Separatist governor was. *(William Bradford)*
- ➤ How often did the Separatists hold an "election"? *(every year)*
- ➤ How many times was Bradford elected governor? *(thirty times)*

Every group of people has laws and leaders. The Indians that were already living in the New World had governments too.

- ➤ How do you think we know what went on so many years ago?
- ➤ Read the last section. *Discuss the information.*
- ➤ *Read the following selection from Governor Bradford's book about how the Separatists must have felt as they got off their ship in the cold, lonely New World.*

> They now had no friends to welcome them nor inns [hotels] to . . . refresh their weather-beaten bodies; no houses or . . . towns to [go to]. . . . It was winter, . . . sharp and violent, [with] cruel and fierce storms. . . . What could they see but a . . . wilderness, full of wild beasts and wild men, . . . full of woods and thickets. . . . If they looked behind them, there was the mighty ocean. . . . What could now [keep] them but the Spirit of God and His grace?

- ➤ How do you know that Bradford trusted God? *(The last sentence of the passage shows he did.)*

Imagine being left on an island with no ship or airplane to take you home. Imagine that the snow is deep and the food almost gone. This is what the Separatists experienced, and yet they did not turn back or complain. They believed that God had sent them and that He would keep them. (BAT: 8d Courage)

Direct a poem reading. Although only men wrote and signed the Mayflower Compact, many women wrote things down. They kept diaries, telling about everyday events in Plymouth. Name some things the diaries might have told about.

A Puritan woman who lived in the town of Boston became famous for writing poems. Explain that you will read a part of a poem that Anne Bradstreet wrote after her house burned down. This poem, using the speech of the Puritans, describes how she felt after the fire.

> I wakened was with thundering noise
> And piteous shrieks of dreadful voice.
> That fearful sound of 'Fire!' and 'Fire!'
>
> . . . .
>
> Then, coming out, beheld a space
> The flame [burn up] my dwelling place.
>
> . . . .
>
> When by the ruins oft[en] I past,
> My sorrowing eyes aside did cast.
>
> . . . .
>
> Here stood that trunk, and there that chest,
> There lay that [thing] that I loved best.
> My pleasant things in ashes lie,
> And them behold no more shall I.
> Under that roof no guest shall sit,
> Nor at that table eat a bit.
>
> . . . .
>
> The world no longer let me love,
> My hope and treasure lies above.

◆ FAMOUS PEOPLE ◆

Anne Bradstreet

Only men wrote the Mayflower Compact.
But women in Plymouth also wrote.
They wrote letters back to England.
They wrote in diaries about things that happened in everyday life.

Anne Bradstreet came over on a later ship to a different town.
She was the first poet in America to have a book published.
Some poems were about her children.

Many of her poems were about her home in the New World.

65

A Family Tree

Some people keep information on everyone who has ever been in their families. They use *family trees* to record information.

Here is a family tree for one person in New England. Do you think it looks like a tree?

179

Discussion Questions

- *If you have seen a house fire, discuss the experience.*
- What things did the woman in the poem remember and miss? *(her trunk, her chest, her pretty things, her table, her house)You may want to reread the fourth stanza and guide your child in listening for these items one at a time. The old English phrases may be difficult for him to understand.*
- *Reread the last two lines of the poem.* The woman decides to think about her heavenly treasures rather than the earthly ones she lost. We should learn to trust God to provide our needs too and not to put too much store in earthly things. (BAT: 7d Contentment)

Day 3

Direct a text activity on page 65 and page 179. Read the text on page 65. Discuss what Anne Bradstreet liked to write about. *(her children and her home in the New World)*

Text Discussion, page 179

- Look at the family tree. Men and women of the early settlements wrote down this kind of important information. A **family tree** is a chart of all the people in one family. This is a family tree for one family that came here on the Mayflower.
- Why do you think it is called a family tree? *(It looks something like a tree trunk with branches.)*

Evaluating the Lesson

Direct the writing of a new law. Ask your child to think of some things he could do in your home to help it become a better place. Guide him in stating these in the form of a rule or law. You may want to suggest some things, such as making his bed when he gets up, putting one toy away before getting another one out, or waiting quietly for his turn.

Choose one rule to write on chart paper or "parchment" paper. You and your child should sign it. Perhaps you could create a name for your agreement, such as the Smith Agreement or Miller Compact. Then ask him to name the agreement that the Separatists made with each other in much the same way. *(the Mayflower Compact)* Explain that a woman would not have been allowed to sign the agreement in Puritan times.

Going Beyond

Enrichment

Encourage your child to make up a poem about everyday things. If you wish, use the following model from Anne Bradstreet.

> Here stands the _______, and there that _______,
> There lay that [thing] that I loved best.

Write the poem down for your child and allow him to illustrate it.

Additional Teacher Information

John Carver was the first governor of Plymouth Plantation. He died the first winter, however, and was replaced by William Bradford. Bradford's thirty terms were not entirely consecutive since he did not serve as governor for five of the thirty-six years he lived in Plymouth. He died in Plymouth in 1657. His account of the crossing and of life in Plymouth, *Of Plymouth Plantation,* has earned Bradford the appellation "Father of American History."

The group of settlers at Plymouth consisted of Separatists and others interested in setting up a colony in the New World. The Separatists called the others strangers. Collectively the group has become known as Pilgrims, perhaps from a clause in Bradford's book: "They knew they were Pilgrims."

Anne Bradstreet, the famous poet and first woman in America to have a book published, was not a member of the Plymouth group but rather came to Massachusetts Bay Colony on the *Arbella* with other Puritans in 1630. The settlers in Massachusetts Bay still held with the Anglican Church and did not consider themselves Separatists. (*NOTE:* See Additional Teacher Information, Lesson 21, for further distinction between the settlements.)

Separatists were willing to risk their lives to separate themselves from the church of England and worship as they wished. It is reported that William Bradford said, "To keep a good conscience and walk in such Way as God had prescribed in his Word, is a thing which I must prefer before you all, and above life itself. Wherefore, since it is for a good Cause that I am likely to suffer the disasters which you lay before me, you have no cause to be either angry with me, or sorry for me. Yea, I am not only willing to part with everything that is dear to me in this world for this Cause but I am thankful that God hath given me heart so to do; and will accept me so to suffer for him."

The Mayflower Compact was an agreement the group felt necessary to their welfare, since they had landed far north of their authorized destination and were beyond the bounds of the Virginia Company, who had sponsored the trip. In the interest of civil order, the men who were heads of families drew up the compact and signed it.

LESSON 24

Living in the New World

Text, pages 67-69, 172, 177
Notebook, pages 27-28

Preview

Main Ideas

- The first winter in the New World was hard for the settlers.
- The Indians gave the settlers food and taught them how to plant and fish.

Objectives

- Pantomime the Indian method of planting corn
- Locate a storehouse on a picture map

Materials

- A small glass of water
- A half slice of bread
- 9 grains of dried corn*
- A Bible

Notes

This is a reminder to be certain that your child completes Notebook page 24, illustrating the step-by-step growth of his plants. See the Evaluating the Lesson section of Lesson 19 for specific instructions.

Day 1

Lesson

Introducing the Lesson

Conduct a demonstration. Give your child the glass of water and the piece of bread.

Demonstration

➤ Imagine that we are on an island and that this is all the fresh water and food you and I will have for a whole day.

➤ Divide the bread and water in fair portions for the two of us.

➤ Think of ways you can make your portion last all day. Remember you cannot go out to a store to buy more food.

➤ How does this shortage of food make you feel?

➤ Imagine that a snowstorm comes to the island today. Describe what it is like outside.

Plymouth Rock

This spot may be where the *Mayflower* landed.

You can visit a new Plymouth Plantation.

172

The first year in Plymouth Plantation was hard.
There was little food.
The Separatists hunted and fished some.
But it was too late in the year to plant
any vegetables.

The winter was cold and hard.
The snow fell, and the wind blew.
The people began to run out of food.
What do you think happened to the settlers?

67

The people of the *Mayflower* had to face two things as soon as they landed in the New World. The first was a cold, snowy winter. The second was having little food. We will be learning some of the ways God cared for them.

> No matter how bad things seem, we can trust God to watch over us. (BAT: 8a Faith in God's promises; Bible Promises: H. God as Father, I. God as Master)

Text Discussion, page 172

➤ Read the top of the page.

The monument stands on the place where it is believed the *Mayflower* landed. Some people believe that the rock inside the monument is the very rock that the first Separatist leaving the ship stepped on. No one can say for sure that it is the exact rock.

➤ Read the bottom of the page.

Modern people have built a new Plymouth Plantation to look as much like the first one as possible. Workers there dress like Separatists and other Pilgrims and speak as they did. People visit the new Plymouth in Massachusetts to see how life back then might have been.

Teaching the Lesson

Direct a text activity on pages 67 and 68. Read page 67. Ask how the Separatists got food the first winter. *(They hunted and fished.)* Although the Separatists may have been hungry and cold and perhaps afraid, they knew that they had done the right thing in coming to the New World. They had faith that God had led them there. (BATs: 1c Separation, 6c Spirit-filled, 8d Courage)

Read a story. Tell your child to listen to this story to find out how God provided for the settlers.

One spring morning when the snow was still on the ground, the men were talking inside one of the new houses. Suddenly a child screamed. The men jumped up to go to the door, but in that doorway a tall Indian appeared. The men stepped back to grab their guns.

The Indian did not move. He said, "Welcome, Englishmen."

Every man stared at the Indian. Had he really spoken to them in their own language?

The Indian bowed to them. "Samoset is friend of Englishmen. Samoset says 'welcome.' "

One of the settlers came forward and held out his hand. The Indian and the Separatist shook hands. "Thank you," said the settler. "How do you know English?"

"I am from north of here," said the Indian. "Englishmen come to fish and trap animals there. I learn from them."

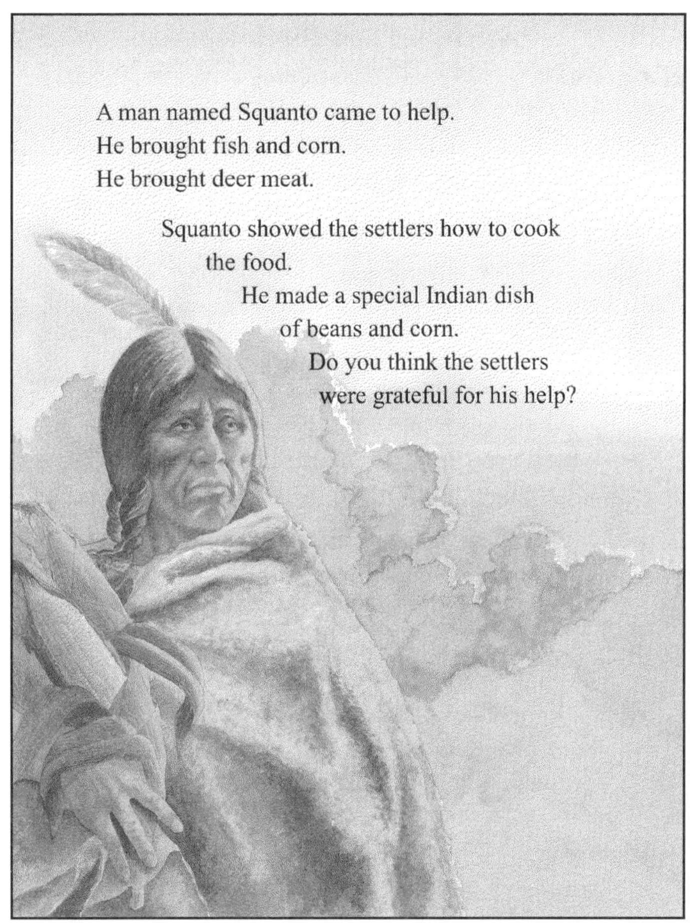
A man named Squanto came to help.
He brought fish and corn.
He brought deer meat.

Squanto showed the settlers how to cook the food.
He made a special Indian dish of beans and corn.
Do you think the settlers were grateful for his help?

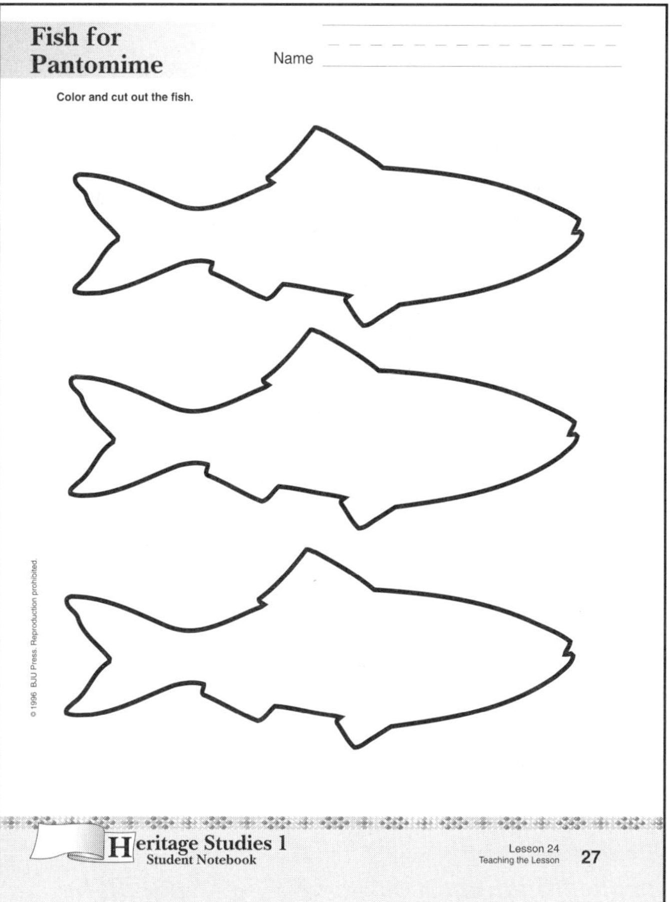
Fish for Pantomime

Name ______________

Color and cut out the fish.

© 1996 BJU Press. Reproduction prohibited.

Heritage Studies 1
Student Notebook

Lesson 24
Teaching the Lesson 27

Samoset stayed all day. That night he slept in the home of one of the families. The next morning he told the settlers that he would bring his friends and his chief to visit Plymouth Plantation.

"One of my friends," he said, "speaks much better. You will like him."

Several days later Samoset came back with his friends. One of them had been to England with the fishermen on one of their ships! This was the friend who spoke very good English!

Discussion Questions

- ➤ Why do you think the settlers were surprised to hear an Indian speak English?
- ➤ Do you think that the family that Samoset stayed with overnight was afraid of their guest?

Although Samoset seemed friendly, he was still a stranger. The leaders of Plymouth Plantation gave Samoset a knife, a ring, and a bracelet when he left. It was the custom of Indians to give gifts, and the Pilgrims wanted Samoset to understand that they were friendly. Samoset was a help to the settlers in return. The friend he brought back turned out to be the best help of all.

- ➤ Read page 68 to find out how God had prepared someone else to help the people get ready for the next winter.
- ➤ What was the name of the man who helped the people? *(Squanto)*
- ➤ What did Squanto do for the people? *(He brought them meat, corn, and fish. He taught them how to cook beans and corn the Indian way.)*

Squanto liked the settlers. He had been captured by other white men. Those men were trappers and explorers looking for better ways to sail to the New World and for ways to get the wealth of the New World for themselves. He escaped from them and at last found himself in England. There an Englishman had been kind to him and helped him get back to his home. God had given Squanto all those travels to make him ready to help the settlers. The settlers considered Squanto and his friends gifts from God.

Day 2

Direct an activity using Notebook page 27. Tell your child to color and cut out the fish for use later in the lesson.

In the spring the Indians taught the settlers how to plant corn.
They taught them how to get cod and clams.
Without Squanto and other Indians, the settlers might have died.

The next fall the Separatists stored much food for the coming winter.
They were grateful to God for their new home.
They were thankful for the people who had helped them.

69

Direct a text activity on page 69. Read the first section on the page. Squanto taught the Separatists not only how to catch fish for eating but also how to use fish for planting. The settlers were glad to learn from their Indian friends.

> You may want to direct your child to do the following pantomime in the room. Or you may prefer to take him outside to actually plant the corn seeds in the ground.

Pantomime and Discussion

- Pretend you are a settler planting corn with fish the way Squanto taught you to do it.
- First dig a hole in the ground.
- Next, put the three grains of corn into the hole. Why do you think they used three seeds? *(Accept any answer, but help to draw the conclusion that three seeds made it more likely that at least one plant would come up there.)*
- Put a fish in the hole with the seeds. Why do you think they put the fish in too? The fish was a kind of fertilizer, a material that helps plants grow well.
- Cover the seeds and fish with soil.
- What do you think the Indians did with any fish that was left?

They may have done more planting; they may have fed it to their animals; they may have eaten it if it was fresh; they may have dried it for later use.

- Decide how you will use your extra seeds and fish.

Text Discussion, page 69

- Read the last section on page 69 to find out whether the seeds that the Indians helped the Separatists plant really did grow. *(yes)*
- Did the Separatists grow more than enough to eat during the summer? *(Yes, they ate some and they stored some.)*

The Bible tells us that it is good to save up for winter. Read Proverbs 6:6-8. The Separatists built a special place for keeping the extra food for winter. It was called a **storehouse.** They stored corn, dried fish, meat, dried berries, and other wild fruits. The Separatists probably had barrels from the ship to store things in.

- How do people today store food for the winter? *(They can it, freeze it, and sometimes dry it.)*

The settlers had now been in their new home for one year. They were not afraid for winter to come. They were probably grateful to have food stored; they surely felt more able to survive than they had before.

- What do you think the Separatists did to show they were thankful for the good crops? They praised the Lord; they thanked their new friends. (BAT: 7c Praise)

Foods the Indians Gave Us
Indians taught the white men what foods to plant.
They gave them seeds for all these foods.
177

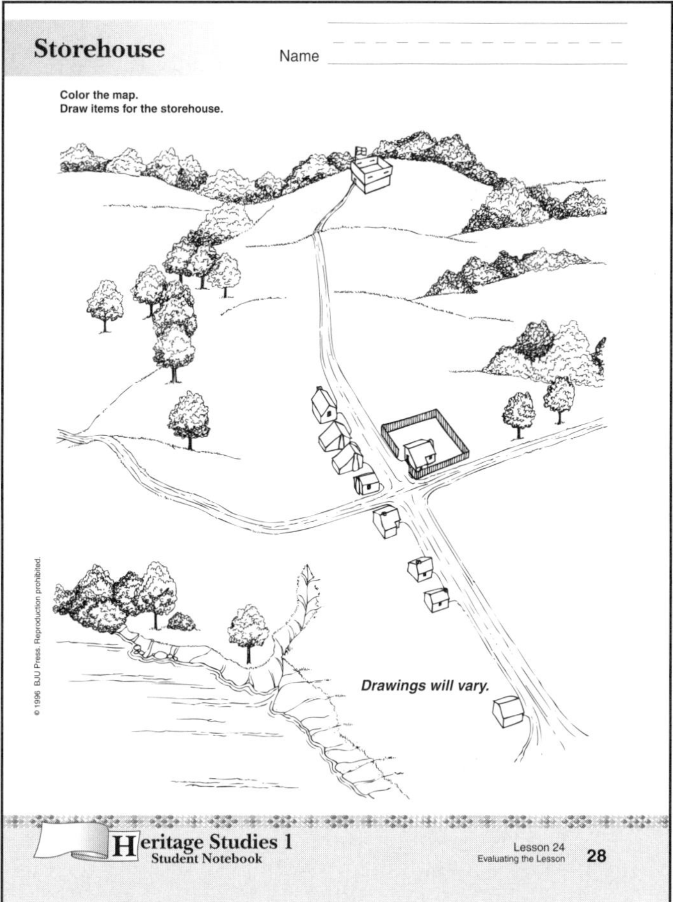

Storehouse
Name
Color the map.
Draw items for the storehouse.
Drawings will vary.
© 1996 BJU Press. Reproduction prohibited.
Heritage Studies 1
Student Notebook
Lesson 24
Evaluating the Lesson
28

Direct a text activity on page 177. Read and discuss the foods pictured on page 177. Ask your child which of these foods from the Indians are his favorites.

Evaluating the Lesson

Direct an activity on Notebook page 28. Direct your child to point to the storehouse on the map. It is the building located the farthest to the south. Suggest that he draw items around the storehouse that would be kept there. Then tell him to color the map.

Going Beyond

Enrichment

Collect small cardboard boxes, such as pudding or cereal boxes or milk cartons. Design a map on a large sheet of paper. Guide your child in creating a replica of the layout of Plymouth Plantation as shown on Notebook page 28 or text page 83.

Additional Teacher Information

Squanto was pleased when one of the settlers, Edward Winslow, asked to be taught Squanto's language. Winslow thought it prudent to be able to communicate with his neighbors himself, in case something were to happen to the trusted interpreter.

In return Squanto asked to be taught to read from the "speaking papers," as he called books. Winslow taught Squanto to read using the Bible.

Lesson 25
Giving Thanks

Text, pages 70-72, 176

Preview

Main Ideas

- The settlers gave a feast after the first harvest.
- People in the United States observe Thanksgiving in different ways.

Objectives

- Describe the first Thanksgiving feast
- List things to be thankful for

Materials

- Ingredients for Indian pudding*

  6 cups milk
  1 cup yellow cornmeal
  $\frac{1}{2}$ cup molasses
  $\frac{1}{4}$ cup sugar
  $\frac{1}{4}$ teaspoon ground ginger
  $\frac{1}{4}$ teaspoon ground cinnamon
  $\frac{1}{4}$ teaspoon ground nutmeg
  $\frac{1}{4}$ cup butter, melted
  $\frac{1}{4}$ teaspoon baking soda
  2 eggs, beaten

- A 2-quart casserole dish, greased*
- A table knife
- Some food to eat on a knife
- The figure of the *Mayflower* (1620) from the History TimeLine Packet
- Maps and More 17, page M10
- Chart paper or a large sheet of paper

To prepare the Indian pudding, simmer the milk and then remove it from the heat. Mix together the cornmeal, molasses, sugar, ginger, cinnamon, nutmeg, butter, soda, eggs, and half the hot milk. Whisk well and blend in the rest of the milk. Pour into the greased dish and bake at 250° F for five or more hours, stirring occasionally, until firm.

The Separatists gave a great feast to show their thankfulness.
They invited all the Indians who had helped them.
Today we call this feast *Thanksgiving.*

Giving thanks always for all things unto God and the Father in the name of our Lord Jesus Christ.
Ephesians 5:20

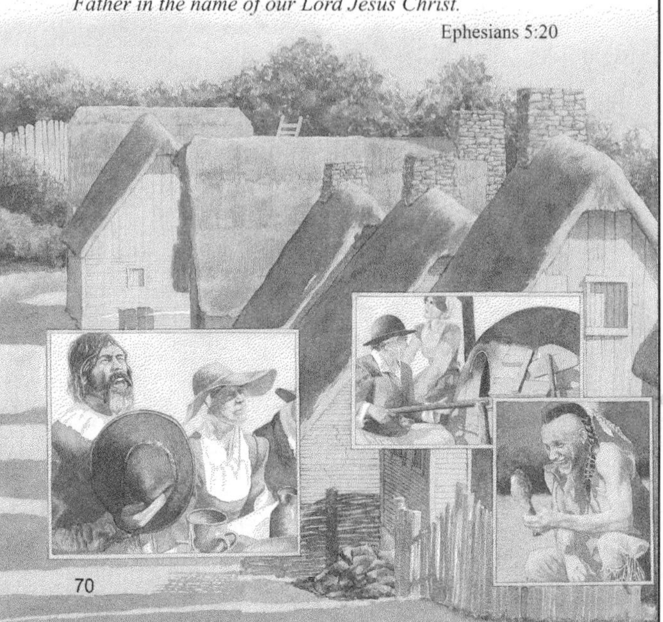

70

Day 1

Lesson

Introducing the Lesson

Direct a discussion. Discuss the names of the various holidays and why we celebrate them. Emphasize that the main reason for holidays is to help us remember important events that happened in the past.

Discussion Questions

➤ Name some holidays that help Christians remember what Christ has done for them. *(Christmas celebrates His birth and Easter His rising again from the grave.)* (BATs: 1a Understanding Jesus Christ, 7b Exaltation of Christ)

➤ Why do you think we celebrate Thanksgiving?

It is important to remember what has happened in the past. People who lived long ago did much to make America what it is today. It is important to remember how others suffered and sacrificed to help begin America and to keep it strong. If Americans forget what the Separatists did and how life was for them, they will not be as grateful as they should be for their country. Thanksgiving is a way of remembering each year that the Pilgrims thanked God for helping them. (BAT: 7c Praise)

◆ THINGS PEOPLE DO ◆

Celebrating Thanksgiving

Many people in the United States eat turkey on Thanksgiving.
Why do you think they do that?
Turkey was part of the first Thanksgiving meal.

The Indians brought deer meat and fish to the feast.
There was probably pumpkin pudding.
Do you have any food made of pumpkin on Thanksgiving?

71

Teaching the Lesson

Direct a text activity on pages 70-71 and 176. Discuss how your family celebrates Thanksgiving.

Text Discussion, page 70

- ➤ Read the text and look at the pictures on page 70.
- ➤ Look at the picture on Maps and More 17.
- ➤ What is similar and what is different about that first Thanksgiving and your Thanksgiving?

The Separatists wanted to celebrate getting in the first harvest. They may have wanted to eat a big feast to make up for all the times that they had had to go hungry or to eat the same thing over and over.

- ➤ Would it have been hard to have good table manners eating in that big group?

In the days of the Pilgrims, table manners were not the same as today. There were no forks—only knives and spoons. Sometimes a clam shell served as a spoon. Many foods were eaten right from the knife. The knives they ate with did not have sharp edges.

- ➤ Name some foods that would be difficult to eat with a knife. *(Answers may include soup and peas.)*
- ➤ Try eating some foods with a knife.

In the days of the Pilgrims, it was not considered bad manners to stick out the elbows when raising food to the mouth. It was also acceptable to eat with one's fingers at that time as well.

- ➤ Name some foods you think the settlers ate at the feast.

The settlers had many kinds of food at their feast. They had clams and eels and other kinds of seafood and fish. They had cranberries (the Indians sometimes called these "bear berries" because bears liked them), maple sugar, corn, turkey, and perhaps quail. The Indians brought five deer. There was much food, but there had to be a lot to eat because ninety-one Indians came to join the Separatists for the celebration.

- ➤ Do you know how long the celebration lasted?

The celebration went on for several days. The settlers and the Indians not only ate but also had shooting contests. The settlers shot their guns and the Indians used bows and arrows. The children played together, running races and competing in jumping contests. The Indians liked the games.

- ➤ Name some things you think the Separatists thanked the Lord for that day. *(Answers may include having enough food, having good friends among the Indians, having houses to live in, having a new home in the New World, and having the freedom to read the Bible and obey God.)* (BAT: 7c Praise)

Text Discussion, pages 71 and 176

- ➤ Read page 71 and answer the questions. Talk about the pictures.

The women of Plymouth Plantation cooked for three days to get the feast ready. They put the food on long tables that stood outside because no house in Plymouth could have held all the people. Children helped carry wood for fires, stirred the pots of corn, and watched over the cornbread as it baked. Everyone in Plymouth had a job to do, and Thanksgiving Day was no different in that respect. (BATs: 2c Faithfulness, 2e Work)

Although many of the foods are the same, they were often prepared differently. Most meats were roasted over an open fire, turning on a stick or spinning on a string. Potatoes were often boiled or baked on glowing coals. Puddings were cooked slowly in covered dishes under hot coals. They were much thicker than the puddings of today.

Squanto had taught the people to cook clams by building a "nest" of hot stones on the beach. He built a fire on the stones to make them sizzle. Then he laid seaweed in the hot embers, then a layer of clams still in their shells, and then more seaweed. Finally he covered all with green branches. This way the clams were steamed until they were fully cooked.

◆ LEARNING HOW ◆

To Make Indian Pudding

1. Take out the ingredients your teacher tells you to get. You will also need a baking dish, a saucepan, a wire whisk, and a place to bake the pudding.
2. Help your teacher mix the ingredients. How do you think the pudding will taste?
3. Bake the pudding. Taste the pudding. Do you think that you would have liked the food at the first Thanksgiving?

72

➤ Look at the pictures on page 176. Tell what you have learned about life for the settlers in the Plymouth Plantation.

Day 2

Direct a *Learning How* activity on text page 72. Read the instructions. Follow the recipe given in the Preview for making the pudding. When the pudding has finished baking, have a tasting session. Talk about how it tastes, relating it to the food served at the first Thanksgiving.

Add a figure to the History TimeLine. Help your child decide where the figure of the *Mayflower* should go on the TimeLine. *(1620)* Place the figure on the TimeLine at the year 1620. Review the events already represented on the TimeLine.

Evaluating the Lesson

Guide a storytelling time. Tell your child to imagine that he ate with the settlers and the Indians at the first Thanksgiving feast. Help him to make up a story, telling what the tables might have looked like filled with food, how the foods tasted, what the people said to each other, and what they thanked God for.

Direct your child to name things that he is thankful for. Write the list on the chart paper. Encourage your child to decorate the chart. Then pray together, thanking God for some of the things listed.

Going Beyond

Enrichment

Plan a time to celebrate an authentic Thanksgiving feast. If weather permits, set up a large table outside. (Planks over sawhorses would be most authentic.) If not, choose a spacious inside place. Ask friends or relatives to join you and to bring corn, succotash, cornbread, roast turkey, venison (if available), whole cranberries, Indian pudding (or a pumpkin pudding), cheeses, apples, and apple cider. Ask some people to be settlers and some to be Indians. They may want to dress in costumes. The settlers should have stools or benches to sit on. The Indians should sit on the ground or logs. Before the feast, the Separatist governor should say a blessing. The Indian guests, out of respect, should bow their heads as the original guests did. Then, if they like, they could eat with spoons and knives.

Additional Teacher Information

When the Separatists invited Samoset and his chief, Massasoit, and a few warriors to the feast, they did not expect the great crowd that arrived. The warriors left and came back with five deer to help accommodate the number of guests. The Wampanoag people had had little food themselves the previous year and were glad to partake in what must have seemed to them a marvelous fare.

Many scholars think the feast was held October 15, 1621, although the exact date is not known. The settlers did not have annual feasts as we now do. Rather, the governor would declare a holiday of thanksgiving as the times warranted.

Thanksgiving was not a national holiday until 1863. Some of the foods served at the first "official" Thanksgiving in 1863 were roast turkey with cranberry sauce, fish pastries, clam chowder, mashed sweet potatoes, creamed onions, and pumpkin and apple pies.

6 LESSONS 26-30

Maps of Old Places

This chapter introduces the features that most settlements have in common: proximity to water, defensibility, and so on. A brief look at archaeology helps combine history your child has seen already (i.e., Plymouth Plantation and Jamestown) with a further study of geography. Your child will be involved in a "dig" and will choose a place to start a "settlement."

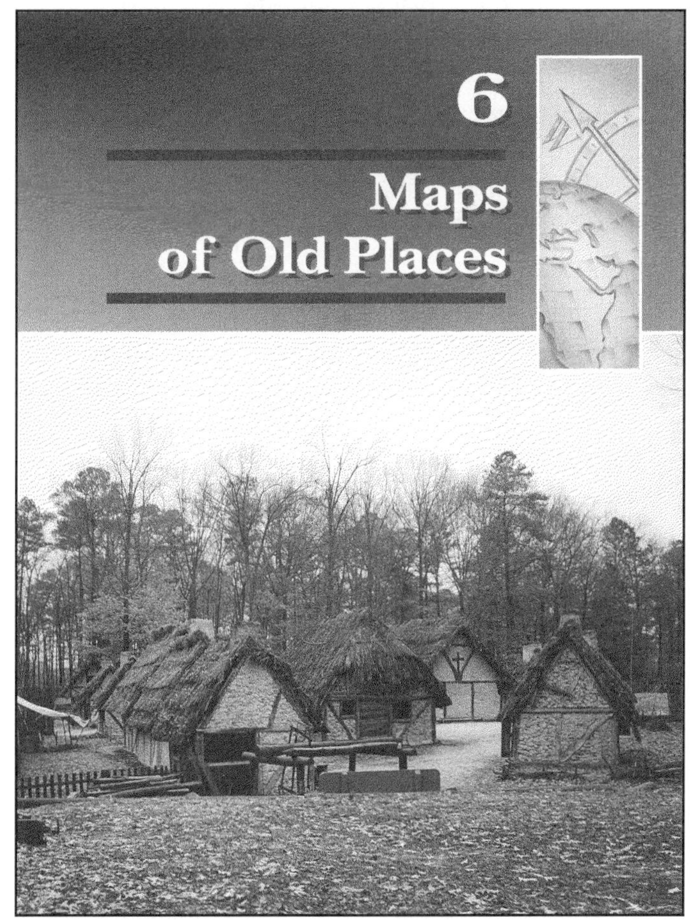

Materials

The following materials must be obtained or prepared before the presentation of the lesson. These items are labeled with an asterisk (*) in the lesson and in the Materials List in the Supplement. For further information see the individual lessons.

- Appendix, page A22 (Lesson 26)
- Brown construction paper (Lesson 27)
- Green construction paper (Lesson 27)
- A brown paper bag or a sheet of tan construction paper (Lesson 27)
- A box or deep tray of soil or sand (Lesson 28)
- A small toy, shell, or other "artifact" (Lesson 28)
- An antique item (Lesson 28)
- Appendix, page A23 (Lesson 30)

Lesson 26
Making Towns and Cities

Text, pages 74-75
Notebook, page 29

Preview

Main Ideas

- Most cities started as small settlements.
- The way a town looks tells what the people there think is important and how they live.

Objectives

- Tell something about your family's own town or city
- Identify clues about the people who live in a certain place

Materials

- Appendix, page A22: Building Graph*
- A highlighter pen
- A telephone book
- Maps and More 18, page M10

Notes

As an alternative for the introduction to this lesson, ask someone who is familiar with the history of your area to talk to your child. In a small town, the speaker might be able to include family names that your child would know. If you are a local history enthusiast, you might take the job yourself. Your community library can probably provide information on the local area.

Day 1

Lesson

Introducing the Lesson

Investigate the history of your local area. Use the resources available at your local library to find out some information about the history of your town or city. Try to find the following information:

- How was your town or city named?
- What was the primary industry at the beginning of your town?
- What important historical events have occurred in your town?

Explain to your child that it is important to know the history of one's hometown.

Cities usually start out as small towns.
Some start out as just a few houses.
A few have begun with one family
settling somewhere.

Do you know how your town or city started?
How could you find out?
One way is to ask someone who has lived in
your town a long time whether he knows how
the town grew.

74

Teaching the Lesson

Direct a text activity on pages 74 and 75. Read page 74. Help your child to answer the questions on the page from your research about your city or town.

Text Discussion, page 74

➤ Often there is someone in a family who keeps records of a family's history, such as births, deaths, marriages, and special honors.

If applicable, tell your child about someone in your family who does this.

Family histories are important to the history of the place where they live. Especially in a small town the history of a family may be an essential part of the town's history.

Text Discussion, page 75

➤ Read page 75. What is happening in the picture? Try to make up a story about the picture.

➤ How is this picture like or unlike the places where we live?

➤ Are there new buildings being built in our area?

➤ What are the new buildings for? One way to know what people in a town think is important is to look at the buildings they build.

Not all towns look alike.
Most towns add buildings as they are needed.
Is there a new building being put up
in your town?

The way a town looks tells us what the people
who live there think is important.
The town can also tell us something about how
the people live.

75

Day 2

Direct a fact-finding and graph activity. Show your child the Building Graph.

Graphing Activity

➤ I want you to help me fill in the chart to find out some things about where we live. How many churches do you think are in our area?
➤ Let's use the yellow pages in our phone book to count the churches. Put an *X* on the chart to show the number of churches in our area.

If your town has more than ten of any of the buildings, add a plus sign at the end of the last segment. In a large city you may want to adjust the quantity to the number of columns or even the number of pages listed for each building. If you live in a small town or village, you may not need the telephone directory.

➤ Let's do the same with the other buildings on the chart. Looking at the chart, how important do you think churches are to our area?
➤ According to our graph, which building is found the most frequently in our area?
➤ What buildings would you build first if you were going to start a town somewhere? *(Answers will vary; lead your child to the conclusion that people would first need shelter for their families. Then perhaps a building that could be used as a church, school, and meeting place should be built.)*

Picture Discussion

➤ Look at Maps and More 18. Point to the castle. What kind of people might live in a place like this?
➤ Why might the castle have been built high like that? *(for safety, for importance, for beauty)*
➤ Point to the apartment building. Who might live there?
➤ What might some of the people in the apartment building do for a living?
➤ Look at the last building pictured. Who do you think might live here?
➤ Why do people choose the houses they do? *(People live in houses that they can afford, that fit their families and the way they live, that they like, that they inherit, or that they build.)* Some people build or buy big houses to make an impression on others.

Emphasize that Jesus never owned a house; He was more concerned with helping others and "being about his Father's business." Though it is necessary for us to have houses and to take good care of what has been given us, we should remember that pleasing God is always more important than caring for houses or other things. (BAT: 7d Contentment)

➤ How many kinds of homes can you think of?

We can tell about people by the way they care for their homes. For example, people who are busy or who do not like flowers may not have any flower boxes or flower gardens. But to someone who thinks flowers are important, they are not too much trouble. People who keep their houses and yards orderly send a different message from those who do not.

Day 3

➤ What are some ways that you can show you care about our home? *(Answers may include putting away toys, bikes, etc.)* You can help make our home have a good impression on others.
➤ You can tell people about yourself without saying anything. What are some ways that you tell people about yourself? *(Answers may include manner of dress, politeness, smiles, and posture.)*

Christians are the Lord's children, and everything they do and say should reflect that. (BAT: 6c Spirit-filled)

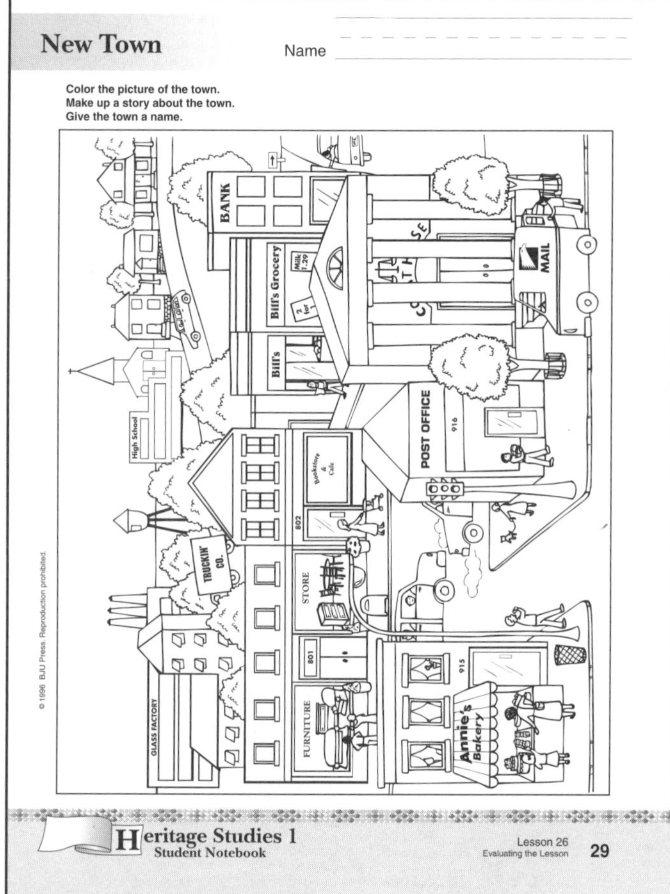

New Town

Name

Color the picture of the town.
Make up a story about the town.
Give the town a name.

Evaluating the Lesson

Direct an activity on Notebook page 29. Instruct your child to follow the directions on the page. Ask questions and encourage speculations about the activities and buildings of the town. Write down your child's information as a story that he can read later.

Going Beyond

Enrichment

Provide magazines that your child may cut up, construction paper, scissors, and tape or glue. Tell him to cut out pictures of different types of houses or dwellings and to affix them to the construction paper. Encourage your child to use clues from the pictures to make up stories about people who might live in the places.

Additional Teacher Information

Most places have historical records in courthouses or town halls. Other sources of local information include libraries (newspapers and books on local history), people, family records (albums, diaries, letters, and so on), and cemetery markers. A little investigation into your area's history can be both rewarding and intriguing.

LESSON 27
Indian Towns

Text, pages 76-79
Notebook, page 30

Preview

Main Ideas

- Different Indian nations lived in different ways.
- The Indians' ways of life reflected their locations.
- Maps can show much information about a place.

Objectives

- Color a map and a key to match
- Get information from a map

Materials

- A $1\frac{1}{2}$" × 12" strip of brown construction paper*
- Four $1\frac{1}{4}$" × 8" strips of green construction paper*
- A brown paper bag or a sheet of tan construction paper*
- Maps and More 19, page M11
- Supplement, page S10: Making a Wigwam

Day 1

Lesson

Introducing the Lesson

Direct an art activity. Ask your child what he remembers about Indian houses. *(Answers will vary.)* Remind him that the different Indian nations lived in different places and that their homes were built for those different types of places.

Art Activity

➤ *Show Making a Wigwam.* This is a **wigwam.** Indians who lived in wigwams built them with small trees and bark. Step 1 shows a circle of saplings or young trees. The saplings are then lashed together. The last step shows the wigwam partly covered with bark.

➤ Here are strips of brown and green construction paper, tan paper, and scissors to make a wigwam.

➤ Glue the green strips together like the spokes of a wheel. *See number 1 in figures on next page.*

➤ Glue the brown strip in a circle.

➤ Glue the ends of the green strips inside the brown circle.

➤ Cut "pieces of bark" (about 1" square) from the tan paper and glue them to the frame. Remember to leave a small space to serve as a door.

Indian Towns

Indians had many kinds of villages and towns.
The Hopi people lived in houses made of clay blocks.
The houses belonged to the women of the village.

Some people made their houses in cliffs.
How do you think they got to their houses?

76

Other Indians made houses from buffalo hides and poles.
The Sioux made such houses.
The houses were called *tipis*.

The Sioux drew pictures of animals on the sides of their tipis.
Often they drew signs of bravery on a house.
Who do you think lived in such a tipi?

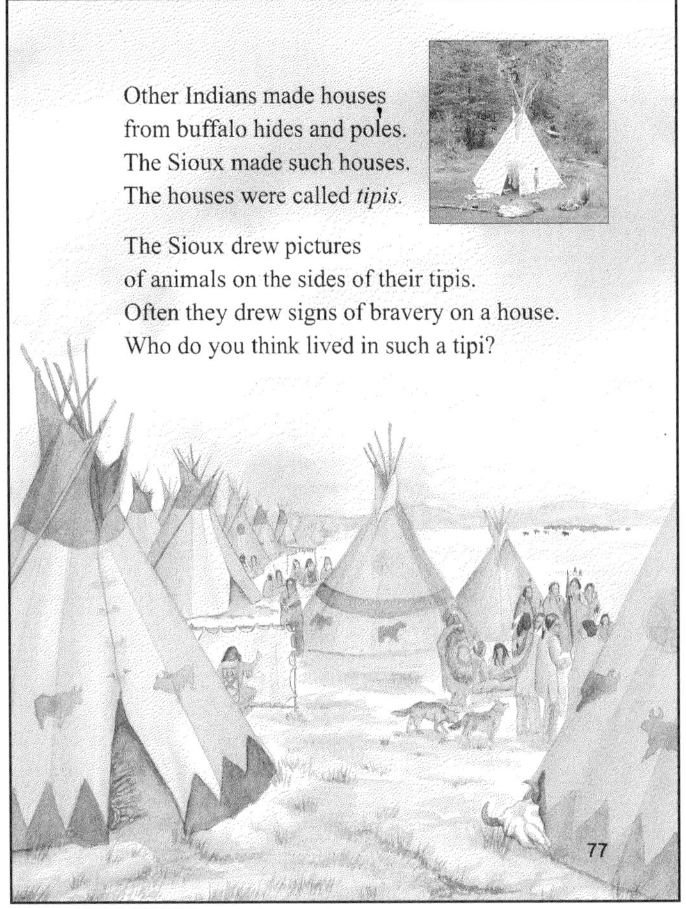

77

The people who lived in wigwams lived in the New World before the *Mayflower* sailed there. Squanto's family lived in a house like this.

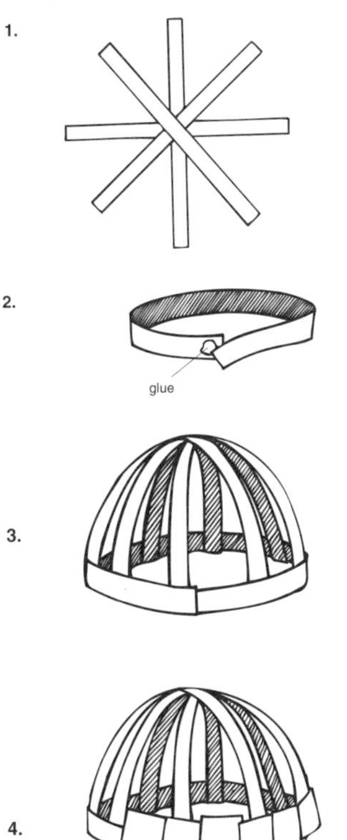

Teaching the Lesson

Direct a text activity on pages 76-79. Invite your child to compare his model of a wigwam with the tipi he made in Chapter 3. Tell him to imagine living in each of the houses and to describe what he thinks the differences would be.

Text Discussion, page 76

- Let's look at page 76. What do you think the Indian homes pictured here are made of? *(clay blocks)* Do you remember talking about these Indians before?
- Read page 76. The Indian people may have gotten to the houses by ladders of rope or wood. *Discuss any experiences you may have had in New Mexico or the area of the Hopi Indians.*

Text Discussion, page 77

- Look at page 77. What were these houses made of? Read the first sentence.
- Do you remember which group of Indians lived in this kind of house? *(Sioux)* Read the next sentence.
- What kind of house is pictured? *(tipi)*
- Read the rest of the page. What kind of markings did you put on the tipi you made earlier?

Squanto lived in a village near Plymouth Plantation. This is a map of his village. The houses are called *wigwams*. How many wigwams do you see?

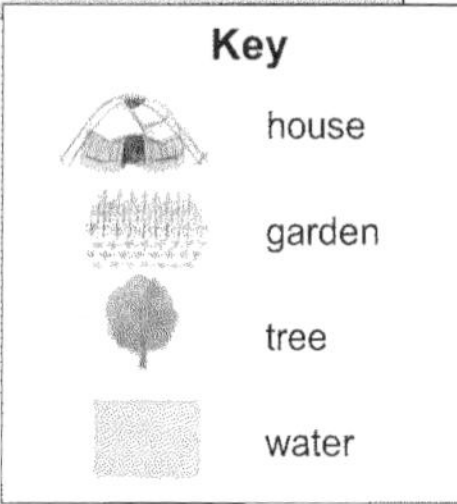

What is growing near each wigwam? Why do you think the Indians built their village here?

78

◆ FAMOUS PEOPLE ◆

Squanto

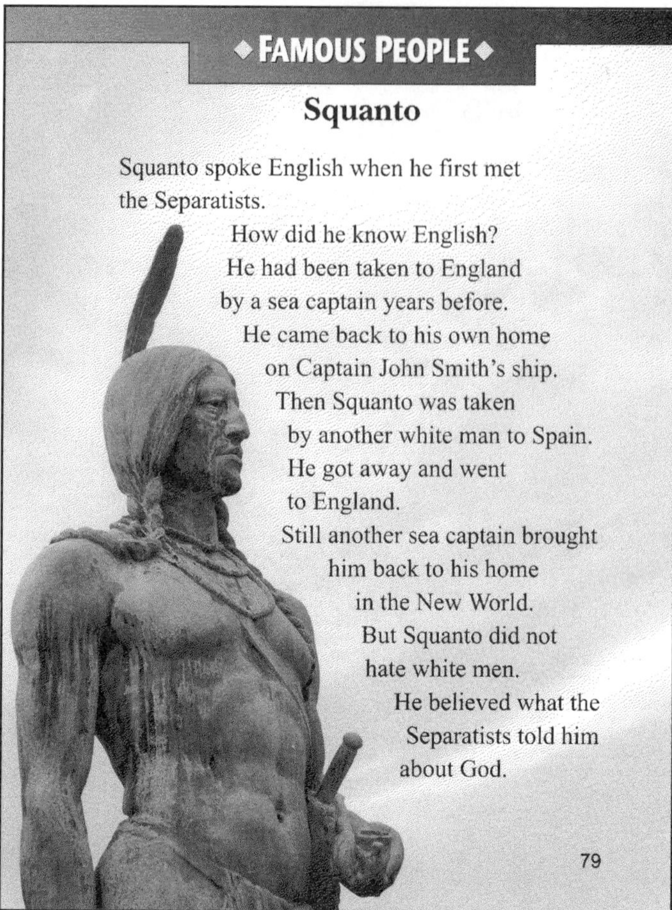

Squanto spoke English when he first met the Separatists. How did he know English? He had been taken to England by a sea captain years before. He came back to his own home on Captain John Smith's ship. Then Squanto was taken by another white man to Spain. He got away and went to England. Still another sea captain brought him back to his home in the New World. But Squanto did not hate white men. He believed what the Separatists told him about God.

79

Day 2

Direct a map activity on page 78. Point to page 78 and show Maps and More 19.

Map Activity Discussion, page 78

- ➤ Read the first section of page 78. What kind of house is pictured? *(wigwam)*
- ➤ Read and discuss the questions at the bottom of the page. *(garden, crop; near water, near trees for building materials and firewood, etc.)*
- ➤ Look at the left side of Maps and More 19. The small box is called a **key.** Why do you think it is called a key? *(Accept all answers; then show how it "unlocks" the meaning of the map.)*
- ➤ What do you think the blue on the key represents? *(water)* Show me where the water is on the left side.
- ➤ Show me the picture on the key that stands for gardens. Count the gardens on the left side. What do you notice about the gardens in Squanto's village? *(Answers will vary; he may note that every house has a garden; he may see that gardens can be in front of a house or around it; he may notice that gardens are different sizes.)*
- ➤ *Point to the tree symbol.* What do you think this stands for? *(forest or trees)*
- ➤ Point to the longhouses on the right side of Maps and More 19. What are some differences between longhouses and wigwams?
- ➤ What is alike and what is different about the keys on the left and right sides of the chart?

Text Discussion, page 79

- ➤ This is a statue of Squanto. Why do you think the people of Massachusetts would erect a statue of Squanto? They respected him; they wanted him to be remembered for helping the early settlers.
- ➤ Read the page except the last two sentences. Do you think you would have been angry if you had been treated as badly as Squanto was?

> Remind your child that God sees everything that happens. If we believe in Him, we should not be angry when things happen that we do not understand. (BAT: 8b Faith in the power of the Word of God)

- ➤ Read the last two sentences.

Squanto did not dislike the white people of Plymouth even though some other white people had mistreated him. It is wrong to think badly of many people because of the actions of a few people. We call this attitude **prejudice,** which means deciding without a good reason that you do not like something or someone. Some people judge all Christians by what one Christian does. Even though it is not right, this fact makes it very important for a Christian to live so that he is a good testimony for the Lord.

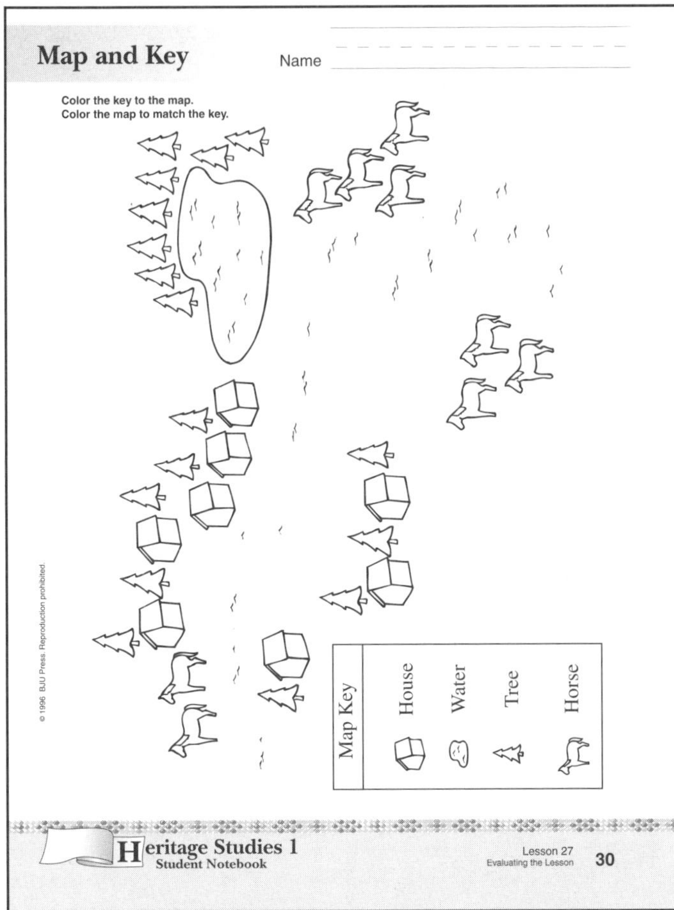

Map and Key
Name
Color the key to the map.
Color the map to match the key.
Map Key
House
Water
Tree
Horse
© 1996 BJU Press. Reproduction prohibited.
Heritage Studies 1
Student Notebook
Lesson 27
Evaluating the Lesson
30

➤ Do you think the Plymouth settlers were good testimonies to Squanto? *(Yes, he believed what they said about God.)* (BATs: 5c Evangelism and missions, 7a Grace)

Evaluating the Lesson

Direct an activity on Notebook page 30. Direct your child to look at Notebook page 30. Point to the map key.

Map Activity

➤ What do the four symbols represent? *(house, water, tree, horse)*

➤ Color the key. Color the map so that it matches the key. You may also add other items to the map and the key.

➤ Where would a person go to see the most horses?

➤ Where are the most houses?

➤ Let's choose one of the houses to be our house. Which one would you choose?

➤ Why did you choose that house?

Going Beyond

Enrichment

Make available some Styrofoam cups, large brown paper, construction paper, crayons, scissors, glue, and transparent tape. Tell your child to decorate the Styrofoam cups as wigwams and then to use the materials and his wigwams to make a three-dimensional model of the map of Squanto's village.

Additional Teacher Information

Another word for *key* is *legend. Legend* comes from words meaning "things for reading." Reading a map is more a matter of interpreting symbols than reading, as your child may think of reading. You may want to explain that "reading" a map is a different way the word *reading* is used.

When Squanto finally returned to his village after his many travels and trials, he found nothing. All of his people had died from an epidemic. All that was left of his village was part of a broken bowl. Squanto was the last survivor of the Patuxet people. He went to live with Massasoit's people. It was in Massasoit's village that he met Samoset and came to know of the Separatists.

Lesson 28
Finding Old Towns

Text, pages 80-82, 184
Notebook, page 31

Preview

Main Ideas

- Extant (existing) records and excavation help us learn about towns that no longer exist.
- Much of what we know about Jamestown comes from excavation finds.

Objectives

- "Excavate" a small area of prepared dirt
- Draw conclusions about the child's "finds"

Materials

- A box or deep tray of soil or sand*
- A pair of tweezers (optional)
- A small, old make-up brush or paintbrush (optional)
- A plastic spoon
- A small toy, shell, or other "artifact"*
- An antique item, such as a kitchen gadget or a piece of jewelry*
- Maps and More 20, page M12

Prepare the "excavation site" by burying an "artifact" in the box of soil. Be sure that the item is covered well but is not overly difficult to find.

Day 1

Lesson

Introducing the Lesson

Direct an inferring activity. Show the antique item.

Inferring Activity

➤ What do you think this was used for?

➤ Do you think that it could be bought at a modern department store? *Name a local store that your child is familiar with.*

➤ Have you ever seen an item like this before? *Tell your child about the item—where you got it, what it is, how old it is, and so on. If it is a functional item, you may want to show how it is used.*

Many things that were used long ago still exist. Many pitchers and cups from Bible times are now in museums. Sometimes whole towns and cities still exist from long ago.

➤ Look at Maps and More 20. Look at the picture of the ancient pottery at the bottom of the page.

➤ Look at the picture at the top of the page. Do you see how the town has many different levels? Why do you think that some older towns are now underground?

Sometimes towns were buried under volcanic ash. Other times, people left towns and the towns were covered after a long while by sand or earth.

Read this verse: "Remove not the ancient landmark, which thy fathers have set" (Proverbs 22:28). Explain that a **landmark** is a fixed marker, something set up to show the edges of property or ownership. Tell your child that the Bible says that it is important to remember what one's ancestors have done. (BAT: 2a Authority)

Teaching the Lesson

Direct a text activity on pages 80-82. Read the first sentence on page 81.

The pages are being discussed out of order to help in the teaching of the lesson.

Text Discussion, page 81

➤ How did the artist know how to draw a town that existed more than three hundred years ago? Much of what we know about Jamestown came from letters the people there wrote and from things we have found there that they used.

➤ Read the next question. Are all the buildings that you see houses? *(no)*

➤ Look at the wall around the town. Read the next question. Walls kept out enemies and wild animals. Do walls protect cities today? *(No, airplanes and new weapons make walls useless.)*

➤ Read the rest of the page and answer the questions. *(The building has a cross on it. It was probably a church.)*

➤ Do you think Jamestown was a big place? Why or why not?

Not long ago, people began to dig up the earth where Jamestown had been. They found where the buildings had stood. They found many objects, such as medals and pieces of armor.

➤ Have you ever found anything buried in the dirt or sand?

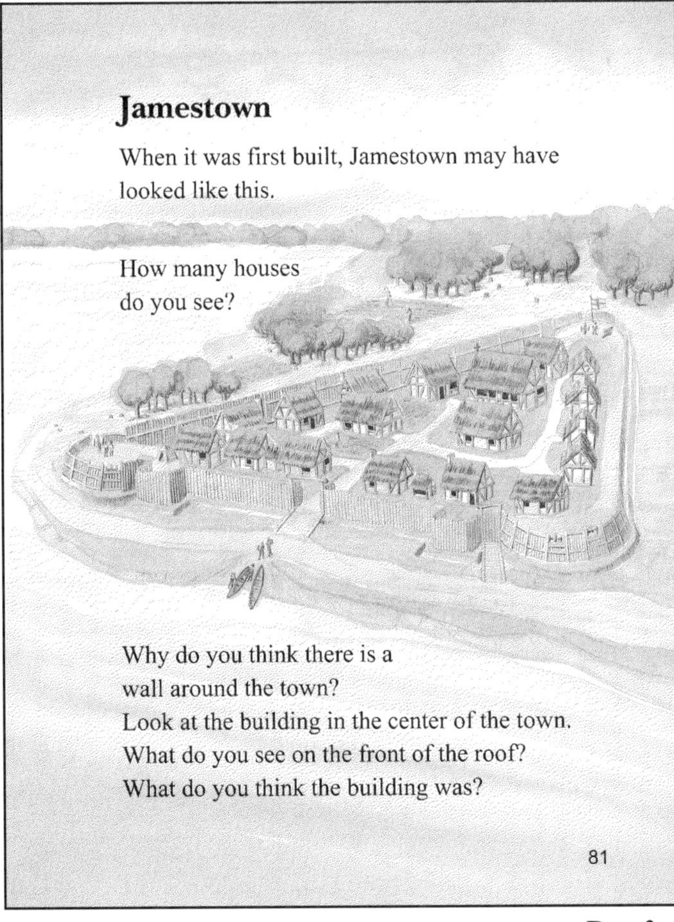

Jamestown

When it was first built, Jamestown may have looked like this.

How many houses do you see?

Why do you think there is a wall around the town?
Look at the building in the center of the town.
What do you see on the front of the roof?
What do you think the building was?

81

◆ THINGS PEOPLE DO ◆

Finding Old Towns

Letters and books of long ago tell of towns that do not stand anymore.
People try to find the old towns with maps from the books.
They have to dig into the ground to find where houses once were.
Sometimes they build a model of the town they find.

80

Day 2

Text Discussion, pages 80 and 184

➤ Read page 80. How do you think Jamestown might have been found?

A man riding his horse in the area came upon the ruins of the town. He had been looking for old places that he had read about in books. He was shocked that people had let such an important town in our history get lost. He began the work to save the town that was left and to unearth the rest of it.

➤ Turn to page 184. Where on this map do you think would be a good place for a settlement? *(Answers will vary, but sites should be near water.)*

Towns often begin in valleys. Such places are protected and often have a good water supply. Also, it is easier to build where the land is not too steep.

➤ We will be learning what things all settlers in a new land look for. What do you think some of those things might be? *(Answers may include water to drink, a place to land a ship, wood to build with, and places to plant crops.)*

People looking for old towns often look in places that have many of the things settlements need, such as water and a good location.

➤ Would you like to help find an old town? **Archaeologists** are people who find old towns and villages.

Text Discussion, page 82

➤ Look at page 82. This is a map of the old town of Jamestown. Read the first two sentences. Why do you think the town was near water?

People need water to live, for drinking, washing, and cooking. If the water is far away from the town, going after it may be dangerous or tiresome. Most villages, towns, and cities grew up near sources of water.

➤ Read the next question. What makes you think that the building you chose is the church? Let's look at the chart at the bottom. Remember we call this part of a map a **key.**

➤ *Point out each symbol and its meaning.* Keys help us read maps.

➤ Read the rest of the page. *Ask other questions using the key and the map.*

This is a map of Jamestown.
Is Jamestown near the water?
Can you find the church on the map?
What do you see in each corner of the town?
Look at the key to find out.

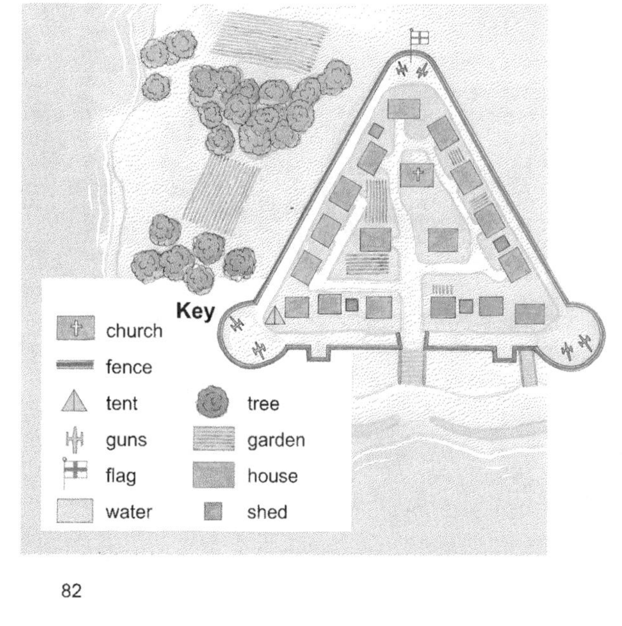

Day 3

➤ What should you do if you find something that looks really old? If it looks like it might break, you should get an adult to help you.

True archaeologists are very careful with what they find. They dig carefully with small shovels and spoons. When they find something, they often dust it off with soft brushes before they take it out of the ground. If the item is small, they use tweezers to pick it up.

➤ Why do you think that the archaeologists are very careful?

It is easy to break things that have been buried for a long time. Archaeologists draw pictures or take photographs of the items they find while they are still in the ground.

➤ Look at Maps and More 20. Point to the drawing of the artifact. Would you like to help draw pictures of a "dig"?

Evaluating the Lesson

Direct an "excavation" using Notebook page 31. Give your child the prepared box, the set of the tools you have chosen to use, and two pencils. Tell him that an object is buried in the box and that he is going to be an archaeologist for a day. Emphasize that he is to search carefully for the item. First, he should use the spoons to scrape the dirt or sand off the object and then any other tools you have given him to dust off the object that begins to appear. Remind him that he should not take the object out of the ground until he has drawn a picture of it on his Notebook page.

As your child is drawing, ask some questions about his find. Ask who might have last seen the object, what it is, or how much it might be worth. Judge his conclusions by how reasonable they are. Ask him whether the object is man-made, what it is made of, or whether he has ever seen something like it. After his drawing is done, encourage him to show his "artifact" and drawing to the family.

Going Beyond

Enrichment

Make a "museum" for the artifact from the evaluation. Allow your child to use a small place card and felt-tip pen to make an identification tag. The tag should tell what the object is, who found it, and the date the object was found. Encourage your child to identify other objects that he may find buried in your yard.

Additional Teacher Information

Many valuable sites have been irreparably disrupted by *pothunters,* irresponsible people who plunder digs and sites for artifacts, only to sell the items for whatever they can get, without regard for historical, scientific, or cultural value. Some pothunters are outright thieves, coming into current sites at night to steal the "good stuff." Some are also vandals. At a site in Oklahoma, pothunters took all they wanted from a rough digging, threw what was left back into the hillside, and dynamited the hill.

Jamestown's recovery was inspired by Benton Lossing, a writer-artist who saw that erosion was taking one of the country's most valuable historical sites. "Look to it, Virginians," he said. That was in 1857. It was not until 1893, however, that the newly chartered Association for the Preservation of Virginia Antiquities began the work of restoring Jamestown, work which continues to this day.

LESSON 29
Old Plymouth

Text, pages 83-84
Notebook, page 32

Preview

Main Ideas

- Jamestown and Plymouth have some characteristics in common.
- Plymouth Plantation changed over the years.

Objective

- Color a map to indicate important sites

Materials

- Maps and More 19, 22, and 24, pages M11 and M13

Day 1

Lesson

Introducing the Lesson

Discuss a verse. Read the verse on text page 83.

Verse Discussion

➤ What does a **watchman** do? *(guards the city by looking for danger)*

➤ What do you think the words *in vain* mean?

The phrase means "for no reason." No matter how well-guarded a place is, it is not safe unless the Lord protects it.

➤ Can you think of a people that we have studied who depended on the Lord to keep them safe? *(Separatists)* (BAT: 8a Faith in God's promises)

Direct a discussion. Show Maps and More 22.

Picture Discussion

➤ What are some things that are happening in this picture? *(Two ladies are talking. A man is cutting wood. Houses are being built.)*

➤ Look at the roof on the completed house.

The roof is a **thatched** roof. It is made of thick layers of straw. Bundles of straw are tied onto the frame of the roof. The settlers built their homes the way they had in England.

➤ How many houses do you think were built in Plymouth the first year?

Except the Lord
keep the city,
the watchman
waketh but in

Psalm 127:1

Plymouth Plantation

The Separatists chose to make their village like this.
Why do you think it is near the water?
Does this village look like Jamestown?
Can you find the fort?
A fort is like a lookout tower with guns.
People can go there to be safe.

83

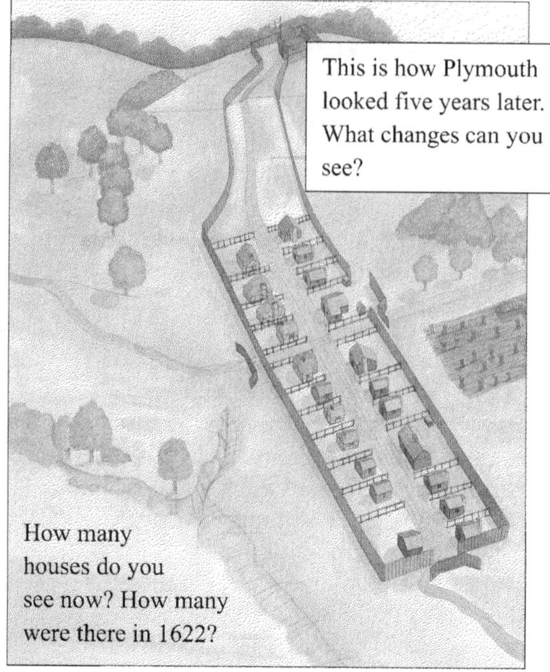

This is how Plymouth looked five years later. What changes can you see?
How many houses do you see now? How many were there in 1622?

Can you find Governor Bradford's house?
Are the corn fields like the ones where Squanto lived?

84

Teaching the Lesson

Direct a text activity on page 83. Direct your child's attention to the map on page 83.

Text Discussion, page 83

- ➤ This a map of Plymouth Plantation just before the first Thanksgiving. Why do you think the people built a fort? *(Answers will vary. It may have been to watch for enemies or for ships coming.)*
- ➤ Do you see the fenced building? That is Governor Bradford's house.
- ➤ Which building do you think is the storehouse? *(The one that is isolated from the other buildings.)*
- ➤ Read page 83, answering the questions as you go along.
- ➤ How many buildings do you see? *(ten buildings: seven small houses, a governor's house, a storehouse, and a fort)*

Everyone lived in the fort until more houses could be built. After that, for a long while, the Separatists went to the fort to hold church services.

Comparison Activity

- ➤ Look at the map of Jamestown on page 82 and the map of Plymouth on page 83. What things are alike and what things are different about the two towns? *(Both have just a few buildings; both are near the water; all of Jamestown is fenced, but only the governor's house is fenced in Plymouth; Plymouth is built in a straight line, but Jamestown is built in a triangle.)*

Text Discussion, page 84

- ➤ Have you seen any changes taking place in our town or city lately? *Remind your child of projects he may have seen or take him on a trip to see changes in progress.*

Towns and cities do not stay the same all the time. New buildings go up; old buildings sometimes are torn down. Sometimes fires and floods change a place.

- ➤ How do you think Plymouth Plantation changed during the five years from 1622 to 1627?
- ➤ Let's read page 84 to find out. This is a map of Plymouth Plantation in 1627.

- ➤ What things are different five years later? Look at page 83 to help you see the differences. *(The later drawing shows more houses, a fence around the town, small fences between the houses, and crops in the fields.)*
- ➤ Why did these changes happen? *(More people came; the people had more time to build houses.)*
- ➤ Look at page 84 again. How many buildings are on the 1627 map? *(twenty-six buildings: a fort, a governor's house, a storehouse, twenty houses, and three outbuildings)*
- ➤ Are there more buildings than there were in 1622? *(yes)*
- ➤ Which house do you think belongs to the governor? The governor had a larger home with an opening, or gate, in the fence. *(fourth from the top on the right)*
- ➤ Which house would you have chosen to live in?
- ➤ Look back on page 82 at the map of Jamestown. Compare Jamestown to Plymouth Plantation in 1627. *(The numbers of buildings are more nearly equal now; both places have enclosing fences.)*
- ➤ Look at Squanto's village on Maps and More 19. Then look at page 84 again. Compare the way crops were planted in Squanto's village to the way crops were planted in Plymouth Plantation. *(The crops in Squanto's village were planted all around the houses. The crops in Plymouth Plantation were planted in a separate field.)*

Map Discussion

- ➤ Look at Maps and More 24. This picture shows some Plymouth household goods and the inside of a house.
- ➤ The settlers at Plymouth Plantation built their fireplaces first and then built their houses around them. Why was the fireplace so important? *(It provided heat for cooking and warming the house, and it gave light.)*

Most early houses in Plymouth had just one room. Above the room was a loft where the children slept.

- ➤ How is this Plymouth home different from our house? *(Answers will vary but should include the differences in furniture, cookware, and number of possessions.)*
- ➤ The drawings of the cradle, chair, and pot show items that were brought to America on the *Mayflower* and that still exist today. Where do you think we might see these items? Such things are in museums for safekeeping.

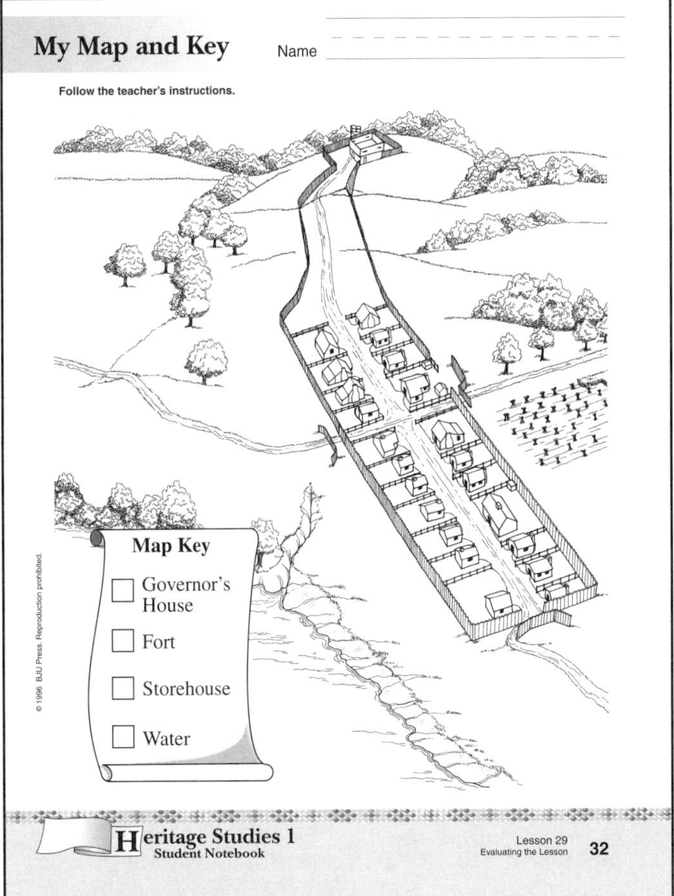

Evaluating the Lesson

Direct a map activity on Notebook page 32. Point out the unfinished key on the page. Tell your child to color the key as he wishes and then to color the map to match. For example, if he fills in the square beside *Governor's House* with green, then he must color the corresponding picture green. After he has completed his coloring, review the map with him.

Going Beyond

Additional Teacher Information

The items pictured on Maps and More 24 are in Pilgrim Hall, Plymouth, Massachusetts. The cradle once held Peregrine White, whose name means "wanderer." Despite his name, he lived more than eighty years without leaving New England. The pot belonged to Miles Standish, the company's military leader. The chair was possibly the property of Elder Brewster.

Because thatched roofs caught fire easily, wooden shingles soon replaced the more English housetop. The reconstructed Plymouth Plantation near modern Plymouth shows both kinds of roofs. Each house, now as then, has a small herb garden and a low fence, giving the impression of privacy and independence in a small, interdependent settlement.

Lesson 30
Planning a Town

Text, pages 85-86
Notebook, page 33

Preview

Main Ideas

- People who settle in new places look for the same necessities: water, food, and protection.
- Choosing a good place for a settlement is important.

Objectives

- Select a site for a house, using a map
- Explain the choice of site

Materials

- Appendix, page A23: Starting a Town*

Notes

To make this lesson relevant for your child, arrange a brief tour of the area around your home. A tour of even two or three blocks will spark enough interest for discussion. Choose a route that has both old and new buildings, if possible, although a newly constructed block or division can be useful as well.

You may decide to research the area briefly yourself. Try to find out which building on the route is the oldest, when it was built, what it was used for (if different from its present use), and who built it. Some good sources for such information are local historical societies, the library, and courthouse or county records. Also, old newspapers often carry information on construction and fires.

Day 1

Lesson

Introducing the Lesson

Direct a short tour. Take your child on a walking or driving tour around the area. Ask your child to point out the buildings he thinks are the oldest. Ask him why he made the choices he did.

Try to accommodate your child's spontaneous interest in things he sees. For example, if he is curious about a particular fence or a turret on a house, ask him why he finds it interesting. Suggest that he try to draw it or look for more examples when he gets back to the schoolroom. You may be able to find in the library books with large color pictures of different styles of architecture.

Teaching the Lesson

Lead a discussion. Ask your child how an old building looks different from most modern buildings.

Lesson Discussion

➤ Why do you think there are so many different kinds of buildings in one town?

A town is not built all at the same time. The buildings will look different from one another. Some will be made of wood, some of brick, some of steel and aluminum. Uses of buildings change as well. For example, an old hardware store may become a restaurant.

➤ Why do you think it might be good to keep an old building even if it is no longer used for its original purpose?

Many old buildings are kept because something important happened in them or because they are very beautiful.

➤ No buildings remain from the first Plymouth Plantation. Why do you think that is?

The settlers there found the need for more buildings and bigger houses; they often used wood and other materials from the older buildings. Also, the early houses with the thatched roofs often burned.

Day 2

Story Discussion

➤ Do you think the people from the *Mayflower* planned the village of Plymouth, or did everyone build his house as quickly as he could wherever he wanted?

➤ Listen to a story of how the village came to be.

When the men got off the *Mayflower* to find a place to build, they saw that the land sloped down toward the sea. They climbed the little hill and found that they could see the whole countryside and much of the sea.

"Ah," said one man, "here is an excellent place for a fort. We can watch for ships coming in and for enemies coming by land."

"And," said another, "there are brooks and springs all about."

They looked off in all directions. On one side was a wide field.

"Look there," said the first man. "Fields already cleared. What a lot of work that will save!"

Another man said, "We can build our houses on the slope down toward the water. Then we will have an easy place to load and unload ships, and our houses will be protected from the weather."

"Yes," said another, "we can build the houses in two rows down toward the sea. We can have an orderly town that way."

One man pointed at the forest a little way off. "We won't have to go far to get wood for our houses," he said.

All the men nodded and began to walk down the hill again. They had found a good spot to start a town.

➤ What are some things that the men thought were important? *(water, a good place for a fort or lookout, cleared fields, an easy place for loading and unloading ships, a protected place for houses, a short distance to get wood to build with)*

➤ Do you think the men were wise in their choice?

Remind your child that the Separatists prayed about everything they did. The morning they set out to find a place for the town, the men prayed for direction from God. (BAT: 6b Prayer)

Direct a text activity on page 85. Read page 85, answering the questions. *(All towns were near the water because people have to have water to live. All grew food but not in the same way or in the same places. For example, Squanto's village had corn growing near each house, and Plymouth's fields were farther away.)* Discuss your child's choice of a town to live in, encouraging him to give his reasons for his choice.

Text Discussion, page 85

➤ Which towns have we studied? *(Squanto's village, Jamestown, Plymouth)*

➤ Look at the map. Find Jamestown and Plymouth.

➤ Where is north on the map? *(at the top)*

➤ Which town, Jamestown or Plymouth, is farther north? *(Plymouth)*

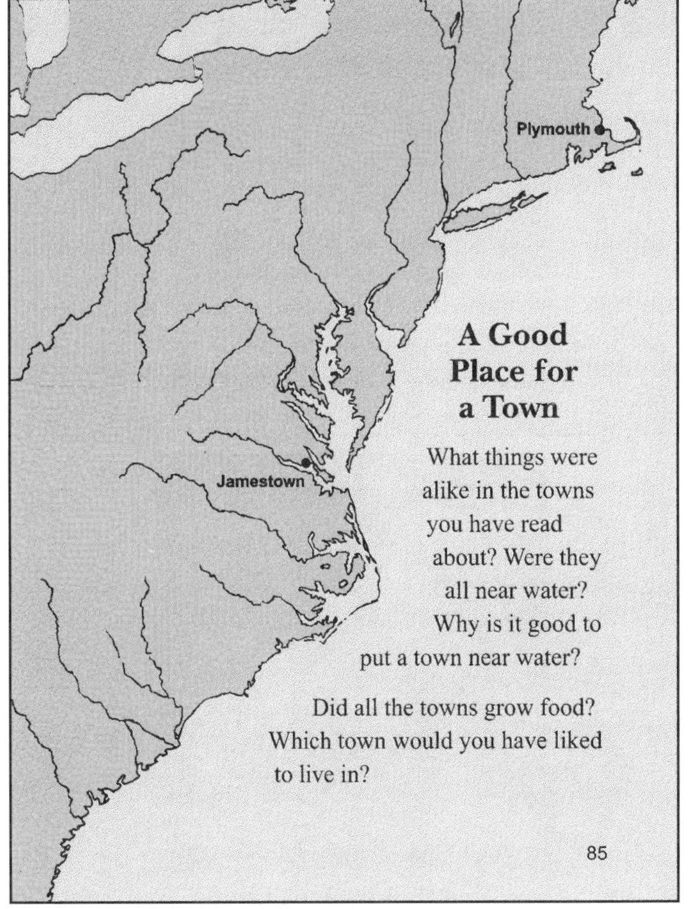

Plymouth
Jamestown
A Good Place for a Town
What things were alike in the towns you have read about? Were they all near water? Why is it good to put a town near water?
Did all the towns grow food? Which town would you have liked to live in?
85

Map Reading Activity

➤ *Point out and read the labels on the map Starting a Town.* The land shown on this page is a good place for a settlement. Where would you choose to build a town?

The best place is probably just northeast of the small hills. The fields will be near, water will be readily available, and access to the bay will be easy. Also, a fort on the hill would be useful. However, let your child come to his own decision, as long as he can give good reasons.

➤ Why would your choice be a good place for a town?

◆ LEARNING HOW ◆

To Plan a Village

1. Get your Notebook page, some scissors, some crayons, some glue, and a felt-tip marker.
2. Color and cut out the model houses, storehouse, and fort.
3. Glue the buildings onto the map. Why did you choose the spots you did? Color the whole map. Name the settlement.

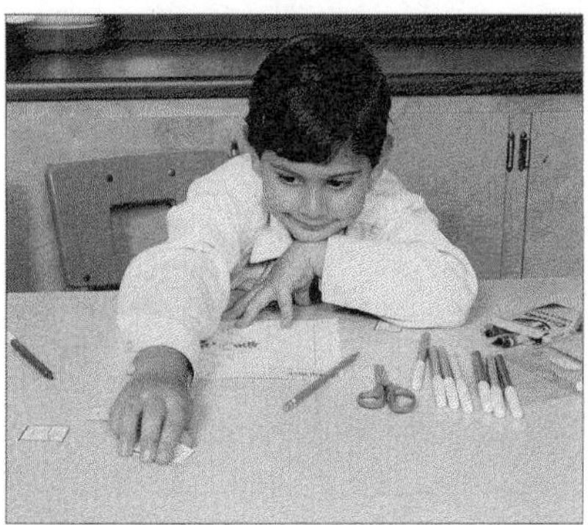

86

Map Work Name ______________

Follow the teacher's instructions.

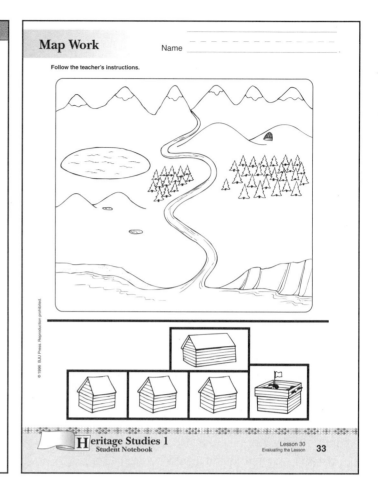

Heritage Studies 1 Student Notebook — Lesson 30 Evaluating the Lesson 33

Evaluating the Lesson

Direct a *Learning How* activity on text page 86 and Notebook page 33. Read the directions on page 86 and allow your child to follow them. Encourage your child to give specific reasons for his choices of spots for each building. Help him to choose and write the name of his settlement.

Going Beyond

Additional Teacher Information

Ten years after the founding of Plymouth, the Massachusetts Bay Company founded Boston. The governor there, John Winthrop, was a wealthy gentleman from Suffolk. The group that came to the New World with him was still in good standing with the Church of England and so had useful connections with those who held high government positions.

From the beginning, the Boston settlement had more resources and more influence than the Plymouth group. In 1636, only six years after the founding of the town, the newer settlers built Harvard College.

7 LESSONS 31-35

Schools Then and Now

The lessons in this unit focus on the history of American schools, mainly the New England schools and the modern schools. One lesson is about the **hornbook,** the famous paddle book from which hundreds of children learned the alphabet and the Lord's Prayer. The chapter also introduces the concept of government influence on schools in the past.

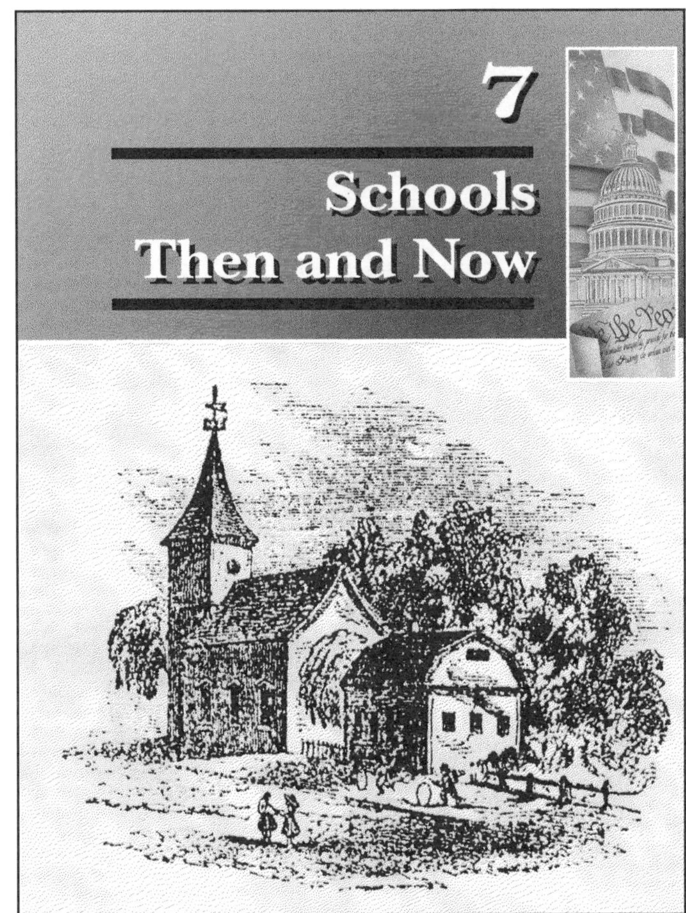

Materials

The following materials must be obtained or prepared before the presentation of the lesson. These items are labeled with an asterisk (*) in each lesson and in the Materials List in the Supplement. For further information see the individual lessons.

- A piece of cardboard (Lesson 33)
- A piece of stiff plastic or plastic wrap (Lesson 33)
- String or ribbon (Lesson 33)

LESSON 31
Schools in America

Text, pages 88-89
Notebook, page 34

Preview

Main Ideas

- School has always been important in America.
- The first schools were in homes.

Objectives

- Draw a picture of the child's school or schoolroom
- Complete a sentence about the importance of school

Materials

- The figure of Harvard College (1636) from the History TimeLine Packet
- A sheet of paper

Day 1

Lesson

Introducing the Lesson

Direct a discussion. On a sheet of paper, write the following headings: *What I like best* and *What is most important.*

➤ Name what you like best about school. *List your child's responses under the first heading, writing them as single words or short phrases:* spelling, math, reading, art, story writing, *and so on.*

➤ What are the most important things that you learn in school? *List his responses under the second heading, using short phrasing.*

➤ Can you find some things that are the same on both lists?

Today we will begin a chapter about schools of long ago and schools of today. In this lesson you will find out what the people of Plymouth thought was the most important thing to learn.

Your child will refer to the lists as he completes his Notebook page.

What kind of school do you go to?
What do you learn in school?
Why do you think it is important to go to school?

School has always been important in America.
Soon after the Pilgrims came,
they began schools.

Seek ye out of the book of the Lord, and read.
Isaiah 34:16

88

Teaching the Lesson

Read aloud Isaiah 34:16 from the textbook, directing your child to listen for one of the things that he may have listed as most important. *(to read)* Ask what "the book of the Lord" is and why it would be important to read it. *(It is the Bible, God's Word. When someone reads it, he finds out what God says.)* (BATs: 6a Bible study, 8b Faith in the power of the Word of God)

Direct a text activity on pages 88-89. Read the first section on page 88 and allow your child time to respond to each question.

Text Discussion, page 88

➤ Does the schoolroom pictured on page 88 look like yours?

➤ Read the rest of the page. Why do you think school was so important to the people of Plymouth?

Some children went to *dame schools* or *kitchen schools.*
Women taught these schools. Women were called *dames* in those days.
These schools were held in the kitchens.

Sometimes children went to a neighbor's house for school.
The parents took turns teaching each other's children.

89

My School Name ____________

Draw a picture of your school.

The most important thing to learn is ____________ *Answers will vary.* .

Heritage Studies 1 Student Notebook — Lesson 31 Evaluating the Lesson 34

Text Discussion, page 89

- ➤ Read page 89. What were women called during this time? *(dames)*
- ➤ What did some of the dames do? *(taught school)*
- ➤ Where did the dames do their teaching? *(in the kitchen)*
- ➤ What other kind of school was there? *(Some parents taught in their own homes. They may have taught neighbors' children as well as their own.)*
- ➤ Is your school like a **dame school** or a **kitchen school?**

Discuss with your child that God expects parents to begin training their children when they are little. Parents are to teach their children to obey, to be truthful, to be kind, to be respectful, and to love God. Home is also the best place for children to learn God's Word. (BATs: 3a Self-concept, 5a Love)

- ➤ The first college in America was Harvard College. Put the figure of Harvard College on the TimeLine at 1636, the year the college was built. *Help your child figure out how many years ago that was.* Harvard College was built by Puritans to train men to be pastors.

Evaluating the Lesson

Direct an activity on Notebook page 34. Read the directions to your child. You may want to suggest that he draw a picture of the outside of his home or of the inside of the room in which you have school. Remind him of the lists made at the beginning of the lesson. He may want to refer to those lists as he completes the sentence on the Notebook page.

Going Beyond

Enrichment

Make a blank book entitled "Things I Have Learned About School." Alternate pieces of blank handwriting paper and plain drawing paper. Invite your child to write and draw on the pages each time he learns something new in this chapter. You might write and draw a few sample pages yourself to inspire your child to contribute. Share parts with the family. Your pleasure with his attempts at authorship will encourage him.

Additional Teacher Information

Dame schools began in England in the sixteenth century. The printed word had made reading a necessity, even for the children of humble families, and the cottage of the local "dame" became the place of learning in many a village. The dame had no special training as a teacher, but she was educated well enough to know her letters, the catechism, and how to count. She was often a poor widow who welcomed the meager pay (often in food and goods rather than cash) in exchange for the lessons.

LESSON 32
Learning to Read

Text, pages 90-91
Notebook, pages 35-36

Preview

Main Ideas

- Parents in Plymouth Plantation were required by law to teach their children to read.
- Plymouth leaders wanted everyone to read the Bible for himself.

Objectives

- Identify the Bible as the most important book to read
- Draw a picture of a Bible

Materials

- A Bible
- A piece of paper

Day 1

Lesson

Introducing the Lesson

Conduct a Bible drill. Following the procedures that you have established for Bible drills in your home, lead your child in a short drill. Use the following verses, which speak of God's Word: John 1:14; Psalm 119:11; Romans 10:17. Give your child as much assistance as needed in looking up the verses and in reading them.

To conclude the drill, explain that he has just done something that was considered of the highest value in Plymouth. Ask him whether he knows what that is. *(He has read portions of the Bible for himself.)*

Teaching the Lesson

Direct a text activity on pages 90-91. Read page 90, asking your child to listen for what the Plymouth law said parents must teach their children. *(how to read)*

Text Discussion, page 90

➤ *Discuss the two questions on the text page.*
➤ *Review the importance of the Bible to the people of Plymouth.* (*NOTE:* See Lesson 21.)

In Plymouth Plantation the law said all parents must teach their children to read.
Why do you think that was the law?

The Plymouth leaders wanted everyone to read the Bible for himself.
Why do you think reading the Bible was important to the people?

90

The king's church in England had not encouraged the people to read the Bible for themselves. The Bible was read only at church. Many people came to Plymouth so that they would be free to read God's Word. (BAT: 6a Bible study)

Text Discussion, page 91

➤ Read the first three sentences to find something that the law in Boston said. *(Towns of one hundred families should build a school.)*

These early schools were one-room buildings, made as inexpensively as possible and furnished simply. All grades were taught in the single room by one teacher. While the teacher was teaching one grade, the other children would be left to study their lessons.

➤ What do you think you would like about going to school in a one-room schoolhouse?
➤ Find the school on the map.
➤ Read the rest of the page. Do you think that the law said that everyone in town had to help pay the teacher? *(Answers will vary. Although the text does not say "paying the teacher was the law," the words* had to give some money *indicate that payment was required.)*

A law in Boston said that towns with one hundred families should build a school. These schools had one teacher for the children of many families.
Can you find the school for many children on the map?

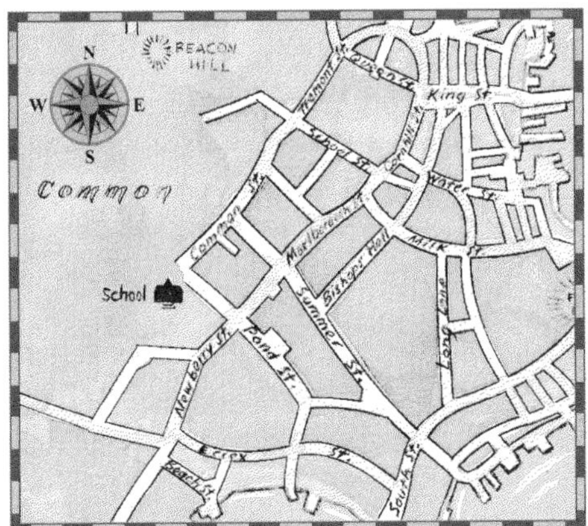

How do you think the towns paid the teachers?
Everyone in town had to give some money to help pay the teacher.

91

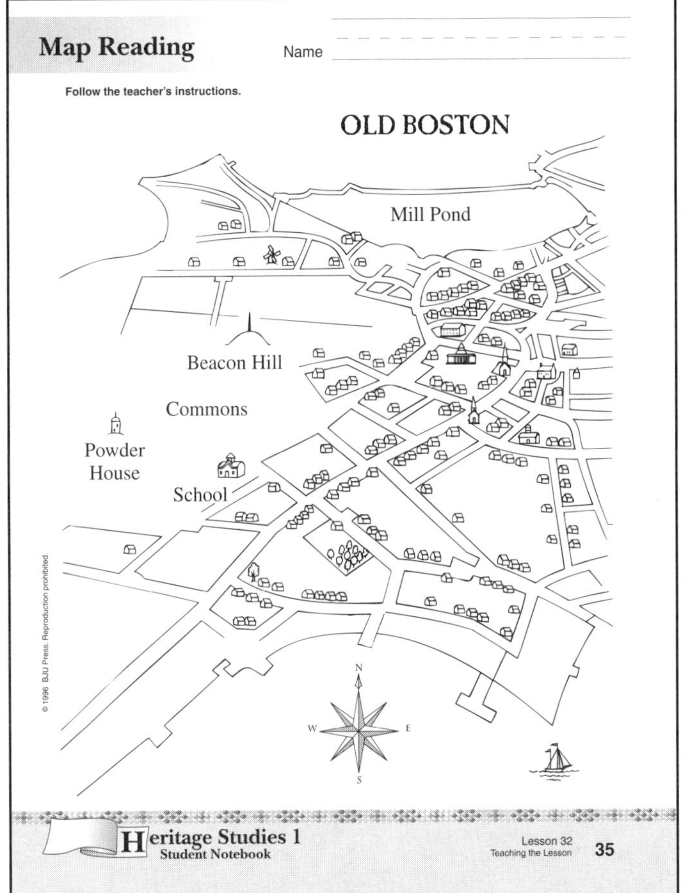

Brief discussion on this point reinforces the higher-level thinking (inferential) skills that you are developing in your reading instruction.

Direct a map-reading activity on Notebook page 35. Write the word *Commons* on a piece of paper. Tell your child to put his finger on the same word on the map.

In the following activity give your child as much help as needed in moving his finger in the correct direction and in reading the words on the map.

Map-Reading Activity

- ➤ Move your finger from the Commons eastward. What important building do you come to? *(a church)*
- ➤ Point to the compass rose on the map. What do the letters stand for? *(north, east, south, and west)*
- ➤ Put your finger on the Commons again. Move your finger south from the Commons. What building does your finger come to first? *(School)*
- ➤ Put your finger on the Commons again. Move your finger to the west. What do you come to if you moved west of the Commons? *(Powder House)*
- ➤ Name something north of the Commons. *(Beacon Hill, windmill, streets, houses)*
- ➤ Look at the compass rose again. I want to show you a new direction term. *Use your finger to trace the diagonal line from the center of the rose between the east and south lines.*
- ➤ What two directions are on either side of the line I traced? *(south and east)*
- ➤ Do you know what direction the new line would be called? *(southeast)*
- ➤ Use your finger to trace the southeast line.
- ➤ *Repeat the procedure, tracing the diagonal line from the center of the rose between the south and west lines.* What two directions lie on either side of the line I traced? *(south and west)*
- ➤ What would this new line be called? *(southwest)*
- ➤ Trace the southwest line with your finger.

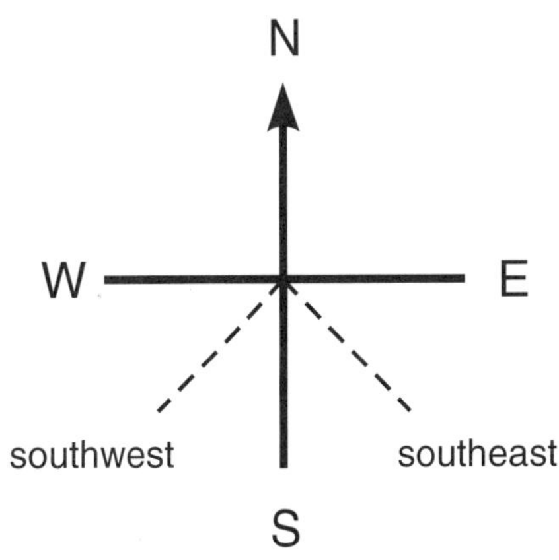

The Most Important Book

Name

Finish this sentence.

The most important book to read is

the Bible or God's Word.

Draw a picture of that book.

Heritage Studies 1 Student Notebook — Lesson 32 Evaluating the Lesson 36

Evaluating the Lesson

Direct an activity on Notebook page 36. Read the directions to your child. He may need help with spelling if he chose the answer *Scripture* or *God's Word.*

Going Beyond

Additional Teacher Information

In 1647 the General Court of Massachusetts Bay passed the Old Deluder Satan Act to establish organized education for the express purpose of insuring that children learn to read the Bible. The act required that communities with fifty families appoint and pay someone to teach the children to read and write. Communities with one hundred or more families were to erect a school building and pay all expenses from the public treasury. But the opportunity and responsibility of educating children still remained in the home.

The act was named for its opening statement, included in the following excerpt:

> It being one chief project of that old deluder, Satan, to keep men from the knowledge of the Scripture, as in former times by keeping them [that is, the Scriptures] in an unknown tongue, so in these latter times by persuading from the use of tongues, that so at least the true sense of the original might be clouded by false glosses [translations] of saint-seeming deceivers, that learning may not be buried in the grave of our fathers in the church and Commonwealth, the Lord assisting our endeavors.
>
> It is therefore ordered that every township in this jurisdiction, after the Lord hath increased them to the number of fifty householders, shall then forthwith appoint one within their town to teach all such children as shall resort to him to write and read.

This law affected all of the Massachusetts Bay Colony but *not* Plymouth, which did not unite with the colony until 1686.

LESSON 33
The Hornbook

Text, pages 92-95
Notebook, pages 37-38

Preview

Main Idea

- Children in early schools learned to read from hornbooks.

Objectives

- Construct a model hornbook
- Demonstrate how the hornbook was used

Materials

- An $8\frac{1}{2}$" × 11" piece of stiff plastic or plastic wrap*

For making the hornbook model, stiff plastic, such as a clear report cover, would be best for conveying the feel and look of the old horn covering.

- An $8\frac{1}{2}$" × 11" piece of cardboard*
- A hole punch
- An 18" length of string or ribbon*
- Maps and More 26, page M14

You may want to find other examples of ways people wrote things down. Some American Indians, for example, wrote and drew on animal skins and strips of bark. The Egyptians covered whole walls with picture writing known as **hieroglyphics.** If there is a living history museum or center nearby, you may want to see whether a reproduction hornbook is available for viewing.

Day 1

Lesson

Introducing the Lesson

Direct a comparison. Show your child Maps and More 26. Ask whether he knows what these things were used for. Explain that they are forms of keeping writing, something like our more modern books. Ask whether he would like to study from scrolls or clay tablets instead of his books.

Do you think the children in schools long ago
had books and paper as you have?
Most schools had a special kind of book called
a *hornbook.*
The hornbook looked like a wooden paddle.
It had a piece of paper on it.
What do you think was on the paper?

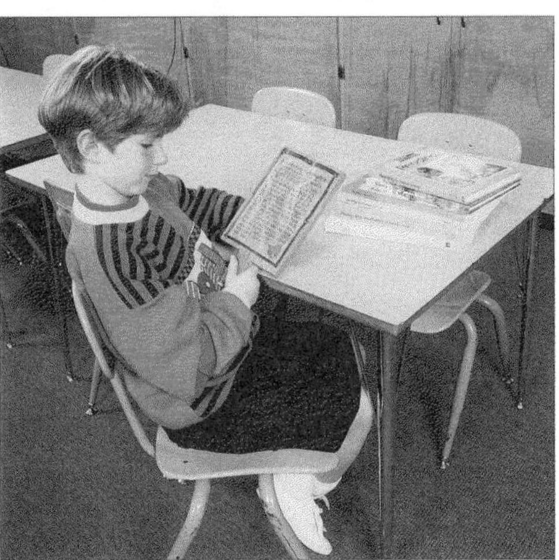

92

Teaching the Lesson

Direct a text activity on pages 92-94. Direct your child to look at the picture on page 92.

Text Discussion, page 92

- ➤ Have you ever seen a book like the one the little girl is holding?
- ➤ Read the page, stopping to answer each question.

Text Discussion, page 93

- ➤ Read the first two sentences. What was written on the **hornbook?** *(the Lord's Prayer and the alphabet)*
- ➤ What did the people of Plymouth think was important for their children to learn? *(learn to read and learn about God)*

You may want to emphasize to your child that he should learn to read and study God's Word just as the Plymouth children did. (BATs: 2a Authority, 6a Bible study)

- ➤ Read the rest of the page to find out why a child might wear a book around his neck. *(to learn his letters while he did chores)*
- ➤ What chores are you asked to do at home?
- ➤ What chores do you think the children of Plymouth did?

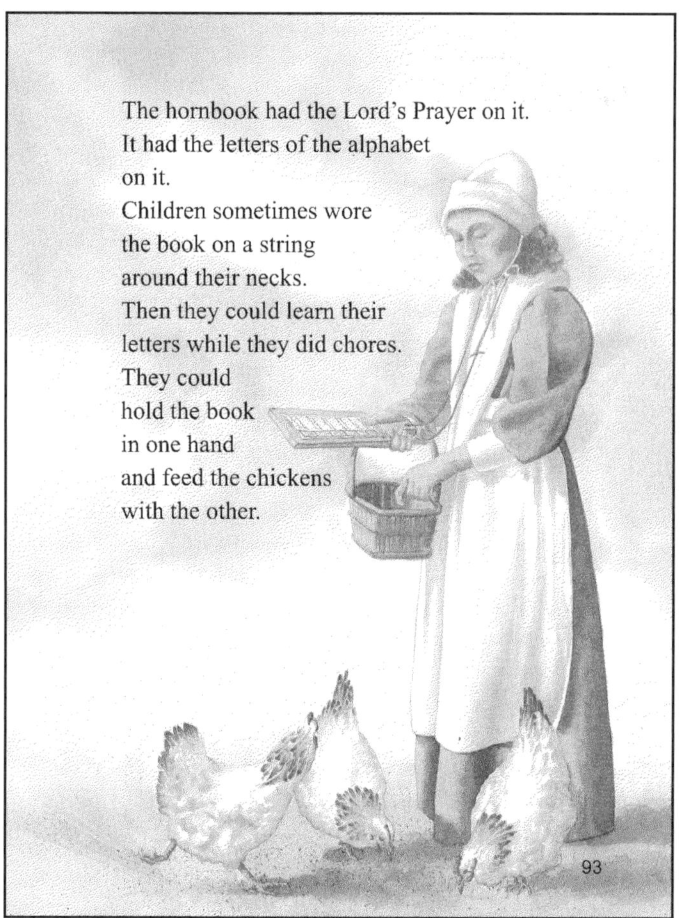

The hornbook had the Lord's Prayer on it.
It had the letters of the alphabet on it.
Children sometimes wore the book on a string around their necks.
Then they could learn their letters while they did chores.
They could hold the book in one hand and feed the chickens with the other.
93

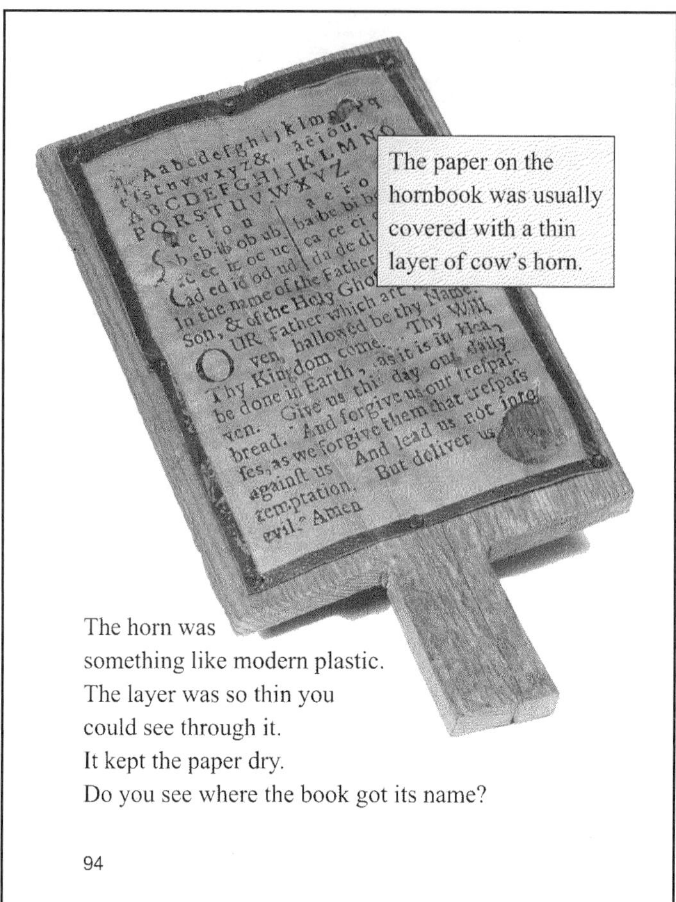

The paper on the hornbook was usually covered with a thin layer of cow's horn.
The horn was something like modern plastic.
The layer was so thin you could see through it.
It kept the paper dry.
Do you see where the book got its name?
94

The Plymouth children were a part of the community life, and it was important for them to do their jobs. They helped carry wood and water, pick berries, tend the cooking, watch younger children, and clean the house. The adults also all had jobs to do. Some hunted for food, some planted and tended crops, and some cooked. Everyone had to help. (BAT: 2c Faithfulness, 2e Work)

➤ How do you think the Plymouth children felt about learning to read?

Although some may not have liked to study, most understood that they were blessed to be in a place where going to school was allowed. Not all children were allowed to read and write at that time. Plymouth children had parents who wanted them to be able to read the Bible for themselves. We are blessed to live in a country in which learning is important.

Text Discussion, page 94

➤ Read page 94. How did the hornbook get its name? *(from the layer of cow's horn)*

➤ Why was the paper covered with the horn? *(to keep the paper dry)*

◆ LEARNING HOW ◆

To Make a Hornbook

1. Get a piece of cardboard, your Notebook pages, a piece of stiff plastic or plastic wrap, a pair of scissors, some string, a hole puncher, and some glue.
2. Cut out the hornbook pattern from the Notebook page. Cut the cardboard using the pattern.
3. Cut out the hornbook page from the Notebook page. Glue it onto the cardboard as your teacher shows you.
4. Punch a hole at the end of the handle. Put the string through the hole and tie the ends.
5. Glue the plastic over the hornbook page. Now hold out your "hornbook."

Can you read the letters?

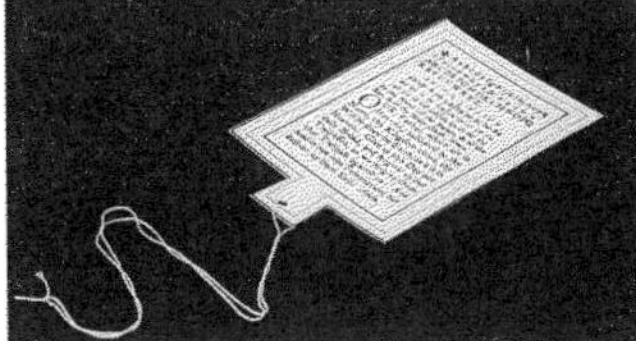

95

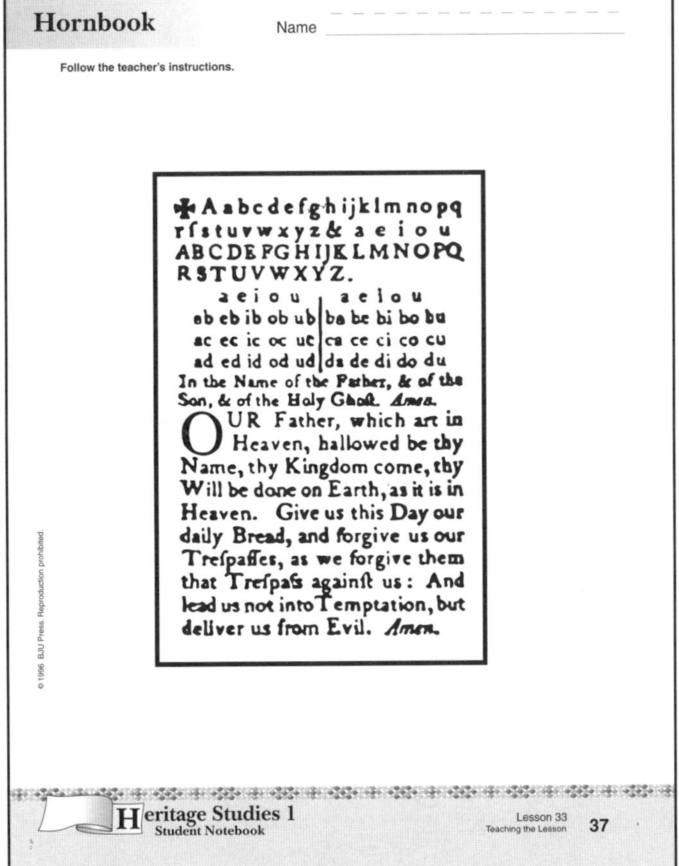

Hornbook Name ______________

Follow the teacher's instructions.

✠ A a b c d e f g h i j k l m n o p q
r ſ s t u v w x y z & a e i o u
A B C D E F G H I J K L M N O P Q
R S T U V W X Y Z.

a e i o u	a e i o u
ab eb ib ob ub	ba be bi bo bu
ac ec ic oc uc	ca ce ci co cu
ad ed id od ud	da de di do du

In the Name of the Father, & of the Son, & of the Holy Ghoſt. *Amen.*

OUR Father, which art in Heaven, hallowed be thy Name, thy Kingdom come, thy Will be done on Earth, as it is in Heaven. Give us this Day our daily Bread, and forgive us our Treſpaſſes, as we forgive them that Treſpaſs againſt us: And lead us not into Temptation, but deliver us from Evil. *Amen.*

Heritage Studies 1 Student Notebook — Lesson 33 Teaching the Lesson — 37

Day 2

The hornbook has been simplified in this lesson for easier production. In its original form, the page was tacked onto the wood.

Direct a *Learning How* activity on text page 95 and Notebook pages 37-38. Direct your child's attention to page 95 as you read the directions. Guide your child as he completes each step. In Step 2 direct him to cut out his hornbook pattern from Notebook page 38 and to glue it onto the cardboard. Then he should cut the cardboard, following the heavy cutting line on his hornbook pattern. In Step 3 he should cut out the hornbook page on Notebook page 37 and glue it onto the prepared hornbook. In Step 5 he should put small dabs of glue on the edges of the plastic, just enough to hold it in place over the paper.

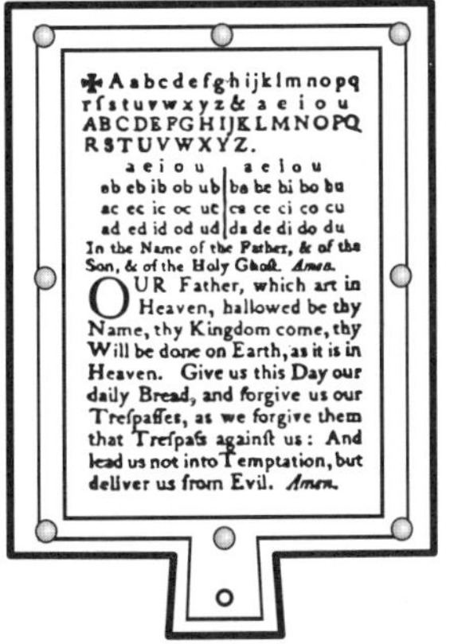

Evaluating the Lesson

Direct a role-playing activity. Give your child "chores" to act out, such as feeding chickens, stacking wood, picking berries, washing clothes by hand, stirring a pot of soup, or carrying water in a bucket. Instruct him to put his hornbook model around his neck. He should then "study" his hornbook at the same time he does his chore. Help him in holding his hornbook correctly and keeping up with his chore. You may want to instruct him to recite the letters of the alphabet as well.

Going Beyond

Additional Teacher Information

The lessons of the hornbook began with the alphabet. At the front of the first line was a +, symbolizing the cross of Christ. This line became known as the Chris-cross row. After studying the alphabet, the student would move on to the syllables and finish with the Lord's Prayer. Before he could go on to the primer, the child would have to learn his hornbook by heart.

LESSON 34
Schools Today

Text, pages 96-97
Notebook, page 39

Preview

Main Ideas

- Schools have changed since early times.
- Schools today still have some things in common with early schools.

Objective

- Make comparisons between the child's school and the early schools

Materials

- Maps and More 27, page M14

Day 1

Lesson

Introducing the Lesson

Conduct an "I am thankful" activity. You and your child should each choose one obvious thing in the schoolroom that you are thankful for, but do not tell what it is. Explain that you will describe the room without the item which you have selected. He is to listen and observe carefully. Encourage him to try to guess the item. Reverse roles, allowing him to describe the schoolroom as you guess his item. Remind him that he should be thankful for all the things the Lord allows him to have. (BATs: 7c Praise, 7d Contentment)

In new or unfamiliar situations, such as the previous activity of describing the schoolroom, it helps your child to see the activity modeled (showing what is to be done) before asking him to do the activity.

Teaching the Lesson

Conduct a comparison activity. Direct your child to look at Maps and More 27 while you read a story about going to school.

> It was eight o'clock in the morning. The snow was still blowing around, but the wind was much quieter than it had been. Richard and Charity stomped their feet outside the schoolhouse door to get the snow off.

Inside, the teacher stood beside his large desk, reading. The fire in the fireplace leaped up as Richard opened the door. One of the older boys was putting another piece of wood on the fire. Charity smiled at her friend Elizabeth on the girls' bench. Elizabeth was always early. When Richard and Charity were seated on the rough benches with the other students, the teacher said, "Good morning. Let's begin with prayer." The students all stood up, and the teacher prayed. Then he read from the Bible.

All morning Richard and Charity sat listening to the older students reading and reciting to the teacher. Since they were six years old and just starting school, they did not read as well as the others. Richard leaned over to his friend William. "When will we get to read?"

"Silence!" said the teacher. Richard ducked his head and blushed. He wanted to lean back, but since the benches had no back, he could only wait until the teacher looked away and then slump a little.

Charity felt sorry for her twin brother. Elizabeth winked at her, and she smiled back. Richard would have to try to remember better about the rule of silence.

Just before eleven o'clock, the teacher said, "It's time for eating and resting. Be back by one o'clock."

Charity and Richard went home for porridge and dried apples. The hot food tasted good to them since the weather was so cold.

After lunch, the older students got out pens made from big feathers and tested the ink in the small round pots. Sometimes the ink froze during the night and had to be thawed by the fire. Today the ink had thawed during the morning.

Richard remembered last summer when his father had gathered bark from maple trees. He and Richard's mother had boiled the bark in a giant iron kettle until the brew was thick and black. Then they had sprinkled some powder in it, and when the stuff had cooled, Richard's father told him that it was ink to take to school. Richard could hardly wait until he was able to use the ink himself. He already had picked out the birch tree he would get bark from for Charity and him to use for paper. No one in his school had real paper because it cost too much.

Until four o'clock the younger children studied the alphabet on their hornbooks and learned verses from the Bible about obedience and God's love. Then the teacher prayed again and let them go home. The only books in the school were a Bible and a hymnbook. Charity and Richard already knew many of the verses and hymns because their father and mother read and sang to them every night.

Ask your child what differences he noticed between the school in the story and his school. *(Answers will vary but could include differences in heating, seats, hours of attendance, and rules.)*

What kind of books do you have in your school?
Do you ever wear them around your neck?
Do you think you would like to learn
from a hornbook?

How else is your school different from the
schools in Plymouth and Boston?
Is anything the same?

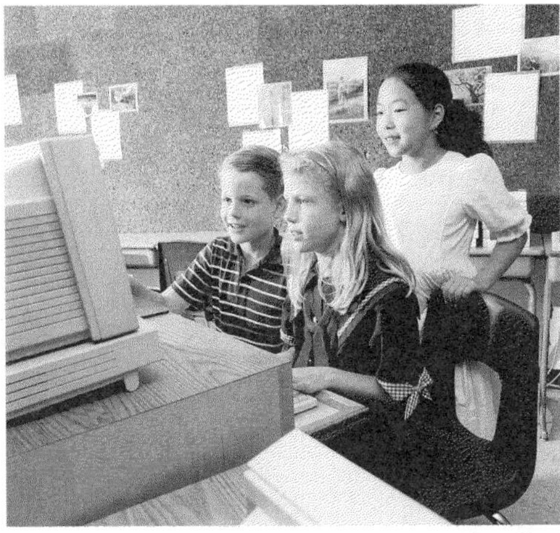

96

Day 2

Text Discussion, page 96

- ➤ Why were the Plymouth students supposed to learn to read? *(so that they could read the Bible for themselves)*
- ➤ Why do you go to school?

I want you to learn to read the Bible for yourself as well as learn other things that will help you as you grow up. I want you to listen and to learn as much as you can, just as the Plymouth parents wanted their children to learn. (BATs: 2a Authority, 6a Bible study)

- ➤ Look at page 96. What are the children in the picture doing? *(working on a computer)*
- ➤ Read the page. *Stop for responses after the questions, especially concentrating on the last question.* Is anything the same? *(Answers will vary. However, your child may mention that school begins with prayer, he has rules to follow, and his parent is his teacher.)*

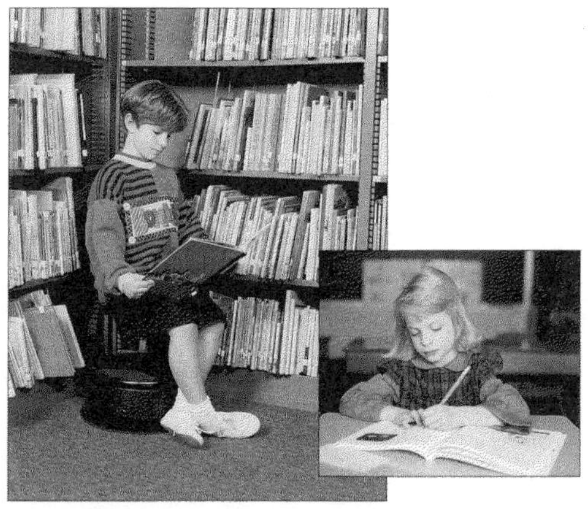

You go to school to learn to read and write.
Why do you need to learn to read and write?

Who is your teacher?
Is your teacher like a kitchen school teacher or
a Boston teacher of many children?

Not all schools are the same today.
Some are like kitchen schools.
Some are like the schools built for
many children.

97

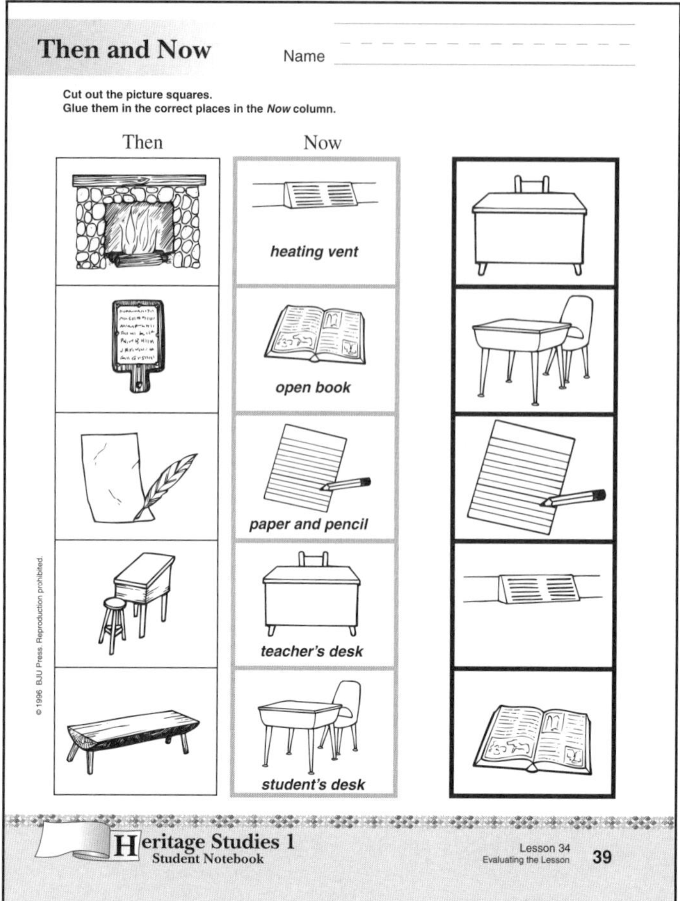

Then and Now Name ______________

Cut out the picture squares.
Glue them in the correct places in the *Now* column.

Then	Now
	heating vent
	open book
	paper and pencil
	teacher's desk
	student's desk

Text Discussion, page 97

- Read the first two sections on the page. *Wait for responses after questions.*
- Read the last three sentences. Some children today go to school in a building with many other children and some go to school at home. *Briefly review the dame, or kitchen, school from Lesson 31.*

Many of the things we do in school today we learned from the early schools. Although our schools are much more convenient and modern, the reason we go to school is still very much the same.

Evaluating the Lesson

Direct an activity on Notebook page 39. Read the directions. Discuss what each picture is before your child begins to work.

Going Beyond

Enrichment

Encourage your child to choose a Scripture passage or a favorite poem to memorize. You may want to make this a family activity. Draw a line with chalk on the floor. Ask the family members to "toe the line" and recite together. (*NOTE:* See Additional Teacher Information for an explanation of "toeing the line.")

Additional Teacher Information

Because learning to read the Bible was the main goal of early schooling, lessons usually began with Bible reading. The most advanced readers would be called upon, one by one, to read the Bible aloud. Upon hearing his name, each student would walk to the assigned place—usually a certain floorboard or a crack in the floor in front of the teacher's desk—and put his toes on the line. We get the expression "toeing the line" or "toeing the mark" from this practice. He would then open the Bible to the assigned passage and read the designated verses.

LESSON 35
Rules About Schools

Text, pages 98-100
Notebook, page 40

Preview

Main Ideas

- Governments make rules about schools.
- Taxes help pay for some schools.
- People vote for laws and for the people who make laws.

Objectives

- Discuss new rules for the schoolroom
- Vote for a rule

Materials

- A small piece of paper for each participating family member
- A sheet of paper, chart paper, or chalkboard
- An empty box
- Supplement, page S11: Children's Survey

Day 1

Lesson

Introducing the Lesson

> Instead of using the Children's Survey found in the Supplement, you may conduct a survey of family, friends, and relatives. A survey of five to ten people is sufficient.

Conduct a survey using Notebook page 40. Tell your child that he is going to be part of a survey. Ask whether he knows what a **survey** is. Explain that it is a way of finding out what people like or what they think about things.

Survey Activity

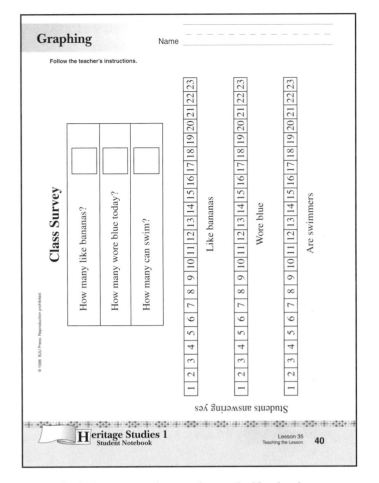

- ➤ Look at the Children's Survey page. Pretend these are friends you have surveyed.
- ➤ Look at the questions in the box on the Notebook page 40.
- ➤ Read the first question.
- ➤ Read the number one response of each child on the survey page. For each *yes* response, put a tally mark in the box next to the question on the Notebook page. *Allow your child to include responses from you and himself for each question.*
- ➤ Read and record the answers to the next two questions in the same way.
- ➤ Count the number of tally marks in each box on the Notebook page and write the number beside the box.

Graphing Name

Follow the teacher's instructions.

Class Survey

How many like bananas?
How many wore blue today?
How many can swim?

1	2	3	4	5	6	7	8	9	10	11	12	13	14	15	16	17	18	19	20	21	22	23

Like bananas

1	2	3	4	5	6	7	8	9	10	11	12	13	14	15	16	17	18	19	20	21	22	23

Wore blue

1	2	3	4	5	6	7	8	9	10	11	12	13	14	15	16	17	18	19	20	21	22	23

Are swimmers

Students answering yes

Teaching the Lesson

Direct a graphing activity on Notebook page 40. Direct your child's attention to the numbered boxes on the Notebook page.

Graphing Activity

- ➤ Each row on the graph stands for one of the questions in the survey.
- ➤ Point to the first row. This row stands for the first question about how many like bananas.
- ➤ What was the total number of *yes* answers for that question? Look at the number written beside the question. Color in the row.

◆ THINGS PEOPLE DO ◆

Making Laws

When people live in the same place, they need laws.
The laws help them live together without fighting.
Most groups of people choose people to make their laws.

The early Americans in Massachusetts had a *General Court.*
The court was made up of several men who were wise.
What law about schools did the General Court make?

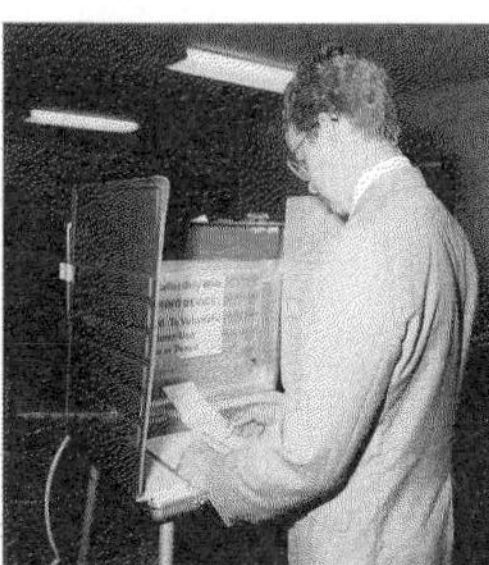

Today our laws are made by people we vote for.
It is important to vote for people who will make good laws.

99

Some teachers of many children are paid by churches.
Others are paid by the towns they live in.
The money paid by towns comes from *taxes.*

Taxes are what people pay to help their towns or cities build schools and pay teachers.
Taxes also help pay for hospitals and fire stations.

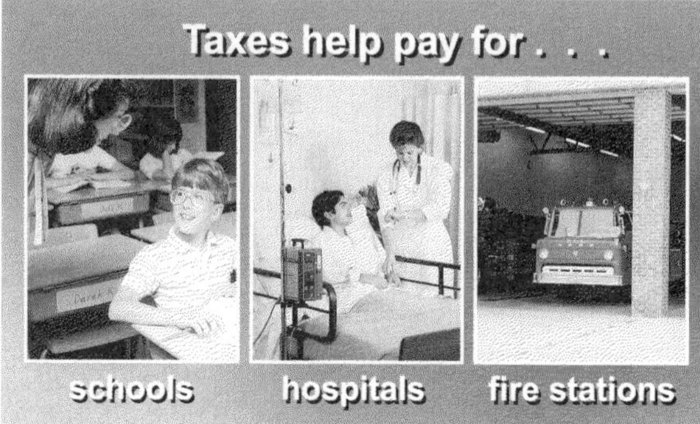

Taxes help pay for . . .
schools
hospitals
fire stations

➤ Do you remember how teachers were paid in early America?

98

➤ Do the same steps with the other two questions.

Because the lesson is introduced with the survey, text page 99 will be discussed before page 98.

Text Discussion, page 99

➤ Sometimes governments take a survey to find out what the people think and how they live. It takes a long time to count all the answers that the people in the United States give.

➤ Another way to find out what people think is to ask them to vote. Voting makes rules based on what most people think.

➤ Do you know what is happening in the picture on page 99? *(A person is voting.)*

➤ Read the first section of the page. Why do you think we have rules in our schoolroom? *(Rules are to help him get along with his siblings and to make things run smoothly while studying.)*

➤ What would happen if there were no rules about playing or talking while it is time for school?

Remind your child that God has made rules for people to live by as well. His rules do not make our lives difficult but help keep us safe and happy. (BATs: 2a Authority, 2b Servanthood)

➤ Read the next section. *Stop after the question about the school law in early Massachusetts.* (*NOTE:* The Additional Teacher Information section in Lesson 32 gives information about the General Court. It ruled that all children were required to learn to read the Bible.)

➤ Read the last section.

If it is a presidential election year, take a few moments to talk about voting for the president of the United States.

Text Discussion, page 98

➤ Read the page.

People make laws about paying for places that nearly everyone uses. Maybe you have wondered who pays the firefighters and the police officers. People pay money to the government. The amount they pay is called **taxes.**

➤ Have you heard the word *taxes* before?

You have probably heard the word because taxes are an important topic with adults. Taxes help pay for roads and fire stations and hospitals.

◆ LEARNING HOW ◆

To Vote About Rules

1. Get a small piece of paper and a pencil.
2. Make up some rules for your classroom. Your teacher will write them out on chart paper or on the chalkboard.
3. Vote for the rule you think is best for your classroom. Write the number of the rule on your paper.

100

➤ Look at the pictures on the page. What other place do you see that sometimes is helped by taxes? *(schools)*

Some schools get money from churches. Christian schools do not get money from taxes. Parents and others give money to help those schools. People give money to Christian schools because they think it is important to have schools that teach the Bible. (BAT: 1c Separation from the world)

Day 2

The following *Learning How* activity requires several participants in order to be successful. The activity has been set up as if you are teaching several children in your home school. If you are teaching one child, consider making it a family activity and voting on a rule to make the home run smoothly.

Evaluating the Lesson

Direct a *Learning How* activity on text page 100. Read page 100 to your children. Tell them that they are going to be like a government in their schoolroom. They are going to discuss rules and then vote on them. Remind them that when they vote, they should try to think of what is best for everyone, not just for themselves.

Learning How Activity

➤ What rules does our schoolroom already have?

➤ Name some other rules we might need.

If no suggestions that are really workable or useful are offered, direct the conversation toward ideas that you have. Write each eligible rule on the chalkboard or paper. Number each rule. When you have two or three, call for a vote. Give each child a small piece of paper to use as a ballot.

➤ *Read the choices again, emphasizing the number that goes with each.* Each of you write the number of the rule you think is best.

➤ Fold the paper without showing it to anyone. Place the paper in the box.

➤ Count the votes. Which rule got the most votes?

Going Beyond

Enrichment

Give your child a copy of the Voting on Rules graph for him to record the votes each rule received. (*NOTE:* See the Appendix, page A24.) You may want to post the results of the voting on a sheet of paper so that he can refer to the tallies as he colors in the graphs.

Additional Teacher Information

The General Court of Boston was made up of a "full assembly of Freemen—Governor and Assistants [who] sat in to pass laws." This body also granted land.

The court adopted a body of laws, the "General Fundamentals," which functioned as a constitution for the colony. Some refer to it as the first bill of rights for America.

Each year, the General Court decided how much money was needed to run the government and apportioned it among the towns. The money was then raised in each town through taxes.

8 LESSONS 36-40

Trading with the Indians

This chapter focuses on trading, specifically settlers trading with Native Americans. Lesson 37 discusses things people make from animal skins. The Canadian fur trapper and explorer Pierre Radisson is highlighted in Lesson 38. In Lesson 40 your child learns about wampum and makes a wampum necklace.

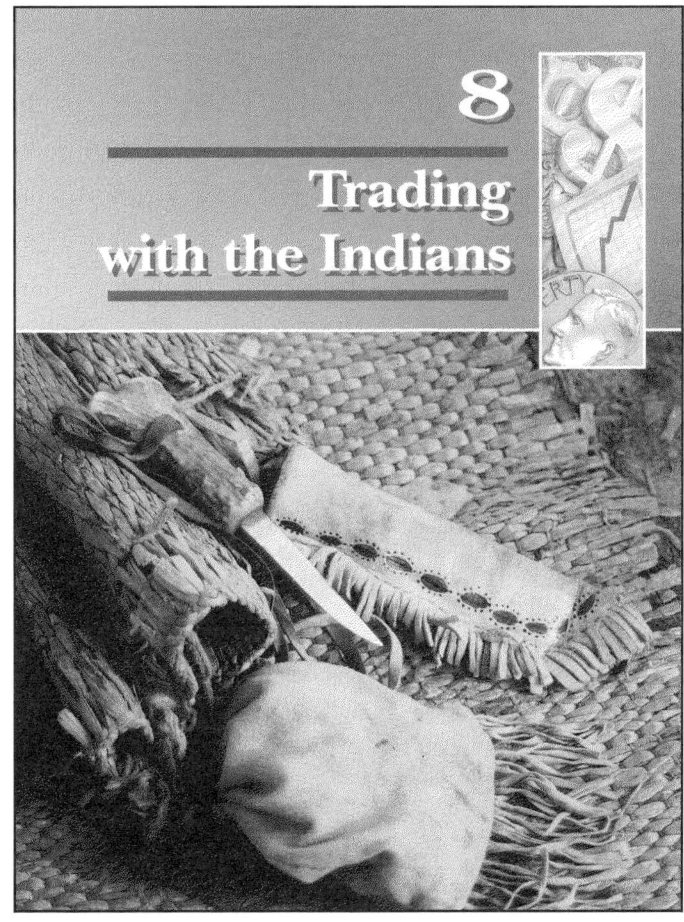

Materials

The following materials must be obtained or prepared before the presentation of the lesson. These items are labeled with an asterisk (*) in each lesson and in the Materials List in the Supplement. For further information see the individual lessons.

- Iron tools (Lesson 36)
- Brightly colored cloth (Lesson 36)
- Items made of fur (Lesson 36)
- Assorted items from the home (Lesson 36)
- Moccasins (optional) (Lesson 37)
- Items made of fur and leather (Lesson 37)
- Brown paper (Lesson 37)
- Poster board (Lesson 38)
- Old ruler or paint paddle (Lesson 38)
- Appendix, page A25 (Lesson 38: 2 copies)
- Macaroni (Lesson 40)
- Food coloring (Lesson 40)
- String or yarn (Lesson 40)

LESSON 36

Early Trading

Text, pages 102-4
Notebook, page 41

Preview

Main Ideas

- Trading means giving one thing to get another thing.
- Traders were looking for goods in the New World.
- The Indians and the settlers traded with each other.
- Some people still trade things today.

Objectives

- Trade certain items for other items
- Distinguish items the Indians traded from items the settlers traded

Materials

- Some iron tools*
- Brightly colored cloth*
- Items made of animal fur (i.e., a collar, a hat, a coat)*
- Items for decision-making activity, such as a glass figurine, a small truck, a doll, a picture book, costume jewelry, a stuffed animal, money, and so on*

Day 1

Lesson

Introducing the Lesson

Direct a decision-making activity. Tell your child to look at the items you have collected one by one. Direct him to select two items that he especially likes. Ask him whether he would be willing to trade something he has in his desk or room for one of those items. Explain that in this lesson he will learn about some groups of people who wanted certain items and had items they thought were valuable for trading. Put away the decision-making items.

Teaching the Lesson

Direct a text activity on pages 102 and 104. Lay the iron tools, cloth, and fur items on the table. Read page 102 to find out about the mapmakers and fishermen that came to the New World.

The men who first sailed to the northern part of the New World were not interested in everything there.
They wanted to make maps of the coast.
They wanted to fish in the cool ocean water.
They wanted to settle along the calm rivers and streams.

Soon the mapmakers and fishermen learned that the Indians wanted things they had.
And the Indians learned that the white men wanted things they had too.
What do you think the men did when they learned these things?

102

Text Discussion, page 102

- ➤ What did the mapmakers and fishermen learn about the Indians? *(The Indians wanted things the white men had.)*
- ➤ What things do you think the Indians might have wanted from the white men?
- ➤ What things do you think the white men might have wanted from the Indians?

The Indians came to the white men first.
They asked the white men for iron tools and brightly colored cloth.
Did the white men just give these things to the Indians?

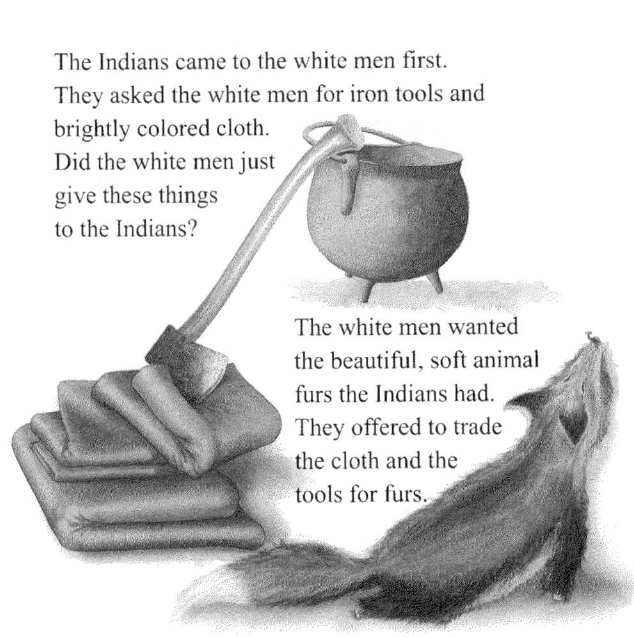

The white men wanted the beautiful, soft animal furs the Indians had.
They offered to trade the cloth and the tools for furs.

The Indians agreed to trade.
They knew where to get more soft furs.
But they did not know how to make the cloth or iron tools.

104

Text Discussion, page 104

- Read the first section on page 104 to find out what the Indians wanted. *(iron tools and brightly colored cloth)*
- Read the second section to find out what the white men wanted. *(animal furs)*
- What plan did the white men come up with? *(They could trade goods with the Indians.)*
- Look at the items on the table. Select what the Indians of long ago might have asked the white men for. *(the iron tools and brightly colored cloth)*
- Select from the table things that the white men of long ago might have wanted. *(the items made of fur)*
- Read the rest of page 104.
- Do you think that trading was a good idea or a bad idea?
- How did trading help both the Indians and the settlers? *(Trading provided goods that each group wanted.)* (BAT: 5c Friendliness)

◆ THINGS PEOPLE DO ◆

Trading Things

And they brought their cattle unto Joseph: and Joseph gave them bread in exchange.
Genesis 47:17

Long ago, people got most things they had to have from the land.
Other things they got by *trading*.

Trading means giving one thing to get another.
Some people still trade things today.
Friends might trade toys.
And sometimes children trade food in the lunchroom.
Have you ever traded anything with someone?

103

Day 2

Direct a trading activity using text page 103. Read and discuss page 103.

Trading Activity

- Divide the tools, cloth, and fur items into two sets, one for the Indians and one for the settlers.
- Choose whether you would like to be an Indian or a settler and take the appropriate set of goods. *You or another child will choose the other.*
- Choose an item that you are willing to trade from your goods. Choose an item that you would like to have from the other set of goods.
- The "settler" and "Indian" may trade goods as often as needed until each has the set of goods he really wants.
- Although this trading is just for fun, the Indians and settlers traded for keeps.

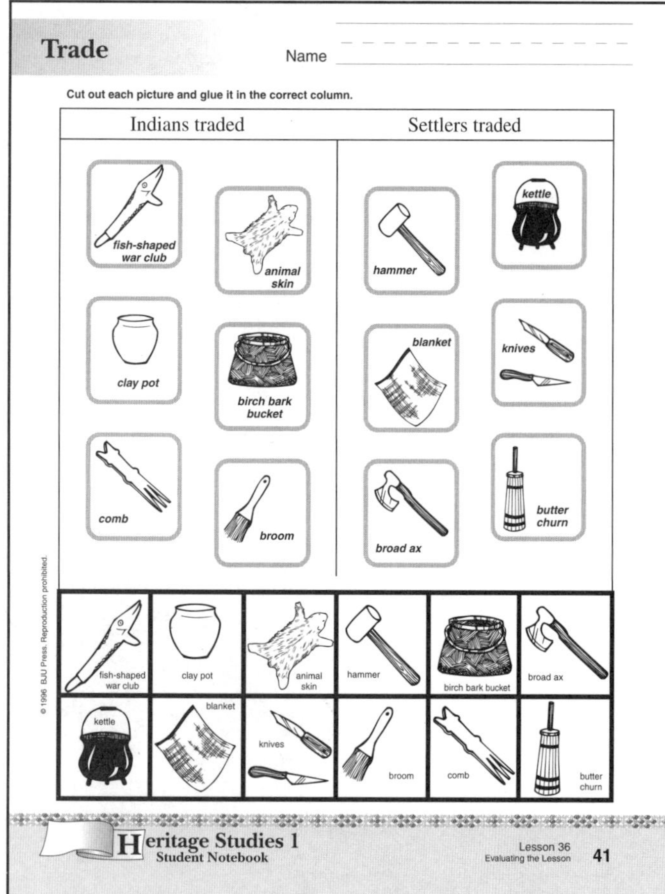

Trade Name

Cut out each picture and glue it in the correct column.

Indians traded	Settlers traded
fish-shaped war club	kettle
animal skin	hammer
clay pot	blanket
birch bark bucket	knives
comb	butter churn
broom	broad ax

fish-shaped war club, clay pot, animal skin, hammer, birch bark bucket, broad ax, kettle, blanket, knives, broom, comb, butter churn

Heritage Studies 1 Student Notebook — Lesson 36 Evaluating the Lesson 41

Evaluating the Lesson

Direct an activity on Notebook page 41. Read aloud the title on each column: *Indians traded* and *Settlers traded*. Read the labels for each of the items pictured at the bottom of the page. Instruct your child to cut out each picture and to glue it under the correct column.

Going Beyond

Additional Teacher Information

Before the settlers came to the New World, Native Americans carved their tools, bowls, and pots out of stone, bone, wood, or shells. To make these necessities, they had to work long and hard to carve them. These items broke easily and had to be replaced often.

In the early days of trading, it was common for one beaver skin to be exchanged for twenty knives. As the European markets demanded more and more furs, the Native Americans demanded a larger variety of merchandise. In 1603 an explorer, Martin Pring, reported that in exchange for barrels of fur, the Indians wanted "hooks, knives, scissors, hammers, nails, chisels, fishhooks, bells, beads, bugles, looking glasses, thimbles, pins, needles, and thread." The Indians also asked for cloth and blankets. The continued trading of Indian furs for European goods, especially ironware, made the Native Americans dependent both upon the Europeans and upon the trading industry.

LESSON 37
Animal Furs

Text, pages 105-6
Notebook, page 42

Preview

Main Ideas

- People work at different kinds of jobs.
- Traders were looking for goods in the New World.
- White men sent most of the furs obtained from the Indians to lands across the ocean.
- The Indians made many things from animal furs.

Objectives

- Make sock covers to resemble moccasins
- Sequence and illustrate events related to the fur trade

Materials

- Moccasins (optional)*
- Two 4" × 11" pieces of brown paper (grocery sack or similar paper)*
- Items made of fur*
- Items made of leather*

Day 1

Lesson

Introducing the Lesson

Direct a moccasin-making activity. Show your child the moccasins or the picture of moccasins on page 186, telling him that Indians of long ago made moccasins of animal skins that they had prepared. Indian moccasins were soft and comfortable. Moccasins enabled the Indians to walk quietly through the forests when hunting or approaching an enemy.

Moccasin Instructions

- ➤ Decorate and color each moccasin (strip of brown paper) using crayons and markers. *(Step a)*
- ➤ On the bottom of each moccasin piece, make small cuts about $\frac{1}{4}$" apart, creating a fringe. *(Step b)*
- ➤ Place the pieces around your ankles, stapling or taping the ends together to fasten the moccasins. *(Step c)*
- ➤ Pretend that you are an Indian walking through the forest.

Do you think the white men kept the warm furs?
The men sent most of the furs to lands across the ocean.
The men traded the furs for food and other things they had to have to live.
They traded the furs for things they wanted.
What do you think they used these things for?
They used them to trade with the Indians again.

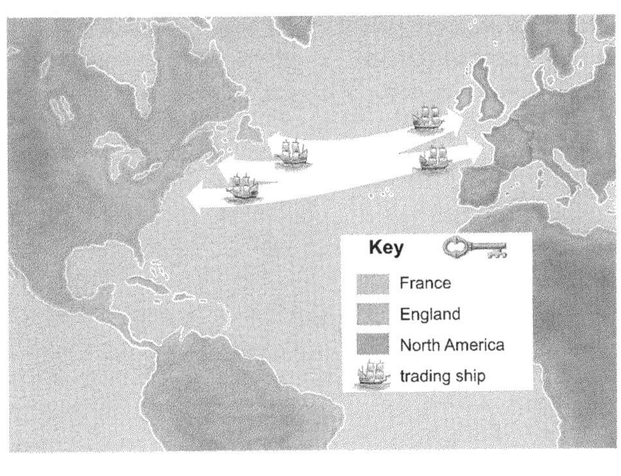

105

◆ THINGS PEOPLE DO ◆

Making Things from Animal Skins

The Indians made many things from the animal furs.
They sewed furs together to make warm blankets and coats.
But most often Indian women scraped the fur from the skin.
They used these skins to make clothes and special shoes called *moccasins.*

Do you think the white men used the furs in the same way?
They did not make many blankets from fur.
They did not scrape the fur from the skins.
But they did make coats from the fur.
What other things do you think they made?

106

a.

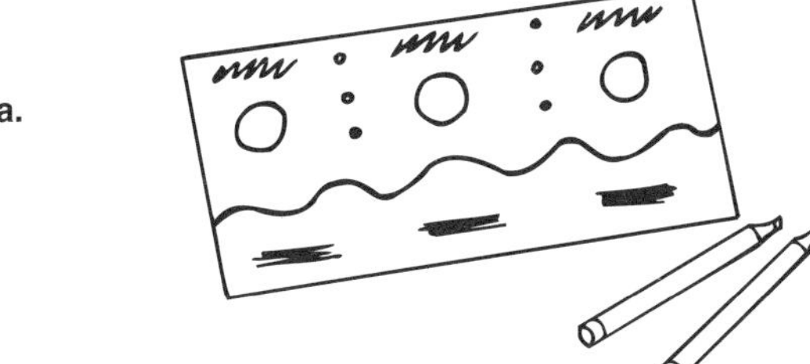

b.

c.

Teaching the Lesson

Direct a text activity on pages 105-6. Read and discuss page 105 with your child.

Day 2

Map-reading Activity

- Look at the map on page 105.
- Name the ocean that is pictured. *(Atlantic Ocean)*
- Point to the key. Tell what dark pink stands for on this map. *(England)*
- Tell what light purple represents. *(France)*

England and France were two countries that sent men to North America. These men traded with the Indians.

- What does the green stand for? *(North America)*
- What is the last symbol? *(a trading ship)*
- Trace the paths of two of the trading ships, telling where the ships were leaving from and where they were going. *(Some ships were leaving England and France and going to North America; others were leaving North America and going to England and France.)*
- What items do you think the ships might have been bringing from England and France to North America? *(Answers might include spices, cloth, and tools.)*

Two Cultures

Name ____________________

Cut out the phrases. Glue them in order in the bottom of the boxes.
Draw a picture to match each phrase.

1. *Indians trapping animals*

2. *Indian women preparing animal skins and furs*

3. *Men loading animal skins and furs onto ships*

4. *People in Europe wearing hats and coats of fur*

People in Europe wearing hats and coats of fur	Indians trapping animals
Indian women preparing animal skins and furs	Men loading animal skins and furs onto ships

- What items do you think the ships were taking from North America to England and France? *(Answers will vary but should include furs.)*

Text Discussion, page 106

- Read and discuss page 106.
- Look at the collection of fur and leather items, all of which were made from skins of animals. Name the items that were made from skins with the fur removed.

> God created the animals and all things on the earth for man's use. God requires Christians to be good stewards of what He has given them. They should use only what they need and always think of the future before they act. (Bible Promises: H. God as Father, I. God as Master)

Evaluating the Lesson

Direct an activity on Notebook page 42. Read the instructions and the phrases at the bottom of the page. Direct your child to complete the assignment, offering assistance as needed.

Going Beyond

Enrichment

Give your child a large sheet of paper or poster board. Encourage him to make a poster of his own, advertising an item that he would like to sell. He may prefer to make an advertisement for something he would like to purchase.

Additional Teacher Information

Native Americans long ago made moccasins out of the skins of buffalo, elk, deer, moose, and reindeer. They would make the leather very soft by oiling the hide, stretching it out, and rubbing it for a long time with a tool made of stone, bone, or wood. Sometimes they smoked the hide over a fire of wet or rotten wood to make it a darker shade of brown, to make it last longer, and to keep it soft. Women sewed the moccasins together with animal sinews or strips of rawhide until thread became available from the traders. Indians carried extra leather and rawhide with them in order to make new moccasins as they were needed.

The largest tribe of the Algonquin family was the Ojibwa. Other tribes called the Ojibwa tribe *Chippewa,* which means "puckered," because of the puckered seams in their moccasins. The Chippewa lands stretched from Lake Huron to Lake Superior and westward. They lived mainly by fishing, hunting, and gathering wild vegetables. The Chippewa were excellent builders of canoes made of birch bark. They lived in round-shaped houses called *wigwams,* which were covered with bark, and in cone-shaped tipis, which were covered with bark or skins.

1-26

Lesson 38
Captured but Not Conquered

Text, page 107
Notebook, pages 43-44

Preview

Main Ideas

- People always live in family groups.
- Many individuals and groups have shaped America's heritage.
- Pierre Radisson was captured and adopted by the Iroquois Indians.
- Pierre Radisson's knowledge about the Indians helped him later in life.

Objectives

- Make a face puppet
- Differentiate between events in Radisson's life as a settler and his life as an Indian

Materials

- The figure of Pierre Radisson (1652) from the History TimeLine Packet
- A 12" × 16" piece of poster board*
- Maps and More 16, page M9
- Appendix, page A25: mask (2 copies)*
- An old ruler or a paint paddle*
- Masking tape

Day 1

Lesson

Introducing the Lesson

Direct a discussion and listening activity. Ask your child to tell what he enjoys about birthdays with your family.

Discussion

➤ Do you know what we are really remembering when we celebrate a birthday? *(when that person was born.)* (BATs: 3a Self-concept, 5a Love) *Talk about the day your child was born.*

➤ What does it mean to be adopted? *If your child knows a person who is adopted or if he is adopted, you might want to discuss that as well.*

➤ Children can be adopted at any time in their lives. A child who is adopted is just as loved by his adoptive family as a child who is born into a family. (BATs: 5a Love, 5b Giving)

When a person receives Christ as Savior, he is adopted into the family of Gód. (BAT: 1b Repentance and faith) As a child of God, the new Christian should strive to do and say things that would please the heavenly Father and bring glory to His name. (BAT: 1c Separation from the world)

Listening Activity

In the spring of 1652 a young Frenchman named Pierre Radisson was captured by a band of Indians. The tribe, called the Mohawks, decided to adopt him as one of their own. Share the following story about the special adoption celebration that took place long ago.

"Get up, our brother," the sisters said as they gently nudged Pierre. He woke quickly, remembering that today was his special day—the day that he was truly to become a member of this family. This was his adoption day!

"Sit here, our brother. We will prepare you for this great day." The sisters gently washed Pierre's face and combed his hair just as dutiful sisters of the village should. They presented him with fine, new clothes made of soft deerskin and decorated with beautiful beads. After Pierre had dressed, his sisters smiled upon him, assuring him that he was handsome and fit to be honored as their new brother. They then took him to the center of the village where a great crowd of visitors had gathered.

Pierre sniffed the air, which was full of the delicious smells of freshly cooked venison, bear meat, persimmon bread, and roasted corn. He liked the persimmon bread best and could hardly wait for the feast to begin. Brilliant colors greeted him everywhere—the red paint on the faces, the yellow feathers in the headdresses, and the elaborate designs of beadwork and wampum.

The drums began to pound as a short, broad woman came out of the crowd. This was Pierre's Indian mother. She offered the corn that had been roasting in the fire to all who stood near. Then turning to Pierre, she bowed, saying, "Here, my son, my own Orimha, my gifts to you I bring." And at that time the gifts were brought to Pierre—new clothes, two necklaces of beads, and a handsome red and blue cape. Then with great glee Pierre's Indian mother began to walk around him, chanting the name of her new son. "Orimha! Orimha! Chagon, Orimha! Be merry, Orimha, my son!"

Next came the Indian sisters who placed bracelets of intricate beadwork on Pierre's arms and legs.

The Indian brother came next, carefully painting Pierre's face with the red marks of the Mohawks. He then put eagle feathers in Pierre's hair.

Next came the chief, Pierre's new father, who presented him with the finest gifts of all! Around Pierre's neck the chief draped a necklace so long that it hung almost to his feet! And in Pierre's hand the chief placed a shiny, new hatchet. Pierre was now an Indian, a Mohawk, a son of the chief!

◆ FAMOUS PEOPLE ◆

Pierre Esprit Radisson

Pierre Radisson was only sixteen years old when he was captured and adopted by Iroquois.
Pierre learned about the Indians while he lived with them.
He learned the Iroquois language.
He learned to hunt for food and to live in the wilderness.
He learned how the Iroquois made war and how they made peace.

When Pierre became a man, he traded with many groups of Indians.
He helped to set up trading companies in New France and New England.
And he helped to build a friendship between the Indians and the Frenchmen.

107

As the feasting and the merriment began, Pierre wondered what life would be like for him as an Indian. What would his Indian family expect of him? Three Rivers, his real home, seemed so far away. Would he ever go back there? Would he ever see his original family again?

Teaching the Lesson

Direct a text activity on page 107. If your child knows a friend or relative who is about sixteen years old, mention that person briefly.

Text Discussion, page 107

- ➤ Is the sixteen-year-old you know a grown-up who lives by himself, works at a job, and takes care of himself all alone? *(probably not)*
- ➤ Read the first sentence on page 107 to find out how old Pierre Radisson was when he was adopted by the Mohawk Indians. *(sixteen)*

The Mohawks were one of the tribes of the Iroquois Nation.

- ➤ Do you think Pierre liked being part of the Indian tribe?
- ➤ Read the rest of the first section to find out some things he learned from the Indians. *(Iroquois language, to hunt for food, to live in the wilderness)*
- ➤ Since the Indians taught him all these things, do you think they treated him kindly?
- ➤ Do you think Radisson lived the rest of his life with the Indians or that he escaped?

Radisson used the training he had learned from the Indians to escape from them less than two years later.

- ➤ Read the last section of the page to find out what Radisson did later in his life. *(traded with Indians, set up trading companies)*
- ➤ Was Radisson a friend to the Indians? *(Yes, he helped make friendships with them and the French.)*

At one time Radisson even sent gifts back to his Mohawk family. He confessed that he actually loved those people.

Day 2

Add a figure to the History TimeLine. Direct your child to tell what each figure represents on the TimeLine. Tell him that about twenty years after the beginning of Harvard in Boston, Radisson was captured by the Mohawks in a land far to the north called Three Rivers, Quebec. This capture occurred in the spring of 1652. Indicate on Maps and More 16 the location of Boston and the location of Quebec. Radisson's adventures continued for many years in this region. Add the figure of Pierre Radisson to the History TimeLine.

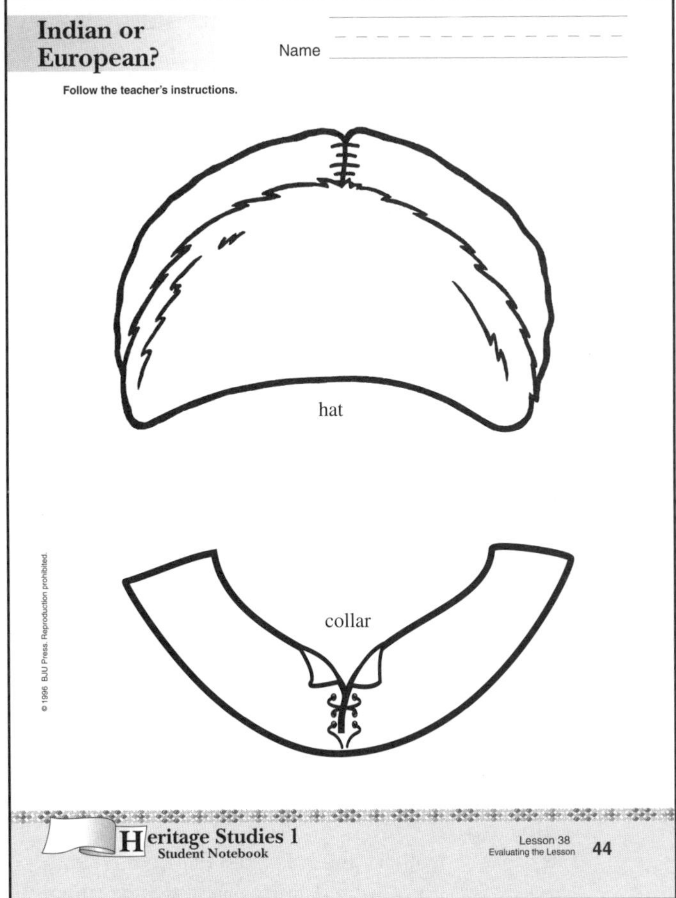

Indian or European?
Name
Follow the teacher's instructions.
hat
collar
© 1996 BJU Press. Reproduction prohibited.
Heritage Studies 1
Student Notebook
Lesson 38
Evaluating the Lesson
44

Evaluating the Lesson

Direct an activity on Notebook pages 43-44. Give your child the poster board, the masks from the Appendix, a ruler, scissors, crayons, and glue.

Activity Instructions

- ➤ Glue both masks onto the poster board and cut them out. Make cutouts for the eyes. *Give help as needed.*
- ➤ Tape the ruler to the back side of one mask.
- ➤ Cover the poster board side of the second mask with glue and press it to the back of the first mask.
- ➤ Color and cut out from Notebook page 44 the items that Pierre Radisson wore when he lived in Three Rivers.
- ➤ Glue these items in the proper places on the one side of the mask.
- ➤ Color, cut out, and glue the Indian items from Notebook page 43 in the proper places on the other side of the mask.

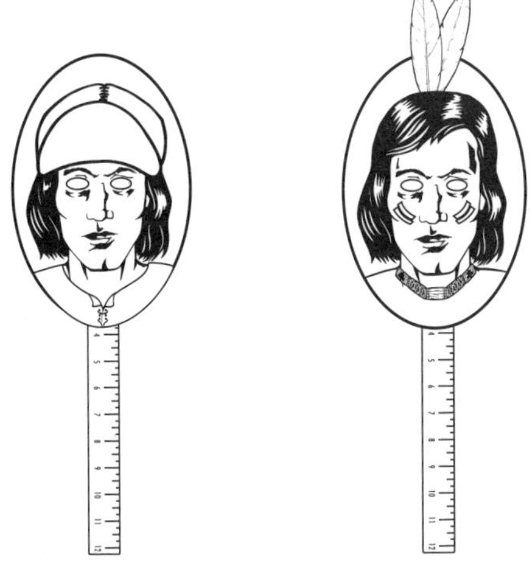

Demonstrate how to hold the mask in front of your face with your eyes showing through the eyeholes in the mask. Direct your child to hold up the mask showing Radisson as a settler; then direct him to turn the mask to show Radisson as an Indian. Tell him that you will read several statements. He is to turn the mask to show Radisson as a settler if the statement refers to that part of his life or to show Radisson as an Indian if the statement refers to that part of his life. Use the following statements.

- Radisson and his friends left Three Rivers to go hunting. *(settler)*
- Radisson's name was changed to Orimha. *(Indian)*
- Radisson was given new clothes, necklaces, a cape, and a hatchet. *(Indian)*
- Radisson lived in a house made of logs. *(settler)*
- Radisson lived in a house made of animal skins. *(Indian)*
- Radisson learned how to live in the wilderness. *(Indian)*

Going Beyond

Enrichment

Plan a pantomime of the story of the adoption of Pierre Radisson. You will need to enlist the help of family or friends. Collect or make props to be used by each character as you reread the story from the lesson. Adapt the following suggestions.

Pierre Radisson: mask from Notebook

Two sisters: washcloth, comb, colorful shirt, bead bracelets

The father: a long bead or paper chain necklace and a hatchet (may be made from construction paper or cardboard)

The brother: feathers and washable felt-tip markers

The mother: corn, folded shirt, colorful cape (piece of cloth or tablecloth), two bead necklaces

A tribal member: drum (may be made from oatmeal box)

Additional Teacher Information

The Iroquois Nation at this time consisted of the Mohawk, Oneida, Onondaga, Cayuga, and Seneca peoples. It was the Mohawks who captured Pierre Radisson and later adopted him into their tribe. His Native American family called him Orimha, meaning "a stone," honoring one of their favored sons who had died. Radisson lived as a member of the Mohawk tribe for two years, learning their language and their customs. His escape came on the morning of October 29, 1653, as he left the Mohawk village with only his hatchet, appearing to go chop wood. He ran all day and on into the evening, not stopping to eat until he saw a Dutch settler working outside his cabin. After a cautious approach, Pierre hid in the settler's house and was helped to get back home safely. He wrote, "I mean not to tell you the great joy I perceived . . . to see those persons that I never thought to see more, and they in like manner . . . thought I was dead long since." Years later when traveling on an expedition, Radisson sent gifts to his Mohawk family—a hatchet for his father, the old chief; two dozen brass rings and two knives for his sisters; and the promise of a blanket for his mother when next he visited their village. Years later Radisson would write, "Friends, I must confesse I loved those poore people entirely well."

For many years thereafter Radisson traveled, explored, and trapped and traded furs along with his brother-in-law, Sire Medard Chouart Groseillers. They provided furs for trading companies in both France and England and set up peace treaties between these trading companies and the Native Americans. Radisson spent his whole life exploring the wilderness. It is said that Radisson was the first white man to explore the West, the Northwest, and the North. His trading brought great wealth to France and England, but Radisson himself lived in poverty.

LESSON 39
Trading

Text, pages 108-9
Notebook, page 45

Preview

Main Ideas
- Traders were looking for goods in the New World.
- The first settlers traded with Indians and with other settlers.
- Sometimes the settlers and the Indians did not want what the other had.

Objectives
- Trade items
- Tell whom the settlers and the Indians traded with
- Name some items that the settlers and the Indians traded with each other

Materials
- 3 or 4 items that your child especially likes (may be food or nonfood)
- 1 or 2 items that your child does not care for

Day 1

Lesson

Introducing the Lesson
Direct a trading activity. Place the items collected on the table. Give your child one of the items he does not care for.

Trading Activity

➤ Are you satisfied with this item? Would you rather have something else on the table? You may trade this item for one of the items on the table.

➤ The Indians had opportunity to trade the goods that they had in abundance. The early trading was done mostly to provide the Indians and settlers with items that helped them survive in the wilderness of the New World; very little trading was done strictly because they were not content with what they had. In this lesson you will learn a little more about trading long ago.

The first settlers traded for things too.
But they did not trade for furs with the Indians.
Mostly they traded with other settlers.
Someone who made lovely cloth could trade
with someone who made sturdy shoes.
Or someone who had extra wood might trade
with someone who had extra food.

The settlers knew that some things were
wanted by many people.
Many people wanted nails, bullets,
and a plant called tobacco.
Things that many people wanted
were worth more.
A settler who had one of
these special things
could trade it for
almost anything.

108

Teaching the Lesson
Direct a text activity on pages 108-9. Direct your child to identify items that the settlers traded with each other as you read page 108.

Text Discussion, page 108

➤ Name the items that the settlers traded with each other. *(cloth, shoes, wood, food, nails, bullets, tobacco)*

➤ Can you think of other items that the settlers might have traded? *(Possible answers include furniture, baskets, and seeds.)*

The settlers decided how much something was worth by looking at how big it was, how heavy it was, or how long it took to make the item.

➤ Do you think these trading methods were fair? (BAT: 4c Honesty)

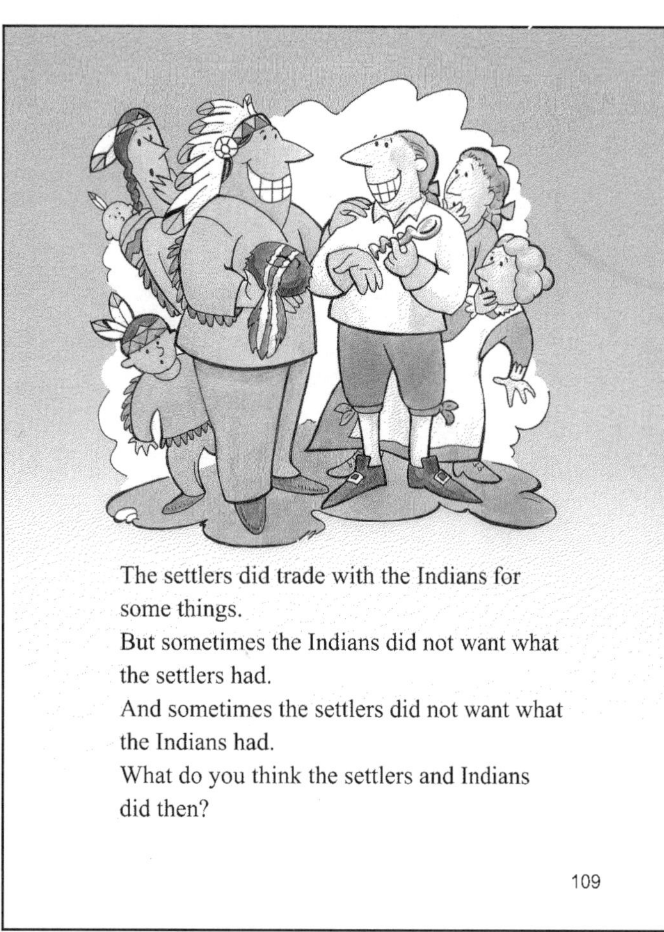

The settlers did trade with the Indians for some things.
But sometimes the Indians did not want what the settlers had.
And sometimes the settlers did not want what the Indians had.
What do you think the settlers and Indians did then?

109

Trading Groups Name ______________

Complete the sentences. *Answers will vary.*

1. Settlers gave ______________ to the ______________ in exchange for ______________.

2. Indians gave ______________ to the ______________ in exchange for ______________.

3. Settlers gave ______________ to the ______________ in exchange for ______________.

Cut out and glue the arrows in the diagram to show trading patterns.

Settlers ⟷ Indians

Settlers ⟷ Indians

Heritage Studies 1 Student Notebook — Lesson 39 Evaluating the Lesson 45

Text Discussion, page 109

- ➤ What items did the settlers want from the Indians? *(furs, jewelry, corn, etc.)*
- ➤ What items did the Indians want from the settlers? *(iron tools, cloth, etc.)*
- ➤ Read page 109 and answer the question.

Usually, the settlers and the Indians went elsewhere to other groups of settlers and Indians, hoping to trade.

- ➤ Look at the cartoon on the page. Tell what you think is happening.

Evaluating the Lesson

Direct an activity on Notebook page 45. Direct your child to cut out the six arrows from the bottom of the page and to glue them in the correct places in the diagram to show which groups of people traded with each other. Then tell him to complete the sentences regarding these trading groups, including items that might have been traded.

Going Beyond

Enrichment

Give your child the trading poem on Appendix page A26. Direct him to fill in each blank with a word that rhymes with the bold word above the blank. Encourage him to illustrate his poem. Post it in a special place.

Additional Teacher Information

The French probably gained more from their trading with the Native Americans than other groups did. The rich furs provided by the Indians were greatly sought after by the European fashion industry. The English traded for furs also, but mostly they wanted the tobacco that the Native Americans grew. The Native Americans traded the riches of their land—animals and plants—for the goods of civilized man. Soon the Native Americans became so accustomed to having these things that they became necessities rather than luxuries. Usually the Indians had no way of knowing the value of the items that they were exchanging with the settlers. Some settlers tried to take advantage of the Indians and cheated greatly in weighing, measuring, and counting.

1-28 a Test

LESSON 40
Wampum

Text, pages 110-12

Preview

Main Ideas

- Many different people and groups have contributed to American culture.
- People work to provide money for goods and services.
- The Indians used their wampum like money.
- Today people use money to trade for things that they want.

Objectives

- Make a wampum necklace
- Answer questions about Indians and wampum

Materials

- Approximately 40 hollow macaroni pieces (Rotini works best.)*
- Red, green, and blue food coloring*
- 4 bowls of water or rubbing alcohol
- Paper towels
- 4 spoons
- Heavy string or yarn, 24" long*

Notes

The actual colors for Indian wampum were purple, black, and white. The text page gives instruction for making red, blue, green, white, and black macaroni beads. Follow the directions in the text or try making purple beads. Assign a value to each of the colors, with black being the most valuable and white the least valuable.

Another way to prepare the macaroni is to use rubbing alcohol and food coloring. Add several drops of food coloring to a quarter-cup of alcohol. Then drop in the macaroni, letting it stand until the macaroni is the desired color. This method makes a brighter color.

Instead of heavy string or yarn, you may want to use elasticized string, available in craft shops specifically for making children's necklaces and bracelets. You may want to tie a large knot in one end or glue a bead on one end of the string to prevent the macaroni from slipping off as the child adds more macaroni beads.

◆ LEARNING HOW ◆

To Make a Wampum Necklace

1. Gather some hollow macaroni pieces, food coloring, a bowl, water, and heavy string or yarn.
2. Fill the bowl with water. Add a few drops of food coloring.
3. Soak the macaroni pieces in the water. (Do not soak the pieces too long or the macaroni will become mushy.) Take the pieces from the water and lay them out to dry.
4. Make a wampum necklace or bracelet by threading the pieces of macaroni on the string. How is your wampum different from the Indians' wampum?

111

Day 1

Lesson

Introducing the Lesson

Direct a *Learning How* activity on text page 111. Explain to your child that he is going to make a necklace similar to an Indian **wampum** necklace.

Learning How Activity

➤ Read and complete step 1.

You will need a total of four bowls and spoons and some paper towels.

➤ Read and complete step 2.

You will want to put a different food coloring in each bowl. To make black, add a few drops of red, blue, and green together. The black beads were rare, so you will want to color just a few of them black.

➤ Read and complete step 3.

Do not soak all the macaroni. Leave some pieces plain to be the white beads. Stir occasionally so that the pieces will color evenly. When the colored beads reach the desired shade, remove them with a spoon. Place them in a single layer on a paper towel to dry.

➤ Allow enough time for the beads to completely dry.
➤ Read and complete step 4.

The Indians had a kind of money with a very long name.
The settlers shortened the name to *wampum.*
They learned to use wampum to get things they wanted.
And they gladly let the Indians trade for things with more wampum.
What do you think the settlers did when they got more wampum from the Indians?

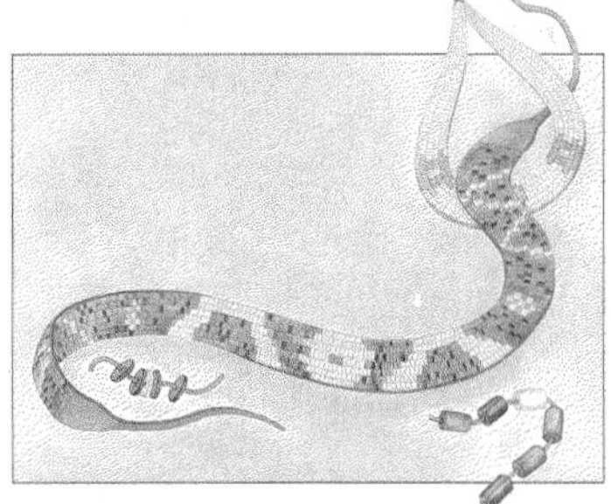

Do you know what the wampum was made from?
The Indians made it from polished seashells.
They cut the shells so that they were all the same size.
Then they put the wampum on strings like beads.
The wampum was purple and black and white.
Which wampum do you think was worth the most? Black was.

110

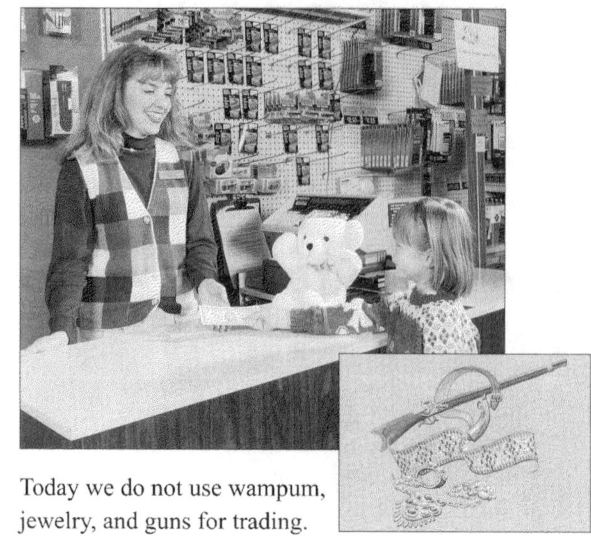

Today we do not use wampum, jewelry, and guns for trading.
But we still trade to get things we want.
What do we use for our trading?
We trade coins and dollar bills for the things we want.
Trading is much easier when everyone uses the same thing.

112

Before you begin to string the beads, plan a pattern. You may select any combination of colors. Use twenty to thirty beads, leaving enough string at both ends to tie.

- To complete the necklace, tie the ends of the string together securely with more than one knot.
- Have fun wearing your new wampum necklace.

Day 2

Teaching the Lesson

Direct a text activity on pages 110 and 112. Ask your child whether he thinks the Indians made their wampum necklaces just for decoration. *(no)*

Text Discussion, page 110

- Read the first section on the page.
- Name some items that the Indians probably "bought" from the settlers with wampum. *(iron tools and utensils, blankets, guns, etc.)*
- Answer the last question from paragraph one. *(Answers will vary.)*
- Read the next section.
- Compare your wampum necklace to a real Indian wampum necklace. *(I have black, white, red, blue, and green beads instead of just the purple, white, and black beads that the Indians had. I made my beads from macaroni instead of real seashells.)*
- Count the number of black beads on your necklace.
- The white beads were worth only half as much as the black ones. Count your white beads and compare them to the number of black beads. Which color do you have more of?
- Do you think your wampum necklace will buy a lot of goods or just a little?

Text Discussion, page 112

- Read the page.
- What might happen if people used many different kinds of things in trading?
- Do you think it would be harder to be fair if everyone was trading with something different? *(probably)*
- Tell about ways you get your own money. *(as a gift, allowance for doing chores, as a reward)*
- Tell about what you do with your money.

God provides everything Christians need and many things that they want. Christians should be thankful for what they have. (BATs: 7c Praise, 7d Contentment)

Evaluating the Lesson

Direct an activity using "wampum." Tell your child that wampum was used as money in trading. It was also used when making an agreement or promise. If the Indian liked the agreement, he would hold out his wampum. If the Indian did not like the agreement, he would drop his wampum belt or necklace to the ground. Tell your child to sit on the floor Indian-style with his legs crossed. Tell him that as you read some statements, he should hold out his wampum necklace in his hand if the answer to the statement is yes. Tell him to place his wampum on the floor next to him if the answer to the statement is no.

- Wampum was made from animals' teeth. *(no)*
- Black wampum beads were the most valuable. *(yes)*
- Indians today still use wampum in trading. *(no)*
- Indians traded wampum for iron tools and copper pots. *(yes)*
- Today we trade coins and paper money for the things that we want. *(yes)*

Going Beyond

Enrichment

Give your child crayons, a pencil, and the wampum questionnaire, Appendix page A27. Guide him as needed to complete the page.

Additional Teacher Information

Wampum is from the Algonquian word *wampompeag,* which means "strings of shell beads." Using only stone knives, the Indians chipped the white beads from conch shells and the black or purple ones from the quahog, a common hard-shelled clam. The black beads were worth twice as much as the white beads. Often Indians spent thirty days making a single bit of shell into a perfect bead. After they carved each bead, they bored tiny holes for threading the beads on leather strings. The designs that were formed using many beads often told a story. Wampum was carried as a string or worn as a belt. It was used as money in trading, as a personal ornament, as a symbol of peace, and as a record of tribal legends and history.

9 LESSONS 41-45

Adventurers

Although this chapter discusses several French and English explorers and their reasons for coming to the New World, it highlights the explorer Robert La Salle and his search for the end of the great Mississippi River. One lesson features King Louis XIV of France, who ordered La Salle to the New World, and describes the king's opulent lifestyle as well as his mistreatment of Christians. In the last lesson, your child learns how places get their names, and he practices making up place names.

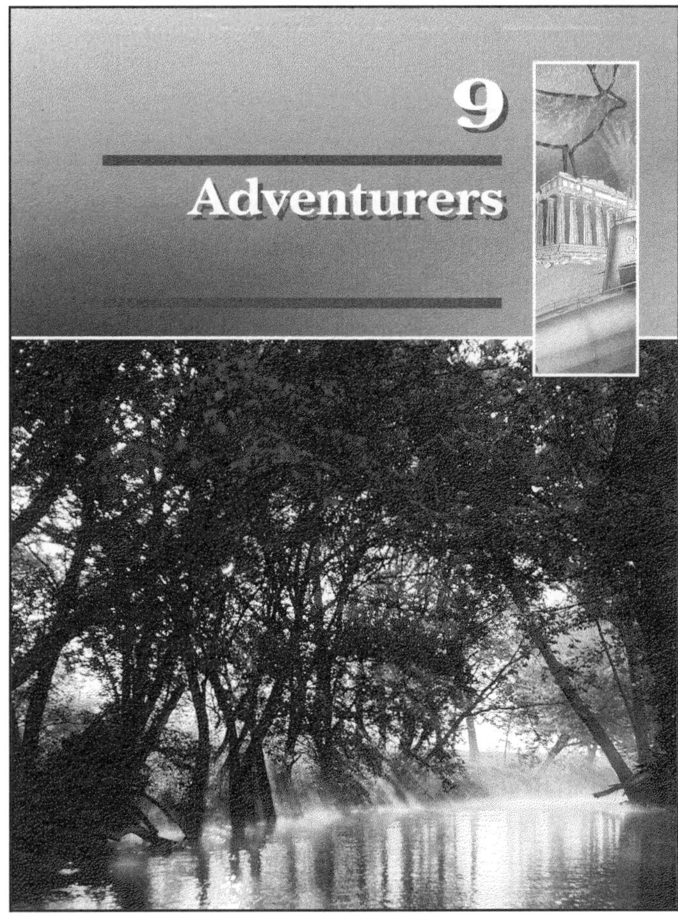

Materials

The following items must be obtained or prepared before the presentation of the lesson. These items are labeled with an asterisk (*) in each lesson and in the Materials List in the Supplement. For further information see the individual lessons.

- Several toys, food items, tools, clothing (Lesson 41)
- Scraps of felt (Lesson 41; optional)
- Small items to hide for a treasure hunt (Lesson 42)
- A chess set (Lesson 43; optional)
- Appendix, page A29 (Lessons 42 and 44)
- Appendix, page A30 (Lesson 44)

LESSON 41
Goods from the New World

Text, pages 114-15
Notebook, page 46

Preview

Main Ideas

- Many explorers were looking for goods in the New World.
- Some New World goods were more popular than others with people in the Old World.

Objectives

- Classify goods sent from the New World to the Old World
- Identify the goods most popular with the people in the Old World

Materials

- Several toys*
- Several tools*
- Several items of clothing*
- Several food items*
- Scraps of felt (optional)*

Notes

In preparation for Lesson 45, contact your city's visitors' center or chamber of commerce for information about anything that makes your town or city unusual or special.

Day 1

Lesson

Introducing the Lesson

Conduct a demonstration. Group the items collected by categories.

Demonstration Discussion

- ➤ *Point to the toys.* What could you call all these things? *(toys)*
- ➤ *Point to the tools.* What could you call this group of things? *(tools)*
- ➤ *Point to the clothes.* What could you call all these things? *(clothes)*
- ➤ *Point to the food.* What could you call this group of things? *(food)*

People in the Old World liked the goods that came from the New World.
They liked the gold, the new kinds of food, and the tobacco.

They especially liked the beautiful furs of beavers and foxes.
What do you think they used the furs for?
People wanted the furs to make clothes.

114

- ➤ Where can you buy food, toys, tools, and clothes? *(store)* We call all things that can be sold at the store **goods.**
- ➤ Is there anything in these groups of items that you especially like?
- ➤ Some of the items that were part of the New World were in great demand by the people of the Old World. Today we are going to talk about some of these items.

Teaching the Lesson

Direct a text activity on pages 114-15. Read page 114. Tell your child to find out what goods the people in the Old World liked. *(gold, food, tobacco, furs)*

Text Discussion, page 114

- ➤ How do you think people in the Old World would use gold? *(Possible answers include to make jewelry and to use as money.)*
- ➤ How do you think they would use furs? *(Possible answers include for trimming or making clothes.)*
- ➤ How do you think they would use tobacco? *(A possible answer is for smoking.)*

Even long ago some people realized that tobacco was bad for a person. King James I of England called tobacco a "stinking weed . . . harmfull to the braine, dangerous to the Lungs." (BAT: 3d Body as a temple)

- ➤ Look at the pictures of the costumed people on page 114. (*NOTE:* The clothing is that of the French nobility, 1650-1700. Women's and men's cloaks were lined and trimmed with fur. Muffs for both men and women were made of fabric—velvet, satin, silk, and cotton—and fur—fox, squirrel, rabbit, and bear. Hats were also of fur.)
- ➤ Are these people from the Old World or New World? *(the Old World)*
- ➤ What makes you think these people are from the Old World? *(Their clothes are fancy, not like the clothes of the settlers in the New World.)*
- ➤ Which parts of the clothing do you think are made from fur?

The man's muff and the linings of the women's capes are made from fur. Although they do not look "furry," the men's hats were made of fur too. The best hats were made of beaver. The fur was shaved from the beaver skins (pelts), matted together, and boiled in acid. It was then beaten and cut to size to make a fabric called felt.

> You may want to tell your child that felt today is made of compressed animal fibers, like wool or fur, often mixed with synthetic fibers. If you have scraps of felt, let him see and feel them.

Day 2

Text Discussion, page 115

- ➤ Look at the explorer on the time line. Is he dressed the same way as the people on page 114 are dressed? *(no)*
- ➤ How is the explorer's fur hat different from the felt hats of the people pictured on page 114? *(The explorer's hat has no trim. The hats of the people from the Old World were larger and made from felt and trimmed with braid and feathers.)*
- ➤ Why were rivers important to an explorer?

A person could travel more easily by canoe or boat on a river than by foot through the thick forests. Explorers spent much of their time, day and night, outdoors, even in the winter. As they traveled, they had to prepare their meals outdoors, often catching fish in the river or trapping animals and cooking the meat over a fire. They also slept outdoors on the ground.

- ➤ Would you have liked to be an explorer?
- ➤ Read the first section on page 115. Where did the explorers go? *(into the forests and down big rivers)*
- ➤ What were the explorers looking for? *(furs and other goods)*

> You will want to review briefly what was learned about the fur trade in Chapter 8.

France and England sent men to explore more
of the New World.
These men went to find more furs
and other goods.
They went into the forests.
They went down big rivers.
They met many different Indian people.

Did these explorers travel before or after
Columbus made his trip?
Was Jamestown already built?

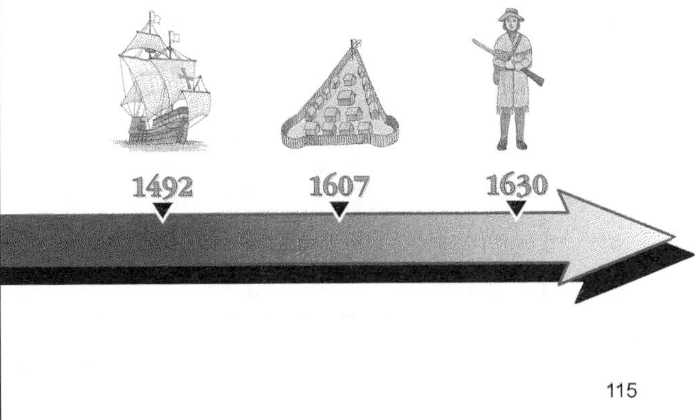

115

- ➤ Read the last section. Use the time line to answer the questions.

Evaluating the Lesson

Direct a classification activity on Notebook page 46. Discuss with your child the goods pictured at the bottom of Notebook page 46 and read the name of each one.

Classification Activity

- ➤ Cut out the picture squares. These goods were sent from the New World to the Old World.
- ➤ Put these pictures into groups. Which of these goods are foods? *(corn, pumpkin, pineapple, tomato, squash, beans)* Glue these on the squares on the first arrow.
- ➤ Into what two groups can we put the remaining pictures of goods? *(skins and flowers)*
- ➤ Glue the four skins onto the squares on the second arrow and the four flowers onto the squares on the third arrow.
- ➤ Draw a line around the goods that the people in the Old World liked best. *(the skins; your child may mark only the beaver and the fox skins)*

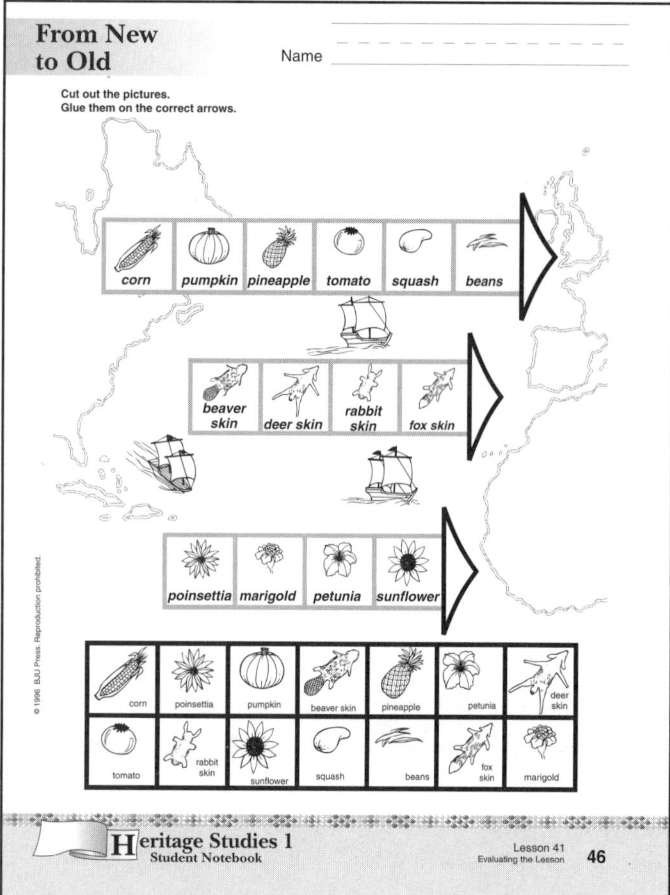

Going Beyond

Enrichment

Obtain a variety of hats, women's and men's. Encourage your child to try on the hats and then talk about who would wear each hat and when it would be worn.

Additional Teacher Information

Among the products that were sent from the Old World to the New World were coffee, wheat, rice, barley, cabbages, turnips, lettuce, peaches, pears, lemons, oranges, bananas, and olives. Gladioli, lilacs, carnations, daffodils, tulips, and daisies also crossed the Atlantic, as did pesky dandelions and crabgrass. Today's razorbacks in the Arkansas Ozarks and piney wood rooters in Georgia's Okefenokee Swamp descend from the swine brought to Florida in 1539 by Hernando de Soto.

Not everything that traveled with the explorers was entirely welcomed on this side of the ocean. Some Old World animals—horses, cows, sheep, and chickens—are accused of carrying smallpox and typhus to the New World. Diseases such as measles and diphtheria, labeled childhood illnesses in Europe, became mass killers once they took hold on the New World continent.

2-2

LESSON 42

Young Robert La Salle

Text, pages 116-18
Notebook, page 47

Preview

Main Ideas

- Explorers took stories of the New World back to the Old World.
- La Salle's goal was adventure.

Objectives

- Complete autobiographical statements
- Draw a picture of what the child would like to be when he grows up

Materials

- A small paper bag or other container
- Small items to hide for a treasure hunt (stickers, pencils, packages of raisins, and so on)—enough for your child to find 3 or 4, as well as 1 of each item for you to show*

Prepare the treasure hunt area—in the house or outdoors—by hiding the small items. Set aside one of each item to show to your child.

- Appendix, page A29: Mississippi River Map*

Day 1

Lesson

Introducing the Lesson

Direct a treasure hunt. Explain to your child that around the room (or outdoors, as the case may be) there are some "treasures" for him to find. Show him a sample of each item that you have hidden. Allow him time to hunt for the treasures and put them in his bag.

Tell him that to most people a **hunt** is a search for things like the treasures he just found. Ask him to name some of those goods that the explorers found. *(gold, food, tobacco, furs—some may name flowers also)* Tell your child that in this lesson he will learn about a young explorer who dreamed of finding something that was not "goods."

The explorers came back to France and England.
They told about their adventures
in the New World.
They told of trees so big that five men could not reach around them.
They told about snow so deep that it could cover houses.
They said hunting was easy because birds and animals were everywhere.

One French boy named Robert La Salle listened to stories about the big forests and the strange animals called buffaloes and moose.
He listened to tales about a river so huge that it looked like an ocean.
The river was called *Mississippi.*
The name came from two Indian words meaning "Big River."

116

La Salle had always wanted to go on an adventure.
In school he had dreamed of sailing to America.
La Salle's brother was already in the New World.
He was a Catholic priest.

When La Salle grew up, he did not want to buy and sell goods.
La Salle did not want to be a priest.
He did not want any gold.
He did not want to be a fur trader.
What do you think he wanted?

117

Teaching the Lesson

Direct a text activity on pages 116-18. Instruct your child to listen for what the explorers told about as you read the first section of page 116. *(big trees, deep snow, easy hunting)*

Text Discussion, page 116

- Do you think the explorers were telling the truth about the size of the trees, the depth of the snow, and the ease of the hunting?

  The explorers may indeed have been exaggerating, but all those facts are true in certain places and at certain times.

- Read the rest of the page. Put your finger on the name Robert La Salle (lə săl′). Listen while I pronounce the name and then pronounce it after me.
- Young La Salle may have been very curious about the Mississippi River because he was used to seeing much smaller rivers like the Seine (sĕn or sān), which flowed through his home city in France. La Salle could hardly imagine a river so wide and so long that it looked like an ocean! (*NOTE:* The Seine is 480 miles long; the Mississippi, 2,350 miles long. At some points, the Mississippi is a mile wide.)
- What does **Mississippi** mean? *(Big River)*
- Did the Indians choose a good name for this amazing river? *(yes, because it is such a big, long river)*
- Would you have liked to listen to the explorers' stories?

Day 2

Text Discussion, page 117

- Read page 117 to find out where Robert La Salle wanted to go. *(on an adventure)*
- What is an adventure? *(Answers will vary.)* An adventure is an unusual or exciting experience.
- Have you ever had an adventure?
- Why do you think La Salle wanted to go on an adventure?
- Do you think the explorers' stories made La Salle want to go on an adventure?

  Although young Robert liked to dream about adventure, he was also an excellent student who studied hard and was an example to the other students because of his good behavior. (BATs: 2c Faithfulness, 2e Work)

- Do you think that La Salle's brother living in America helped to encourage La Salle's desire for adventure? His brother Jean (John) lived in Montreal, in what was called New France.
- What are some things that La Salle did not want? *(gold, to be a fur trader, to buy or sell goods, or to be a priest)*

La Salle wanted to see parts of the New World that no white man had ever seen.
He wanted to be the first to find where the Mississippi River ended.

King Louis wanted everyone to know he was a powerful king.
The king told La Salle to take men and ships to the New World.
He told La Salle that any land he saw first would belong to France.
He ordered La Salle to build forts on the new lands.

118

La Salle and Me Name ______________

Read the sentences about Robert La Salle. Then complete each sentence about yourself.

1. Robert's home was in a city named Rouen.
   My home is in ______________ *Answers will vary.*.

2. Robert's best subject in school was math.
   My best subject is ______________ *Answers will vary.*.

3. Robert wanted to be an adventurer.
   I want to be ______________ *Answers will vary.*.

Draw a picture of what you want to be.

Heritage Studies 1 Student Notebook — Lesson 42 Evaluating the Lesson 47

Text Discussion, page 118

➤ Read the two sentences at the top of page 118. What did Robert La Salle want to do? *(to see parts of the New World that no white man had ever seen; to be the first to find where the Mississippi River ended)*

➤ Do you think La Salle got what he wanted?

The remainder of page 118 will be read and discussed in Lesson 43.

Direct a map activity. Show your child the Mississippi River on the Mississippi River Map. Point out the *X* that shows the Mississippi River's beginning near Lake Itasca, Minnesota. Tell your child to trace the river from the *X* to the mouth at the Gulf of Mexico using a blue crayon. At the time that Robert La Salle heard about the great river, no man had traveled its whole length. According to reports from Indians, no one knew whether the river flowed north to south or turned and flowed west at some point.

Save this map to use again in Lesson 44.

Evaluating the Lesson

Direct an activity on Notebook page 47. Read the statements about Robert La Salle and the sentence starters. Help your child to finish each sentence. Direct him to draw a picture about what he wants to be when he grows up.

Going Beyond

Enrichment

You may want to visit a library to find children's books about different careers.

Additional Teacher Information

A whole generation of French explorers thrilled to the possibilities of the Mississippi River's being a long-sought waterway. They had already discovered the great lakes that lay to the southwest of the Saint Lawrence. If there was a link between those lakes and the Mississippi, the French would have within their grasp the Northwest Passage to Asia and, thereby, great wealth. Even if the Mississippi flowed south rather than west, France would have water access to trade with Mexico.

Lesson 43
The Sun King

Text, pages 118-20
Notebook, page 48

Preview

Main Ideas

- Louis XIV was a proud king.
- King Louis XIV made life difficult for Christians in France.

Objective

- Complete a sentence telling one thing about King Louis XIV

Materials

- A chess set (optional)*
- A sheet of paper

Notes

If your child is interested in learning more about the game of chess, you may want to refer to the book *Chess for Children Step by Step,* by International Grandmaster William Lombardy and Bette Marshall, published in 1977 by Little, Brown and Company.

Day 1

Lesson

Introducing the Lesson

Direct a discussion. Discuss with your child his procedures for getting up in the morning. Use questions such as the following:

- Do I wake you up or do you get up on your own?
- What time do you get up?
- How long does it take you to get ready to start the day?

Explain that you need his help as you read to him about how a certain king of France started his day. Tell your child that he is to be the king's servant, or **valet,** who answers the royal door of the royal bedchamber. Tell him that each time you put your finger to your lips he is to whisper "Shhh, His Majesty is sleeping." Read the following story to your child.

> Bong, bong, bong, bong, bong, bong, bong rings the royal clock in the hall outside the royal bedchamber. The valet opens the door for the Royal Fire-Bearers.
>
> *"Shhhh, His Majesty is sleeping."*
>
> The fire-bearers tiptoe into the golden room and light the fire in the royal fireplace.
>
> The valet opens the door for the Royal Watchmaker.
>
> *"Shhhh, His Majesty is sleeping."*
>
> The watchmaker tiptoes into the great golden room and winds the royal clock.
>
> The valet opens the door for the Royal Wigmaker.
>
> *"Shhhh, His Majesty is sleeping."*
>
> The wigmaker tiptoes into the great, glittering, golden room carrying the king's royal wigs.
>
> Bong, bong, bong, bong, bong, bong, bong, bong rings the royal clock in the hall outside the royal bedchamber.
>
> The valet tiptoes to the royal bedside. "Sire, it is time," he whispers into the king's royal ear.
>
> In the next room, the royal family and the royal courtiers hear the news. King Louis XIV is officially awake!

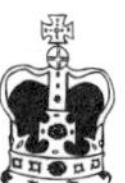

If you are teaching a second child, you may want to allow the second child to say the bongs for the clock.

Story Discussion

➤ You have just helped tell what really happened over and over, day after day, in the life of King Louis (lo͞o´ ē) XIV.

This was the first part of what was called the king's **lever** (lə vā′), or getting-up ritual, a ceremony that took two hours. The lever involved many servants and **courtiers.** The courtiers were rich men called French noblemen who lived at Versailles (vər sī′), the king's spectacular palace in the country.

➤ Why do you think the noblemen lived at the king's palace?

These men stayed near the king, performing even the simplest tasks and attending every formal event in order to win his favor. Much of a courtier's time was spent in simply watching the king as he got ready for the day, ate, played billiards, or got ready for bed. Whenever King Louis prayed in his chapel, strolled in his vast gardens, listened to a concert or a play, he expected all the courtiers to accompany him. Knowing where everyone was at all times made the king feel powerful and in complete control of his country.

➤ Do you think you would like to be King Louis XIV for a day?

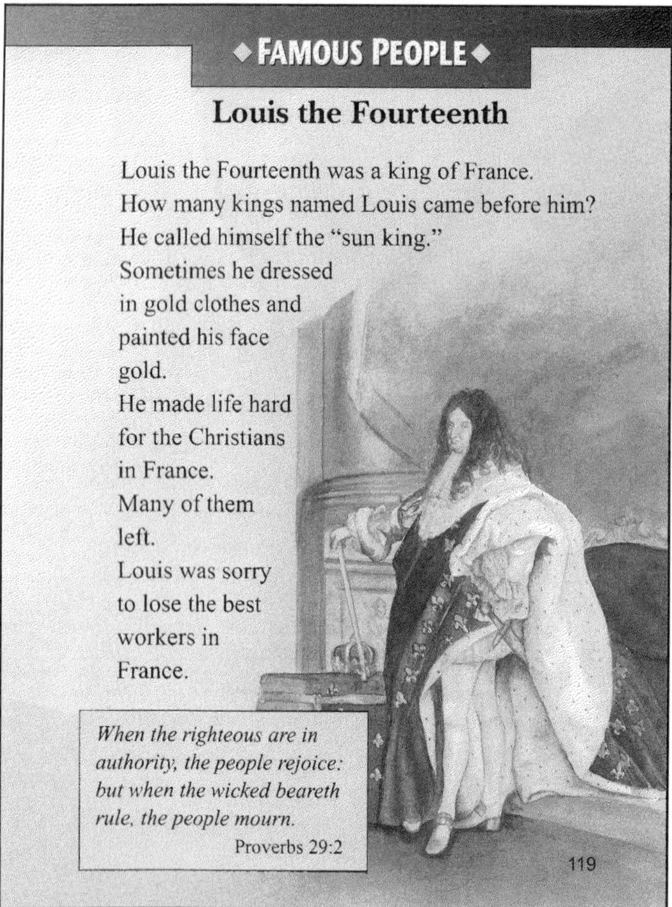

◆ FAMOUS PEOPLE ◆

Louis the Fourteenth

Louis the Fourteenth was a king of France.
How many kings named Louis came before him?
He called himself the "sun king."
Sometimes he dressed in gold clothes and painted his face gold.
He made life hard for the Christians in France.
Many of them left.
Louis was sorry to lose the best workers in France.

When the righteous are in authority, the people rejoice: but when the wicked beareth rule, the people mourn.
Proverbs 29:2

119

◆ THINGS PEOPLE DO ◆

Playing Chess

Most people play chess on a game board similar to a checker board. King Louis the Fourteenth played on a much bigger one. His chess board was a whole lawn.
His chess pieces were real people and horses.

Day 2

Teaching the Lesson

Direct a text activity on pages 118-20. Tell your child to listen for the nickname that King Louis gave to himself as you read page 119. *(the Sun King)*

Text Discussion, page 119

➤ Why was the king sorry that many Christians left France? *(He hated to lose the best workers.)*

For eighty-seven years the French Protestants (Huguenots) had had equal rights with the Roman Catholics as citizens and in freedom to worship God. Then, forty-two years after Louis XIV became king, he took that freedom away. Thousands of Christians, many of them the best-educated citizens, left France. Some of the lands where the Huguenots settled were enemies of France, and those countries welcomed the people who fled King Louis's persecution.

➤ Would you have liked to live in France when King Louis XIV was king?

Read Proverbs 29:2 on page 119. The verse means that when a good man rules, the people are glad but when a bad man rules, the people are sad.

➤ Was Louis XIV a good king or a bad king?
➤ Look at the picture of King Louis. Describe the king.

Some who write about Louis XIV say that his wigs were the curliest, his robes the richest, his jewels the rarest, and his shoes the fanciest in all of France.

➤ What do you remember about the clothes that the wealthy people in the Old World wore? *(They were fancy, often trimmed with gold or trimmed and lined with fur.)*
➤ Look at the design on King Louis's robe and on the stool beside him. What does it look like? *(a flower)*

This design is called a **fleur-de-lis** (flûr′də lēs′), which means "flower of the lily." In 1376, Charles V chose the symbol for his coat of arms. Since then, the fleur-de-lis has been the symbol of French royalty. Whenever the fleur-de-lis appeared on any of the king's clothing or flags or furniture, it was made of pure gold. Also made of gold were his jewelry and the buckles on his shoes, which were set with diamonds.

You may want to refer to Maps and More 14 to remind your child what a coat of arms is.

La Salle wanted to see parts of the New World that no white man had ever seen.
He wanted to be the first to find where the Mississippi River ended.

King Louis wanted everyone to know he was a powerful king.
The king told La Salle to take men and ships to the New World.
He told La Salle that any land he saw first would belong to France.
He ordered La Salle to build forts on the new lands.

118

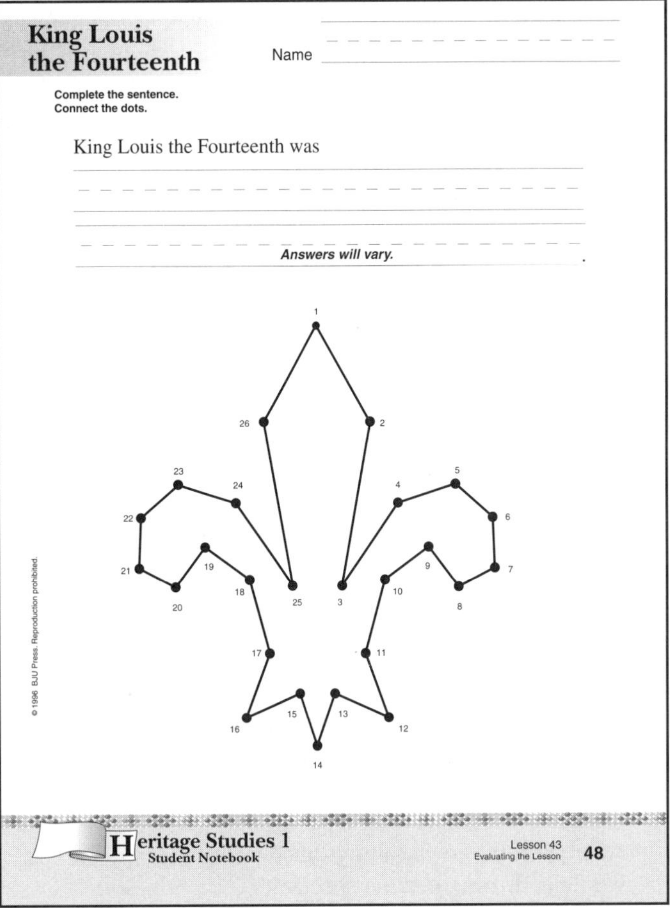

King Louis the Fourteenth Name ______________

Complete the sentence.
Connect the dots.

King Louis the Fourteenth was ______________________________

Answers will vary.

Heritage Studies 1 Student Notebook — Lesson 43 Evaluating the Lesson — 48

Text Discussion, page 120

➤ Look at the chess set (if available). Do you know anything about how this game is played?

Although the game of chess has been played around the world for many years, it was Benjamin Franklin who made it popular in the United States.

➤ Read page 120. Look at the picture. What is different about the way most people play chess and the way the king played? *(The king played, not with figures, but with real people and real horses.)*

➤ Do you think the king showed love and respect for his people by making them be chess pieces? *(no)*

When the king played chess on this outdoor chessboard, the servants and horses who were the game pieces had to stand in the hot sun for hours, waiting to be told where to move. They were treated like toys.

> When a person, even a king, does not love God, he often does not love others either. A person who loves God should show love to others by what he does and says. (BATs: 3c Emotional control, 5a Love, 5d Communication)

Day 3

Text Discussion, page 118

➤ Read the second section of page 118.

➤ What things did King Louis XIV tell Robert La Salle to do? *(to take men and ships to the New World; to claim for France any land that he saw first; to build forts on the new land)*

➤ Why did the king tell the explorer to build forts? *(Answers will vary.)* The forts were built to protect the land from Indians and explorers from other countries who might try to take the new land away from the French.

Evaluating the Lesson

Direct a writing activity on Notebook page 48.

Notebook Activity

➤ *Write* King Louis XIV *in the center of a sheet of paper and circle it. Write* fleur-de-lis *to one side.*

➤ Name words and phrases that tell something about King Louis. *Write the words your child gives you around the circled name. (Answers might be as follows: Sun King, powerful, gold, fur, food, chess, servants, courtiers, royal, valet, wigs, jewelry, diamonds, mean to Christians, selfish, fancy shoes, lever, Versailles, palace.)*

➤ Look at the Notebook page. Complete the sentence to tell one thing that you have learned about King Louis XIV. You may use any of the words from the paper.
➤ Complete and color the dot-to-dot drawing of the fleur-de-lis.

Going Beyond

Enrichment

Make a copy of the dot-to-dot crown page in the Appendix, page A28. Let your child decorate his completed crown drawing. You may want him to memorize Proverbs 20:28. It is a promise to a good and faithful king.

Additional Teacher Information

Of all the events of King Louis's day, his meals were perhaps the most spectacular. The dinner, or *Petit Couvert,* was served at one o'clock in the afternoon, and the supper, or *Grand Couvert,* took place after ten o'clock at night. Although some of the dinner meals were termed "private," Louis was never alone when he dined. Servants and guests always stood by, watching and waiting to cater to the king's every whim. During a "public" dinner, visitors at the palace would parade past the king as he ate. At supper, the royal family dined with the king, and the whole court watched the spectacle.

Five hundred servants were involved in the preparation and serving of each meal. Before any dish left the kitchen, it was tasted by two men to make sure that it was "fit for the king." Then the dishes, covered with elaborate golden lids, were carried single file down the long corridors that led from the kitchens to the king's apartments. Anyone standing in the halls as the dishes passed by had to bow to the king's food. The dinner menu often included many soups, meats, salads, pastries, and fruit. For supper, as many as forty different dishes were brought to the royal table.

After King Louis's death, the autopsy revealed that His Majesty's royal stomach was twice the size of an average man's stomach, a fact that did not surprise anyone who had seen or heard of the eating habits of the monarch.

The preceding information was taken from *The King's Day* by Aliki, published in 1989 by Thomas Y. Crowell. Although it depicts (on a double-page spread) the king's mistresses and the children they bore him, the book gives an excellent description—in word and picture—of King Louis XIV.

LESSON 44
La Salle's Dream Come True

Text, pages 121-23
Notebook, page 49

Preview

Main Ideas

- Indians helped La Salle and his men.
- La Salle found the end of the Mississippi River.

Objective

- Identify as true or false statements about La Salle's journey down the Mississippi

Materials

- Maps and More 30, page M15
- Appendix, page A29: Mississippi River Map (used in Lesson 42)*
- Appendix, page A30: Indian sign language and canoes*
- The figure of La Salle (1682) from the History TimeLine Packet

You may want to allow your child to lightly color the canoes needed in the map activity before they are cut out. This will make them easier to see on the map. Because they are small, you may prefer to cut out the canoes yourself. The Indian sign language chart found on the same page as the canoes may be used in the Enrichment section of this lesson.

Day 1

Lesson

Introducing the Lesson

Conduct a review. Discuss with your child some of the ways that the new settlers had contact with the Indians in the New World.

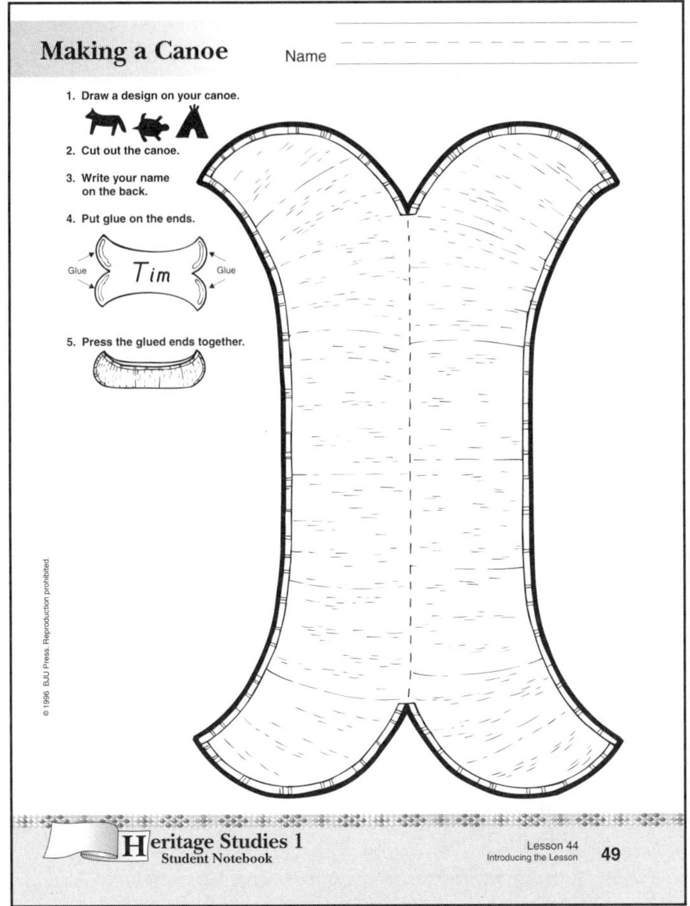
Making a Canoe Name

1. Draw a design on your canoe.
2. Cut out the canoe.
3. Write your name on the back.
4. Put glue on the ends.

Glue Tim Glue

5. Press the glued ends together.

Heritage Studies 1 Student Notebook — Lesson 44 Introducing the Lesson 49

La Salle and his men traveled into
the New World.
They canoed down streams and rivers.
The winter snows came, and the food ran out.
Some men wanted to go back.
La Salle refused to give up.
What do you think he did?

He asked the Indians for help.
The Illinois Indians fed La Salle and his men.
La Salle gave the Illinois Indians axes and
knives in return.
He learned to speak different Indian
languages well.
He always kept his promises with everyone.

121

Review Discussion

➤ Who helped the early settlers in both Jamestown and Plymouth? *(Indians helped in both cases; your child may mention Squanto by name.)*

➤ How did the Indians help the white men? *(They gave the settlers food and taught them how to plant crops and to fish.)*

➤ Were the settlers grateful to the Indians? *(Yes, the settlers in Plymouth invited the Indians to their feast of thanksgiving to God.)*

Explain a procedure. Tell your child that the explorers of the Mississippi River were also grateful to the Indians. Men like Robert La Salle, who depended on traveling along rivers, learned from Indians how to make the canoes in which they traveled. Point to the appropriate drawing on Maps and More 30 as you relate the following procedure:

1. The young Sauks (săk) cut down a tall birch tree with stone axes. (*NOTE*: The Sauk were Indians that lived in Illinois.)
2. Then they slowly and carefully peeled the bark off with wooden wedges.
3. Next they made a strong frame of wood.
4. They sewed the bark onto the frame with roots.
5. They filled any cracks with pitch, or sap, from pine trees.
6. Finally, they decorated the canoe with porcupine quills or paint.

Ask your child how long he thinks it would take to make a canoe. *(at least a week)* Tell him that he is going to make a canoe, but his will take much less time to make.

Direct an art activity on Notebook page 49. Follow the instructions on the Notebook page for making the canoe. Help your child as needed.

Teaching the Lesson

Direct a text activity on page 121. Read the first section of page 121.

Text Discussion, page 121

➤ What problems did La Salle and his men face as they traveled? *(It snowed, and the food ran out.)*

➤ What would you have done if you were La Salle?

➤ Read the second section of the page to find out what La Salle did. *(asked the Indians for help)* What did the Indians do to help La Salle? *(fed La Salle and his men)*

➤ How did the axes and knives help the Indians to make canoes? *(Answers will vary.)* Indians had used stone axes to cut down trees and wooden wedges to strip off the bark. Probably the white man's metal axes and knives were sharper and lasted longer.

➤ What did La Salle learn? *(to speak different Indian languages)* He mastered Iroquois and could speak seven or eight other Indian languages.

The Indians trusted La Salle.
They told him how to find the Mississippi River.
La Salle and a few men went down the big river in canoes.
At last they came to the end.
La Salle found what he was looking for.

122

➤ La Salle also kept his promises to everyone. Is keeping a promise important? Christians should always keep promises and be honest. (BATs: 2c Faithfulness, 4c Honesty)

Text Discussion, page 122

➤ Read page 122 to find out another way that the Indians helped La Salle. *(They told him how to find the Mississippi River.)*

➤ What was La Salle looking for? *(the end of the Mississippi River)* Did he find it? *(yes)*

➤ Look at the picture. What do you think is happening? It represents La Salle and his party claiming the area or territory along the banks of the Mississippi for France.

➤ Look at the flag. What is on it? *(the fleur-de-lis)*

➤ Whose flag do you think it is? *(the flag of King Louis XIV or the flag of France)*

Day 2

Direct a map activity. Tell your child that you will guide him in using his canoes to follow La Salle's route south on the Mississippi River.

Map Activity

➤ Find Lake Huron, Lake Erie, and Lake Michigan on the Mississippi River Map. *Give your child help as needed.* Color the lakes blue.

At first La Salle planned to build a large ship to travel down the Mississippi. He had built a big ship before to sail on the lakes. La Salle decided instead to use the lightweight, sturdy birch-bark canoes that the Indians had taught him to make. Canoes would take much less time to build, and they could be lifted out of the river and **portaged,** or carried, along the shore if the river were blocked at some point.

➤ On February 13, 1682, La Salle and his men launched their canoes at the mouth of the Illinois River, where it meets the Mississippi River.

➤ Point to the spot where the Illinois River joins the Mississippi River. Do you know what the **mouth** of a river is? The mouth of a river is the place where it empties into a larger river, a bay, or an ocean.

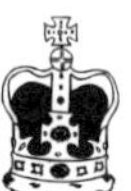

During the map discussion, encourage your child to use the compass rose to help in identifying compass directions. Help your child to place the canoes on the map so that they will not cover the names of the rivers.

➤ Find the canoe that says *February 13, 1682,* and glue it at the place where the Illinois and the Mississippi Rivers join.

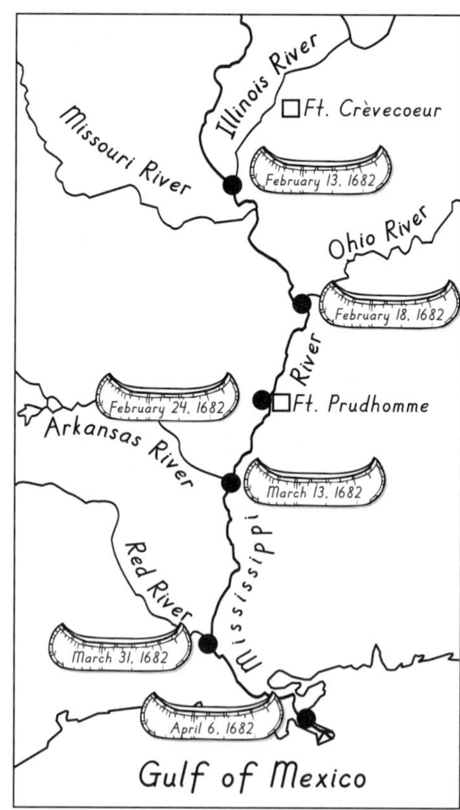

➤ In the evening of that same day, the canoes passed the mouth of the Missouri River. Find the Missouri River. At that place the Mississippi River becomes nearly twice as wide.

➤ A few days later, on February 18, La Salle's party (or group) passed another large river. Which river do you think it was? *(the Ohio River)*

➤ Is the Ohio River north or south of the Missouri River? *(south)*

➤ Glue the canoe that says *February 18, 1682,* where the Ohio River meets the Mississippi River.

La Salle knew that soon he would be traveling beyond where any other Frenchmen had gone on the great river. For a few days, the party did not see anyone along the banks. Then about halfway between the Ohio River and the Arkansas River, La Salle ordered the party to pull the canoes ashore and make camp. It was February 24. The Indians left the rest of the party to search for food, and the Frenchmen built a small fort, which they named Fort Prudhomme after one of the men in the group.

➤ Glue the canoe that says *February 24, 1682,* at Fort Prudhomme.

Up to this point in their trip, La Salle's party had been traveling during extremely cold weather. Now spring was coming. The waters of the river moved smoothly along, making paddling easier. On March 13, one month after they had begun their trip, the explorers drew near the mouth of the Arkansas River.

➤ Attach the canoe that says *March 13, 1682,* at the mouth of the Arkansas River.

At that place, La Salle's party went ashore at the village of some friendly Quapaw (kwô pô) Indians and held a ceremony. La Salle set up a large wooden cross with the coat of arms of King Louis XIV of France. He made a speech in French, saying that all the land he stood on belonged to France. The Quapaw Indians smiled and nodded. They did not understand a word of what was said about the land they thought was their own. After three days, La Salle and his party left the village and paddled on down the river. They stopped along the way, visited with other friendly Indians, and held ceremonies saying the land belonged to France, as King Louis had instructed La Salle.

➤ On March 31, 1682, the explorers paddled by the mouth of the last big river that flowed into the Mississippi. Which river do you think this was? *(the Red River)* Glue the canoe that says *March 31, 1682,* at the point where the Red River and the Mississippi River meet.

➤ Six days later, on April 6, 1682, La Salle and his party reached a place where the Mississippi River divided into three wide parts.

➤ Glue the last canoe at the mouth of the Mississippi River. As La Salle continued down the river, he realized that he had finally found what he was looking for: the end of the great Mississippi River.

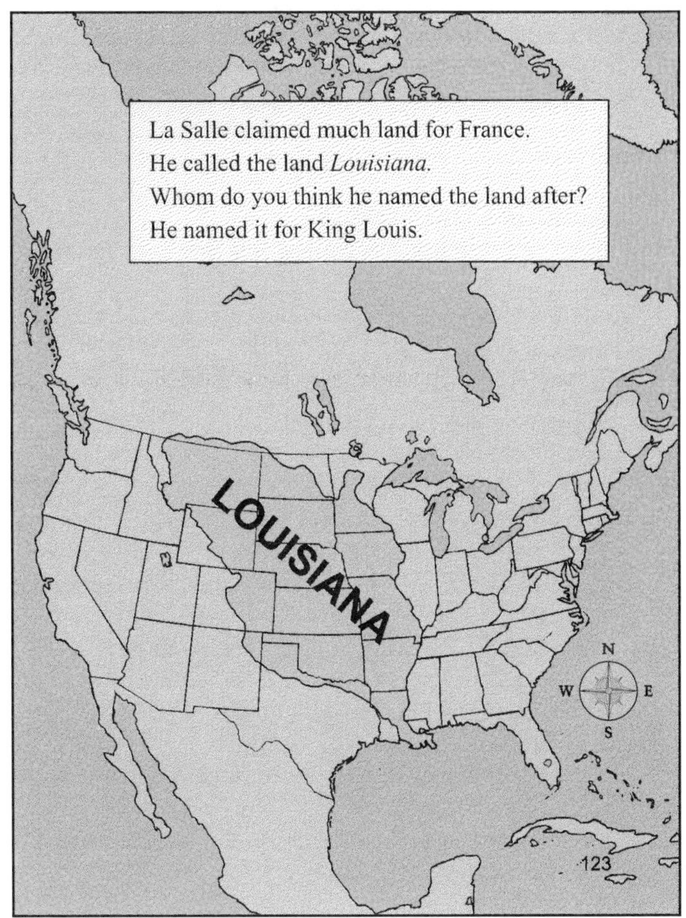

La Salle claimed much land for France.
He called the land *Louisiana.*
Whom do you think he named the land after?
He named it for King Louis.
LOUISIANA
N
W
E
S
123

Day 3

Text Discussion, page 123

➤ Listen for the name that La Salle gave to the land he claimed for France as I read page 123. *(Louisiana)*

➤ Can you find the name *Louis* in the name of the territory on the map? Point to the name.

The land included in La Salle's "Louisiana" today includes all or parts of the states of Arkansas, Missouri, Iowa, Minnesota, North Dakota, South Dakota, Nebraska, Oklahoma, Kansas, Montana, Wyoming, Colorado, and Louisiana.

➤ *Show the state of Louisiana on the map.*

You may want to refer to the map on pages 180-81 of the text to identify Louisiana.

On April 9, 1682, La Salle and his men held a final ceremony on the banks of the Mississippi. They fired their guns into the air and shouted, "Long live the king!" Then La Salle made a grand speech in which he said that France owned all the land he had traveled through and, as the map shows, much more.

Add a figure to the History TimeLine. Tell your child that when La Salle reached the end of the great river, it was the first time a European explorer had traveled the river from the north to its end in the south. Place the La Salle figure at 1682 on the TimeLine.

Evaluating the Lesson

Conduct a true-false oral review. Tell your child that you are going to make some statements about La Salle's trip down the Mississippi. If the statement is true, he should make a motion as if he were paddling his canoe. If the statement is false, he should put his paddle in his lap.

- La Salle and his party used canoes to travel down the river. *(true)*
- They ran out of food. *(true)*
- La Salle gave up and went home. *(false)*
- La Salle asked other French settlers for help. *(false)*
- La Salle spoke many different Indian languages. *(true)*
- La Salle broke many of his promises. *(false)*
- The Indians did not trust La Salle. *(false)*
- The Indians told La Salle how to find the Mississippi River. *(true)*
- La Salle and his men turned back before they came to the end of the river. *(false)*
- La Salle was looking for the end of the Mississippi River. *(true)*
- La Salle found what he was looking for. *(true)*

Going Beyond

Enrichment

Give your child the Indian sign language chart from Appendix, page A30. Explain that in parts of the country where many different languages were spoken, the Indians often used sign language to communicate with one another. The signs on the chart were used by the Plains Indians. Encourage your child to learn a few of the signs.

Additional Teacher Information

La Salle was first commissioned to search out the Mississippi River for France in 1670, but being an independent spirit, he disappeared into the wilderness, possibly trading with the Native Americans and learning their languages and customs. In 1672, not having heard from La Salle, France chose Louis Jolliet, a Canadian fur trader, and Father Jacques Marquette, a Jesuit priest, to explore the river. Along with five others, Marquette and Jolliet entered the Mississippi at its juncture with the Wisconsin River. They descended the river and traveled past the mouths of the Illinois, the Missouri, and the Ohio Rivers. Just above the mouth of the Arkansas River, the party encountered an initially hostile group of Arkansas people with whom they spent several days. After inquiring about the distance to the sea (it was merely seven hundred miles to the Gulf of Mexico), Marquette and Jolliet decided to leave the Arkansas village and return to Wisconsin. They based their decision on three factors: the realization that the Mississippi emptied into the Gulf of Mexico rather than into the great ocean to the west, the worry of trespassing in the territory of Florida and exposing their party to capture by the Spanish, and the threat of Native Americans skilled with firearms and sympathetic to the English. Their decision gave La Salle a second chance to fulfill his dream.

LESSON 45

How Places Get Their Names

Text, pages 124-26
Notebook, page 50

Preview

Main Ideas

- Cities in the United States differ from one another.
- Some places are named for people, some places for how they look.

Objectives

- Make up a place name after being given a description of the place
- Cite a reason that your family's town is special

Materials

- Supplement, page S12: Map of Pennsylvania
- A sheet of handwriting paper with *What Makes Our Town or City Special?* written on it

Notes

In preparation for this lesson, you may want to make a list of cities and towns in your area that are named for people or for their geographical characteristics.

The supplemental lesson for Chapter 3 gives state names taken from Indian words, and Lesson 17 lists towns named after presidents. You may want to review some of those names with your child.

Day 1

Lesson

Introducing the Lesson

Tell a story. Show your child the Pennsylvania map. Point out the town of Cogan House and read the following story of how the town got its name.

> In 1825 David Cogan, wanting to get away from city life, traveled into the middle of Pennsylvania and built his house off Williamson Trail. According to stories that were told, as travelers made their way west, they often stopped at Cogan's house. Not wanting to turn a traveler out in the cold, Mr. Cogan would give everyone a bed and a meal. Those who stayed with Cogan passed the word along to other travelers that Cogan's house was the place to stop. Out of necessity, Cogan added rooms to his house until he finally realized that he didn't really have to provide food and lodging to every stranger who knocked on his door. Cogan sold his house to John Carter, who kept the name Cogan's House and continued to take in travelers. When a town began to grow up around the house, the people adopted the already well-known name, dropping the apostrophe and the *s*.

◆ THINGS PEOPLE DO ◆

Naming Places

Did you ever wonder how towns and mountains
and rivers got their names?
Sometimes places are named for people.
Can you think of a place named for a person?
Sometimes places are named for how they look.
How do you think the river Big Muddy looks?
How do you think the city on this map
got its name?

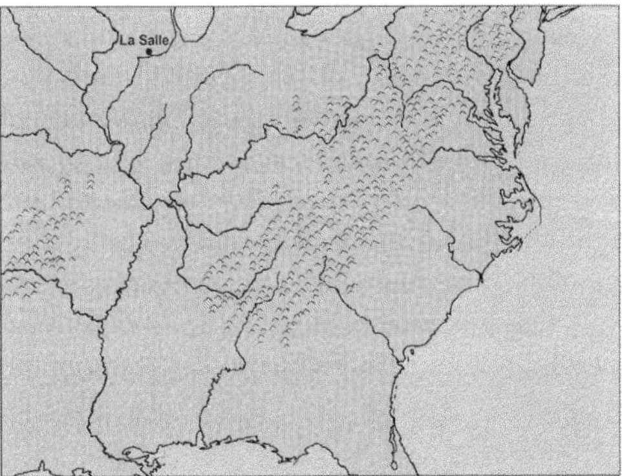

124

Tell your child that there are many interesting stories behind the names of towns and cities. Half of the states in the United States have names that come from what the Indians called their land. Nine states are named for the main river that flows through them. Washington is the only state named in honor of an American.

Teaching the Lesson

Direct a text activity on page 124. Read page 124 and answer the questions on the page.

Text Discussion, page 124

- ➤ Do you remember the person for whom Jamestown was named? *(King James I of England)*
- ➤ Do you think Big Muddy is a real river?

"Big Muddy" is a nickname for the Missouri River. As the river travels through seven states, it picks up dirt called **silt.** The water is so dirty that at the place where the Missouri flows into the Mississippi River, a person can tell which water is from the Missouri and which is from the Mississippi. The dirty water of the Missouri can be seen flowing beside the clean Mississippi water for over one hundred miles.

◆ LEARNING HOW ◆

To Name Places

1. Get your Notebook and a pencil.
2. Make up names for the places your teacher tells you about.
3. Tell the names of your places to a friend. Can he guess why you chose the names you did?

125

Naming Places Name

Listen as the teacher reads.
Invent names for each place.

© 1996 BJU Press. Reproduction prohibited.

Heritage Studies 1
Student Notebook

Lesson 45
Teaching the Lesson 50

If you have made a list of places in your area named for people or for how the places look, discuss those now with your child.

Direct a *Learning How* activity on text page 125 and Notebook page 50. Follow the directions on page 125 using the following place descriptions.

1. Pine trees grow along both sides of the river. The air smells of fresh pines. What name would you give to this river? *(Answers will vary; perhaps Pine River.)*
2. Captain Meriwether Lewis explored the Louisiana territory in 1804-6. He spent part of one winter in this town, and the people wanted to name it in his honor. What name would you suggest for the town? *(Answers will vary; perhaps Lewis, Lewistown, Lewisville, Meriwether, etc.)*
3. Many black bears have been seen in the woods covering these mountains. One trapper says that the bears are grizzlies. What would you name the mountains? *(Answers will vary; perhaps Bear Mountains, Black Bear Mountains, Grizzly Mountains, etc.)*
4. This lake has an unusual shoreline. From the air, its shape is like an oval. What would you name the lake? *(Answers will vary; perhaps Oval Lake.)*
5. Pretend you were the first person to climb to the top of a hill where your family went camping. The people who live nearby want to name the hill after you. What name would you suggest for the hill? *(Answers will vary; any name should include the child's first and/or last name.)*

After discussing the place names, tell your child that people can have names that have meanings as well. Explain that the title *Christian* comes from Christ's name. It means "like Christ." Ask what that name should tell about a person who goes by it. *(He should be like Christ.)* (BAT: 1c Separation, 3d Body as a Temple; Bible Promise: D. Identified in Christ)

What do you think makes cities different from each other? People bring different ways to places. They bring different ways of cooking and speaking. How do you think the cities La Salle started were different from Jamestown?

People who live on ocean shores have different ways of making money than people who live on the plains. Some people fish. Some people farm. Some people make clothes or cars. All the cities in the United States make up one country that is different from all other countries in the world. What makes your town or city special?

126

Day 2

Text Discussion, page 126

- ➤ Read the first section on text page 126. Where did La Salle come from? *(France)*
- ➤ Where did the people in Jamestown come from? *(England)*
- ➤ Would the people in the cities that La Salle started speak the same language as the people in Jamestown? *(no)*
- ➤ Do you think they would eat the same kinds of food?
- ➤ What was different about the location of the cities? *(Jamestown was on the eastern seacoast, and the places established by La Salle were along the Mississippi River.)*
- ➤ What was different about the reasons the French and the English came to the New World?

King Louis had ordered La Salle to build forts as he explored the land; therefore, most of what La Salle established began as forts rather than what we would call cities. Among the forts he built were Fort Crèvecoeur (crĕv′cœr), which means "heartbreak," Fort Prudhomme (wise man), and Fort Miami (Indian).

- ➤ Read the last section of the page. What are some ways that people make money? *(fish, farm, make clothes or cars)*
- ➤ What are some other jobs that people have?
- ➤ What is the name of our town? Let's write about things that make our city special.

Evaluating the Lesson

Conduct a writing activity. Read the title on the sheet of paper you prepared from the Materials list. Ask your child to give you sentences telling about your city. Write these on the paper. You may want to post this in your schoolroom and read it again with your child. You may also want to allow your child to add illustrations to the story.

Going Beyond

Enrichment

Give your child a map of your state or country and some lined index cards. Encourage your child to find towns and cities with unusual names and to copy those names onto the index cards.

Additional Teacher Information

Many words used today in American cooking are words that come from the French. Some of the more common ones are as follows: *croissant* (krwä sänt′), "a rich, crescent-shaped roll"; *quiche* (kēsh), "an egg custard, often including cheese and vegetables, baked in a pastry shell like a pie"; *omelet* (ŏm′ lĭt), "a dish consisting of beaten eggs cooked and folded"; *mousse* (mo͞os), "a chilled dessert made with whipped cream and gelatin"; *crêpe* (krāp), "a thin dessert pancake usually rolled with fruit and topped with powdered sugar"; *gourmet* (go͝or mā′), "a connoisseur of fine food"; *cuisine* (kwĭ zēn′), "a certain style of preparing food."

10 LESSONS 46-49

The One True God

This chapter focuses on how religious beliefs affect the way people live. The Puritan and the Separatist religions were not the only ones influencing early America. Other beliefs of the time are discussed in the light of Scripture. The chapter includes a Puritan hymn for your child to sing.

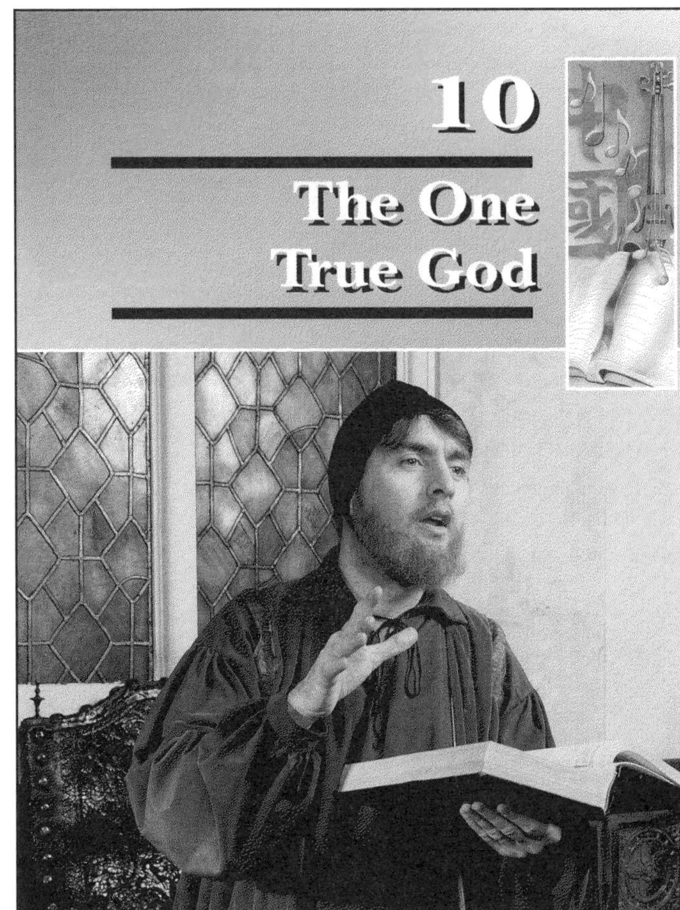

Materials

The following materials must be obtained or prepared before the presentation of the lesson. These items are labeled with an asterisk (*) in the lesson and in the Materials List in the Supplement. For further information see the individual lessons.

- *HERITAGE STUDIES Listening Cassette A* (Lesson 48)
- A cassette player (Lesson 48)
- A bag of dried beans (Lesson 48)

LESSON 46
Other Gods in the New World

Text, pages 128-30, 178
Notebook, page 51

Preview

Main Ideas
- Religions are the different beliefs people have about God and heaven.
- Religious beliefs help shape cultures.
- The Indians believed there were many gods.

Objective
- Write about the child's Christian heritage

Materials
- A Bible

Day 1

Lesson

Introducing the Lesson
Direct a picture activity. Ask your child to turn to page 36 in his text.

Picture Discussion
- ➤ What do you see in the picture? *(buffalo)*
- ➤ Look at page 102. What do we call the body of water in the picture? *(a river)*
- ➤ Look outside. What shines to give us our daylight? *(the sun)*
- ➤ Would the sun, the buffalo, or the river be able to understand you if you asked it a question? *(no)*
- ➤ Could any of the objects make you better if you were sick? *(no)*
- ➤ Who created each of these things? *(God)*

Even though the Indians had no churches, some Indians worshiped these objects and many other objects during special festival and feast times. They bowed down and prayed to the sun and moon, rivers, trees, and animals.

- ➤ Do you know what the word **idol** means? *(a false god)*

How do you believe people can get to heaven?
Not everyone believes the same way.
There are many beliefs about God and about how to get to heaven.
There are even many different beliefs about what heaven is.
The beliefs about God and heaven are called *religions*.

I am the Lord, and there is none else, there is no God beside me.

Isaiah 45:5

128

Just like the Indians who worshiped the sun, moon, and trees, people today have false gods, or idols, too. An idol can be anything that a person loves more than God or in place of God.

- ➤ Name some things that children or adults might love more than God and might use as idols. *(toys, clothing, a new bike, a car, a boat, etc.)*

Even though people today may not bow down and worship these things, they are still idols because they take the place of God. (Bible Promises: F. Christ as Intercessor, H. God as Father)

Teaching the Lesson
Direct a text activity on pages 128-30 and 178. Read the verse on page 128.

Text Discussion, page 128
- ➤ Do all people believe the same about God? *(no)*
- ➤ Read the page to find out what we call a person's belief about God. *(religion)*
- ➤ Can you name some religions? *(Jewish, Catholic, Muslim, Buddhist, etc.)*

Neither is there salvation in any other: for there is none other name under heaven given among men, whereby we must be saved.
Acts 4:12

The Bible says that God is the only God.
The Bible says that believing on Jesus is the only way to heaven.
Some religions say that doing good will help get you to heaven.
Is that true?

129

Other Gods in the New World

Many Indian peoples lived in the New World. None of them knew about the God of the Bible.

Some tribes worshiped the stars and the moon. Some worshiped animals or carved pieces of wood.

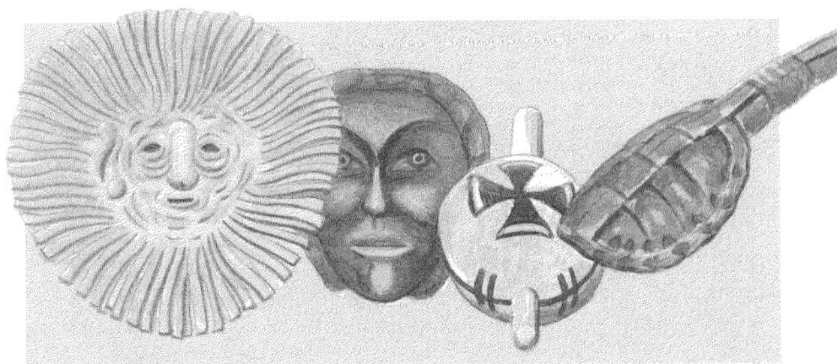

People coming to the New World brought other ideas about gods.
People called *Vikings* had gods of thunder and wind.
People from Africa and Mexico had stone gods.

130

Text Discussion, page 129

➤ Read the page. What is the only way to get to heaven? *(believing on Jesus)* (BATs: 1a Understanding Jesus Christ, 1b Repentance and faith, 7a Grace; Bible Promises: A. Liberty from Sin, B. Guiltless by the Blood)

➤ Read the verse on page 129. Whose name is the verse speaking about? *(Jesus Christ's)* (Bible Promise: D. Identified in Christ)

Text Discussion, pages 130 and 178

➤ Read the first two sentences on page 130. Why did the Indians not know about God? *(No one had ever told them.)*

➤ Do you know of anyone today who has never heard about God?

You may want to take time for your child to tell about a time when he told someone (a neighbor, a friend, a relative) about God. (BAT: 5c Evangelism and missions)

➤ Read the next two sentences. Name some of the things Indians worshiped. *(sun, moon, stars, rivers, trees, rocks, animals)*

➤ A few tribes made large carvings on poles to stand outside their villages. These poles were called **totem poles.**

➤ Look at the picture of the totem pole on page 178. What is on the top of the totem pole? *(an animal)*

This animal was usually the good luck mascot, or totem animal, of the family. The carved faces of fish, birds, and other animals may have represented the spirits of the Indians' dead relatives. Some Indians believed that these totem poles would help them to remember their relatives and that the spirits would continue to help them.

➤ Can spirits help anyone? *(no)*

➤ Was it right for any of the Indian tribes to worship the spirits of their relatives? *(no)*

➤ Who is the only one to be worshiped? *(God)* (Bible Promise: H. God as Father)

Day 2

➤ The Indians were not the only ones who had their own ideas about gods. Every group of people who came to the New World brought with them their own ideas about whom and what to worship.

➤ Read the last section on page 130. What gods did the Vikings worship? *(gods of thunder and wind)*

➤ What kind of gods did some people from Mexico and Africa worship? *(gods made of stone)*

➤ Could these gods heal the sick and answer the prayers of the people? *(no)*

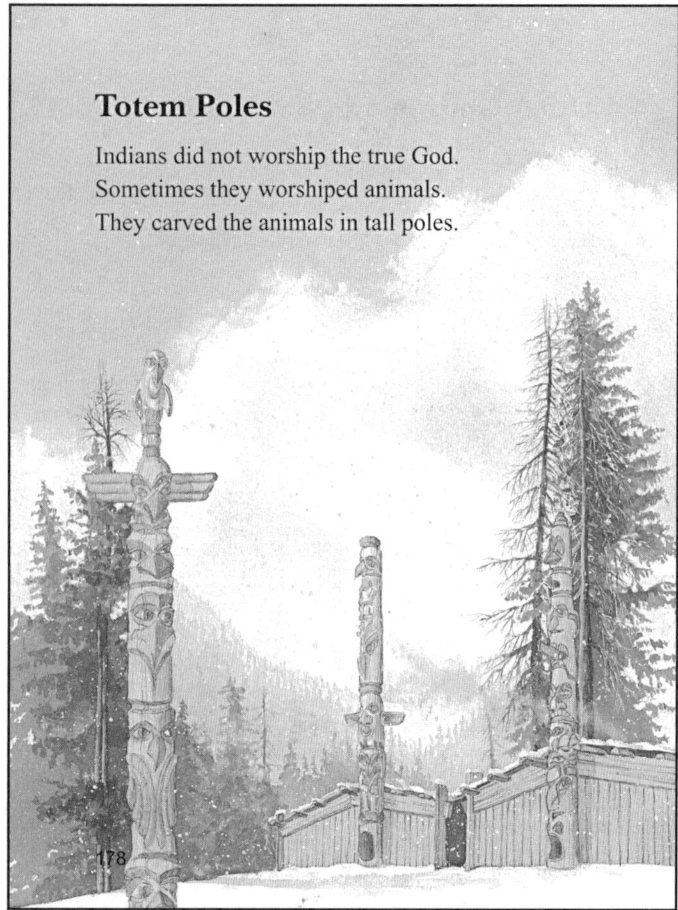

Totem Poles

Indians did not worship the true God. Sometimes they worshiped animals. They carved the animals in tall poles.

178

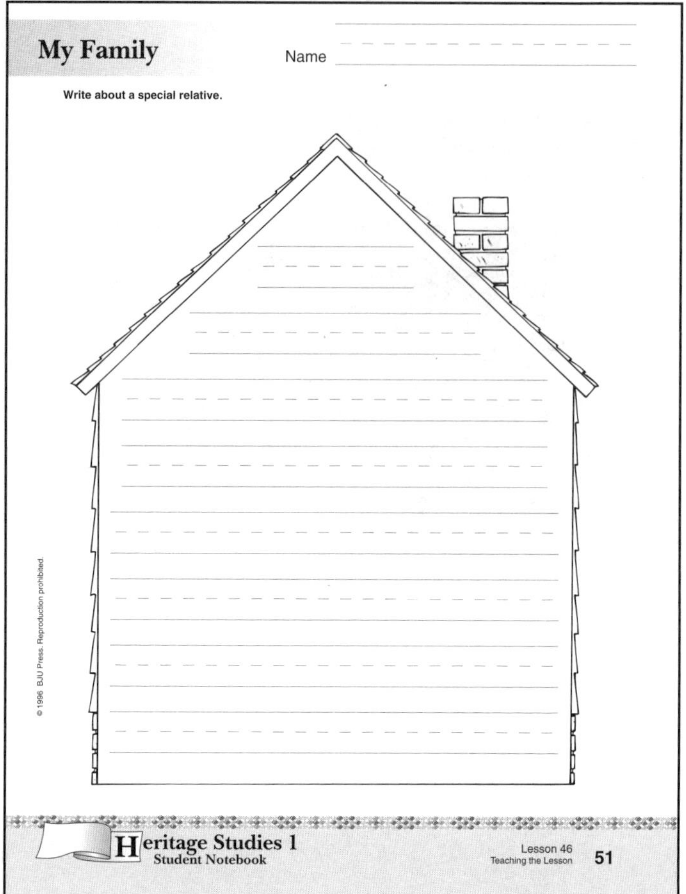

My Family Name

Write about a special relative.

Heritage Studies 1 Student Notebook Lesson 46 Teaching the Lesson 51

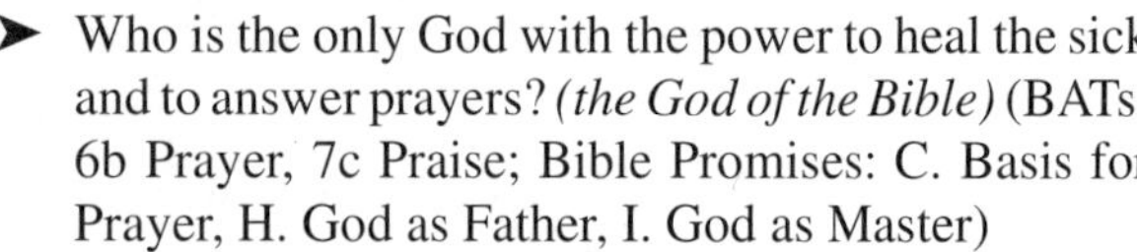

➤ Who is the only God with the power to heal the sick and to answer prayers? *(the God of the Bible)* (BATs: 6b Prayer, 7c Praise; Bible Promises: C. Basis for Prayer, H. God as Father, I. God as Master)

Evaluating the Lesson

Direct an activity on Notebook page 51. Ask your child whether the spirits of the Indians' relatives ever helped any Indians. *(no)*

Notebook Activity

➤ Was it all right for the Indians to remember special things about their relatives? *(yes)*

The stories that some older Indians told about their relatives probably helped the younger Indians to understand more about their families.

➤ Do we worship our relatives? *(no)*

➤ Do you like to hear special things about your relatives, such as how life was when Grandma and Grandpa were children? Our relatives help us to learn how to worship God. Sometimes they teach us a song.

➤ Has your grandparent, an aunt or an uncle, or a parent taught you something special about God?

➤ Write a few sentences about this person on the outline of the house on Notebook page 51.

Try to make this an enjoyable activity. Help your child with spelling. You may need to ask some questions to help him get started.

Going Beyond

Enrichment

Label a file box *Please Pray.* Give your child some index cards. Ask him to make prayer cards for family members, friends, or neighbors that need to be saved. Tell him that he may attach a photograph or draw a picture of the person if he wishes. Instruct your child to place the prayer cards in the box. Select several prayer cards each day to remember for prayer during devotions, Bible time, or dinner time. You may want to include other prayer requests and missionary prayer cards in the file box.

Additional Teacher Information

Native Americans had special songs for their many religious ceremonies. They sang when death was near. They sang to the spirits for good luck in hunting and planting. They sang to their many gods to please the spirits or to make requests of the spirits.

Religion and superstition were often entwined for the Native American. Indians used paint on their bodies to please the spirits who were thought to live in the mountains and to cause the spirits to grant their desires. For instance, a Native American would paint as much of his body red as possible when he was going to gather berries, hoping to please the spirits and thereby gain more berries.

The Indian's dance was often a prayer to the god of corn, rain, or sun. Some of these dances lasted many days. The Hopi snake dance was a prayer for rain in August so that the crops would be good. Snakes were handled by snake priests in this elaborate ceremony and then were sent back to the desert to carry the prayers to the rain gods.

2-18

LESSON 47

Religions in the New World

Text, pages 131-32

Preview

Main Ideas

- People came to the New World for many reasons.
- Religious beliefs help shape cultures.

Objective

- Memorize a Bible verse to use in witnessing

Materials

- A Bible

Day 1

Lesson

Introducing the Lesson

Direct a discussion. Ask your child to close his eyes and to use his imagination as you read to him the following.

> Pretend you are sitting under a large oak tree in the front yard looking at a picture book. The little boy who lives across the street wanders over. He asks whether you have heard about the ice-cream truck that will be coming. It will be a big blue truck. The first five people will get free ice cream. While you are considering the ice-cream truck, you see a young girl running down the sidewalk. She yells to you to watch out for the ice-cream truck.

➤ Would you believe the ice-cream truck is giving away free ice cream? Why or why not?

➤ What could you do to check the information to find out whether it is really true? *(ask your mother or father, wait to see whether an ice-cream truck really comes, ask the ice-cream truck driver)*

➤ Sometimes other people try to convince us that false ideas are true. If you think information is not true, you should always try to check it out. What do you think you should do to find out whether the information is true?

Teaching the Lesson

Direct a text activity on pages 131-32. Read page 131, instructing your child to find out about some of the traders' beliefs concerning God.

Religions in the New World

Many of the white men who traded with the Indians had their own beliefs about God.
Some traders were Roman Catholics.
They said that Jesus Christ is God and that He died for our sins.
They believed that you get to heaven by believing in Christ and by belonging to the Catholic Church.

> *Not by works of righteousness which we have done, but according to his mercy he saved us.*
> Titus 3:5

131

Roman Catholics have a leader called the *pope*.
Many believe that some things the pope says are as true as what the Bible says.
Is any man as wise as God?

Most Indians kept their old religions.
They did not take the white man's gods.
Others took part of the Roman Catholic religion.

Today many people in America think that to get to heaven they just have to live a good life.
These people need to hear the truth.
How will they hear?

132

Text Discussion, page 131

- ➤ What religion were some of the early traders? *(Roman Catholic)*

> Other religions brought to the New World during this time were Puritan, Separatist, and Anglican. These will be discussed in the next lessons.

- ➤ How did Catholics think they could get to heaven? *(by believing in Christ and by belonging to the Catholic Church)*

> Read Titus 3:5 from the text. Explain that this verse means that a person cannot get to heaven by doing good works. Ask your child whether he knows what "doing good works" means. Explain that it means going to church, reading your Bible, obeying your parents, and doing any other activity in hope of getting to heaven. Ask what the only way to get to heaven is. *(salvation through Jesus Christ)* (BAT: 1b Repentance and faith; Bible Promise: A. Liberty from Sin)

Text Discussion, page 132

- ➤ Read the first sentence on page 132. What is the Roman Catholic leader called? *(the pope)*
- ➤ What do we call the leaders of our church? *(Possible answers are pastor, preacher, reverend.)*
- ➤ Read the rest of page 132. Did most of the Indians accept the traders' beliefs? *(no)* Even though most of the Indians did not believe, they needed to hear about the one true God from the traders.
- ➤ Are there people today who do not know the truth of salvation? *(yes)*
- ➤ How can these people hear the truth of salvation? *(by Christians' going to tell them)*
- ➤ Can you think of ways you can help people hear the truth of the gospel? *(tell people about Christ, pray for the unsaved, give money to send missionaries to go tell these people about Christ, provide Bibles for these people in their languages)*

Evaluating the Lesson

Memorize a verse. Read Titus 3:5 again to your child. Direct him to read the verse with you several times. Help him to memorize the verse to use whenever he witnesses for the Lord. Your child may need several days to completely memorize the verse.

Going Beyond

Additional Teacher Information

In the early 1600s, the Dutch claimed a large region of land that they called New Netherland. It included parts of what are now Connecticut, Delaware, New Jersey, and New York. In 1621, merchants in New Netherland formed the Dutch West India Company, especially to develop the profitable fur trade with Native Americans. The government of the Netherlands gave the company all rights to trade in New Netherland for the next twenty-four years. Thirty families, sponsored by the company, established a Dutch settlement at the mouth of the Hudson River in 1624 and later founded New Amsterdam, now named New York City. The company, under the leadership of Peter Minuit, bought Manhattan Island from the Native Americans in 1626 for goods worth about twenty-four dollars. The Dutch traders set up trading posts at the places that became Albany, New York; Hartford, Connecticut; and Trenton, New Jersey. The leaders of New Netherland were harsh and set up strict rules, allowing no religious freedom and quarreling among themselves and with neighboring settlements. They severely mistreated the native people, so they were often in danger of attack. The rivalry in trade was fierce between the Dutch and the English; this rivalry led in 1664 to the capturing and claiming of New Netherland by the English.

Native Americans called the region around the Saint Lawrence River valley *Canada,* from their word meaning "group of huts." In the early 1600s, a Frenchman, Samuel de Champlain, explored the regions in the eastern part of Canada. In 1608, he founded Quebec, the first permanent Canadian settlement. He discovered the lake that was later named for him and explored the interior near Lake Huron. In 1642, Montreal, at first named Ville Marie, was founded as a missionary center. For more than sixty years, most of Canada was controlled by the fur-trading companies of France. The French called their North American settlements *New France.* Ruling New France were a governor and the chairman of the Sovereign Council, which served as a court and law-making branch of government. An important member of the Council was the Roman Catholic bishop of Quebec, who was in charge of the religious needs of the people. The governor's main duty was defense against the Native Americans with their Dutch and English allies.

2-23

LESSON 48
The Puritans

Text, pages 133-34
Notebook, pages 52-53

Preview

Main Ideas

- Man's view of God determines his philosophy and history.
- Religious beliefs help shape cultures.
- Puritans wanted to make the Church of England pure.

Objectives

- Sing a Puritan hymn
- Label the Atlantic Ocean and the countries of England, France, and Spain on a map

Materials

- A Bible
- Maps and More 8, page M5
- A cassette player*
- *HERITAGE STUDIES Listening Cassette A**
- A pan
- A bag of dried beans*
- A small toy such as a block
- A sheet of paper with the following words written on it: *England, France, Spain, Atlantic Ocean*

Notes

Place the beans and the toy block in the pan before beginning the lesson.

HERITAGE STUDIES Listening Cassette A includes songs and readings for grades 1, 2, and 3. Though this is the only lesson in grade 1 which specifically uses Cassette A, you may find other songs appropriate for use in your first grade studies.

Day 1

Lesson

Introducing the Lesson

Read a story. Tell your child to imagine a king dressed in red robes and fur and a wide, feathered hat. Ask where he thinks this king might have ruled. Read the following true story.

The Puritans and the Separatists

Many of the countries that sent people to the New World were Roman Catholic. Most of the French people were Roman Catholic. Most of the Spanish people were Roman Catholic. Those countries followed the pope. England had some Roman Catholics. But England did not follow the pope. England had its own church.

Some people in England believed the Bible. These people wanted to make the English churches completely different from the Roman Catholic churches. These people said they wanted to make the churches in England pure. They were called the *Puritans.*

133

A long time ago, a rich and famous king in England decided that he did not want the people of his country to go to the Roman Catholic Church any more. He told his people that he was going to become the leader of a new church in England. He told them that he would let them have their own Bibles.

"This will be the Church of England. We will not have to wait for priests to read the Bible to us anymore."

The people could not believe their ears. As far back as anyone could remember, everyone in England had belonged to the Roman Catholic Church.

This king was named Henry, and he had his own reasons for wanting to make a new church. But the people did not care what his reasons were. They were just happy to be able to have their own Bibles.

The leader of the Roman Catholic Church was not happy. He wanted to make King Henry stay true to the Roman Catholic Church.

However, King Henry built his own churches, and he made all his people go to his church. Even the pope could not stop the new church in England.

Teaching the Lesson

Direct a text activity on page 133. Read the first section on page 133.

Text Discussion, page 133

- ➤ What religion were many of the people that came to the New World? *(Roman Catholic)*
- ➤ What country had some Roman Catholics as well as its own church? *(England)*

Map-reading Activity

- ➤ Look at Maps and More 8.

You may want to use a globe for this map-reading activity.

- ➤ Point to the continent that France and Spain are on. *(Europe)*
- ➤ Point to the island that is directly to the west (left) of the word *Europe.* This island is England. The people that live in England are called English. England is a part of the continent of Europe also.
- ➤ Point to the area directly south of England. This is France. The people that live in France are called French.
- ➤ Look at the area to the south of France that sticks out a little to the west. This is Spain. What do you think we call the people who live in Spain? *(Spanish)*
- ➤ What body of water did the people from these countries have to cross in order to reach the New World? *(Atlantic Ocean)*

Day 2

Text Discussion, page 133 (cont.)

- ➤ Read the rest of page 133.
- ➤ Look at this pan of dried beans. Before these beans are cooked, I need to make sure that there is nothing dirty or unwanted with the beans. Do you see anything that I need to remove before cooking the beans? *(yes)*
- ➤ What needs to be removed? *(a toy block)* By removing the block from the pan, we are making the pan of beans **pure.** The pan will contain only what we want.
- ➤ Read the last two sentences again. The Puritans wanted to make the Church of England pure by removing some of the people or by changing some of the ways people believed and some of the things people did in the church.

◆ LEARNING HOW ◆

To Sing a Puritan Hymn

1. Take out your Notebook.
2. Listen to the tune your teacher sings or plays for you.
3. Sing the words of the Puritan hymn with the tune. Where do you think the words of the hymn come from?

134

Puritan Hymn Name ____________

Compare this hymn to Psalm 23.

Psalm 23

Text from the Psalter

1. The Lord's my shepherd, I'll not want;
He makes me down to lie,
To lie in pastures green; He leadeth me
The quiet waters by.

2. My soul He doth restore again;
And me to walk doth make,
To walk doth make within the paths of righteousness,
E'en for His own name's sake.

3. Yea, though I walk through death's dark vale,
Yet will I fear no ill;
For Thou art with me, and Thy rod
And staff me comfort still.

4. My table Thou hast furnished
In presence of my foes;
My head Thou dost with oil anoint,
And my cup overflows.

5. Goodness and mercy all my life
Shall surely follow me;
And in God's house for evermore
My dwelling place shall be.

Heritage Studies 1 Student Notebook — Lesson 48 Teaching the Lesson 52

Direct a *Learning How* activity on text page 134 and Notebook page 52. Read Psalm 23 from the Bible to your child.

Learning How Activity

➤ Read the steps on page 134. The words for this hymn are on page 52 in your Notebook.

➤ Read silently the words to Psalm 23 from your Notebook page as you listen to the song on the cassette. (*NOTE:* If you have not purchased the cassette, you may read the Notebook page together.)

➤ Answer the question in Step 3. *(The words in the hymn are similar to the words in Psalm 23 in the Bible.)*

In 1640 the first book was printed in the New World by the Puritans of Massachusetts Bay. This book contained the Psalms set to music; it was called the *Bay Psalm Book*.

Evaluating the Lesson

Direct an activity on Notebook page 53. Direct your child's attention to Notebook page 53. Place the sheet of paper prepared for the Materials list in front of your child. He may need to refer to the spellings when labeling his map.

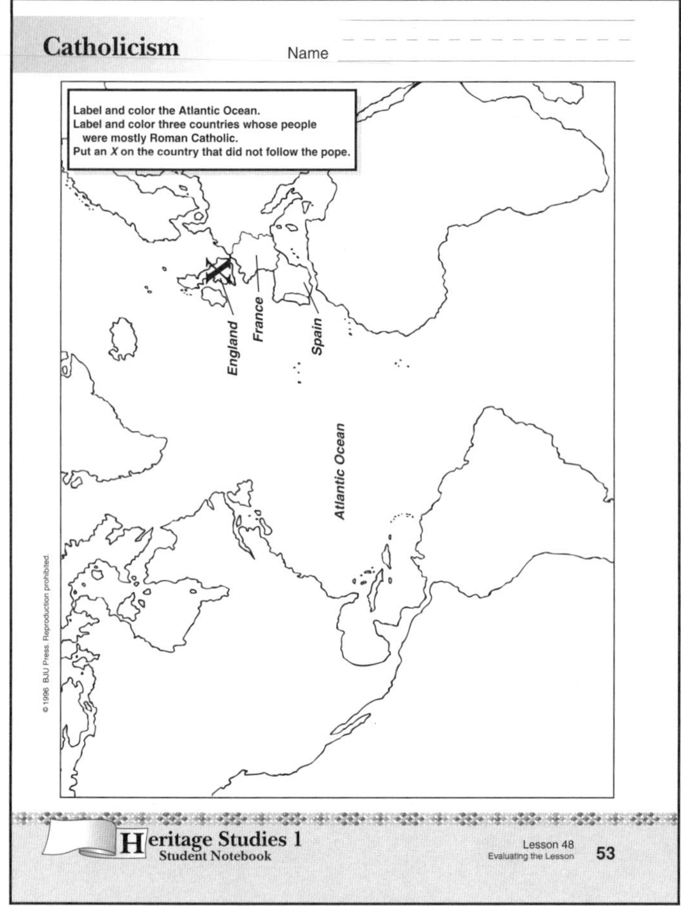

Catholicism
Name
Label and color the Atlantic Ocean.
Label and color three countries whose people were mostly Roman Catholic.
Put an X on the country that did not follow the pope.
England
France
Spain
Atlantic Ocean
© 1996 BJU Press. Reproduction prohibited.
Heritage Studies 1
Student Notebook
Lesson 48
Evaluating the Lesson
53

Notebook Activity

- Find the Atlantic Ocean. Label the ocean by writing *Atlantic Ocean* in the middle of the area.
- What are the three countries where most of the people were Roman Catholics? *(England, France, and Spain)*
- Write the name of each country on the map. There is not enough room to put the name of the country on the country itself. You will need to write the name beside the country and then draw a line from the name of the country to its location.
- Put an *X* on the country that did not follow the pope. *(England)*
- Color the three countries green and color the Atlantic Ocean blue.

Going Beyond

Enrichment

Encourage your child to memorize Psalm 23. To help in this endeavor, provide a fill-in-the-blank study sheet for him. (*NOTE:* See Appendix, page A31.) Direct your child to use his Bible to help him fill in the missing words in the first three verses.

Additional Teacher Information

John Winthrop, a lawyer, was the leader of the Puritan migration to America. He was selected to be the governor of the Massachusetts Bay Colony in 1630. Like many other Puritan men, the wealthy and prominent Winthrop traveled to the New World for three main reasons: religious freedom, ambition to do well in his profession, and a desire to reap financial profit. Making the long voyage across the Atlantic aboard the *Arbella,* John Winthrop faithfully recorded the events of each day in his diary, *Journal,* which was later entitled *The History of New England.* The *Arbella* was one of sixteen ships that was readied to carry one thousand Puritans, their provisions, equipment, trading goods, and cattle from England to America. The voyage took seventy-six days, reaching Salem on June 22, 1630. These newly-arrived Puritans did not settle in one small community but rather established numerous settlements in regions surrounding Salem.

The laws governing the Puritans of the Massachusetts Bay Colony were severe, with whipping posts and pillories in every town. Those who disobeyed the laws were publicly punished rather than jailed out of sight. Church attendance was compulsory, with fines charged to any who did not attend. Swearing was punishable by a fine of ten shillings or humiliation in the stocks. There were also laws against smoking, first in public, then later also in private, though these laws were impossible to enforce. In 1634, the General Court passed laws forbidding all lace or silver or gold thread on clothing. Ruffs, beaver hats, and fancy needlework on hats were also forbidden.

The leading men of Massachusetts Bay were well educated. Their most important concerns were to educate their ministers and to make sure that the people could read the Bible for themselves. In 1634, the Boston Latin School was founded; then in 1636, the General Court gave money for the establishment of a college for Massachusetts Bay. This college was named for the Reverend John Harvard, a young Puritan minister who died at the age of thirty-one, leaving half of his estate and his library of four hundred books to the new Harvard College.

The *Bay Psalm Book* of 1640 was originally entitled *The Whole Booke of Psalmes Faithfully Translated into English Metre.* Only thirteen different tunes were used in the singing of the Psalms in the *Bay Psalm Book*. Seventeen hundred copies of the *Bay Psalm Book* were published, but only eleven remain—five complete copies, the others lacking some pages. In 1947, a copy sold in New York for $151,000, the highest price ever paid for a book in the English language.

LESSON 49
A Separatist Sunday

Text, pages 135-38
Notebook, page 54

Preview

Main Ideas

- People came to the New World for many reasons.
- The Separatists separated from the Church of England.
- Religions influence governments.
- The Pilgrims included the Separatists, merchants, and runaways.

Objectives

- Identify whether the Separatists came to the New World before or after Columbus
- Locate the words *IN GOD WE TRUST* on a coin and be able to tell why they are there

Materials

- A coin
- A sheet of paper with the words *IN GOD WE TRUST* on it

Day 1

Lesson

Introducing the Lesson

Examine a coin. Point to *IN GOD WE TRUST* on the paper, reading the phrase to your child. Give him a coin.

Discussion

➤ Look at the coin closely and find the words *IN GOD WE TRUST.*

➤ Why do you think America's coins have these words on them? When our country was started, belief in God and giving honor and glory to Him were very important.

➤ Do you remember what the Pilgrims promised when they signed the **Mayflower Compact?** *(The people promised to obey the rules they made.)* The Mayflower Compact gave honor and glory to God. (*NOTE:* See Lessons 22-23 to review information about the *Mayflower.*)

➤ Do the people of America still go along with this agreement? *(Some do; some do not.)*

The Puritans could not make the churches pure. So some Puritans decided to leave England and go to a new place. Do you remember who these people were?
Why do you think they were called Separatists?
They "separated" from the church they did not think was pure.
Some of them came to the New World.

Look at the line on this page.
Did the Separatists come to the New World before or after Columbus?

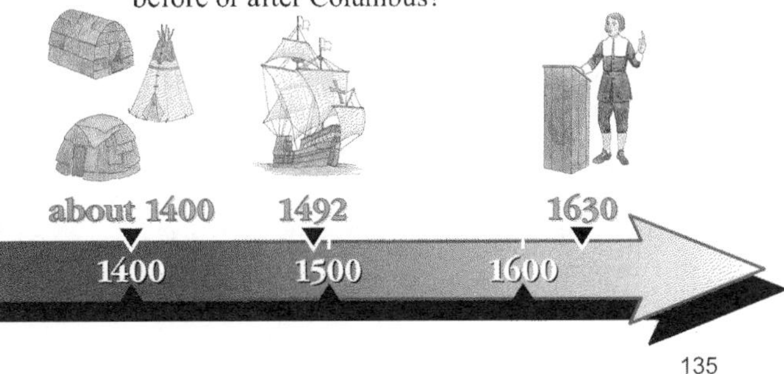

135

Teaching the Lesson

Direct a text activity on pages 135-37. Read and discuss page 135.

Text Discussion, page 135

➤ Why did some Puritans decide to leave England? *(because they could not make the churches in England pure)*

➤ Look at the time line on the page. Name the year where the Puritans or Separatists are shown on the time line. *(1630)* Did the Separatists come to the New World before or after Columbus? *(after)*

Text Discussion, page 136

➤ Read the page.

➤ Do you remember traveling to another town, state, or country for vacation? People who travel can also be called **pilgrims.**

➤ Why did the Separatists come to the New World? *(to worship God as they wanted)*

➤ Why did the people who sold things come to the New World? *(to make money)*

➤ Why did the people who were running away come to the New World? *(to be free)*

➤ Look at the picture. What is the name of the ship? *(the* Mayflower*)*

➤ Were all the passengers on the *Mayflower* men? *(No, women and children also sailed.)*

Some people call the Separatists *Pilgrims.*
Pilgrims are people who travel to other places.
There were other travelers on the *Mayflower*
besides Separatists.
Some Pilgrims were people who sold things;
some were people who were running away from
hard masters.

136

The Separatists believed that faith in Christ was
the only way to heaven.
The Separatists built their own churches.
They sang hymns.
They heard sermons about how God
wants people to live.
They read the Bible and obeyed God.

The church leaders helped make rules
for the towns.
Today our coins say "In God we trust."
Why do you think our country began with
a belief in God?

137

Text Discussion, page 137

- ➤ Read the page.
- ➤ How did the Separatists believe they could get to heaven? *(by putting their faith in Christ)*

This means that a person must believe that Jesus died for his sins, confess his sins to Him, and accept Him as his Savior. (BAT: 1b Repentance and faith) This is the only way to heaven.

Day 2

Direct a listening activity. Direct your child to listen as you read a story of what a Separatist Sunday was like. Listen for ways their Sundays were different from your Sundays.

Wrestling Brewster rolled out of bed. He jumped when his bare feet touched the cold floor. "Ooh! That's cold!" he warned his older brother Love, still in bed. Wrestling tiptoed quickly across the room, hurried down the small, winding staircase, and ran to the big open fireplace in the middle of the parlor. He sat down on the floor facing the flames and pushed his feet toward the warmth. It felt good. He wiggled his toes.

Mother was setting out the large bowl of cooked cereal that she had prepared the day before. "Would you like to take a pan of coals with you to the church service this morning, Wrestling?" she asked her son. "Perhaps you and Love could share one. You have both worn out your last pair of stockings, and your bare feet are going to get very cold, even with your shoes on. You can set the pan at your feet during the meeting."

"Oh, yes!" said Wrestling. "It will be almost like taking the fireplace with me!"

Wrestling brought his Sunday clothes down to the fireplace so that he could dress where it was warm. He didn't mind that his shirtsleeves were two inches too short. He hardly even noticed the big patch in the knee of his breeches. None of the other children had nice clothes to wear on Sunday either. It had been nearly two years since he had worn new clothes.

After breakfast, the family was ready to walk to the fort where the Separatists met for church. Wrestling's father, William Brewster, carried his big Bible under one arm and his musket in the other. "Do you think the Indians will attack us today, Father?" asked Wrestling. He asked that question every Sunday.

"I hope not, Son," said Father. "But the other men and I have our muskets to fire at them if they attack. Don't worry. The Lord who brought us to this great land will keep on protecting us, Wrestling."

Wrestling glanced at the woods surrounding them, wondering whether any Indians were listening. He walked closer to his tall father.

Other families were coming from all across the settlement. Wrestling smiled when he saw some of his friends, but they were not allowed to talk to each other. This was a time for worshiping God, not for chatting.

Inside the fort, Wrestling and Love sat down with the other children on the long wooden benches at the back of the building. The men all sat on one side of the church; the women sat on the other. Wrestling watched his mother go to sit down beside Mrs. Allerton. His father walked straight up the aisle to the front of the room. He was the preacher.

Love elbowed him sharply. "Hey, Wrestling! Do you have the pan of coals?"

"Yes."

"Well, stop keeping it all to yourself. My feet are cold!"

Wrestling opened his mouth to reply, but he suddenly felt a brisk tap on the top of his head. He looked up to see Deacon Fuller's quiet gray eyes fixed on him, his long birch rod still poised in the air. "This is the Lord's house," the deacon said. "We must keep absolutely still in His presence. No more talking, boys."

Wrestling felt a pink blush rising to his ears. He slid the pan of coals toward Love and folded his hands. None of the other children dared to smile or giggle. They all feared Deacon Fuller and his big birch rod.

Father stood up behind the wooden table at the front of the church and welcomed the people. "Let us begin by singing a hymn of praise to our God."

Wrestling looked expectantly at Captain Standish. The captain always started the hymns because they had no musical instruments to set the proper pitch. The strong tenor voice of Captain Standish rang out on the opening notes, and the rest of the people immediately joined in. Wrestling loved the words to this hymn; they were taken from Psalm 23: "The Lord's my Shepherd, I'll not want." He sang out loudly and eagerly.

After the hymn, Father prayed. He thanked God for bringing them to this land. He prayed for God to provide food for them and to protect them from the Indians. He prayed for sick people in the community. He prayed for England, their homeland, and for friends who were still there, waiting to come and join them here in America. Sometimes Father's prayers were very long. But Wrestling tried to keep his hands and feet still and listen.

When Father finished praying, he opened his big Bible. "Our text today is found in the book of Daniel," he said.

Wrestling listened as Father read about the brave Daniel who trusted God so much that he was willing to be thrown into a den of lions. God honored Daniel's faith and closed the lions' mouths. Father said that God could protect the Separatists in the very same way. It made Wrestling feel very safe.

At last the service was over. Wrestling's back was stiff from sitting up straight on the wooden bench. His stomach was growling. He could almost taste Mother's hot bean porridge and rye bread. He could hardly wait to get home for Sunday dinner.

On the way out of the church, Wrestling looked up and saw the guard still at his post on the roof of the fort. Thus far the Indians had been peaceful, but the settlers had to be ready just in case, so the men of the community took turns guarding during the church services.

The Separatists worked hard.
Their towns grew. They made money.
They knew that every blessing came
from God.

Later settlers also
worked hard.
America became
a rich, strong
country.

How do you think the early settlers helped
make America what it is?
Do you think that Americans still believe
that hard work will bring good results?

138

Wrestling looked up at his father. "When can I take a turn as guard during church, Father?"

"Not until you're a little older, Son."

"I can hardly wait. I'm going to be brave—just like Daniel!" (BATs: 6b Prayer, 7c Praise; Bible Promise: I. God as Master)

Story Discussion

- Is your Sunday the same as the Sunday that Wrestling and Love had? *(Answers will vary.)*
- What are some of the differences between a Separatist church service and your church services? *(The Separatists had no musical instruments; children sat on benches at the back; their clothes were old and patched; the men carried muskets to ward off Indians; they heated themselves with a pan of coals.)*
- How did the Separatists show that they trusted in God? *(Answers will vary.)* (BAT: 8a Faith in God's promises)

Direct a text activity on page 138. Read and discuss page 138.

In God We Trust

Name

Follow the teacher's instructions.

Heritage Studies 1 Student Notebook

Lesson 49 Evaluating the Lesson 54

Evaluating the Lesson

Direct an activity on Notebook page 54. Tell your child to write the words *IN GOD WE TRUST* in the proper place on the picture of the coin.

Activity Discussion

- ➤ Why do we have these words on our coins? *(The people who made our coins wanted us to remember that the reason our nation is successful is that it was founded on God.)*
- ➤ Can you find the word **liberty** on the coin? Liberty means freedom. It was the main reason the settlers came to the New World.

Going Beyond

Enrichment

Provide a sheet of drawing paper with lines drawn to divide the paper into six "windows." Instruct your child to draw a picture in each window of a special activity that he does with his family on Sunday.

Additional Teacher Information

The *Mayflower* sailed with 102 passengers. At least thirty of these people were children, from babies to age fifteen. This long voyage in cramped quarters took nine weeks.

The motto *In God We Trust* dates back to 1861 when the Secretary of the Treasury, Salmon P. Chase, wrote the Director of the Mint and urged that the "trust of our people in God be declared on our national coins." The first coin to actually bear the words *In God We Trust* was a two-cent piece issued in 1864. It was not until 1955 that Congress passed a law making it official for the motto to appear on all coins of the United States.

11 LESSONS 50-54

People Have Needs and Wants

This unit will help your child distinguish wants from the four basic needs: food, shelter, clothing, and love. He will learn that everyone has the same needs but different wants. He will see that money has to be budgeted to meet needs first and then wants. He will learn what it means to save money and to spend wisely.

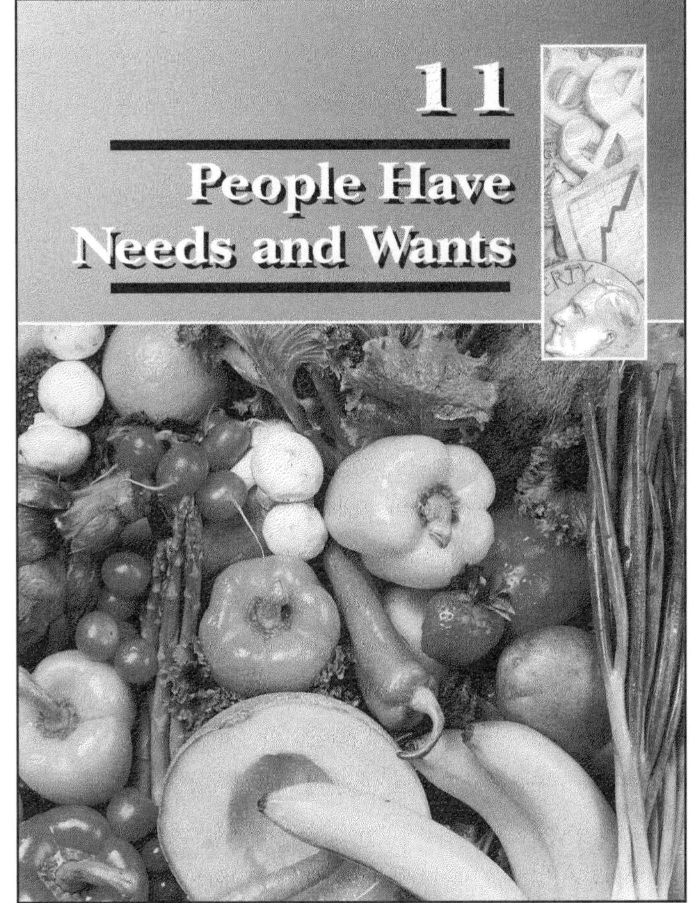

Materials

The following materials must be obtained or prepared before the presentation of the lesson. These items are labeled with an asterisk (*) in each lesson and in the Materials List in the Supplement. For further information see the individual lessons.

- Several camping items (Lesson 50)
- A picture of a man dressed for construction or farm work (Lesson 52)
- A picture of a man dressed in formal clothes (Lesson 52)
- Play or real money (Lesson 53)
- Items to make a piggy bank (Lesson 54)
- Appendix, pages A34-A35 (Lesson 54)

LESSON 50
Things People Need

Text, pages 140-41
Notebook, pages 55-56

Preview

Main Ideas

- Needs are things people must have to live.
- All people have the same basic needs.

Objectives

- Differentiate between things that are needed and things that are not needed
- Distinguish among the four basic needs of people

Materials

- Several camping items (a flashlight, matches, a sleeping bag, and so on)*
- Several miscellaneous items not needed for camping
- A large cardboard box in which you place the above items

Notes

In the first part of this chapter you have the opportunity to help your child understand the complex question of why God allows Christians to have needs. The most important part of this concept is the fact that God supplies your child's needs. His desire is for His children to trust Him completely with every need and to watch Him work in their lives.

Day 1

Lesson

Introducing the Lesson

Direct a classifying activity. If your child has ever been camping, allow a few moments for him to tell about his trip. Show the box filled with the collected items. Explain that in the box are some things that would be important on a camping trip and some things that would not be important.

Classifying Activity

➤ Take out all the items that would be important on a camping trip.

➤ Why did you leave some things in the box? *(They are not important for a camping trip.)*

➤ Tell me why you chose each camping item.

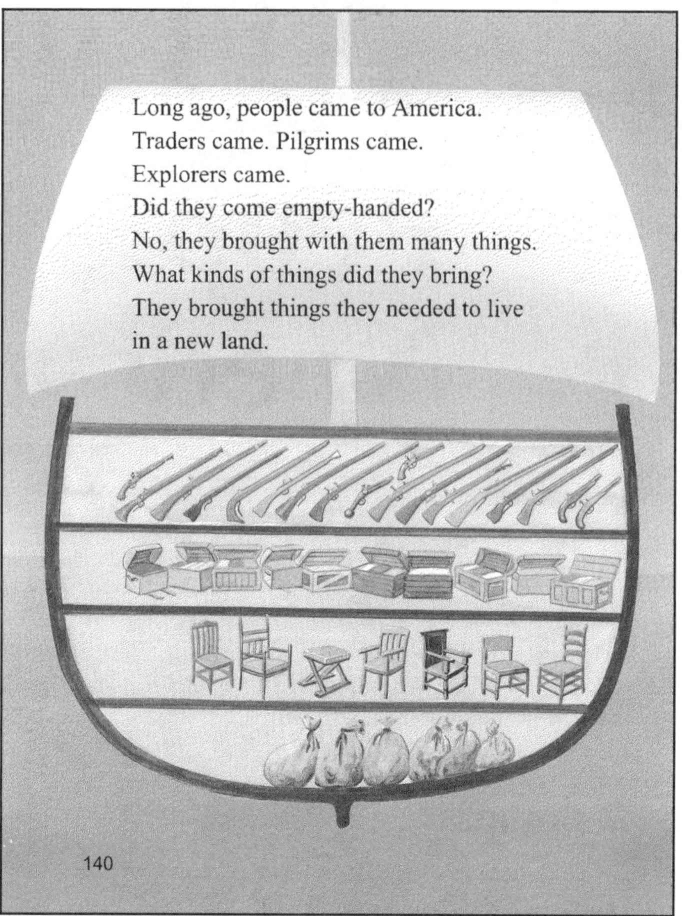

Long ago, people came to America.
Traders came. Pilgrims came.
Explorers came.
Did they come empty-handed?
No, they brought with them many things.
What kinds of things did they bring?
They brought things they needed to live
in a new land.
140

➤ What would the camping trip be like without these things? *(chilly, dark, etc.)* These things are necessary to make the camping trip comfortable and enjoyable.

Teaching the Lesson

Direct a text activity on pages 140-41. Remind your child that the people who came to the New World had to choose what to take on the ship with them.

Text Discussion, page 140

➤ How do you think coming by ship instead of coming by wagon would change what the people could take with them?

➤ Different ways of traveling mean different ways of getting ready. How would your camping trip list change if you had to go by bicycle instead of car or truck?

➤ Read the first five sentences on page 140. Then read sentence six to find the answer. *(No, they brought many things with them.)*

➤ Read the next question. Name a few things the people might have brought to their new homes.

➤ Read the last sentence to find the answer. Look at the pictures on the page. What did the settlers bring? *(guns, chests, chairs, bundles)*

➤ Why do you think these were important to the settlers? *(Answers will vary; guns—safety and food; chests—clothing; chairs—home.)*

Things People Need

People everywhere have needs.
Needs are the things people must have to live.
What things do you need to live?
You need food.
You need a place to live.
You need clothes to wear.
And you need care and love
from other people.

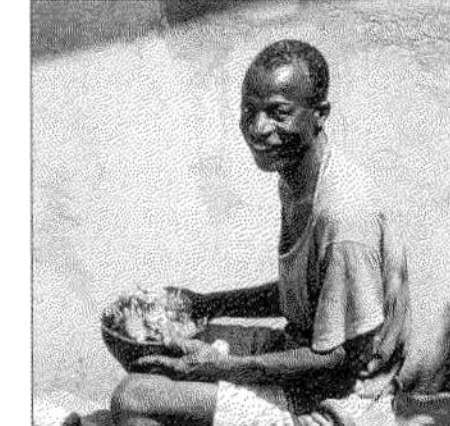

For your heavenly Father knoweth that ye have need of all these things.
Matthew 6:32

141

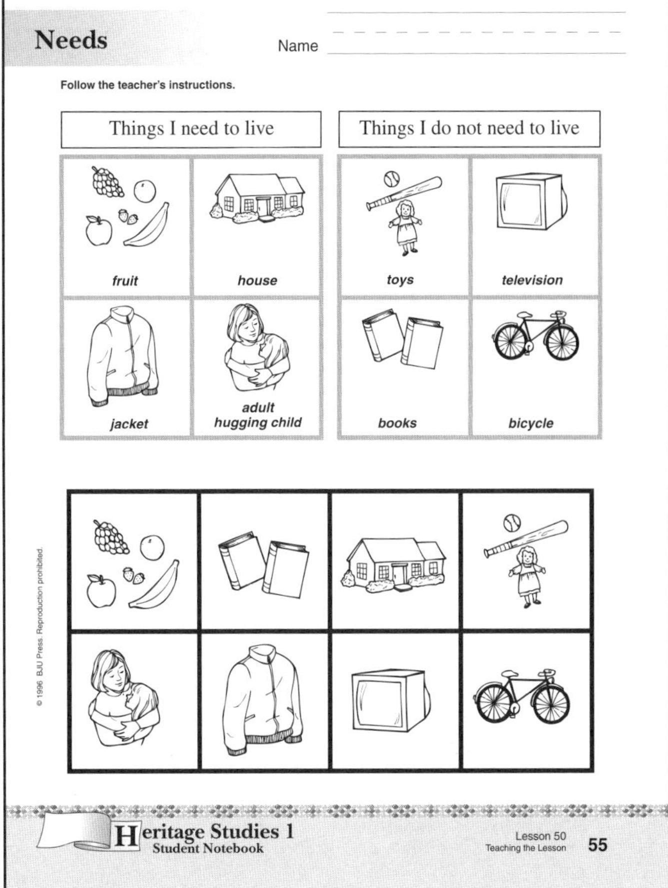

Needs Name

Follow the teacher's instructions.

Things I need to live		Things I do not need to live	
fruit	house	toys	television
jacket	adult hugging child	books	bicycle

Heritage Studies 1 Student Notebook — Lesson 50 Teaching the Lesson 55

Day 2

Text Discussion, page 141

➤ Read the first three sentences. Name some things that you think we need to live today. Read the rest of the page to find out what we truly need in order to live. *(food, clothing, home, and love)*

All people have the same basic **needs,** but the things used to meet those needs may be different.

➤ Name some of the things the Indians in the New World needed to live. Do we need these things today? Why do we not need some of the items? *(Answers will vary.)*

➤ Why were guns more necessary to the settlers than to us? *(We do not have to hunt for food or stand guard in a fort.)*

➤ Why do we have to eat? *(to stay healthy)*

➤ Who provides your food? *(God provides all food; parents provide for their children from what God has given them.)*

➤ Name some different kinds of houses that people live in.

A place to live is called **shelter.** There are many kinds of shelters, but the size and kind of house is not as important as the love and care that the people in it have for each other. (BATs: 5a Love, 7d Contentment)

> Read the verse at the bottom of page 141. Ask why God allows us to have needs. *(Answers will vary.)* Lead your child to the conclusion that God wants us to trust Him to meet our needs. Guide a discussion about the ways in which God meets our needs, such as providing us with loving parents or sending rain to help the food grow. Discuss our responsibility to be grateful to God. (BATs: 7c Praise, 8a Faith in God's promises; Bible Promise: H. God as Father)

Direct an activity on Notebook page 55. Read the two headings to your child. Allow him to color the pictures and then cut them out. Instruct him to glue each picture under the appropriate heading.

Four Basic Needs

Name

Color and cut out the pictures.
Glue the needs in the correct columns.

Food	Shelter	Clothing	Love
fruit	apartment house	gloves	adult reading to child
bread	trailer	sweater	adult and child holding hands
pizza	house	shoes	child kissing mother

Heritage Studies 1 Student Notebook

Lesson 50 Evaluating the Lesson 56

Evaluating the Lesson

Direct an activity on Notebook page 56. Review the four basic needs as you point to each heading. Explain to your child that he will complete a chart of the four basic needs. Instruct him to color and cut apart the squares of pictures at the bottom of the page. Direct him to glue each picture in the column of the need that it would meet.

Going Beyond

Enrichment

Provide the basic needs story page for your child. (*NOTE:* See the Appendix, page A32.) Allow him to cut a picture from a magazine to complete each square. Instruct him to make up a story using the pictures he has chosen. Allow your child to share his story with the family.

Additional Teacher Information

The modern housewarming party is a variation on a much earlier tradition. When a family finished building a home in pioneer times, they would invite their friends to be with them when they lit the first fire in the fireplace. To be invited to this ceremony bespoke the warmth of the friendship. It was an especially appropriate gathering if the neighbors had helped build the house or clear the land. Today's version is a time for getting to know new neighbors or for inviting old friends to visit a new home.

3-4

LESSON 51
People Need Food and Shelter

Text, pages 142-45
Notebook, pages 57-58

Preview

Main Ideas

- People need food.
- People need a place to live.

Objectives

- List two different ways people get food
- Match different types of homes with the people who live in them

Materials

- A garden vegetable or fruit that contains seeds
- A prepackaged food, such as a can of vegetables
- A knife

Day 1

Lesson

Introducing the Lesson

Direct an activity on Notebook page 57. Direct your child's attention to the drawings under the Saturday heading on the Notebook page. Ask what foods are pictured. *(soup, crackers, a drink, and grapes)* Explain that these foods show what a child ate for lunch on Saturday. Tell him to choose a meal he has eaten that week and to draw it in the appropriate square. You may need to help him find the right square.

Teaching the Lesson

Direct a comparison activity. Ask your child where he thinks his food comes from.

Comparison Activity

➤ *Show the fresh vegetable and the canned vegetable.* Which one might have come straight from a garden, and which might have been bought in a store? *(Answers may vary. The food bought in a store was also grown in a garden at one time, but some worker in a factory prepared it and put it in a package to sell.)*

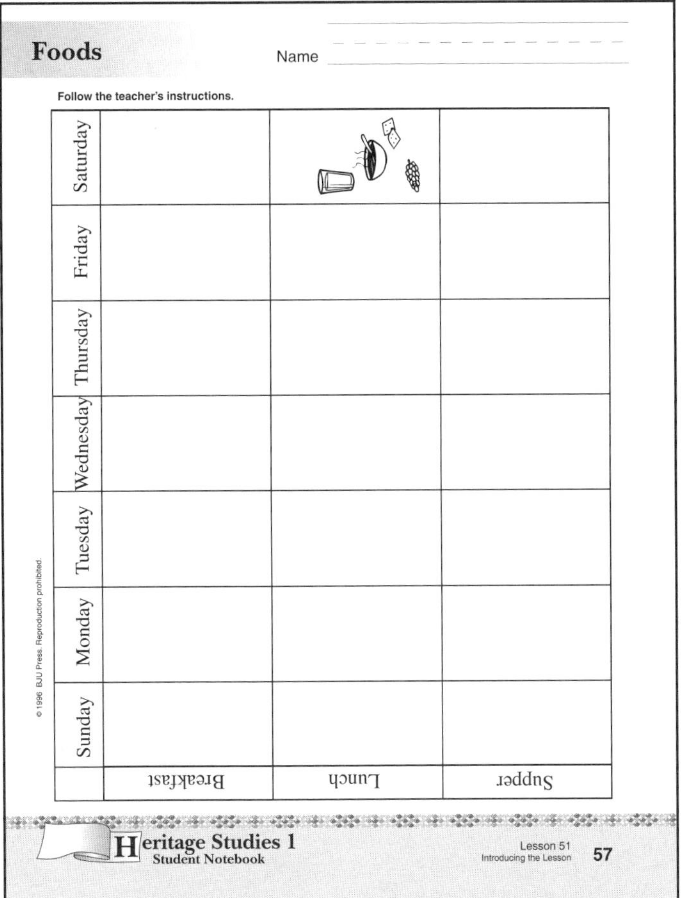

Foods Name

Follow the teacher's instructions.

	Breakfast	Lunch	Supper
Saturday			
Friday			
Thursday			
Wednesday			
Tuesday			
Monday			
Sunday			

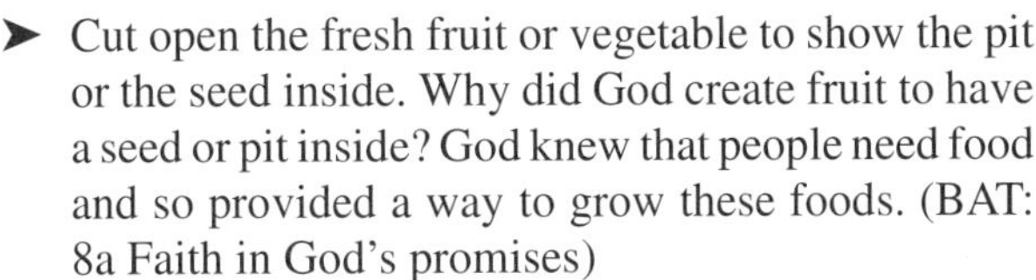

Heritage Studies 1 Student Notebook — Lesson 51 Introducing the Lesson 57

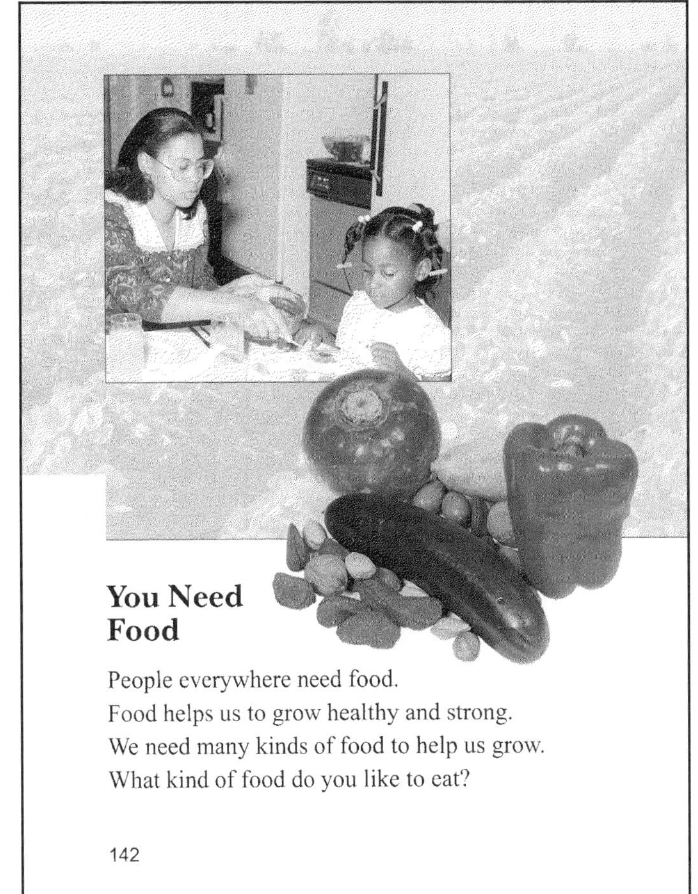

You Need Food

People everywhere need food.
Food helps us to grow healthy and strong.
We need many kinds of food to help us grow.
What kind of food do you like to eat?

142

- ➤ Cut open the fresh fruit or vegetable to show the pit or the seed inside. Why did God create fruit to have a seed or pit inside? God knew that people need food and so provided a way to grow these foods. (BAT: 8a Faith in God's promises)
- ➤ What will happen if you plant the seed? *(A plant will grow.)*

Direct a text activity on pages 142-45. Read pages 142-43.

Text Discussion, pages 142-43

- ➤ Look at the picture of the little girl at the supper table. Where do you think the family got the food? *(from the store or from a garden)*
- ➤ Tell about some foods you like.
- ➤ Which foods shown on the page might have come from a garden?

> You may want to talk about gardens, reminding your child that God created each kind of food. (Bible Promise: H. God as Father)

- ➤ What does God give us to help a garden grow? *(rain and sunshine)* In giving rain and sunshine, God is actually supplying our need for food. (Bible Promise: H. God as Father)
- ➤ Why is it important for people to eat? *(to grow, to stay healthy)*
- ➤ What would happen if a person did not eat? *(Answers will vary.)*

All people need four main things to live. One of those things is food. Water is included as part of the food category.

> Christians need spiritual food to stay healthy. Ask where Christians get this "spiritual food." *(the Bible)* Ask your child whether Christians get this spiritual food by really eating it. *(no, by reading God's Word)* (BAT: 6a Bible study)

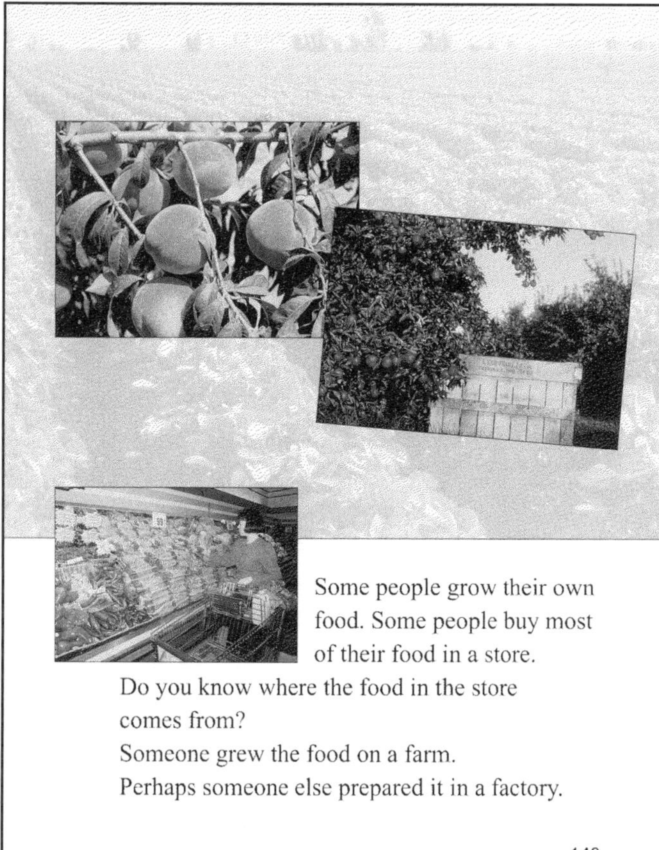

Some people grow their own food. Some people buy most of their food in a store.
Do you know where the food in the store comes from?
Someone grew the food on a farm.
Perhaps someone else prepared it in a factory.

143

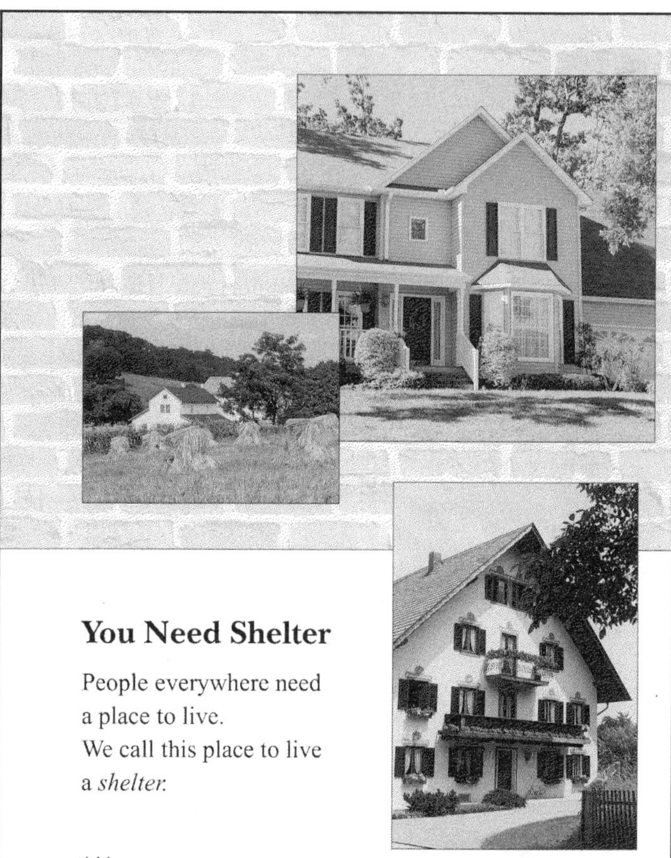

You Need Shelter

People everywhere need a place to live.
We call this place to live a *shelter.*

144

Day 2

Text Discussion, page 144

➤ Read page 144. Another basic need is shelter. What is a shelter? *(a building or other place in which people can be protected from the cold, rain, heat, etc.)*

➤ Name some different kinds of shelters. *(apartment, house, castle, tent, tipi)*

The pictures on the text page show kinds of shelters. Houses are different from each other on both the outside and the inside.

➤ Name some of the differences. *(Answers will vary: made of different materials, different sizes, different shapes, different colors.)*

Text Discussion, page 145

➤ Read and answer the first question.

➤ Read the rest of the page. What can a shelter protect you from? *(cold, rain, heat, snow, wind)*

The way a house is built sometimes depends on the kind of weather the people have most of the time. In parts of Japan where it is hot and rainy much of the time, the houses have doors that slide into the walls. This arrangement lets breezes sweep through easily, drying out the air inside.

➤ Do you remember Leif Ericson, the Viking?

His people lived where it is cold much of the time. They made tiny holes in the walls of their houses called *wind eyes* that let in fresh air but not too much cold wind. Our word *windows* comes from the Viking word.

➤ What do you think was most important for the settlers at Plymouth to do when they came to the New World? *(Answers will vary but may include find water and build shelter.)*

➤ The settlers had the same needs as you and I have. How did they meet their needs for food and shelter?

The settlers did not have restaurants and grocery stores or hotels or houses waiting for them. (*NOTE:* Refer to Lessons 24, 29, and 30 for more details.) The settlers had to meet their needs with the things they found around them.

➤ Do you remember how the settlers chose the place they lived in? *(It had clean water and trees for building houses, among other advantages.)*

➤ People build houses out of the material they have near them. Look back at the picture on page 42. Do you think the Hopi people had many trees to build with? *(no)* They used the clay that was all around them.

What does your home
look like?
Your home is a shelter.
It protects you from cold weather.
It protects you from rain.
It keeps you dry and warm.
What things do you do in your home?
145

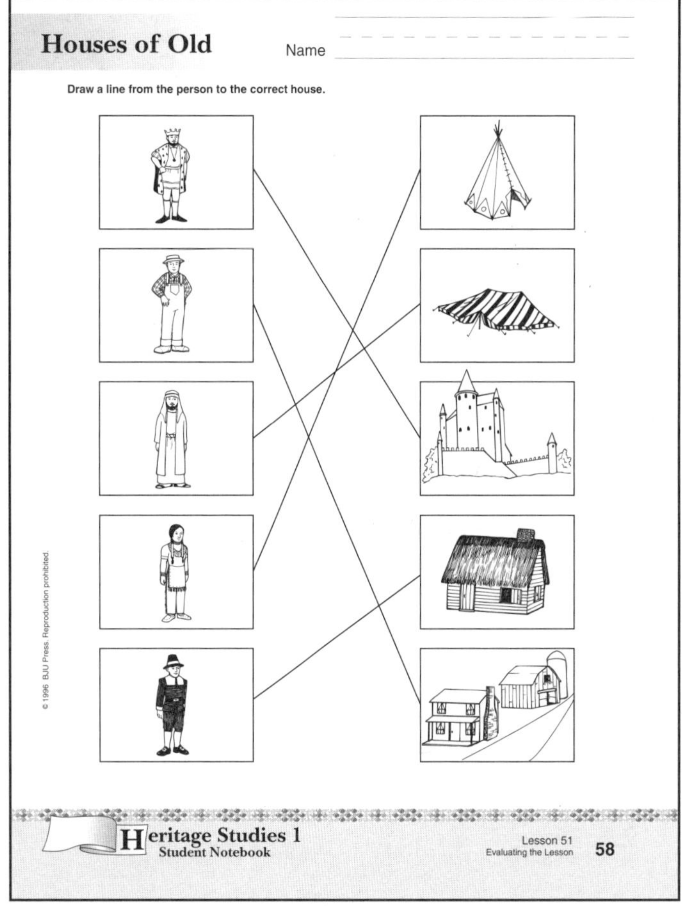

Houses of Old
Name
Draw a line from the person to the correct house.
© 1996 BJU Press. Reproduction prohibited.
Heritage Studies 1
Student Notebook
Lesson 51
Evaluating the Lesson
58

Evaluating the Lesson

Direct an activity on Notebook page 58. Just as modern houses are different from each other, the houses of people long ago were different too.

Notebook Activity

- Name the kinds of houses on the page. *(tipi, tent, castle, thatched-roof house, modern house/farm)*
- Why do you think each group of people made their houses in a different way?

  Each group used the materials around them. Pilgrims used wood and straw, and Indians used buffalo skins.

- Draw lines on the Notebook page matching each person to the house in which he would live.
- Which of these shelters might be used today? *(farm, possibly castle)*
- Look at the History TimeLine. In what year could we find the Plymouth house? *(1620)*
- Do you think that the Bible-time tent was made before the Plymouth house? *(yes)* The people in the Old Testament lived long before the Separatists.
- Draw on the back of the Notebook page a picture of what you think a house might look like in the future.

Going Beyond

Additional Teacher Information

Although we often see pictures depicting the Pilgrims and early settlers in North America living in log cabins, this assumption is incorrect. The first settlers built framed houses out of planks or timber and used thatched roofs. Log cabins were never built in the Massachusetts Bay Colony or the Virginia Colony. They were not introduced by the English settlers but rather by the German and Swedish settlers.

Log cabins were a primary housing for only some of the early Americans. It was not considered prestigious, nor was it as comfortable and idealistic as we imagine. As soon as was possible, settlers built new, more modern homes to replace the log cabins. Log cabins have taken a bigger role in folk stories than they actually held in history.

LESSON 52
People Need Clothes and Love

Text, pages 146-49
Notebook, page 59

Preview

Main Ideas

- People need clothes.
- Some people make their clothes.
- Some people buy their clothes already made.
- People need love and care.
- God loves and cares for people everywhere.

Objectives

- Describe what type of clothing is worn in specific seasons
- List some ways in which people show love

Materials

- A picture of a man dressed for construction or farm work*
- A picture of a man dressed in formal clothes*
- Maps and More 10 and 32, pages M7 and M16

Day 1

Lesson

Introducing the Lesson

Direct a discussion. Explain to your child that there was a man who was on his way to his friend's wedding to be the best man.

Discussion

➤ *Show the picture of the man dressed for physical work.* Do you think this man is ready to be in a wedding? *(probably not)*

➤ Another man was going to do some hard work. He was going to get a little dirty, so he dressed for the job. *Show the picture of the man in formal attire.* Does the man look ready to do hard work? *(no)*

➤ Do you think I got the pictures mixed up? *(yes)* Why?

➤ People wear different clothes for different occasions and activities. Would you go to church in your pajamas? *(no)*

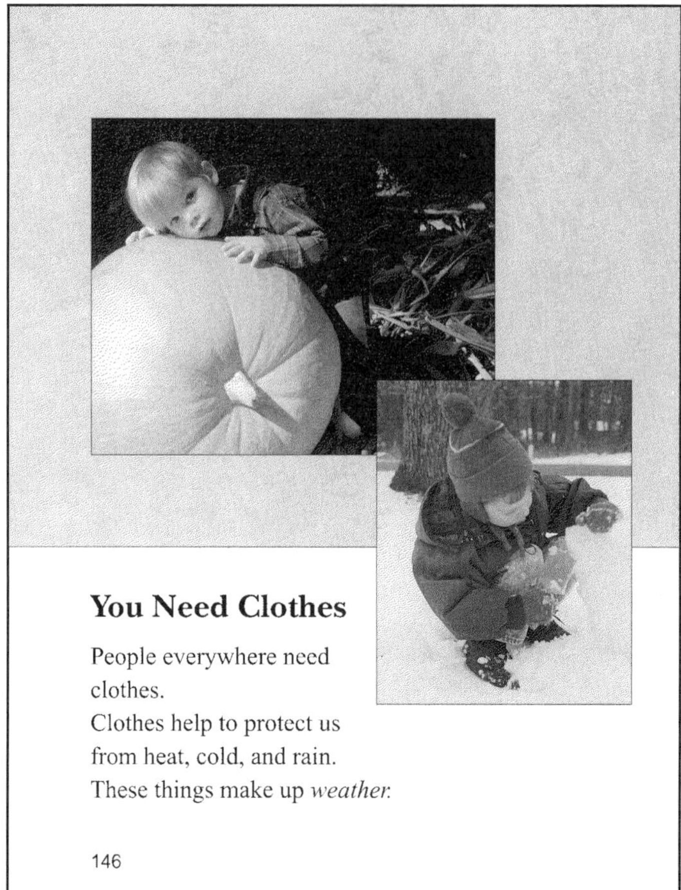

You Need Clothes

People everywhere need clothes.
Clothes help to protect us from heat, cold, and rain.
These things make up *weather.*

146

➤ Would you wear your church clothes to bed? *(no)*

➤ Why do people wear different types of clothes? *(Answers will vary but may include keeping warm and looking stylish, etc.)*

Teaching the Lesson

Direct a text activity on pages 146-49. Show your child Maps and More 32, directing him to notice the different types of clothing that the people are wearing.

Text Discussion, page 146

➤ One of the four basic things people need is clothing. What two other needs did we learn about in our last lesson? *(food, shelter)*

➤ Read page 146. What kind of clothes must children put on before they go out into the snow? *(warm clothing such as gloves, scarves, coats, etc.)*

➤ People wear different clothing depending upon the climate or weather conditions. What is the climate like in Florida? *(hot)*

➤ What type of clothing do people who live in Florida wear? *(Answers will vary; probably lightweight.)*

➤ How would the kind of clothes that someone must wear in Alaska be different from the Florida clothing? *(Answers will vary; they would probably be much heavier.)*

Some people must have clothes for warm weather and cold weather.
These people live where the weather changes with the seasons.
The seasons are winter, spring, summer, and fall.
Does the weather change with the seasons where you live?
Do you have clothes for more than one season?

Where do people get the clothes they need?
Some people buy their clothes in a store.
These clothes have been made by other people.
Some people make their own clothes.
Do you have any clothes that were made especially for you?

147

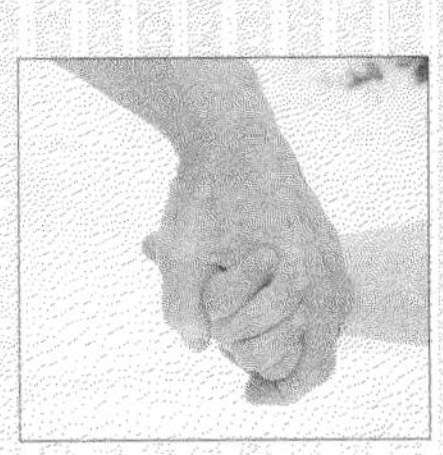

You Need Love and Care

People everywhere need love and care.
They need to love and care for others too.
Who loves and cares for you?
Your family and friends do.
God loves and cares for you too.

148

Text Discussion, page 147

- Read the first section on the page. Look at Maps and More 10. Name the seasons of the year. *(spring, summer, fall, winter)*
- Do you have different clothes for different weather? *(Answers will vary.)*
- Read the second section. Where did you get the clothes you are wearing? *(Answers will vary; mother made them, bought them at a store, somebody gave them as a gift, etc.)*
- Why do you like certain clothes?

You may want to use this opportunity to point out that clothes are not as important as advertisements, television commercials, and peer pressure would have us believe. Remind your child that character is more important than how we look. (BATs: 7d Contentment, 7e Humility)

- Have you ever watched your clothes being made?

When clothes are made at home, the seamstress usually uses a pattern and has fittings to make sure the clothes will fit right. The seamstress usually uses a sewing machine with a needle and thread that makes stitches to hold the clothes together. Even the clothes that are bought in a store are made from patterns and are sewn together. The clothes that are bought in the store are usually made by a worker in a factory; others are made in the home by the mother or another family member.

Sometimes someone makes clothes at home because those in the store are not suitable. Sometimes it saves money to make clothes at home. Often the clothes made at home fit better, and they can be just the color and style the person wants.

Dorcas, a kind, good woman in the Bible, made clothes for people who needed help. (*NOTE:* See Acts 9:36-42.) Explain that many times someone sews for another out of love. (BAT: 5a Love)

Day 2

Text Discussion, pages 148-49

- Read the pages. How are the people in the pictures showing love and care?
- Why did God give us families and friends? *(He knew that people need others around to give love and care.)*
- Who takes care of you? *(usually parents)*

Someone has cared for you since you were born. As a baby, you could not do much for yourself, but as you have grown, you have learned to do some things on your own.

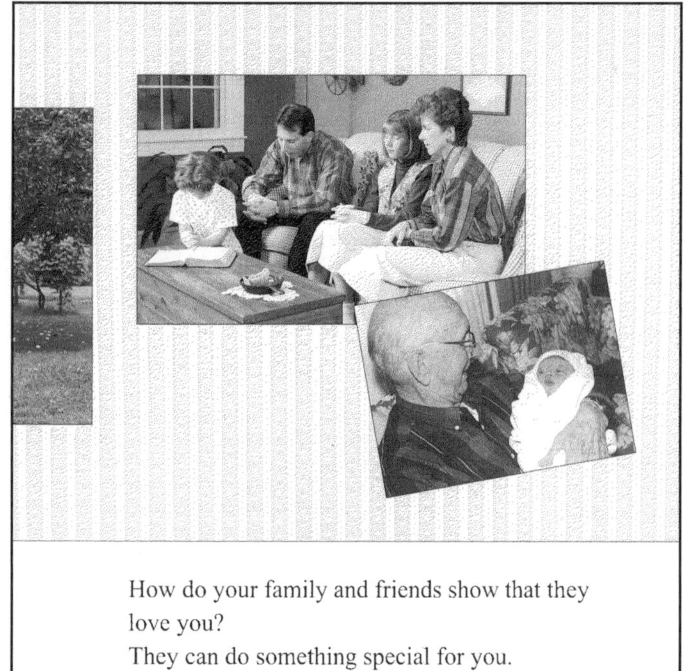

How do your family and friends show that they love you?
They can do something special for you.
They can do something special with you.
People have many ways to show others that they care. How can you show people that you love and care for them?

149

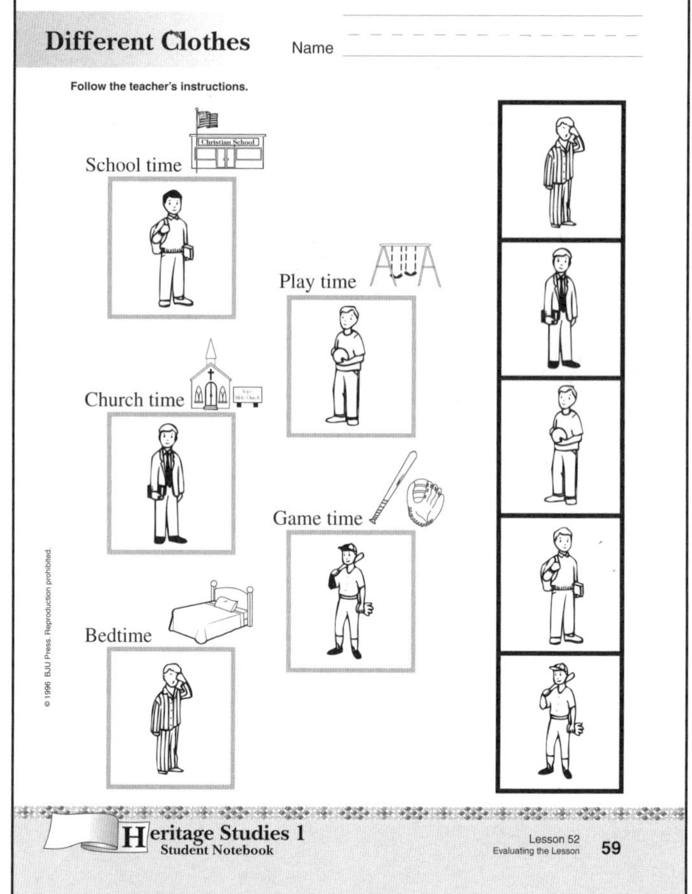

Different Clothes Name

Follow the teacher's instructions.

School time

Play time

Church time

Game time

Bedtime

© 1996 BJU Press. Reproduction prohibited.

Heritage Studies 1 Student Notebook

Lesson 52 Evaluating the Lesson 59

- ➤ What things must you do on your own now? *(make the bed, get dressed, etc.)*
- ➤ What things do your parents or family still do for you? *(cook meals, take to church, etc.)*
- ➤ Name some of the things that your friends do to show that they love you. *(share with him, play with him, do special things with him)*
- ➤ Can you name some ways that you can show your love to your family and friends each day?
- ➤ Can you name the last of the four basic needs? *(love)*
- ➤ There is someone who loves us more than anyone else and who understands and provides for all our needs. Who do you think that someone is? *(God)*

Lead a discussion about how your child can know that God loves him and how God shows His love. Read I John 3:16: "Hereby perceive we the love of God, because he laid down his life for us." (Bible Promise: E. Christ as Sacrifice) Remind your child that we can know for sure that God loves us and that we should show Him we love Him. Encourage him to name ways he can show God that he loves Him. (BATs: 1c Separation from the world, 4b Purity, 6a Bible study, 7c Praise, 8a Faith in God's promises; Bible Promise: H. God as Father)

Evaluating the Lesson

Direct an activity on Notebook page 59. Read the phrases beside each picture. Ask your child to color the clothes in colors that he would like to wear. Instruct him to cut out the pictures. Allow him to choose which activity he will match with each outfit. Direct him to glue the pictures on the correct locations.

Going Beyond

Enrichment

Give your child a copy of the story "Camping Out." (*NOTE:* See the Appendix, page A33.) Read the dialogue with him. At each underlined word, instruct him to circle which of the four basic needs that word represents. *(food, shelter, food, clothing, love, love)*

Additional Teacher Information

Clothing has been an important cultural aspect in every civilization. Many civilizations have had unique social standards of dress. In early Rome, peasants were allowed to wear only one color. Most citizens wore a cream color, the natural color of the wool used to make the garments. Royal members could wear six or more colors in their garments. Purple and gold could be worn only by the nobility or high-ranking officials. Footwear was also limited in later Rome. Sandals and shoes were decorated with paint or even jewels, but only red, green, yellow, or white shoes could be worn by women.

In Greece, where simplicity was admired as much as beauty, borders were the only decorations on the garments. The Greeks wore purple for festivities and black for mourning. Early French women were forbidden to cut their hair after they were married and had to cover their head with a sheer veil as a religious symbol of repentance for Eve's sin. However, by late Middle Ages, veils were a sign of social class. Plebeians wore only waist-length veils, but upper-class women wore floor-length veils. Also, in the late Middle Ages, the accepted color for a wedding dress was red.

3-11

LESSON 53
Things People Want

Text, pages 150-51

Preview

Main Ideas

- People have the same basic needs but different wants.
- People work to get money to buy the things they need and want.

Objectives

- Distinguish the difference between wants and needs
- Show that we use money to pay for wants and needs

Materials

- A one-dollar bill
- A quarter
- Food, clothing, toy houses (or pictures of houses), toys, books, and other items that a child might want to buy
- A sheet of paper
- Blank stickers or Post-It Note Pads
- Play or real money*

You will need to put price tags on the items using the blank stickers. When pricing the items, consider the denominations of the play money bills you have and the goal of teaching your child to distinguish between wants and needs. Make most needs more affordable than the wants.

Day 1

Lesson

Introducing the Lesson

Direct a vocabulary activity. Write the word *desire* on a piece of paper. Say the word.

Vocabulary Activity

➤ What do you think the word *desire* means? *(Answers will vary.)* It means "a wish for something."

➤ Let's make a birthday (Christmas) list on this sheet of paper.

➤ Do you think that there is anything on your list that you will not get? *(Answers will vary; probably yes.)*

➤ Do you think the things you will not get are needs?
➤ Do you need any of the things you listed in order to live? *(probably not)*

Sometimes we might think that we need these things to live, but most things we wish for are not needs. They are wants. Wants are desires. (BAT: 7d Contentment)

Read Psalm 37:4: "Delight thyself also in the Lord; and he shall give thee the desires of thine heart." Ask your child whether he thinks that God wants us to have *some* of the things that we desire. *(yes)* Ask whether he thinks God will give us *all* of the things we want. *(no)* Ask why not. *(They would not be good for us. He has something better for us.)* Explain that God loves us and wants to give us what is best. (Bible Promise: H. God as Father) Sometimes what we think is best and what God says is best are not the same, but God is all-knowing. We should trust Him to supply not only our needs but also our wants. (BAT: 8a Faith in God's promises) God wants us to talk to Him and to tell Him the things we would like to have, but He also wants us to be content with the things He has given us. Discuss with your child some of the wants God has already given him. Remind him that we should be thankful for the way God cares for us. (BAT: 7d Contentment)

Teaching the Lesson

Direct a text activity on page 150. Read the page.

Text Discussion, page 150

➤ What is a **want?** *(a thing that we would like to have)*
➤ Look at the chart. Which row has the most things that interest you? *(probably the second)*
➤ Compare the other rows to the second one. *(Answers will vary; he may notice that a stuffed animal appears in the first and second rows and that a bicycle appears in the second and third rows.)*
➤ What other things would you put in the rows of the chart?
➤ *Show your child how to make the letters* W *and* N *in sign language. Three fingers up is* W*; two fingers down is* N*. (See the figure below.) Practice with him a few times.*

W

N

Things People Want

People everywhere have wants.
Wants are things that we would like to have.
But we do not need them.
Do you get everything you want?
You must often decide which things you want the most.

Do you want the same things that your friend wants? Probably not.
All people have the same needs, but they do not always have the same wants.

150

➤ The *W* stands for *want* and the *N* stands for *need.* I will say a word. Show a sign telling me whether it is a want or a need. *Use words such as the following:* bread, socks, necklace, soccer ball, car, jacket.

Day 2

Direct a text activity on page 151. Read the first section.

Text Discussion, page 151

➤ Remember that the Indians traded many things, or goods, such as animal skins. Why would a trader want an animal skin? *(to sell, to make clothing)*
➤ Did the traders and Indians have paper money or coins like those we have? *(no)*

Early traders set their prices according to the things they were trading. For example, a gold necklace could cost one or two beaver skins. A beaded necklace could cost one or two iron tools. The trader then could trade the skins or the tools with other Indian tribes or with settlers for the products they made that someone else needed or wanted. The settlers and Indians hunted, made, or grew the things they used for "money." People still depend on each other to make or grow things that they do not make or grow themselves.

Getting Needs and Wants

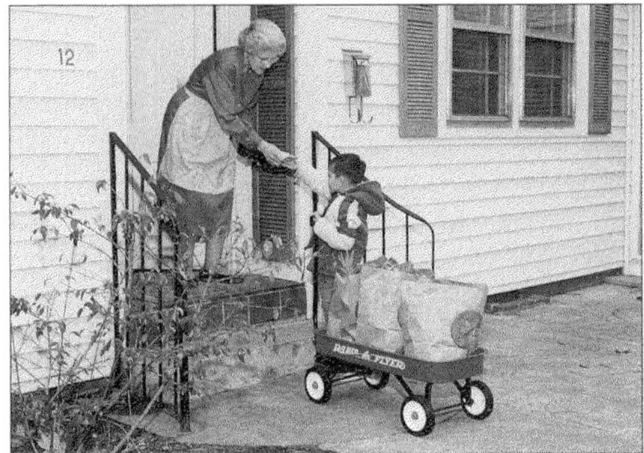

Long ago, people traded things they made or grew to get other things.
In this way, they got the things they needed and wanted.

Today we use money to pay for the things we need and want.
But we cannot grow money or make money.
How can we get money?
People get money by working.

151

- ➤ Do remember the wampum you made (Chapter 8)? Later the Indians traded wampum for goods from the settlers. Would you like to use wampum instead of dollars and coins?
- ➤ *Show a dollar bill and a quarter.* Do you know the names of these pieces of money and how much each is worth?
- ➤ Read the first two sentences of the second paragraph on page 151 to find out what we use money for. *(to pay for things we need and want)*
- ➤ What are some things you have bought?

In the United States people have the freedom to choose what they want to buy and to decide what they need. Not every country lets its people make as many choices as ours does.

- ➤ Read the rest of the page.

Most adults today get money by working for it. Most children do not work at a job. God gives children parents who work to buy what the children need. There are many different types of work that parents do.

Evaluating the Lesson

Direct a market day. Lay the items with the price tags along the kitchen counter or table. Tell your child that you are going to give him some money to go to the "market-place" to purchase the items he thinks he should buy. Explain that you will be the cashier and that you will be looking to see that he purchases at least one item that meets a need. Ask him to identify which item meets a need. If your child selects more than he can pay for, help him choose the item he will put back by asking, "Which item do you not need?"

Going Beyond

Enrichment

Give your child some old magazines that he can cut and a large piece of construction paper. Instruct him to cut out people to make a family and to glue the figures on the construction paper. Next tell him to cut out pictures that might represent the needs and wants of this family. Instruct him to try to find at least one picture for each of the four basic needs as well as some of the things that the family might want. Instruct him to glue these pictures on the paper also.

Additional Teacher Information

Many of the coins that we have today have been around for a long time, although most of them have undergone many changes in design and material. One of the earliest issued coins was the silver dollar, first minted in the 1790s. However, the silver dollar was out of issue for thirty-five years during this century, until it was reissued in 1975. The dime was first introduced in 1796 and has been produced every year except one since then. The quarter was also issued in 1796. The nickel and the penny are the latecomers, the nickel not appearing until 1866.

Pennies are made of copper, and up until 1965 all dimes, quarters, and silver dollars were made of silver. Today, copper that is covered by a layer of nickel is the main material in dimes, quarters, silver dollars, and nickels.

Each coin, excluding pennies and nickels, has a ridged edge. Before 1965, when coins were made of pure metals, people would trim off the edges of the coin. Then they could melt the metal and sell it. The ridges on the edges of coins were designed to keep people from stealing metal from the coin.

Lesson 54
Saving and Spending Money

Text, pages 152-54
Notebook, page 60

Preview

Main Ideas
- People save some of their money.
- People plan how to spend their money.
- A plan for spending money is called a budget.

Objective
- Distribute spending money into budget categories

Materials
- Appendix, page A34: a spending chart*
- Appendix, page A35: price tags for items (cut apart)*
- An empty, well-rinsed plastic jug (milk or liquid detergent)*
- A chenille wire*
- Two buttons (optional)*
- Four small empty spools*
- Felt-tip pens*
- Construction paper (optional)
- A sheet of paper
- Various coins in the amount of 50¢
- A calculator (optional)

Day 1

Lesson

Introducing the Lesson
Direct an art activity. Guide your child in making the piggy bank following the steps in the figures at the right. Encourage him to decorate his pig with eyes, ears, mouth, a tail, and any other decorations he wishes to make. Ask him how he can get his money out when he needs it. *(by opening the cap to dump out the coins)*

1. Turn the jug on its side.

2. Draw a rectangle on the jug for the coin slot.

3. Cut out the coin slot.

4. Decorate the bank. The tail may be made from chenille wire. The eyes may be made from buttons or drawn with a felt-tip pen. The mouth is drawn with a felt-tip pen. The ears may be made from construction paper or drawn with a felt-tip pen.

5. Glue on the spool legs.

Day 2

Teaching the Lesson
Direct a text activity on pages 152-53. Show the piggy bank.

Text Discussion, page 152
➤ Do you have some money saved?
➤ What does it mean to "save" money? *(to keep money for later)*
➤ Read page 152. Point to the picture that shows where most adults save their money. What is the place or building called? *(a bank)*
➤ A bank is a safe place to keep money.

If your child says that banks are sometimes robbed, explain that people can still get the money they had in the bank. The United States government pays if something happens to the bank.

◆ THINGS PEOPLE DO ◆

Saving Money

Have you ever needed or wanted something that cost a lot of money?
How might you get enough money to buy it?
You could save small amounts of money.
Soon you would have enough to buy what you wanted.

Adults save money in buildings that look like this.

Children save money in places like that too.

More often children save money in places like this.

What do we call these kinds of places? We call them *banks.*
Banks are a safe place to save money.

152

Many people make a plan for spending their money.
This plan is called a *budget.*
When people follow their budget, they can buy the things they need.
They may even have money left to buy some of the things they want.

Delight thyself also in the Lord; and he shall give thee the desires of thine heart.

Psalm 37:4

153

➤ It is important for us to be wise with our money because we need it to meet our needs, but God does not want Christians to be always worrying about money. God promises to take care of His people if they are obeying Him. While we should be wise with the money we have, we should not love money. (BAT: 7d Contentment; Bible Promise: H. God as Father)

God has a safe place for us in heaven in which to keep our treasures. Read Matthew 6:20-21: "But lay up for yourselves treasures in heaven, where neither moth nor rust doth corrupt, and where thieves do not break through nor steal: For where your treasure is, there will your heart be also." Invite your child to name some heavenly treasures. *(kind deeds, souls led to Christ, etc.)* (BATs: 4a Sowing and reaping, 5c Evangelism and missions, 8a Faith in God's promises)

Text Discussion, page 153

➤ Read the page. What do we call a plan for spending money? *(a budget)*

➤ Look at the Spending Chart. The biggest box shows all the money that we have. We must decide how to spend our money. A **budget** helps us make a plan.

➤ What is the first thing that we should do with our money? *(Answers will vary.)*

We should give God something first. (BAT: 5b Giving) Find the circle on the chart that shows we have given some money to God.

➤ Which box is almost as big as the Money-on-Hand box? *(money for needs)*

In a budget, the needs must be put first. Only if there is money left over after planning for all the needs can we think about what we want.

➤ Why do you think the needs box is almost as big as the box for the money at hand? *(because most money goes for needs)*

➤ What do we spend our money on after we have paid for our needs? It is found in the next largest box. *(our wants)*

➤ After we have decided what to spend for needs and wants, where does the money go? *(money to save)*

Evaluating the Lesson

Direct a budget activity. Give your child 50¢ in various coin denominations. Place the price tags and the Spending Chart in front of him.

◆ LEARNING HOW ◆

To Make a Budget

1. Get a pencil and your Notebook.
2. Pretend that you earn a 50-cent allowance each week. Make a list of the things you need. Make another list of the things you want. Decide how you should spend your money each week.
3. Write the things you need and want. Record the amount of money you can spend on each thing during the week. Remember to give some of your money to God. Make sure that you do not spend more than 50 cents during the week.

154

My Budget Name ____________

Follow the teacher's instructions.

Money to spend			50¢
For God			– ¢
		Money left	¢
For needs			
	1.	¢	
	2.	¢	
	3.	¢ All needs }	– ¢
		Money left	¢
For wants			¢
For savings			¢

The purpose of the following activity is to show your child how a budget is developed. A small amount of money that he can visualize has been chosen. The amounts designated and manipulated for the items that he is purchasing are intentionally unrealistic. Your child will need your help in making adjustments between the categories. It is recommended that you use a calculator so that your child can focus on the budget activity and not the math.

Budget Activity

- ➤ Put all your money on the Money-on-Hand box.
- ➤ What is the first thing we should do with our money? *(give some to God)* Decide how much money you will give to God and put it on the circle.
- ➤ Sort the items on the price tags into two sets: needs and wants. Select several items from the needs category. Use a calculator to add up the cost of the items you need. Take the money from the Money-on-Hand box and put it on the Needs box.

You may ask your child to choose something from each of the categories—food, shelter, and clothing. If he has a specific want, you may add a picture of it to the set of wants.

- ➤ Now select an item or items that you want. Add the cost of the item(s) and put this money on the Wants box.
- ➤ How much money are you going to save? Put the money on this box.

Going Beyond

Enrichment

Use the *Learning How* activity on text page 154 and Notebook page 60 to help your child develop a personal budget. (*NOTE:* You may want to change the amount on the Notebook page to reflect the amount of allowance your child receives.) Follow the steps on page 154.

Additional Teacher Information

We quite logically think that the piggy bank acquired its name because of its shape. In fact, the reverse is true; the bank takes its shape from its name. In early America, people saved coins by placing them in a pot or jar. Glass and tin were used at first, but in the 1700s people began using a new clay material to make jars and pots. This material was called *pygg;* soon the colonists referred to all containers as "pygg jars." Eventually someone made the connection between a pygg jar and the plump, four-legged animal. Once the coin holder became known as a piggy jar, potters began making special coin banks in the shape of a pig.

12 LESSONS 55-60

Families Together

This final chapter discusses the importance of the family. The uniqueness of your child and his family is emphasized. Art activities, discussion, and role-playing help your child to express the ways in which your family is special. The last two lessons deal with the fact that each family has a history. Your child will work with a family tree and a personal time line to understand his place in his family history.

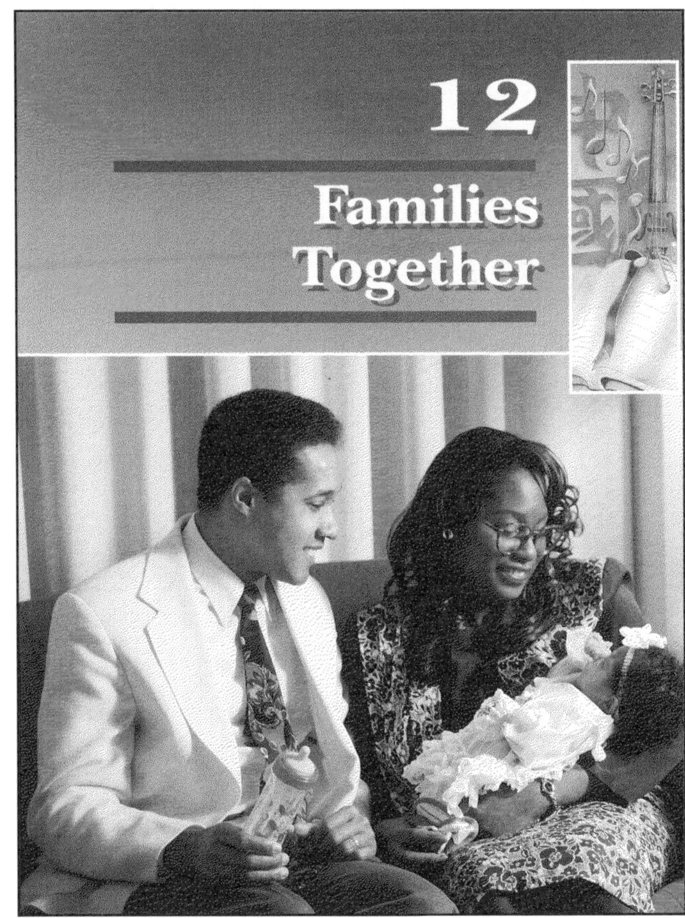

Materials

The following materials and items must be obtained or prepared before the presentation of the lesson. These items are labeled with an asterisk (*) in each lesson and in the Materials List in the Supplement. For further information, see the individual lessons.

- A large piece of chart paper or butcher paper or a growth chart (Lesson 55)
- 1 or 2 books listing the meanings of first names (Lesson 55)
- *If Everybody Did* by JoAnn Stover (Lesson 57) (optional)
- *Pulling Together* by Dawn Watkins (Lesson 58) (optional)
- An item that has been in your family for a long time (Lesson 59)
- 3 to 4 photographs of yourself at different ages (Lesson 60)
- Four sheets of construction paper (Lesson 60)
- Photos of several important events in your child's life (Lesson 60) (optional)

Lesson 55
You Are Special

Text, pages 156-58
Notebook, pages 61-62

Preview

Main Ideas

- God made each person different from every other person.
- A person changes as he grows older.
- A person learns to do new things as he grows older.

Objectives

- Locate the child's name in a book listing the meanings of first names
- Match sentences with the children they describe

Materials

- A large piece of chart paper or butcher paper at least 4 feet long or a growth chart*
- A yardstick
- Tape or Plasti-Tak
- 1 or 2 books listing the meanings of first names*
- A piece of drawing paper

Notes

You may want your child to make a "My Family and Me" book. Several of the art and writing activities suggested throughout the chapter, as well as appropriate Notebook pages, may be included in the book. This book will not only be enjoyable for your child and family but is also an important first step in learning about your family's history. If you choose to make this book, you will want to keep your child's work in a folder until the end of the chapter.

To enhance the introduction for Lesson 59, you will need an older person to tell about his life when he was growing up. If a grandparent or older friend cannot come to your home, perhaps you can ask one of them to write a letter or make an audio tape about his experiences and send it to your child.

Day 1

Lesson

Introducing the Lesson

Direct an activity on Notebook page 61. Read the sentence starter at the top of the page. Point out to your child that this phrase begins each of the questions on the top part of the page. Then read the sentence starter at the bottom of the page; this phrase begins the remaining questions on page 61 and on the back. Instruct your child to answer each question about himself. When he has finished, allow him to share his answers.

That's Me! Name ______________

Answer each question about yourself.

What is your favorite . . . *Answers will vary.*

color? ______________

subject in school? ______________

book? ______________

game? ______________

animal? ______________

Bible story? ______________

place to visit? ______________

What do you . . .

like to do on weekends? ______________

Heritage Studies 1 Student Notebook — Lesson 55 Introducing the Lesson — 61

This work can be included in the "My Family and Me" book.

Teaching the Lesson

Direct a text activity on pages 156-58. Call attention to the children pictured on the page. Read page 156.

Text Discussion, page 156

- ➤ Why are we different from each other? *(Answers will vary; God created us that way.)*
- ➤ Look at the word ***individual.*** This word means that there is no one else just like you anywhere in the world. How does that make you feel?
- ➤ God gave you special things that you could do well when He created you. What things do you think you do well? *(Answers may include help Mom or Dad, play an instrument, or play a sport.)*
- ➤ What does God want you to do with the abilities that He has given you? *(practice to get even better, use them for Him)* (BAT: 3a Self-concept; Bible Promise: H. God as Father)

Is there anyone on Earth just like you?
No, you are special.
What things about you are special?
No one looks just like you.
No one thinks just like you.
No one acts just like you.
God made you different from everyone else.
You are an *individual*.

156

◆ LEARNING HOW ◆

To Make a Height Chart

1. Get a yardstick, a roll of paper, tape or Plasti-Tak, and a pencil.
2. Fasten the paper to the wall using tape or Plasti-Tak. Stand with your back to the paper. Make sure that your heels are against the wall.
3. With the help of your teacher or a friend, mark your height on the paper. Place the yardstick on top of your head and let it touch the wall to show where to draw a line. Write your name and the date next to the mark.
4. Use the yardstick to measure from the floor to the line. How tall are you?

158

Day 2

Learning How Activity, page 158

- Read and follow the instructions given to find out how tall you are.
- How long do you think we should wait before measuring your height again? *(Answers will vary; several months.)*

If you have a special place in your house where you mark your children's height, you may want to use this place rather than the piece of chart paper.

Research Activity

- Look at the book that gives the meaning of first names. The names are in alphabetical order and are divided into a section of boys' names and a section of girls' names. Find your name in the book.
- Draw or paint a picture illustrating the meaning of your name, using the drawing paper and your art supplies.
- Write your name and its meaning on the paper.

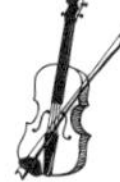

This work can be included in the "My Family and Me" book.

Text Discussion, page 157

- Have you always been the height that you are right now? *(No, he has probably grown some even during this year.)*
- How long do you think you will be the height that you are right now?
- Let's read the first section of page 157. These pictures represent the same person from a baby to adulthood.
- You look different from the way you looked two years ago and in another year you will look different from the way you look now.
- We become different as we get older. Some of the ways that we are different cannot be seen in a photograph.
- What are some ways that we change that we cannot see? *(Answers may include things we know, things we can do, how we behave, and our understanding of God.)*
- Read and discuss the remainder of the page.

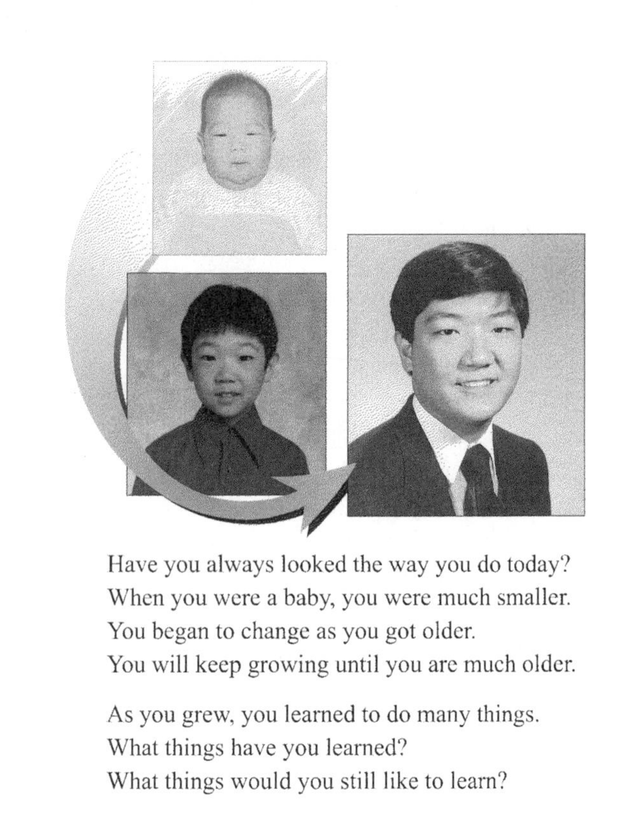

Have you always looked the way you do today?
When you were a baby, you were much smaller.
You began to change as you got older.
You will keep growing until you are much older.

As you grew, you learned to do many things.
What things have you learned?
What things would you still like to learn?

157

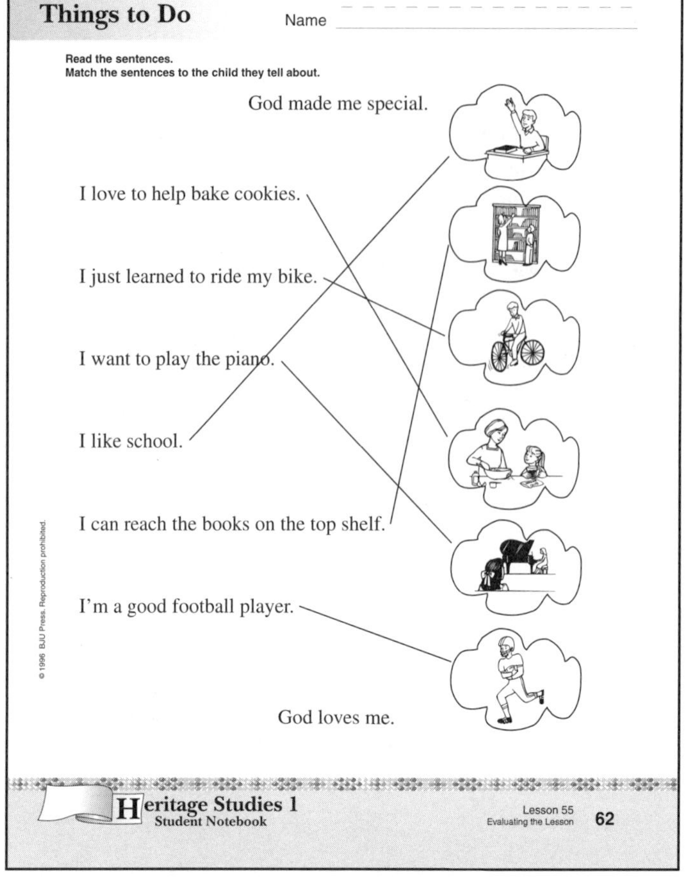

Things to Do Name

Read the sentences.
Match the sentences to the child they tell about.

God made me special.

I love to help bake cookies.

I just learned to ride my bike.

I want to play the piano.

I like school.

I can reach the books on the top shelf.

I'm a good football player.

God loves me.

© 1996 BJU Press. Reproduction prohibited.

Heritage Studies 1
Student Notebook

Lesson 55
Evaluating the Lesson 62

Evaluating the Lesson

Direct an activity on Notebook page 62. Read all the sentences on the page. Instruct your child to draw a line from each describing sentence to the child the sentence describes. Tell him that when he has finished, he should circle the statements that best describe himself.

This work can be included in the "My Family and Me" book.

Going Beyond

Enrichment

Explain to your child why you gave him the name you did. Provide him with writing paper and instruct him to write a few sentences telling about how his name was chosen.

This work can be included in the "My Family and Me" book.

Additional Teacher Information

The United States government places only one legal restriction on names given to children. The name must be composed of letters; numbers or other characters are not allowed. Several other countries regulate the naming of children to a greater extent. In some countries it is illegal to give a child a name that obviously had its origin as a surname, such as Parker or Delaney. And according to a law written in 1813, children in France must be named for a Catholic saint or a person of importance in ancient history.

Recent studies show that about 70 percent of the people living in the United States today bear names that honor someone. Many children are named after family members or close family friends.

Some children have been named for famous people or for special events. For example, following the victories of World War II, many baby girls were given the name Victoria, and boys were named Douglas or Dwight after Generals MacArthur and Eisenhower. Today some children are given names of popular politicians, television characters, or people mentioned in the Bible.

LESSON 56
A Family Is Special

Text, pages 159-61
Notebook, page 63

Preview

Main Ideas
- Every family is different.
- God gave us our family.
- God has a plan for families.
- Families change over time.

Objectives
- Name some ways in which the child's family is different from other families
- Tell how the child's family has changed

Materials
- No new materials required for this lesson

Day 1

Lesson

Introducing the Lesson

Direct a poetry-reading activity. Before reading the first poem below, ask your child whether he has ever wanted you to watch him do something. Then tell him to listen to find out what the child in the poem wanted his mother to watch him do.

Mommy, Watch Me

"Mommy, watch me throw this ball.
Mommy, watch me play.
Mommy, come and see the flip
I learned to do today."

Mommy always watches;
Mommy always likes to see.
And even when I'm quiet,
Mommy likes to look at me.

Read the following poem to your child. Allow him to create sound effects for this poem. Encourage him to laugh as he thinks this child's dad would laugh.

My Dad

My dad has a funny laugh,
Like a motor starting up;
Once he broke into a roar,
And scared our beagle pup.

We all get to giggling,
'Til we nearly fall in half;
But though he does sound funny,
I love to make him laugh.

A Family Is Special

A *family* is a special group of people.
A family is special because each person in the family is an individual.
No other family is just like your family.
God gave you your family.

Some families are very large.
Some families are very small.
How many people are in your family?

159

Teaching the Lesson

Direct a text activity on pages 159-61. Read the first section on the page, placing emphasis on the last two sentences.

Text Discussion, page 159

➤ What does the word *individual* mean? *(There is no one else just like me anywhere in the world.)*

➤ God made each person special, or one of a kind. He made each **family** group different from all others. (BAT: 3a Self-concept; Bible Promise: I. God as Master) What things in our family make us special or unique?

➤ Look at the picture on the page. How is this family different from our family? *(Answers will vary but may include the size of the families.)*

➤ Read the rest of the page.

God created the first man and woman.
Adam and Eve became the first family.
Do you remember the names of their children?

People have always lived together as families.
God planned for families to live and work together.

160

A Family Changes

A family changes as time goes by.
Change means that things are different from what they were before.
In what ways has your family changed?

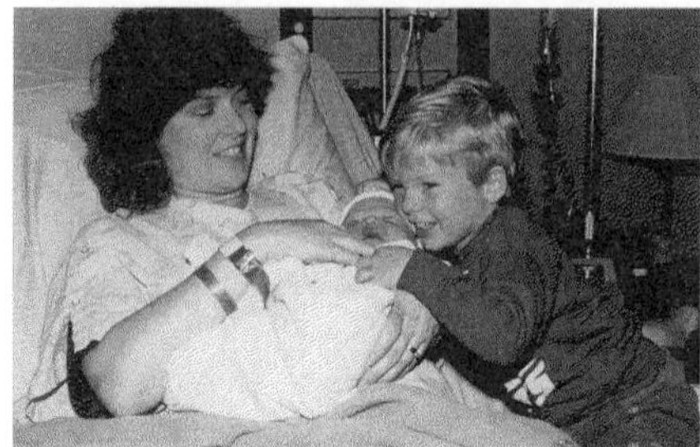

Families change in many ways.
Adding a new brother or sister can change a family.
Moving to a new home brings changes too.
All families change in one way.
They change as the people in the family grow older.

161

Day 2

Text Discussion, page 160

➤ How many people are in this family? *(three)*

➤ Read the first section on page 160 and answer the question. *(Cain, Abel, and Seth: Genesis 4:1-2, 25)*

➤ How do we know so much about the very first family? *(God's Word tells us.)*

TimeLine Discussion

➤ Reread the first two sentences on page 160. Do you think that there was ever a time when people did not live in family groups? *(no)*

➤ Point to each person pictured on the History TimeLine. Did each one of these live together in a family? *(yes)*

➤ Read the second section of page 160. God's Word tells us how families should live and work together. (Bible Promise: I. God as Master)

➤ What verses do you know that tell what children should do in a family? *(Answers will vary but may include "Children obey your parents" and "Honour thy father and thy mother.")*

➤ The Bible gives instructions to parents. Do you know a verse that tells parents what to do? *(Answers will vary but may include "Train up a child in the way he should go" and "Husbands, love your wives.")*

Text Discussion, page 161

➤ Read page 161. What changes have happened to our family? *(birth of a new baby, marriage of an older sibling, death of a family member, moving to a new house, grandparent living with the family, etc.)*

God was not surprised by any of these changes. He knows about everything that happens to us and to our family; these things are part of His plan for our family. (BAT: 3a Self-concept)

Evaluating the Lesson

Direct an activity on Notebook page 63. Ask your child what the page looks like. *(a notebook, a photo album)* Point out that each "photograph" in the album has a **caption,** or description, beneath it. Read the captions; instruct your child to draw pictures of his family to illustrate the captions.

This work can be included in the "My Family and Me" book.

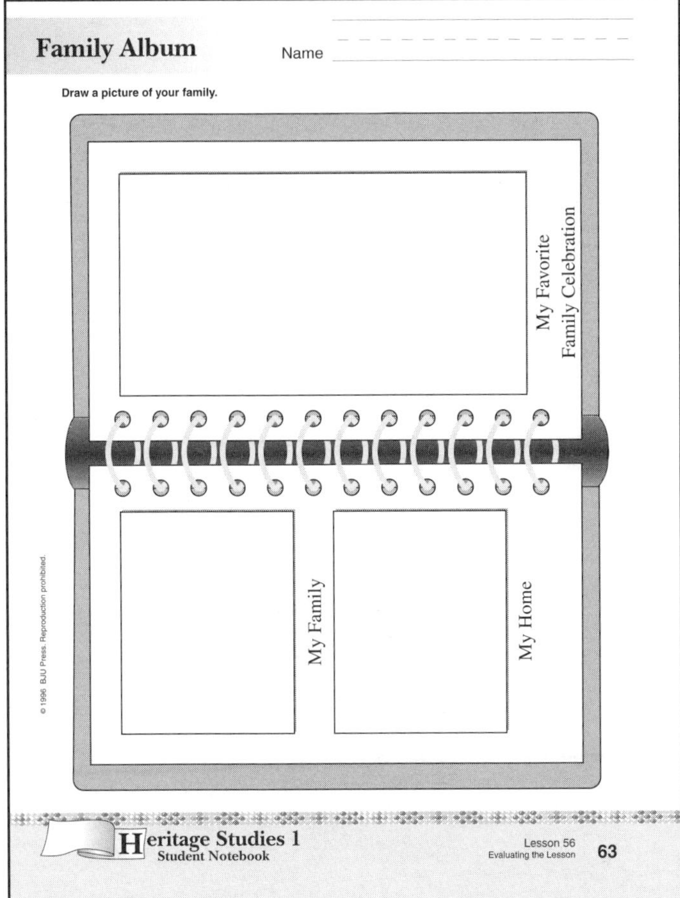

Family Album Name

Draw a picture of your family.

My Favorite Family Celebration

My Family

My Home

© 1996 BJU Press. Reproduction prohibited.

Heritage Studies 1 Student Notebook

Lesson 56 Evaluating the Lesson 63

Going Beyond

Enrichment

Give your child a copy of the simplified family group sheet from the Appendix, page A36. Explain that people who study families begin their work by completing a form similar to this one. Tell your child to fill in each blank at the top of the page with information. Point out that he should write the last name his mother had *before* she was married. Then he should write the full name of each child in the family at the bottom of the page. Tell him to write the children's names in order of their births.

When the family group sheet is completed, your child could include it in his "My Family and Me" book along with photos of the people.

Additional Teacher Information

European surnames, or family names, originated in the Middle Ages from one of four sources. The most common source of a family name is a location. A location name may have been a description of the land near a local resident's home. If an Englishman lived near a forest, he and his descendants may bear the last name of Woods or Forrest. In Germany, the same man would have been known as Mr. (or *Herr*) Wald. A location name might also be related to the name of a town or country from which a new resident moved; for example, Di Napoli means "from Naples."

The second most common source of family names is known as *patronymics.* The Latin word *pater* means "father"; these names were given after the father. Leif, the son of Eric, became known as Leif Ericson. Originally these names were changed with each successive generation. Eventually one name was decided upon and passed down regardless of the name of the child's actual father. Suffixes such as *s, acs,* and *escu* and prefixes such as *Ben, Fitz,* and *Mc* mean "son of" or "descendant of."

About 15 percent of family names in America today come from the occupation of an ancestor. Smith is an obvious example, as are Baker, Cooper, and Taylor. These names are of English origin, but examples exist in other languages as well.

The last 15 percent of American surnames are based on personal characteristics. These names may describe physical characteristics (Short) or behavioral ones (Savage).

Surnames did not become popular among all ethnic groups at the same time. Chinese surnames have a much longer history than European names. Jewish and African-American surnames originated in the 1600s–1700s.

LESSON 57
A Family Has Rules

Text, pages 162-64
Notebook, page 64

Preview

Main Ideas

- We need rules.
- Rules can be changed.
- Voting is one way to change a rule.

Objective

- Distinguish between children following family rules and children disobeying family rules

Materials

- Some dirty laundry
- A laundry basket
- A sheet of paper
- *If Everybody Did* by JoAnn Stover (BJUP) (optional)*

Day 1

Lesson

Introducing the Lesson

Direct a discussion. Scatter a few pieces of dirty laundry around the room.

➤ What is scattered around the room? *(dirty laundry)* This is what would happen if each of us did not pick up our clothing and put it where it belongs.

➤ Let's use the basket to pick up the dirty laundry and put it where it belongs. What would happen if we did not wash our dirty clothes? *(Answers will vary but may include that there would not be clean clothes to wear.)*

➤ What would happen if none of us washed the dishes? *(Answers will vary but may include that there would soon be no dishes for anyone to use.)*

➤ What would happen if we kept driving our car and did not take time to put gas in it? *(Answers will vary but may include that it would stop running.)*

➤ There are many rules that we have to follow to make things work smoothly in our family.

A Family Has Rules

All families have rules.
Rules can help you know what you should do.
Rules can help you know what you must not do.

Do you know why we need rules?
Rules help us get along with others.
And rules help to protect us from harm.
What rules does your family have?
Who makes your rules?

Children, obey your parents in the Lord: for this is right.
Ephesians 6:1

162

The book *If Everybody Did* by Jo Ann Stover is a good follow-up to a discussion about what happens when everyone disobeys the little rules in a family. The book *If Everybody Did* can be purchased from Bob Jones University Press.

Teaching the Lesson

Direct a text activity on pages 162-64. Read page 162. Write the following titles on a sheet of paper: *Rules for getting along* and *Rules to protect us from harm.*

Text Discussion, page 162

➤ What are some rules that we have in the house to help us get along with each other? *(Answers may include speaking quietly, respecting others' property, and doing chores responsibly.)* *Write the rules under the first heading.*

➤ What are some rules we have that help protect us? *(Answers may include not running with things in our mouths, not playing with matches, picking up toys and items from stairways, and holding scissors in a proper way.)* *Write the rules under the second heading.*

Sometimes families need to make new rules or change old ones.
How does your family decide on changes like these?

A family might talk about the reasons for changing a rule.
They might list the reasons for the change.
Each family member may even *vote* for or against the new rule.
Have you ever helped to make a rule?

163

◆ THINGS PEOPLE DO ◆

Voting

In some countries, people choose the rules they think are right.
They choose the leaders that they think will make the best rules.
People make their choices known by *voting*.

A person can vote by writing his choice on a piece of paper.
A person can vote by raising his hand.

When a choice must be made by many people, a special day is set aside for voting.
People mark their votes on special pieces of paper or special machines.

164

- ➤ Do you think that different families have different rules? *(Answers will vary; though there would be some differences, many rules would be the same.)*
- ➤ Why do parents usually make the rules for a family?
- ➤ Part of God's plan for families is that parents are responsible for their children. What does **to be responsible** mean? *(to take care of, to protect, to provide for)*

One of the ways parents take care of their children is by making rules that help to protect them from harm. Children also fit into God's plan for families.

- ➤ Read the verse at the bottom of the page. Repeat this verse with me. (BAT: 2a Authority; Bible Promise: H. God as Father)

Day 2

Text Discussion, pages 163-64

- ➤ Read the first section on page 163. Do you remember any changes we have made in our family's rules?
- ➤ Each family has its own special way of making family rules. What are some ways that we make rules?
- ➤ Read the remainder of page 163 and answer the question.

Sometimes children cannot vote on family rules because their parents know they would not choose what is best for them. Adults have to make the difficult decisions about changes and new rules. Adults can even decide about changes in rules for the whole country.

- ➤ Which set of rules would affect more people: family's rules, school rules, or a country's rules? *(a country's rules)*
- ➤ Read page 164. How do adults change a country's rules? *(by voting)*
- ➤ Why do you think it is important for a country to have good rules and good leaders?

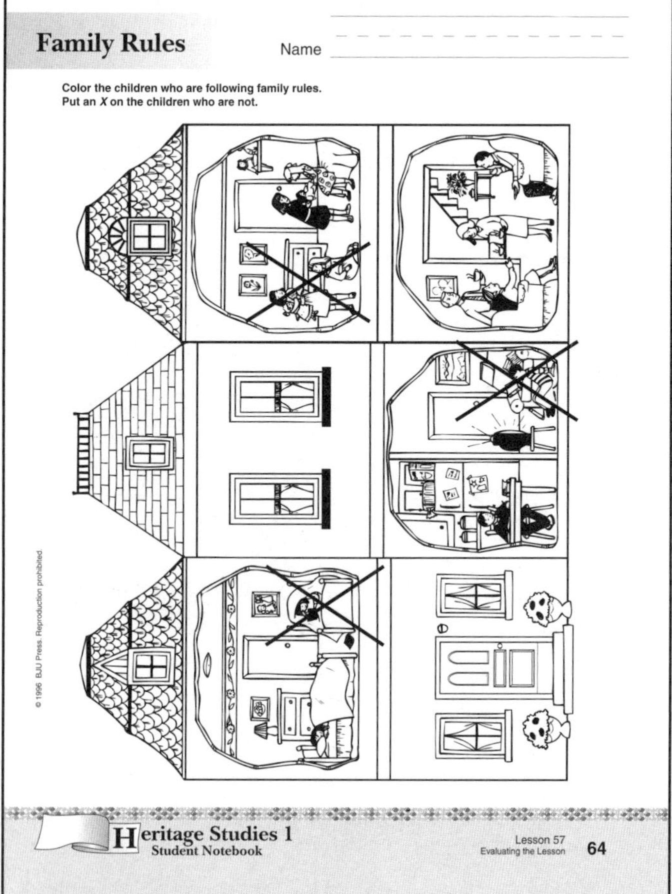
Family Rules Name

Color the children who are following family rules.
Put an *X* on the children who are not.

© 1996 BJU Press. Reproduction prohibited.

Heritage Studies 1
Student Notebook

Lesson 57
Evaluating the Lesson 64

Evaluating the Lesson

Direct an activity on Notebook page 64. Direct your child to look carefully at the Notebook page. Some of the children in the picture are following family rules and some are not. Follow the instructions given on the page.

This work can be included in the "My Family and Me" book.

Going Beyond

Additional Teacher Information

Today in the United States American citizens over the age of eighteen are permitted to vote. But it has not always been so. During the American colonial period, voting privileges in most colonies were limited to adult white men who owned land. Some colonies permitted non-landowners to vote if they owned a certain amount of personal property. It was believed throughout Europe at the time that men who owned land were more interested in law, order, and government. Restricting voting rights protected the good of the colony from the poor and uneducated.

After the War for Independence, many restrictions still applied. A few states changed the restrictions somewhat, allowing all taxpaying men to vote. And in Vermont, every male citizen within the state could vote. As more states were added to the Union, each was allowed to set up its own voting regulations. By the mid-1800s, native-born white men over the age of twenty-one had the right to vote in all states. But in some states restrictions applied that prevented Jews, Catholics, and paupers from voting. In 1870 the Fifteenth Amendment gave black men the right to vote, at least in theory if not always in practice. Women were given this right in 1920 after the ratification of the Nineteenth Amendment. With the ratification of the Twenty-sixth Amendment in 1971, young men and women eighteen years and older were given the privilege and responsibility of voting.

LESSON 58

3-18

A Family Works and Plays Together

Text, pages 165-66
Notebook, page 65

Preview

Main Ideas

- Families do things together.
- A job is work that you do.
- Christian families worship God together.

Objective

- Pantomime a family activity

Materials

- *Pulling Together* by Dawn Watkins (BJUP) (optional)*

Day 1

Lesson

Introducing the Lesson

Direct a listening activity. Read aloud the following excerpt from *Pulling Together* by Dawn L. Watkins. Tell your child that this story might have taken place when his grandparents' parents were children. Instruct your child to listen for the things each member of the family does.

Pulling Together can be purchased from Bob Jones University Press.

Luke was waiting at the barn. He waved when he saw them.

"Papa," he said. "I fixed the latch on the coop."

"Good, Son." John Briggs sprang down from the seat.

"I drove part of the way," Matthew said.

"Sure enough," said Luke.

Thunder boomed again, closer this time. Behind the barn the sky was dark gray. A little wind kicked up.

"Luke, let's get the wagon unloaded. Matt, can you drive onto the barn floor?"

"Yes, sir!"

Matthew lifted the lines and clicked his tongue. Ben and Dolly walked through the wide doorway.

"Whoa, there," said Matthew.

Luke jumped onto the wagon. He hefted a sack up and handed it to his father.

John Briggs carried the sack into the granary. He whistled as he went. He came out and passed Luke coming in.

Matthew sat in the wagon, watching. "Can I help, Papa?"

John Briggs shouldered a sack. "Not with this, Son. What I need is for you to unhitch the horses. I think I'll leave the wagon here."

* * *

Another little roll of thunder sounded.

Shortly his father came and led the team out of the barn. Matthew ran ahead to open the pasture gate.

His father slowed up and studied the sky. "Better put them in tonight," he said.

The chains of the traces dragged and jingled. Matthew followed his father and the team to the lower part of the barn.

John Briggs took off the harness and the collars and put everything away. Matthew fed the horses and put down new straw. Luke milked the two cows.

When they came out of the barn, it was dark. Black clouds covered half the sky. Thunder banged almost overhead. The apple trees rustled in the orchard in front of the barn.

"Will it be a big one?" Matthew said.

"Could be," said John Briggs.

Matthew's mother [Addie] came out on the porch. Her long apron blew out sideways, and her skirt stirred around her ankles.

"Come on, men," she said. "Supper's ready."

John Briggs climbed the steps two at a time. He took off his hat. He put his arm around his wife and kissed her.

"Did you miss me?" he said.

"I might have," she said.

Matthew took his father's hat. He pulled it at an angle across his eyes and grinned at Luke.

The lamp was lit, and the table was set. Matthew smelled ham. He tried to hang up the hat, but the peg was still a few inches too high. His father picked him up, and Matthew dropped the hat into its place.

Luke set down his pail. Addie dipped the fresh milk into cups for each of them.

They all sat down at the table. Matthew put his hands out. His father took one and his mother took the other. They took Luke's hands, too, and made a circle. Matthew closed his eyes, but he could still feel the warmth of the lamp in the center.

"Our Father," John Briggs said, "we've come to the close of another day. We thank You for Your good gifts. I thank You that the oats are in. Thank You for this food, and for my fine family around this table. I ask that You keep us well, if it be Thy will. Amen."

A Family Works and Plays Together

Families do things together.
The people in a family do things for each other.
They show their love for each other.

Families work together.
Working together makes the work easier.
Working together gets the job done faster.

Any work you do can be called a *job.*
What jobs do you do for your family?

165

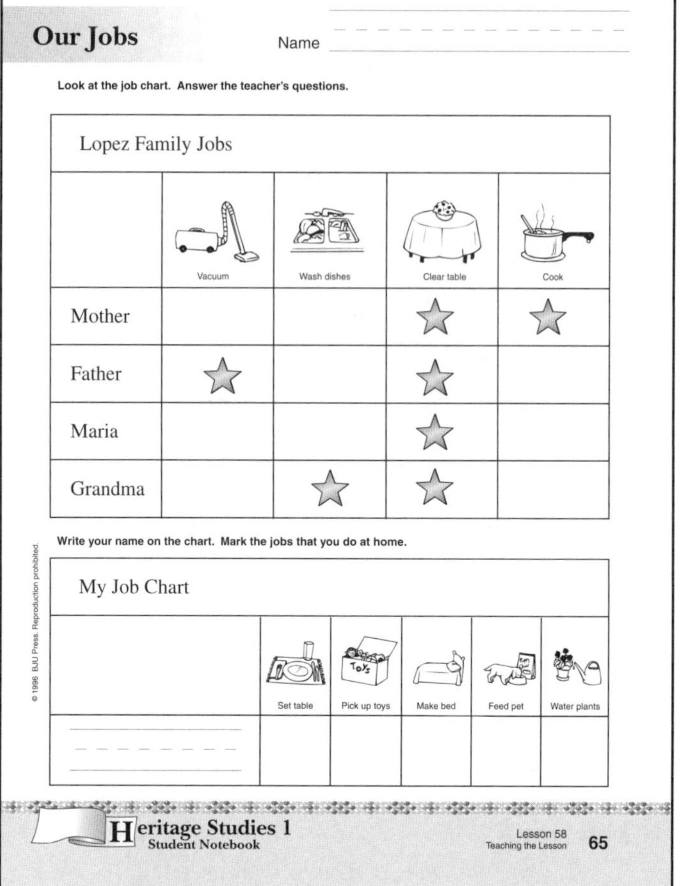

Our Jobs Name ______________

Look at the job chart. Answer the teacher's questions.

Lopez Family Jobs	Vacuum	Wash dishes	Clear table	Cook
Mother			☆	☆
Father	☆		☆	
Maria			☆	
Grandma		☆	☆	

Write your name on the chart. Mark the jobs that you do at home.

My Job Chart	Set table	Pick up toys	Make bed	Feed pet	Water plants
______					

Heritage Studies 1 Student Notebook — Lesson 58 Teaching the Lesson 65

Story Discussion

➤ How many people made up this family, and what were their names? *(four: John Briggs, Addie, Luke, and Matthew)*
➤ What time of day was it? *(late afternoon, evening)*
➤ Did each member of the family have a job to do as he prepared for the end of the day? *(yes)*
➤ Do we have to do any of these things at the end of the day?
➤ In this lesson we will learn about some of the things that families today do together.

Day 2

Teaching the Lesson

Direct a text activity on pages 165-66. Point to the photograph on the page. Allow your child to tell what this family is doing together. *(painting)* Then direct him to listen as you read page 165 to find out about things that families do together.

Text Discussion, page 165

➤ Look at the word ***job.*** What jobs, or work, do you have to do at school? *(reading, math, etc.)*
➤ What kinds of jobs do you have to do around the house, with or for other family members?

God wants us to do all our jobs. We should be dependable and willing workers; we should do our work with a smile. (BATs: 2e Work, 2f Enthusiasm)

➤ Which family job do you enjoy helping with most?

Direct an activity on Notebook page 65. Remind your child that charts can show many different things. Explain that this chart shows jobs the members of the Lopez family do.

Notebook Activity

➤ Read the names of the family members and then read the jobs across the top of the chart.
➤ On this chart the stars show the jobs each person does.
➤ Which jobs do Mother, Father, Maria, and Grandma do?
➤ Which job does everyone do? *(clear table)*

If your child is having difficulty reading the graph, show him how to put his finger on a name and run it across to a star and then up to the job.

Families play together.
What things does your family do together for fun?

Christian families do something else together. They worship God together. How do we worship God?

166

➤ Look at the empty job chart at the bottom of the page. Write your name in the proper place on the chart. Mark the boxes beneath the jobs you do.

This work can be included in the "My Family and Me" book.

Day 3

Text Discussion, page 166

➤ Read the first section on page 166. Listen for another thing families do together. Discuss times your family has played together.

➤ Why do families do things together? *(because they love each other, because they enjoy being together, to help each other)* (BAT: 5a Love)

➤ God loves you even more than your family does. What kinds of things can you do with or for God? *(pray, witness, read His Word, etc.)*

➤ Read the rest of the page. Look at the picture at the bottom of the page. How is the family in the picture worshiping God? *(reading the Bible in church)* (BATs: 3e Unity of Christ and the church, 6a Bible study, 6b Prayer, 7c Praise)

Evaluating the Lesson

Direct a pantomime activity. Encourage your child to think about something the family has done together. Explain that the activity could be work, play, or worship. Tell him to pantomime the activity while you guess what he is doing. Continue as time and interest allow.

If you have several children, you may wish to allow everyone to participate in this activity.

Going Beyond

Enrichment

Have available large sheets of construction paper, scissors, glue or paste, and magazines that can be cut. Encourage your child to find and cut out pictures showing families or family members working and playing together. Instruct him to glue his pictures to the construction paper to form a collage. Encourage him to think of a title for his collage and to write it on his paper. Display the collage if you wish.

Additional Teacher Information

Until the early part of the nineteenth century, the American economy was based on agriculture and other family businesses. Families worked together to make their own clothing, produce their own food, and provide for other necessities. Sometimes three generations of family members lived and worked together. Aunts, uncles, and cousins combined with grandparents, parents, and children to form a close-knit extended family.

The Industrial Revolution brought a change to the family pattern. As factories sprang up, young people left their farms to move to the cities. Because success in the workplace was based on competency and efficiency, more time was devoted to a job that took men away from their families. The nuclear, or immediate, family became more important. A smaller family group was more mobile; it could respond more easily to the demands industrialization placed upon it.

Other changes came to the family as a result of the Industrial Revolution. Education, communication, health, transportation, and welfare affected the family. Most families do not completely cut ties with their relatives. But these relationships are a matter of choice, not social tradition.

Lesson 59
A Family Has a History

Text, pages 167-68
Notebook, page 66

Preview

Main Ideas
- History is the story of people and the things they have done.
- Every family has a history.

Objective
- Use pictures to complete a family tree

Materials
- An item that has been in your family for a long time*
- Maps and More 36, page M16

Day 1

Lesson

Introducing the Lesson
Introduce a special speaker. If you have a grandparent or older person who is able to come speak to your child, introduce him and ask him to tell your child about his childhood. If you were able to get a letter or tape from a grandparent, read or play it for your child. If none of these options were available, tell your child a story about your childhood or a story that you heard from your parents or grandparents.

Try to allow time for your child to ask questions of your special guest or to ask questions of you concerning the tape, letter, or your own story.

Tell your child that family stories are special because they remind us of the people we love. They help us learn what our families were like long ago.

Day 2

Teaching the Lesson
Direct a text activity on pages 167–68. Point to the pictures at the bottom of page 167.

Text Discussion, page 167
➤ Do you think these pictures were taken recently or many years ago? *(many years ago)*

A Family Has a History

History is the story of people and the things they have done. We often think of history as the story of famous people.

Famous people have a history.
But people who are not famous have a history too.

All families have a history.
Your family's history is the story of the people in your family who came before you.
Those family members are called *ancestors*.
Your parents and grandparents are your ancestors.
What do you know about the things they have done?

Learning about your ancestors helps you understand the things that happened long ago.

167

➤ Why might these people have been photographed together? *(Answers will vary; they are family or close friends.)*

➤ Read the first section of the page. Tell in your own words what **history** is. What are the names of some of the famous people or groups of people whose stories you have learned throughout the year? *(Leif Ericson, Christopher Columbus, the Indians, the Separatists, the Jamestown settlers, etc.)*

➤ These famous people make up the history of our country. Tell me about some of these people as I point to them on the TimeLine.

➤ Reread the last sentence in the first section. Do the people pictured on the bottom of the page have a history? *(yes)*

➤ Read the rest of the page. Can you pick a person in the picture that might be the **ancestor** of someone else in the picture?

The stories of people who are not famous at all, like the ones in the pictures, are part of a country's history as well.

➤ What are some names of your ancestors?

➤ Are you parents and grandparents your only ancestors? *(no)*

Each person's ancestors include man people—too many for him to count—who lived a very long time ago.

THINGS PEOPLE DO
Studying Family Histories
YOUR GREAT-GREAT-GRANDPARENTS
YOUR GREAT-GRANDPARENTS
YOUR GRANDPARENTS
YOUR PARENTS
YOU
People record the things they learn about their families on special charts.
This chart is called a *family tree.* How do you think it got that name?
168

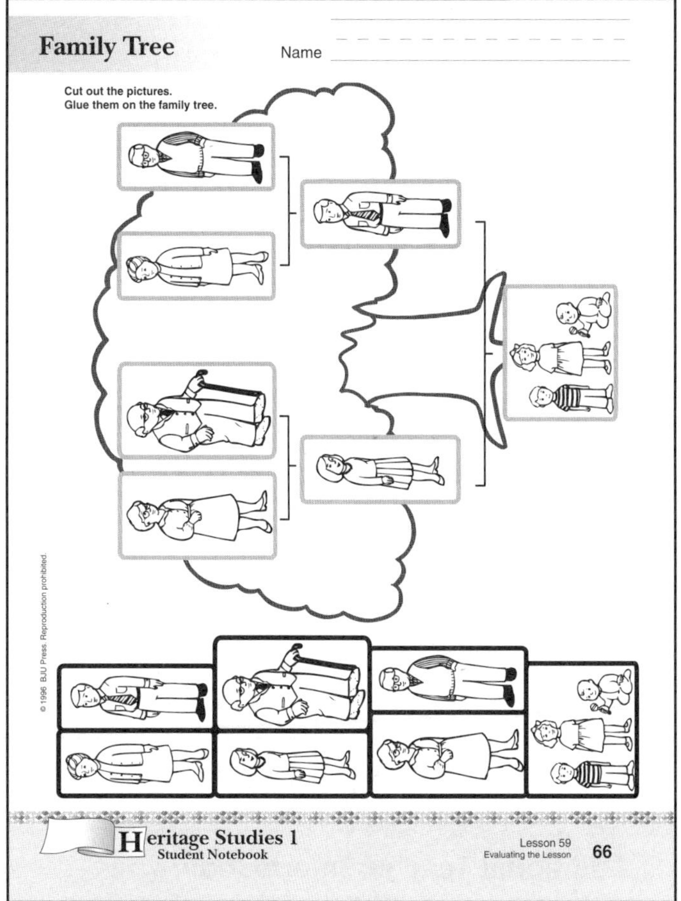

Family Tree
Name
Cut out the pictures.
Glue them on the family tree.
© 1996 BJU Press. Reproduction prohibited.
Heritage Studies 1
Student Notebook
Lesson 59
Evaluating the Lesson
66

- ➤ Show Maps and More 36. Each person has a mother and a father, and each of his parents has a mother and a father, and those parents (the child's grandparents) have mothers and fathers, and so on.
- ➤ Notice that each new group of mothers and fathers is larger than the group before. Point to the top group of mothers and fathers. Would you like to count this group?
- ➤ Do you think this chart includes all of this person's ancestors? *(no)*
- ➤ If you knew the names of all of his ancestors, you could make a list of people that reached all the way back to the very first family. Who were in the first family? *(Adam and Eve)*
- ➤ Adam and Eve are the first ancestors of everyone. Why is this so? *(They were the first parents; all families on the earth came from them.)*

Many people today do not know much about their ancestors. They do not know where their ancestors lived or what they did to earn money. Often they do not even know their names.

- ➤ Do you know all your ancestors? *(no)*
- ➤ Do you think you could find out more about your ancestors?

Sometimes old pictures help us learn about family history. Sometimes special items that have been in the family a long time help teach about a family's history.

- ➤ *Show the family item. Tell a story associated with the item.*

Text Discussion, page 168

- ➤ How might you find out about your ancestors? *(Answers may include asking grandparents and looking at old picture albums.)*

Sometimes people write down things they learn so that they will remember the names and history of their ancestors.

- ➤ Read page 168. What kind of information is on this **family tree?** *(ancestors)*
- ➤ Do you see the lines leading from the child to the parents in each place on the tree? What do you think they mean?

God brought many people—your ancestors—together to make you the person you are. God has a special plan for you. (BAT: 3a Self-concept)

Evaluating the Lesson

Direct an activity on Notebook page 66. Point to the drawing on the page. Review with your child what this drawing is called. *(a family tree)* Tell him that people usually write names in the blanks on a family tree. But some family trees have pictures instead. Call attention to the pictures of the people on the page. Discuss each picture with your child, allowing him to tell the family relationship he thinks each picture represents. Then instruct him to cut out each picture and glue it in the proper place on the family tree. Allow your child to look at the family tree on page 168.

Going Beyond

Enrichment

Give your child the family tree form in the Appendix, page A37. Encourage him to complete the tree with the information he knows for sure (i.e., his full name and possibly his parents' full names). Tell your child to write in the correct places what he calls each grandparent.

This work can be included in the "My Family and Me" book.

Additional Teacher Information

Genealogy is a fast-growing hobby. In the past twenty years, more and more people have become interested in learning about their families. But genealogy, the study of families, is not a new science. Ancient people learned family history through oral tradition—poems and songs recited at gatherings of family and friends. Some cultures in Africa and New Zealand still learn about their family histories in this way.

At the time of Christ, the Hebrews, Greeks, and Romans were all interested in genealogy. The Greek and Roman people tried to trace their family lines back to their gods and goddesses. The Bible contains several Hebrew genealogies, tracing family lines back to Adam, Abraham, and David.

Americans have always been interested in genealogy. Early American genealogists hoped to trace their roots to the colonial settlers or Revolutionary soldiers. Today most genealogists pursue their hobby because they enjoy learning about life long ago. And they are proud of their family's contribution, whatever the size, to the history of America.

3-19 & Test

LESSON 60

You Have a History

Text, pages 169-70

Preview

Main Ideas

- You are part of your family's history.
- The things you do each day are important.

Objective

- Construct a time line showing events from the child's life

Materials

- Maps and More 36, page M16
- 3 to 4 photographs of yourself at different ages, arranged in sequential order*
- Plasti-Tak or transparent tape
- Several pieces of art paper
- Photos of several important events in your child's life (optional)*
- Four sheets of construction paper prepared for a time line and taped together as shown below*

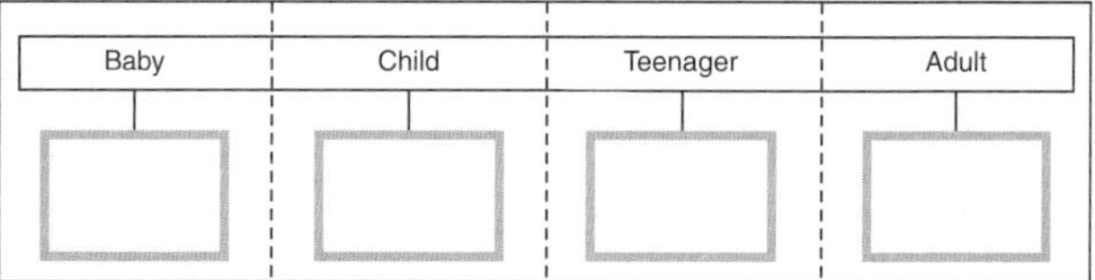

Day 1

Lesson

Introducing the Lesson

Direct a time line activity. Direct your child to look at the first photo of yourself. Tell him a story associated with the photograph. Follow the same procedure with the other photographs. Then explain that you told the stories in the order that they happened. The pictures represent the events in order. Ask your child to look around the room to find another thing that shows the order in which things happened. *(the History TimeLine)*

Display your taped construction paper. Allow your child to help you make a time line using the photographs. Fasten the photographs onto the time line, emphasizing that the photograph on the left shows what happened first, the next photograph shows what happened next, and so on. When your time line is completed, explain that it shows some of your history.

Teaching the Lesson

Direct a discussion. Remind your child that your family has a history.

Family History Discussion

- ➤ What is a history? *(the story of people and the things they have done)*
- ➤ Look at Maps and More 36. What do we call our family members who came before us? *(our ancestors)*
- ➤ Point to the pictures representing the child's parents *(second row from the bottom)* and the child's grandparents *(third row from the bottom).*

Family history is not just interesting stories. The people in family stories and the things they did make each person the special person he is.

- ➤ What might have happened if your first ancestor to come to America had decided not to leave the Old World after all? *(Answers will vary; the family history would have been very different; they might still live in that other country.)*

Even though you did not live through these parts of our family's history, the decisions your ancestors made and the things that happened to them helped to make you the person you are.

Day 2

Direct a text activity on page 170. Remind your child that the things his ancestors did became part of his family history.

Text Discussion, page 170

- ➤ Read the first section of page 170 to learn how you affect your family history too.
- ➤ The things that you do are part of our family's history. What are some things that you have done this last week?
- ➤ Do the things that you do each day affect people other than yourself?
- ➤ Read the second section on page 170.
- ➤ Let's read the verse at the bottom of page 170. What do you think the verse means?

Your family's history is your story too.
You have done things.
You may not have discovered a new land or led a group of people, but you have a history.
What do you know about your history?

Each day you make a little more of your history.
The things you do become part of your history.
They become part of your family's history.
What kind of story will people tell about you?

Even a child is known by his doings, whether his work be pure, and whether it be right.
Proverbs 20:11

170

People all around are watching the things you do. When you are very old, your family members will want to know about the things you did when you were young, just as you now want to learn about things your grandparents and parents did.

- ➤ What kinds of things would you like people to know about you? *(that you love the Lord, are a good worker, are kind, etc.)* (BATs: 1c Separation from the world, 2e Work, 4c Honesty, 5a Love, 6c Spirit-filled) Even as a young person it is important that your work be pure and right.
- ➤ Let's say the verse together a few times. Now I'm going to say the first part, and I want you to complete the verse.

◆ Learning How ◆

To Record Your Personal History

1. Take out a pencil, some crayons, several sheets of paper, and some tape or yarn.
2. Draw pictures showing things you have done and things that have happened to you.
3. Put your drawings into the order that they happened. Hang your drawings in this order, or make your own personal history book.

169

Evaluating the Lesson

Direct a *Learning How* activity on page 169. Help your child in following the directions on the page. Instruct him to label his pictures with a description or the age he thinks he was when the event took place.

You may want to substitute actual photographs that you have showing different important events in your child's life rather than having your child draw pictures.

Provide space for your child to hang his completed time line, perhaps on one wall of the schoolroom. If space is not available, allow him to tape his time line together and fold it into an accordion book.

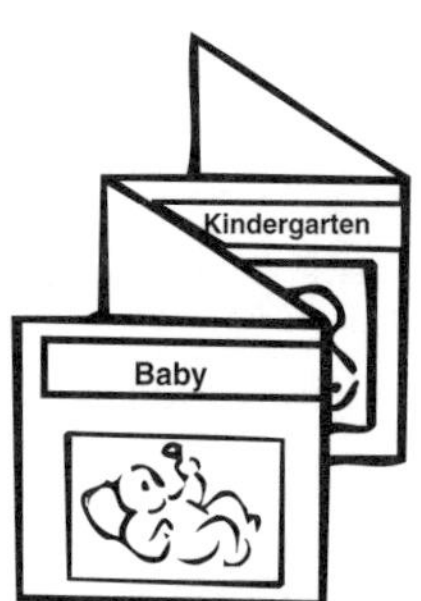

Going Beyond

Enrichment

Give your child the pages you have collected for his "My Family and Me" book. Provide materials for making a cover for his book. Covers could be made from wallpaper scraps, construction paper, or three-hole paper folders. Encourage your child to decorate the cover as he chooses.

This activity is the completion of the book your child has been compiling throughout this chapter.

Additional Teacher Information

Genealogists follow a simple rule: begin with what you know and let it lead you to what you do not know. The personal time line is considered by many genealogists as the important first step to learning the history of your family. As much information as possible should be included on this time line.

Upon completion of the personal time line, the beginning genealogist is ready to learn similar information about his parents and grandparents. Information can be gleaned from official documents, family treasures and photographs, and family Bibles. Interviews with the family members themselves, or someone who knew them well, are the most interesting sources. Further information can be obtained from census records, state and federal archives, old newspapers, and reference books at the local library.

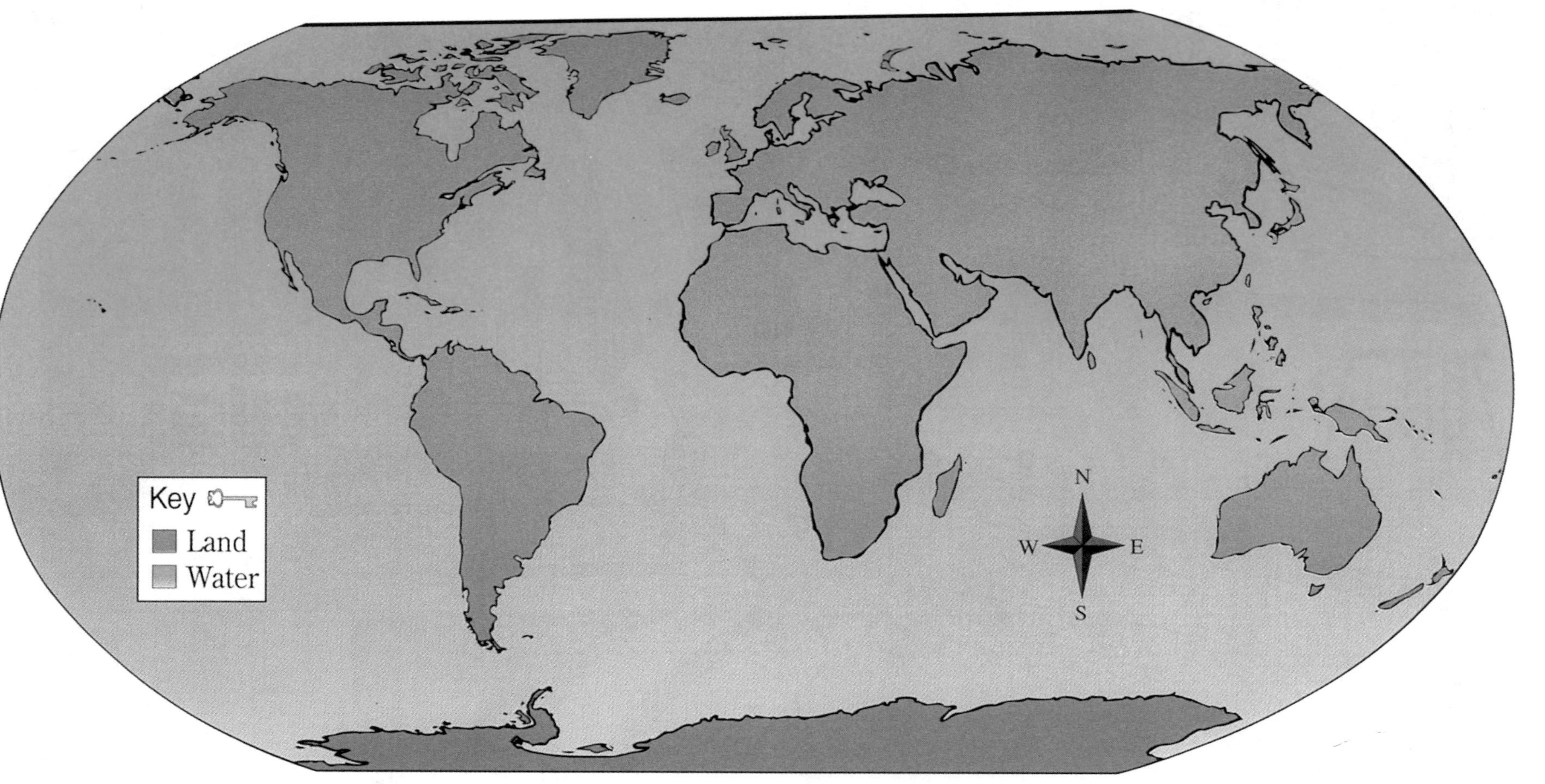

Maps and More: 1

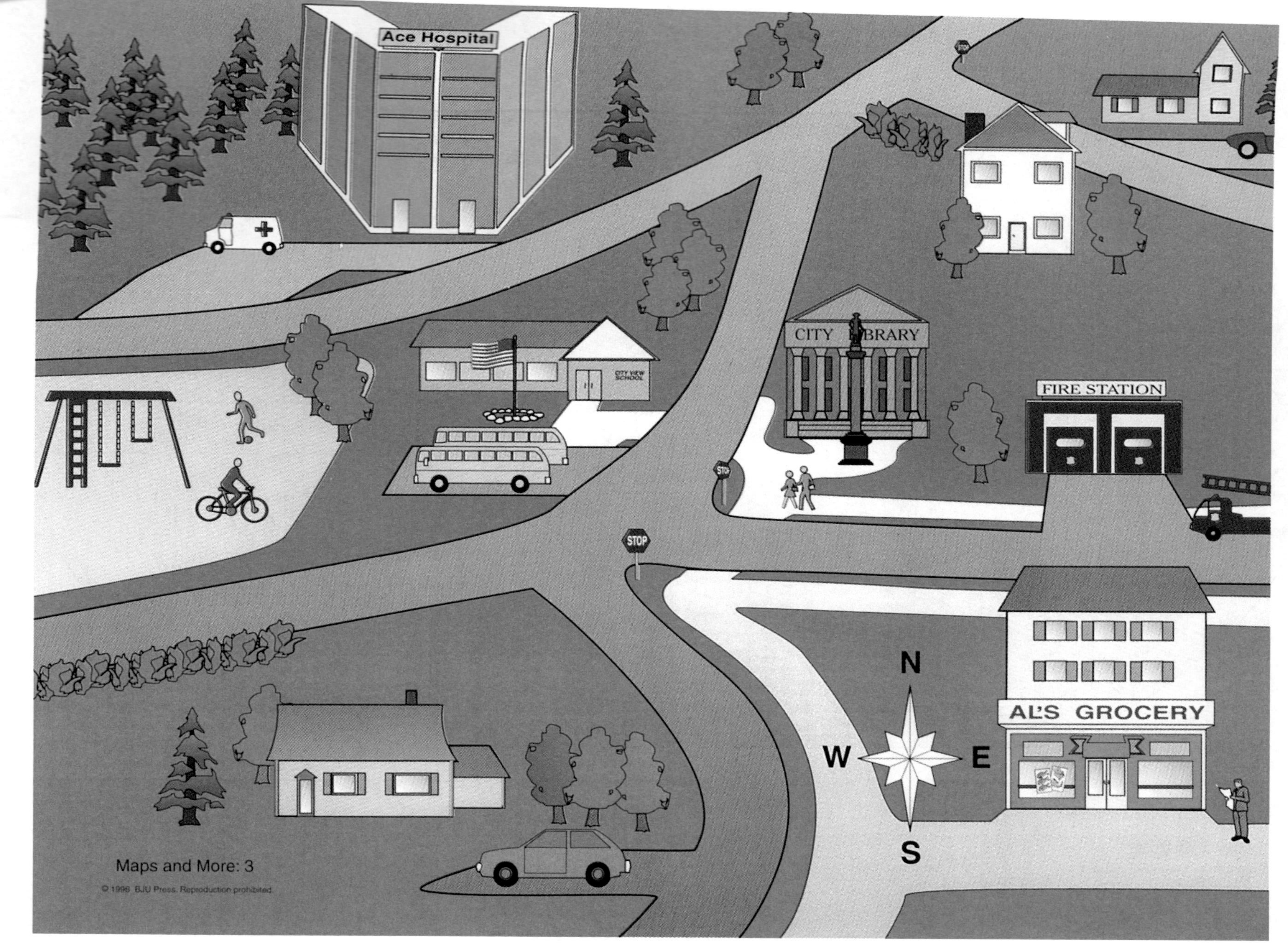
Ace Hospital
CITY VIEW SCHOOL
CITY BRARY
FIRE STATION
STOP
STOP
STOP
AL'S GROCERY
N
W
E
S
Maps and More: 3
© 1996 BJU Press. Reproduction prohibited.

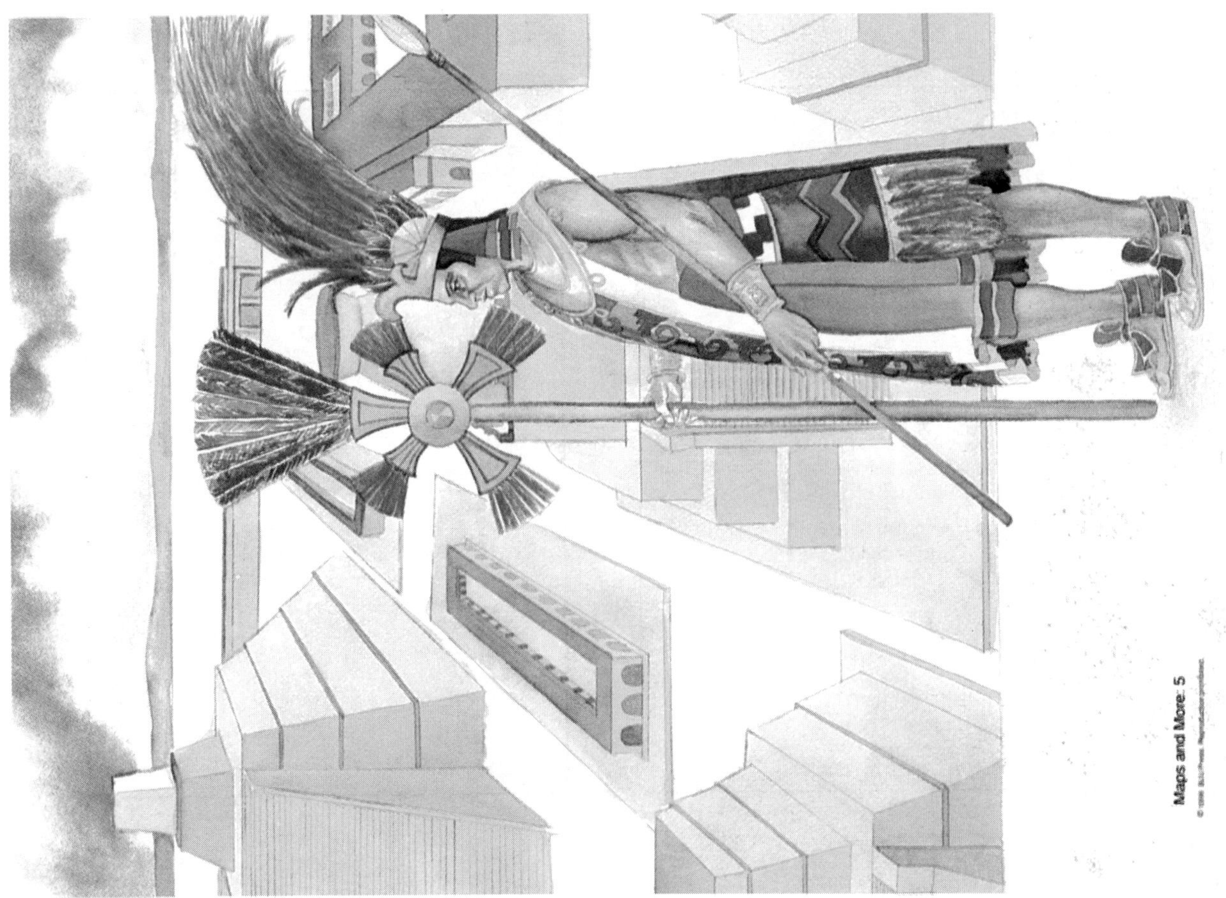

Maps and More: 4

Maps and More: 12

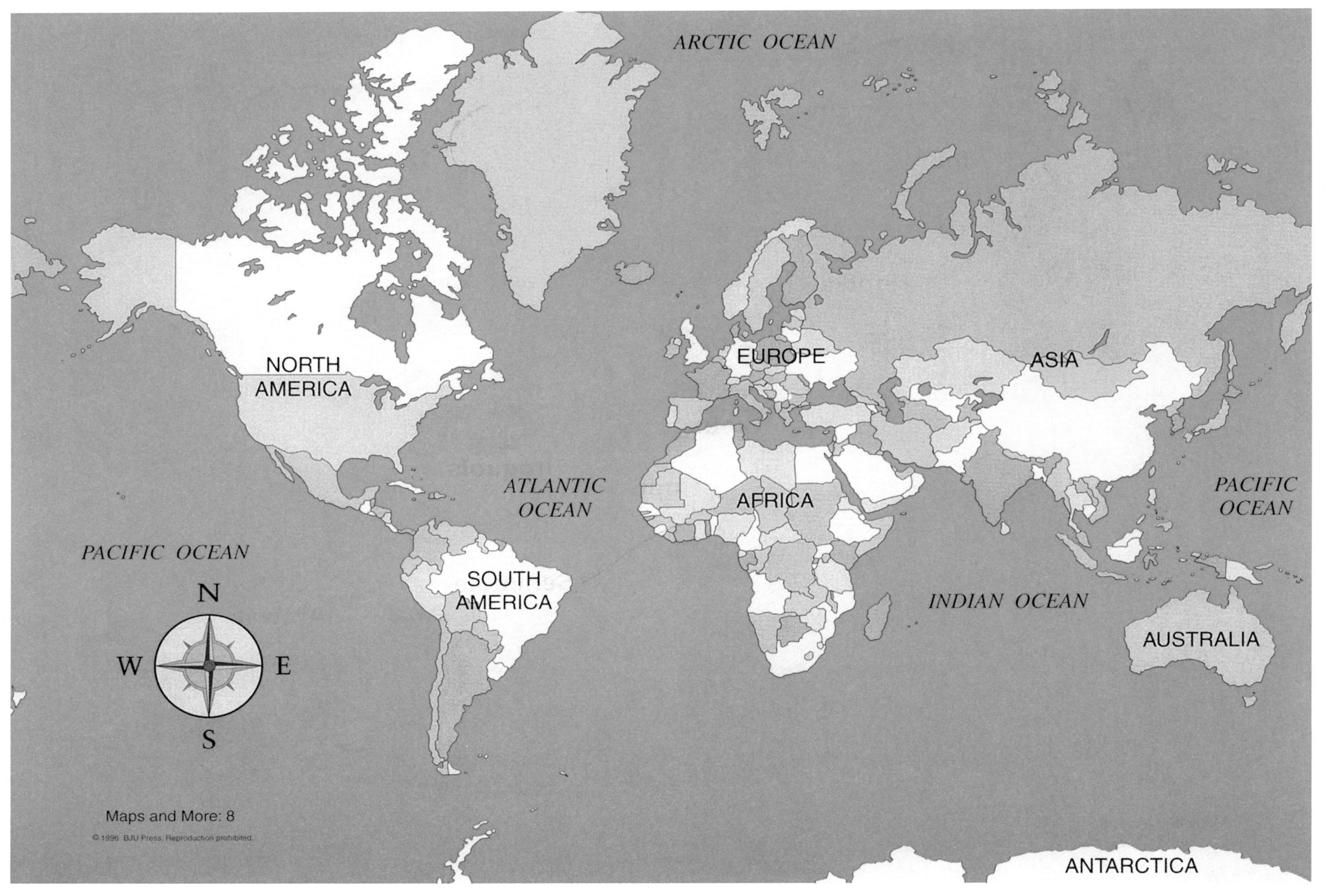
ARCTIC OCEAN
NORTH AMERICA
EUROPE
ASIA
ATLANTIC OCEAN
AFRICA
PACIFIC OCEAN
PACIFIC OCEAN
SOUTH AMERICA
INDIAN OCEAN
AUSTRALIA
N
W
E
S
Maps and More: 8
© 1996 BJU Press. Reproduction prohibited.
ANTARCTICA

N

Inuit

Nootka

Sioux

Iroquois

Hopi

Seminole

Arawak

Maps and More: 9

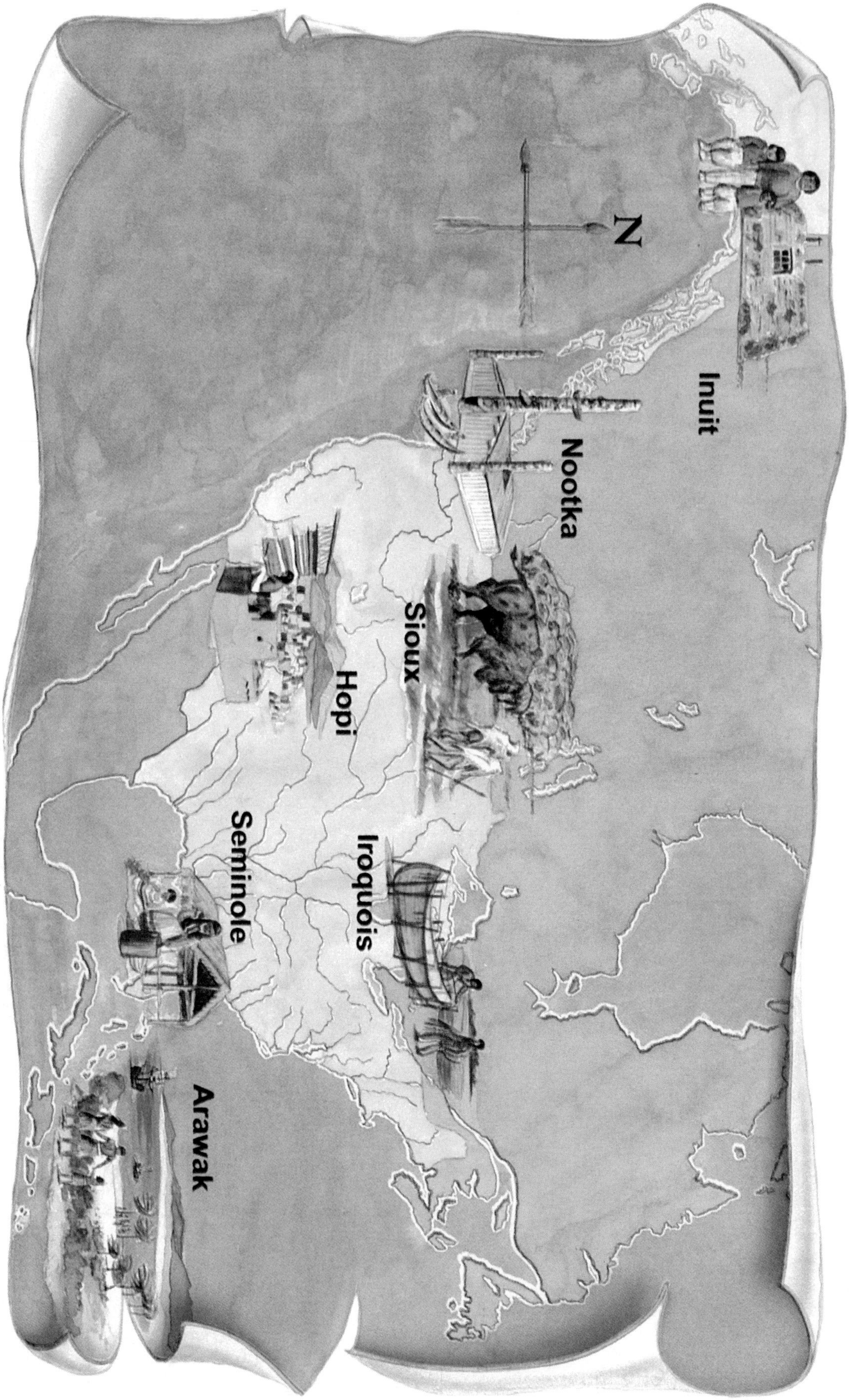

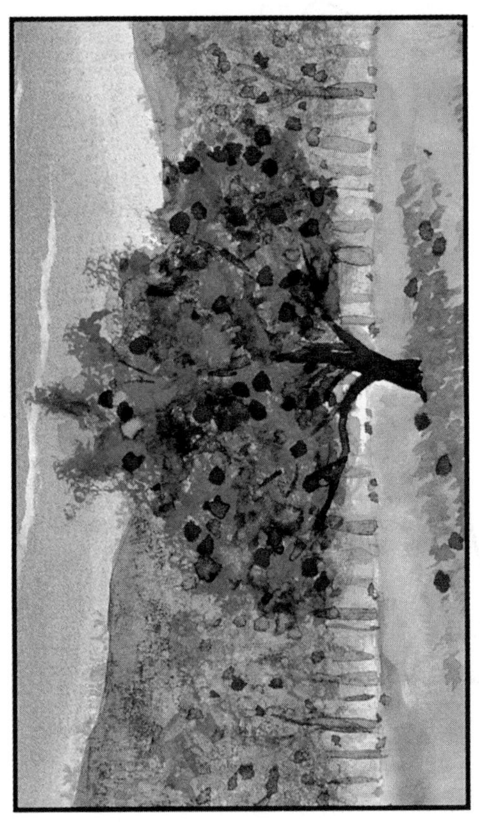

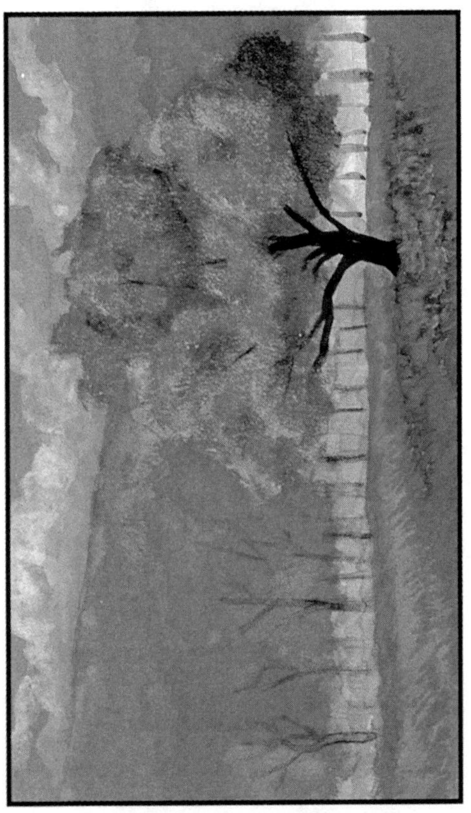

Maps and More: 10

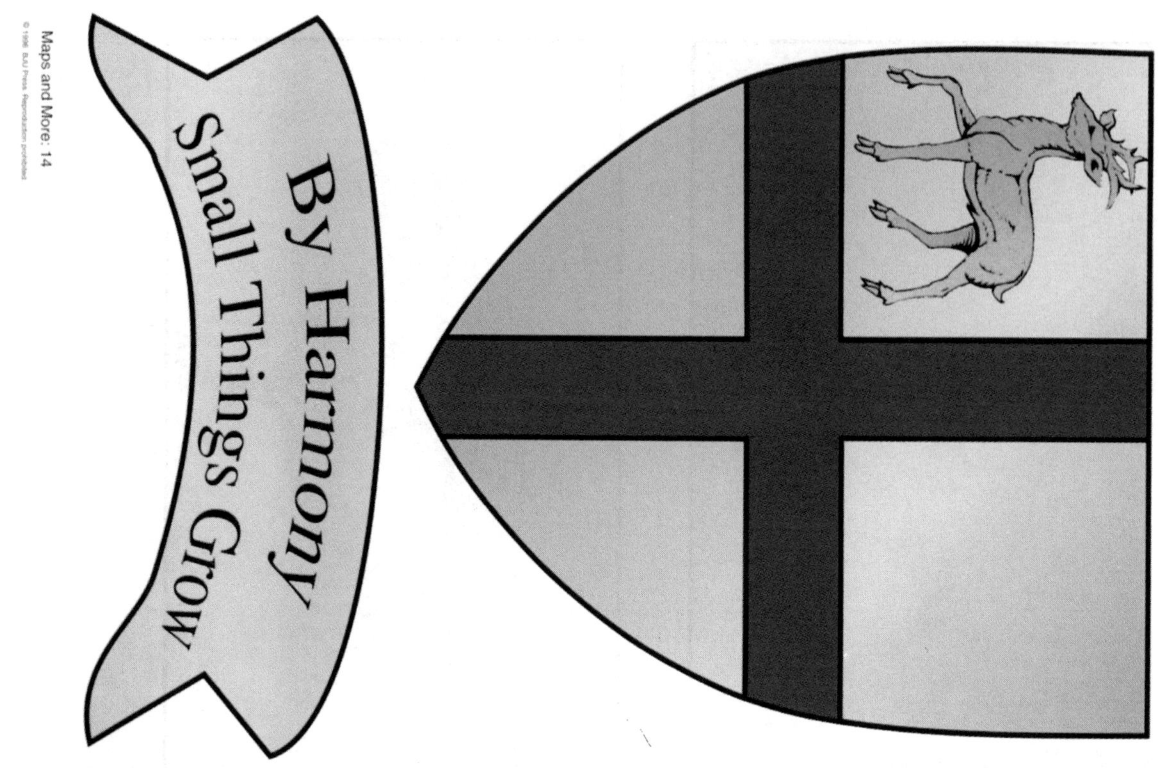

Maps and More: 15

Washington
Oregon
California
Nevada
Idaho
Montana
Wyoming
Utah
Arizona
Colorado
New Mexico
North Dakota
South Dakota
Nebraska
Kansas
Oklahoma
Texas
Minnesota
Iowa
Missouri
Arkansas
Louisiana
Lake Superior
Lake Michigan
Wisconsin
Michigan
Lake Huron
Illinois
Indiana
Mississippi
Alabama
Tennessee
Kentucky
Ohio
Lake Erie
West Virginia
Virginia
North Carolina
South Carolina
Georgia
Florida
Quebec
Vermont
Lake Ontario
New York
Maine
New Hampshire
Boston
Massachusetts
Rhode Island
Connecticut
Pennsylvania
New Jersey
Delaware
Maryland
Alaska
Hawaii
N
W
E
S
Maps and More: 16
© 1996 BJU Press. Reproduction prohibited

Maps and More: 17

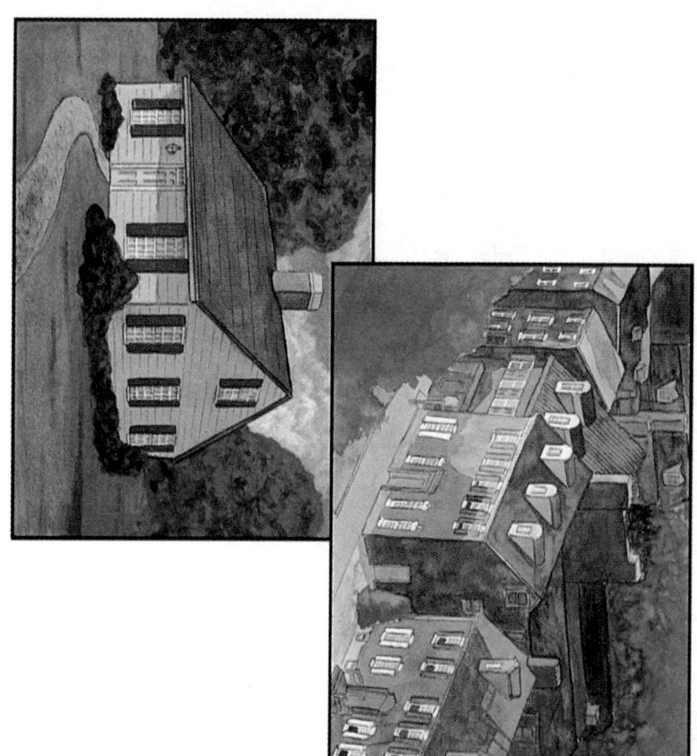

Maps and More: 18

Maps and More: 19

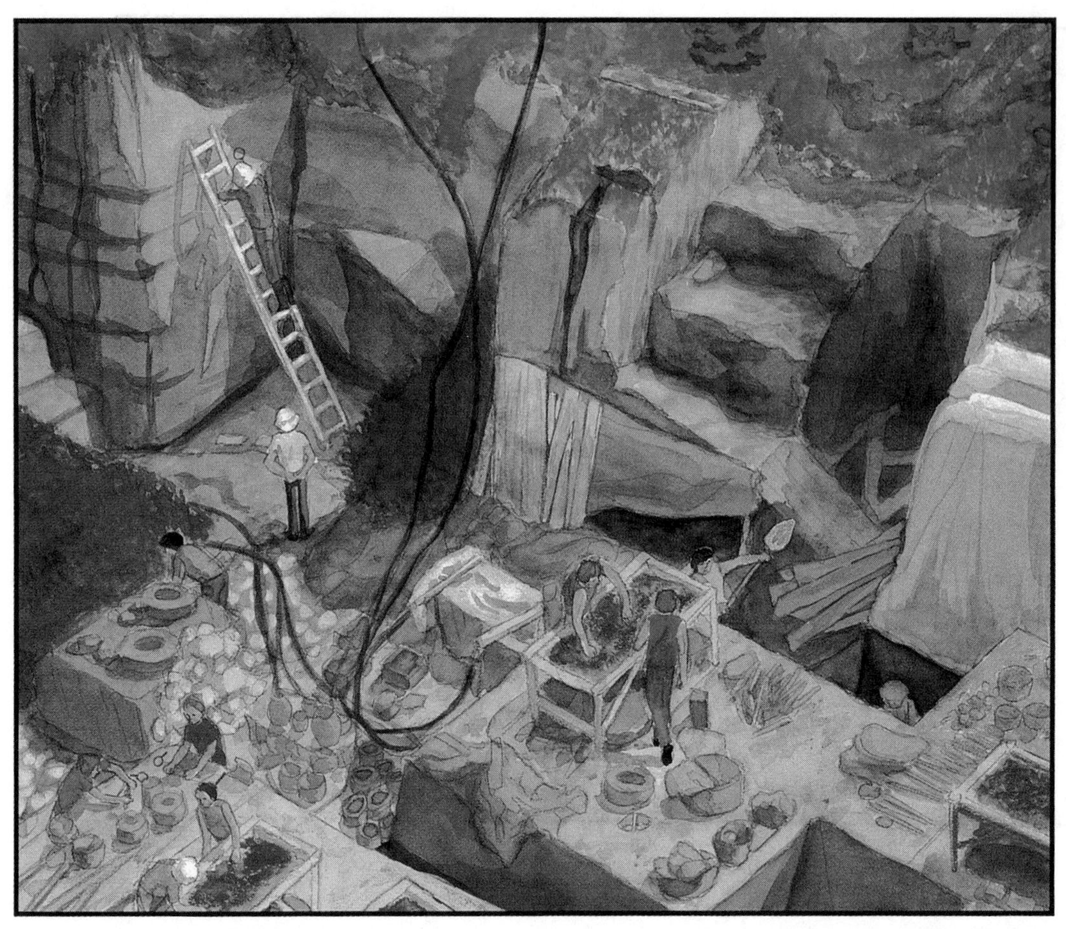

Maps and More: 20

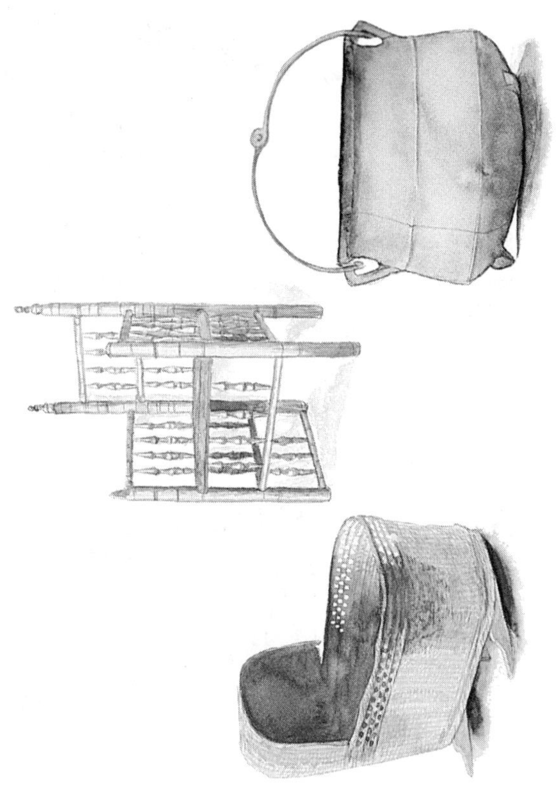

Maps and More: 24

Maps and More: 22

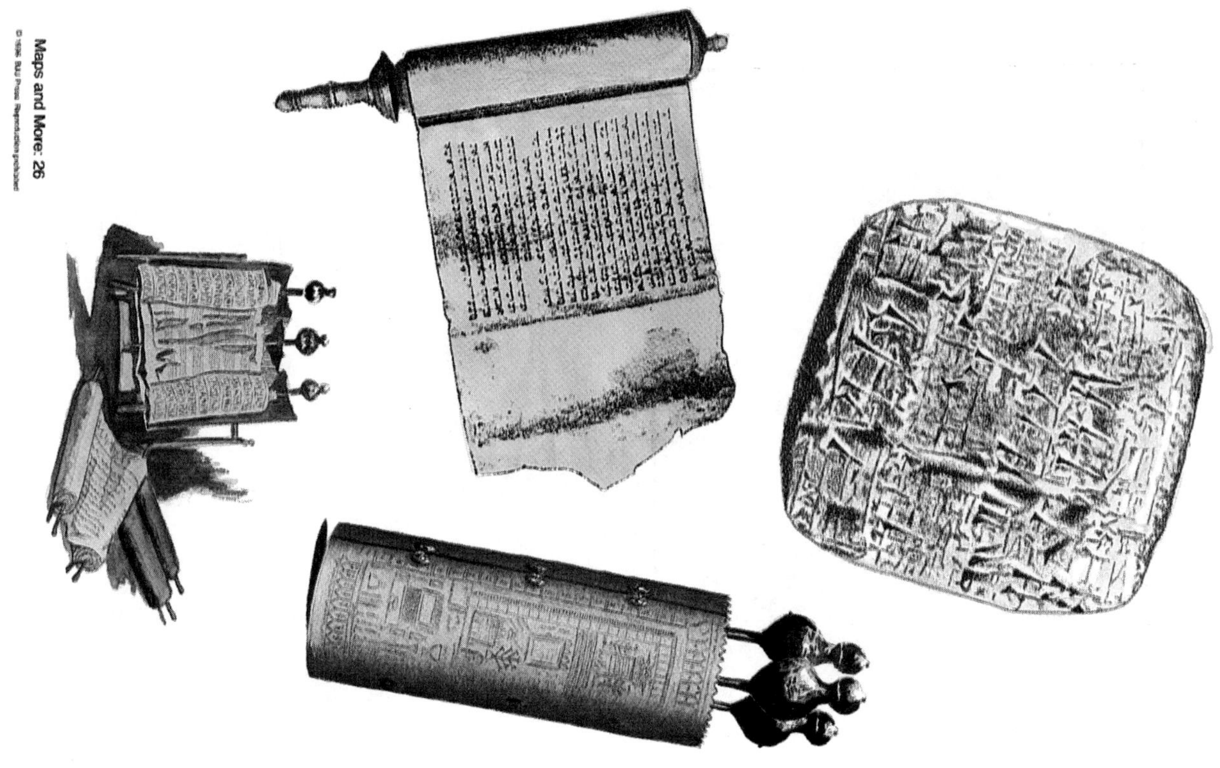

Maps and More: 27

Maps and More: 30

Maps and More: 32

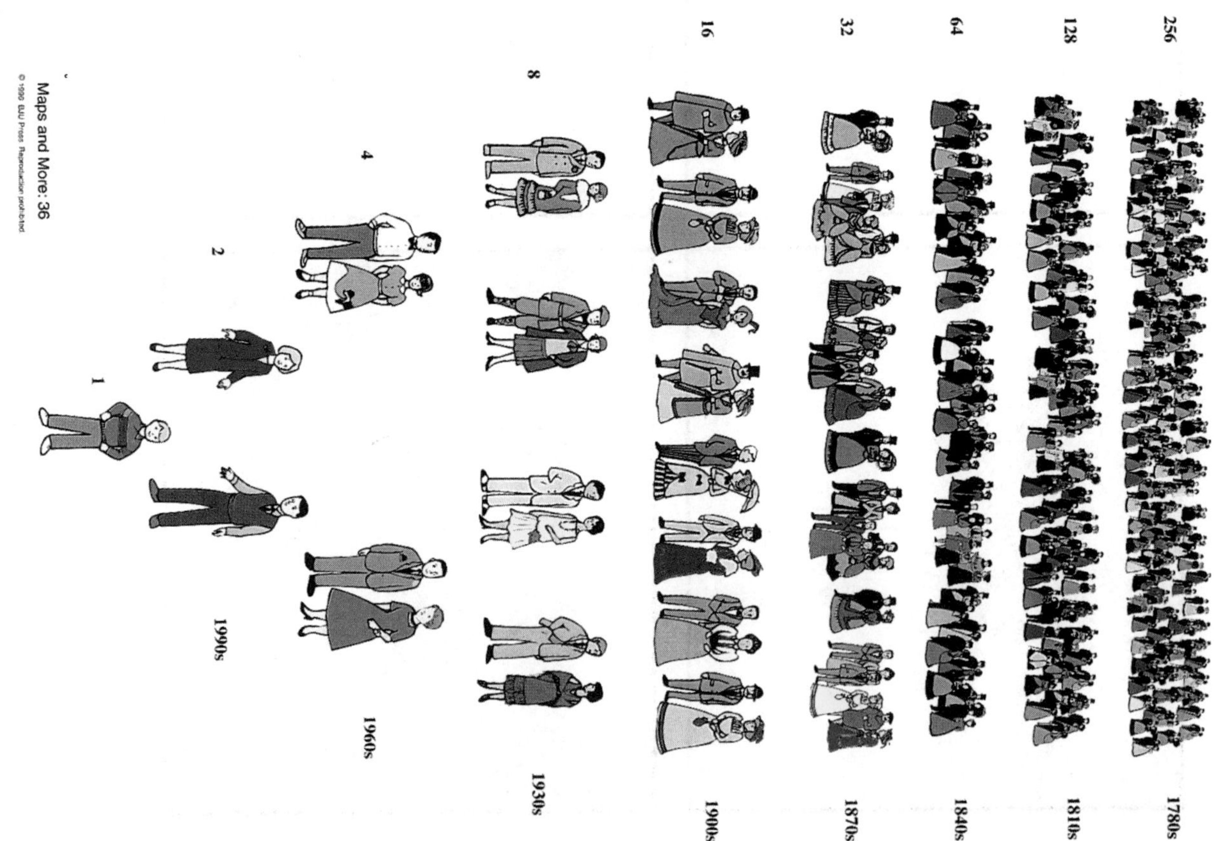

SUPPLEMENT

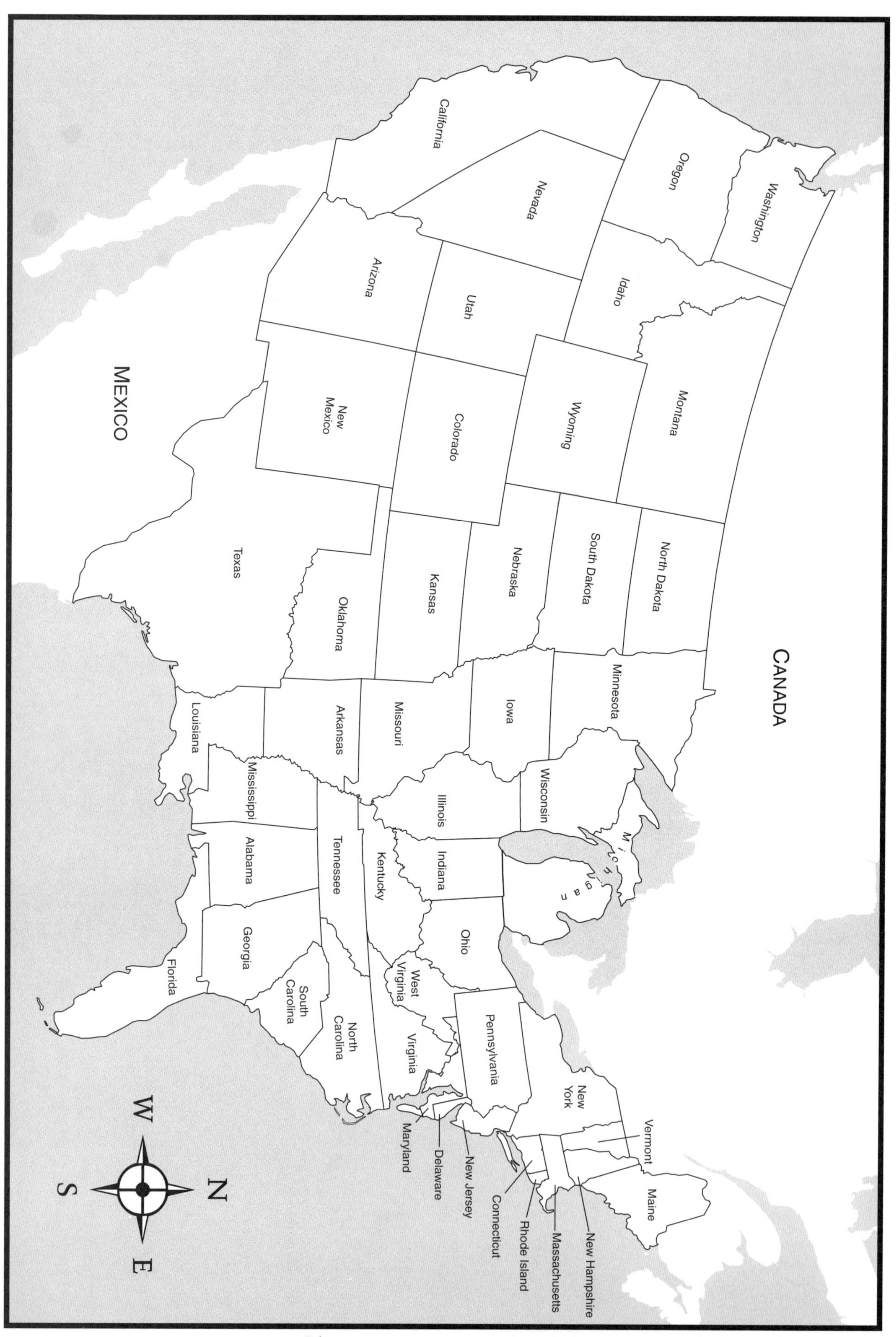
MEXICO
CANADA
California
Oregon
Washington
Nevada
Idaho
Arizona
Utah
Montana
Wyoming
New Mexico
Colorado
Texas
Oklahoma
Kansas
Nebraska
South Dakota
North Dakota
Minnesota
Iowa
Missouri
Arkansas
Louisiana
Wisconsin
Illinois
Michigan
Mississippi
Alabama
Tennessee
Kentucky
Indiana
Ohio
Georgia
Florida
South Carolina
North Carolina
West Virginia
Virginia
Pennsylvania
New York
Vermont
Maine
New Hampshire
Massachusetts
Rhode Island
Connecticut
New Jersey
Delaware
Maryland
N
S
E
W

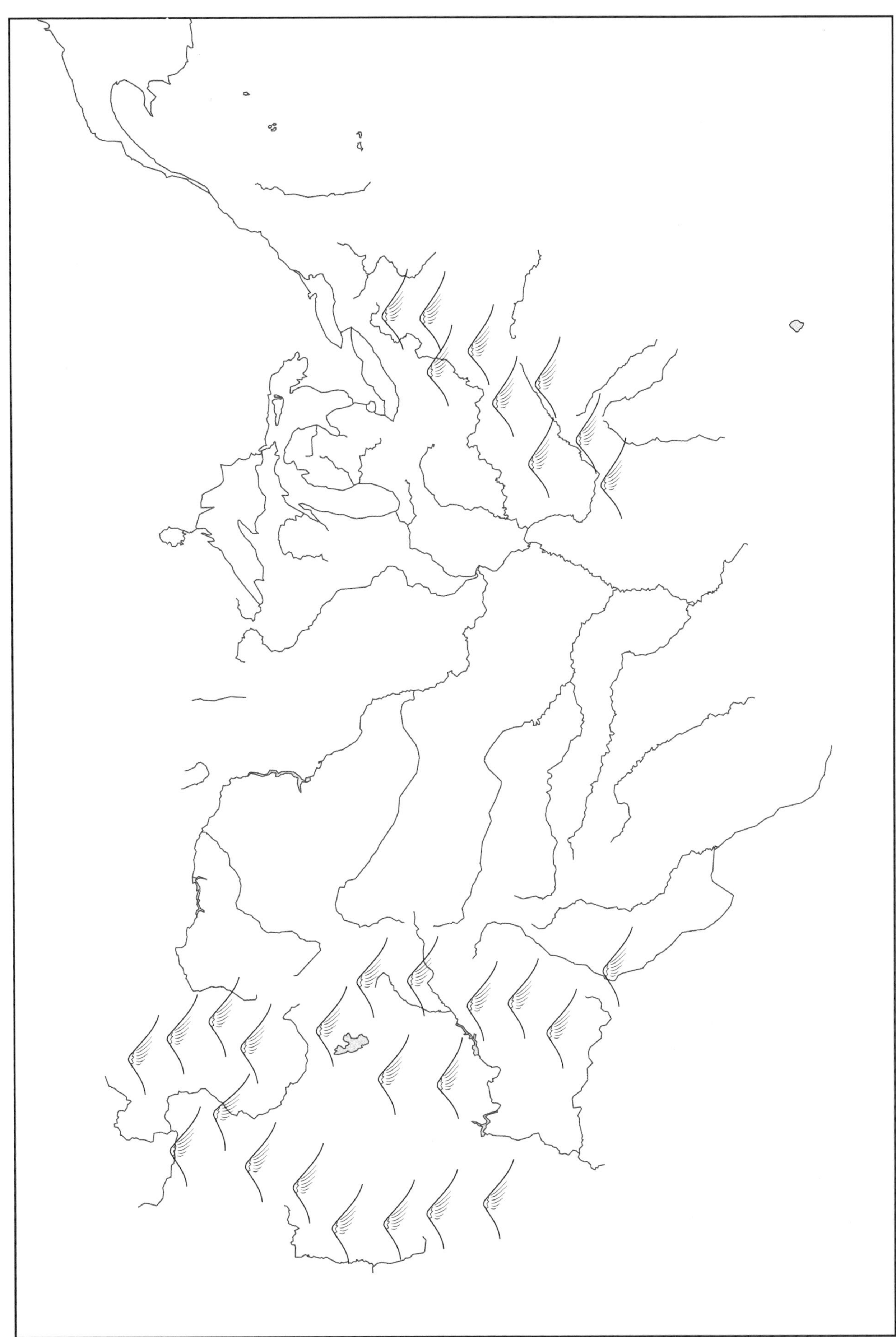

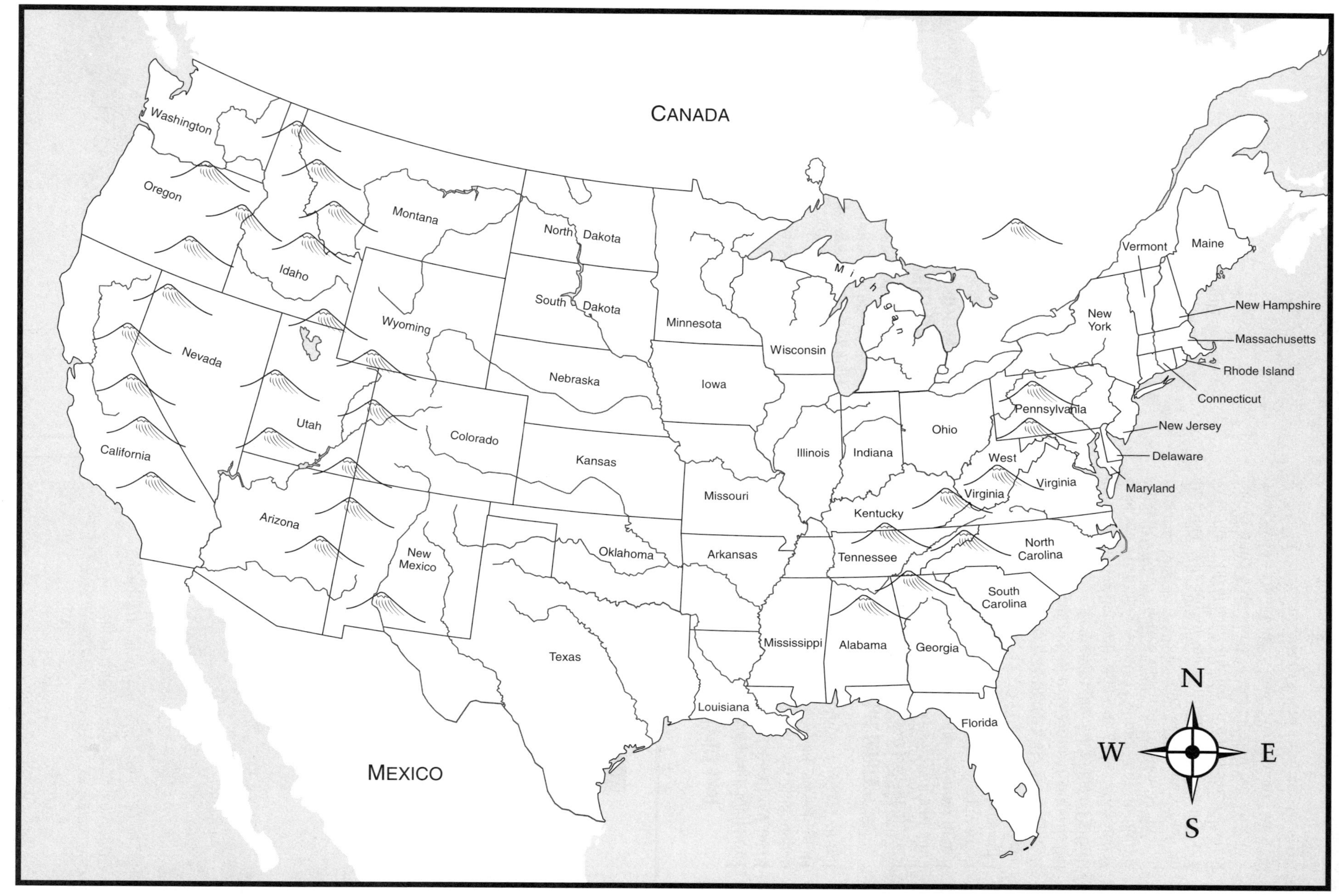
CANADA
Washington
Oregon
Montana
North Dakota
Idaho
South Dakota
Minnesota
Wyoming
Wisconsin
Michigan
Vermont
Maine
New Hampshire
New York
Massachusetts
Rhode Island
Connecticut
Nevada
Nebraska
Iowa
Utah
Pennsylvania
California
Colorado
Ohio
Illinois
Indiana
Kansas
New Jersey
Delaware
West Virginia
Virginia
Maryland
Missouri
Kentucky
Arizona
New Mexico
Oklahoma
Arkansas
Tennessee
North Carolina
South Carolina
Mississippi
Alabama
Georgia
Texas
Louisiana
Florida
MEXICO
N
W
E
S

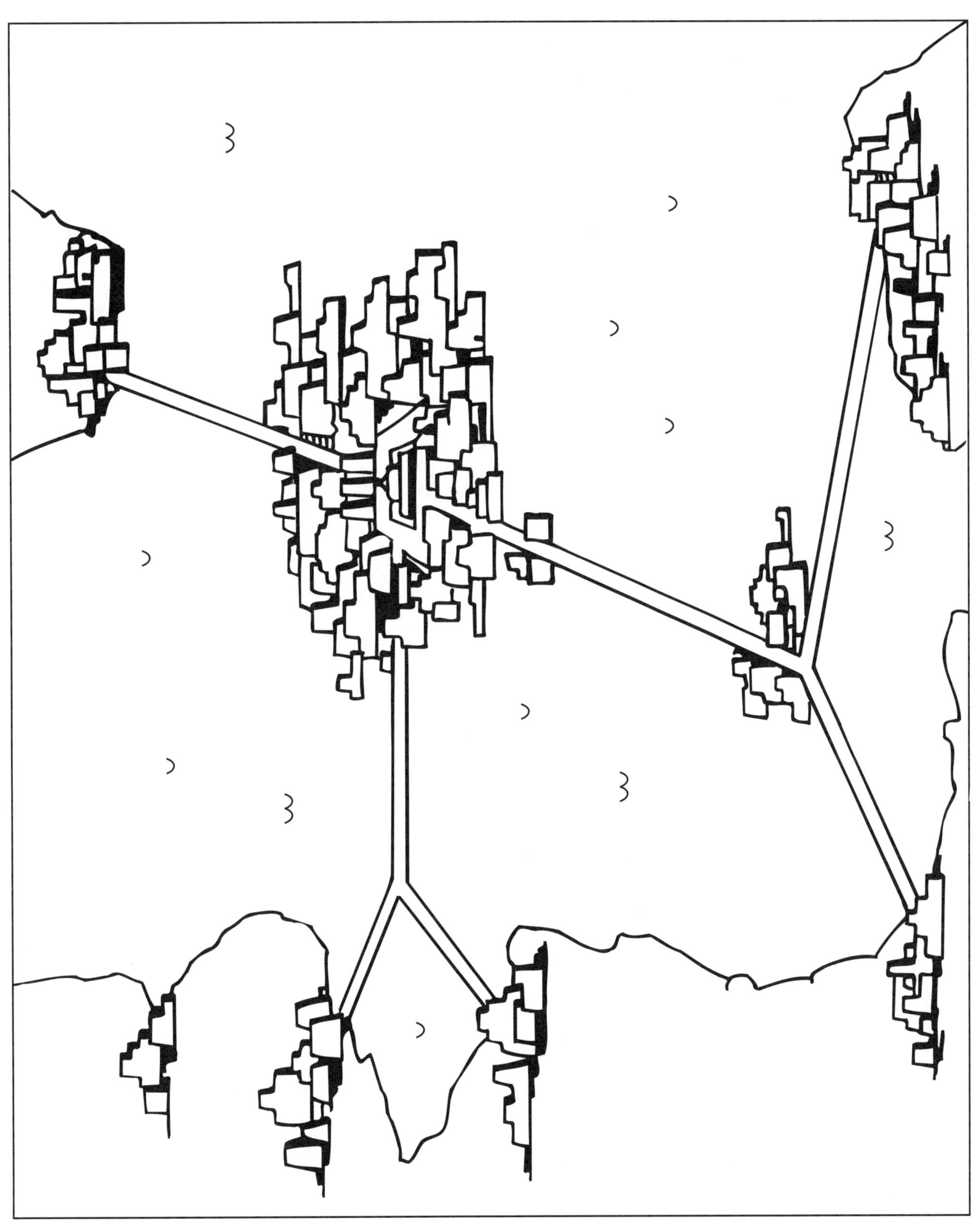

 Use with Supplemental Lesson in Chapter 1.

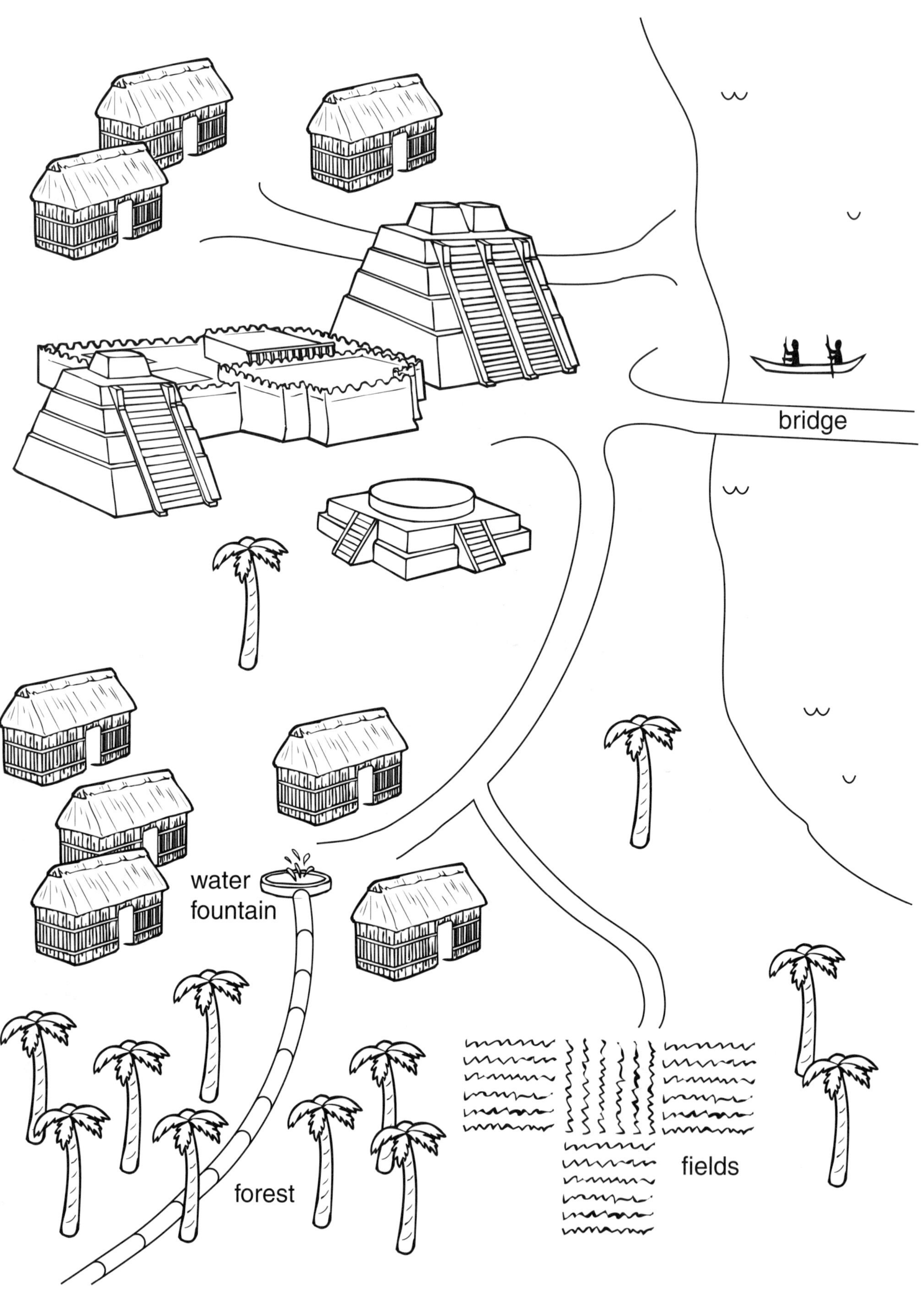
bridge
water
fountain
forest
fields

Columbus went to sea, sea, sea
To see what he could see, see, see.
But all that he could see, see, see
Was the bottom of the deep blue sea, sea, sea.

HONOR FEATHERS

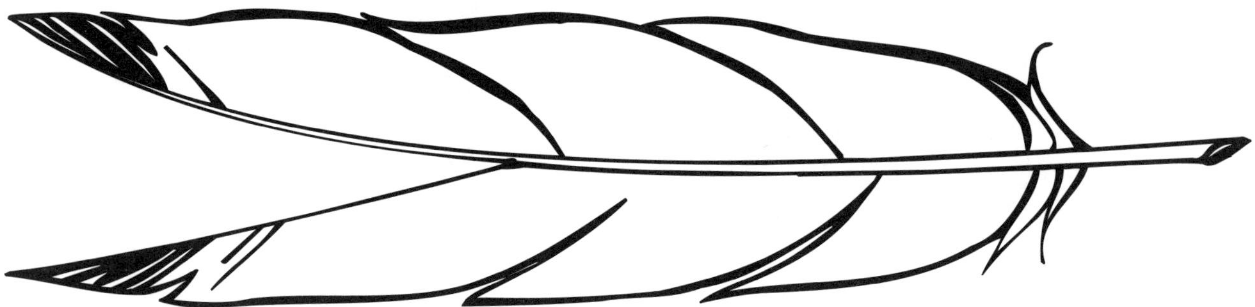

many wounds

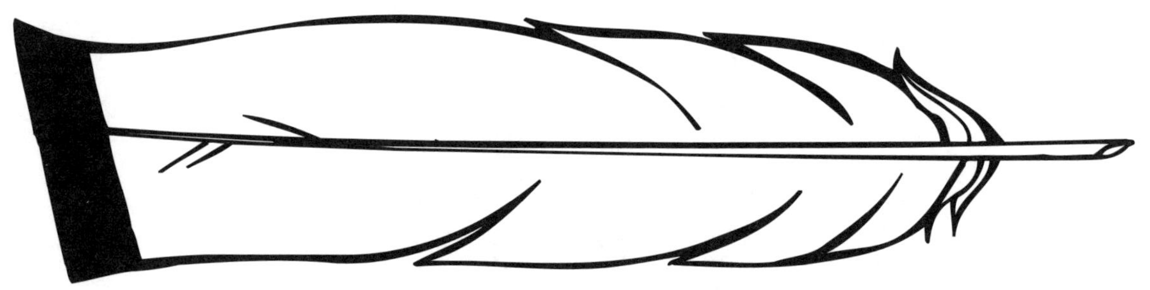

cut enemy's throat

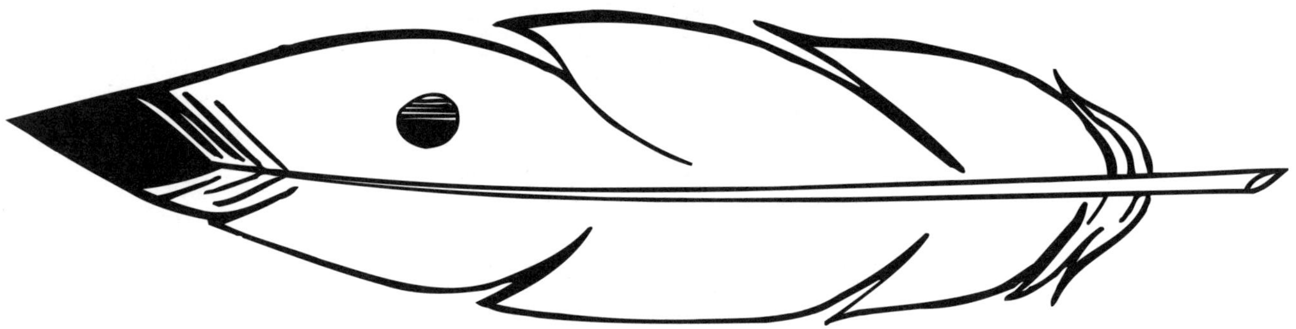

killed an enemy

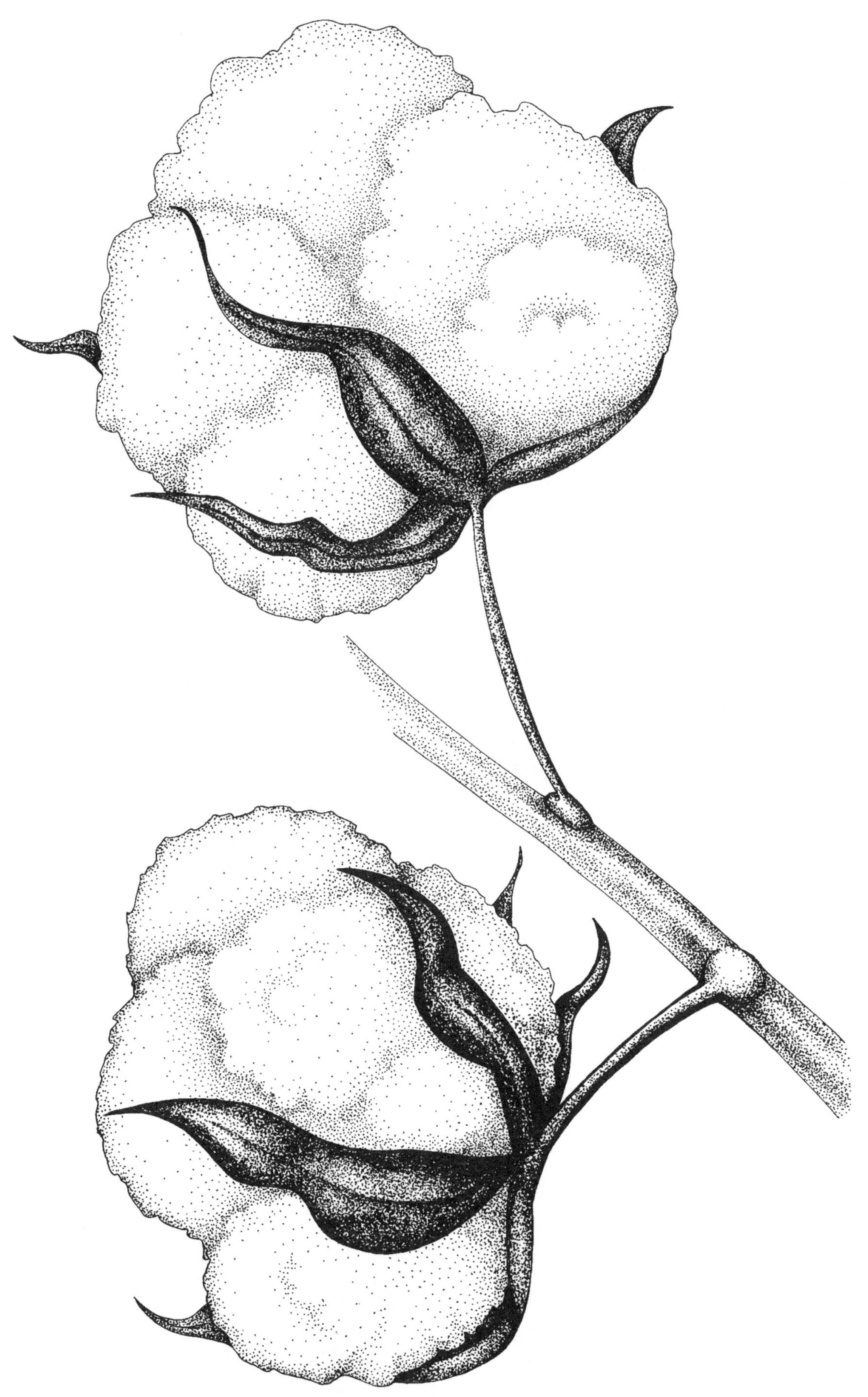

Making a Wigwam

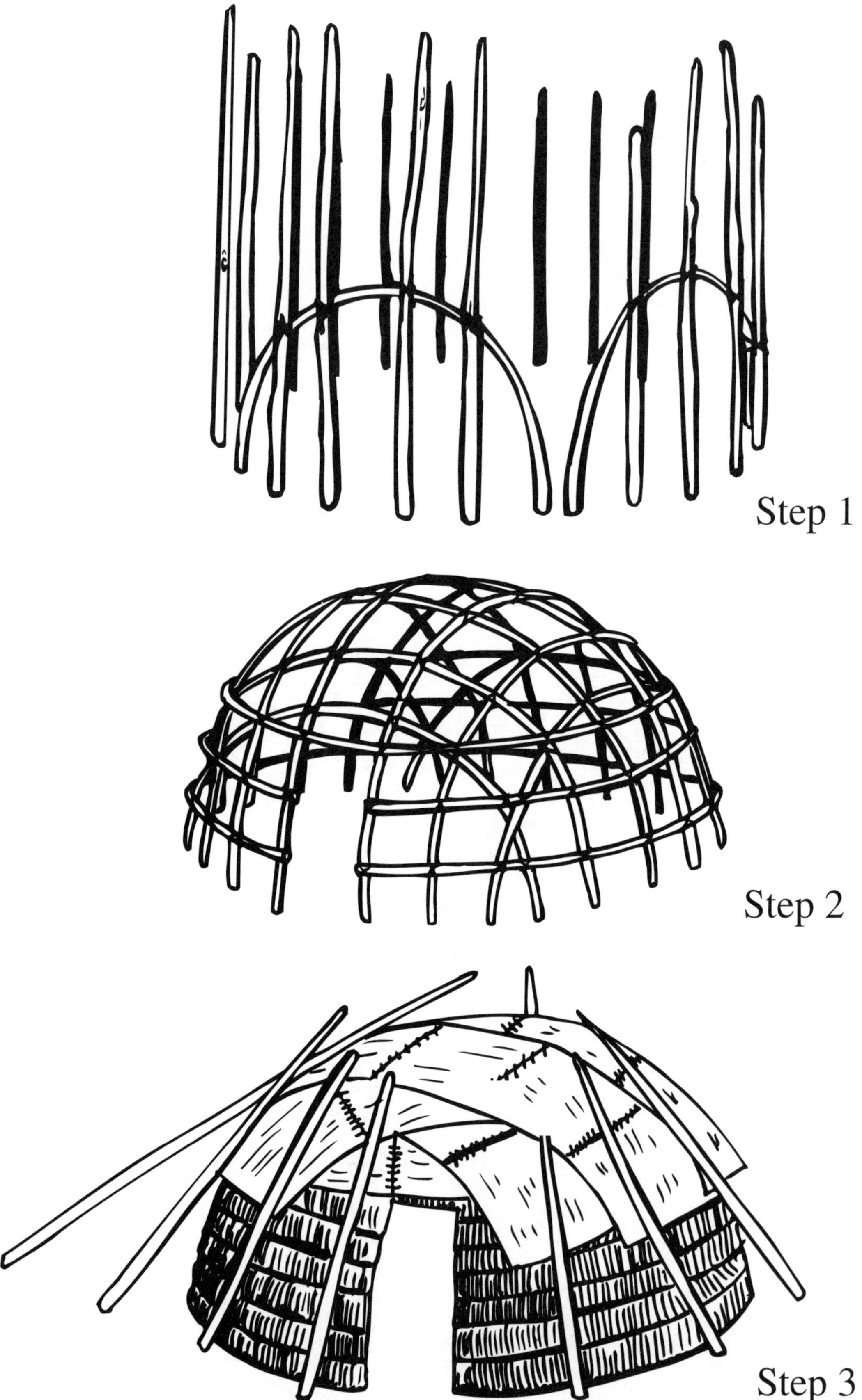

Children's Survey

1. I like bananas.
2. My dress is blue.
3. I cannot swim.

1. I hate bananas.
2. My socks are blue.
3. I love to swim.

1. I like bananas.
2. I have no blue.
3. I cannot swim.

1. I like bananas.
2. My vest is blue.
3. I cannot swim.

1. I like bananas.
2. My top is blue.
3. I can swim.

1. I do not like bananas.
2. I have no blue.
3. I can swim.

1. I do not like bananas.
2. My belt is blue.
3. I cannot swim.

1. I like bananas.
2. My pants are blue.
3. I cannot swim.

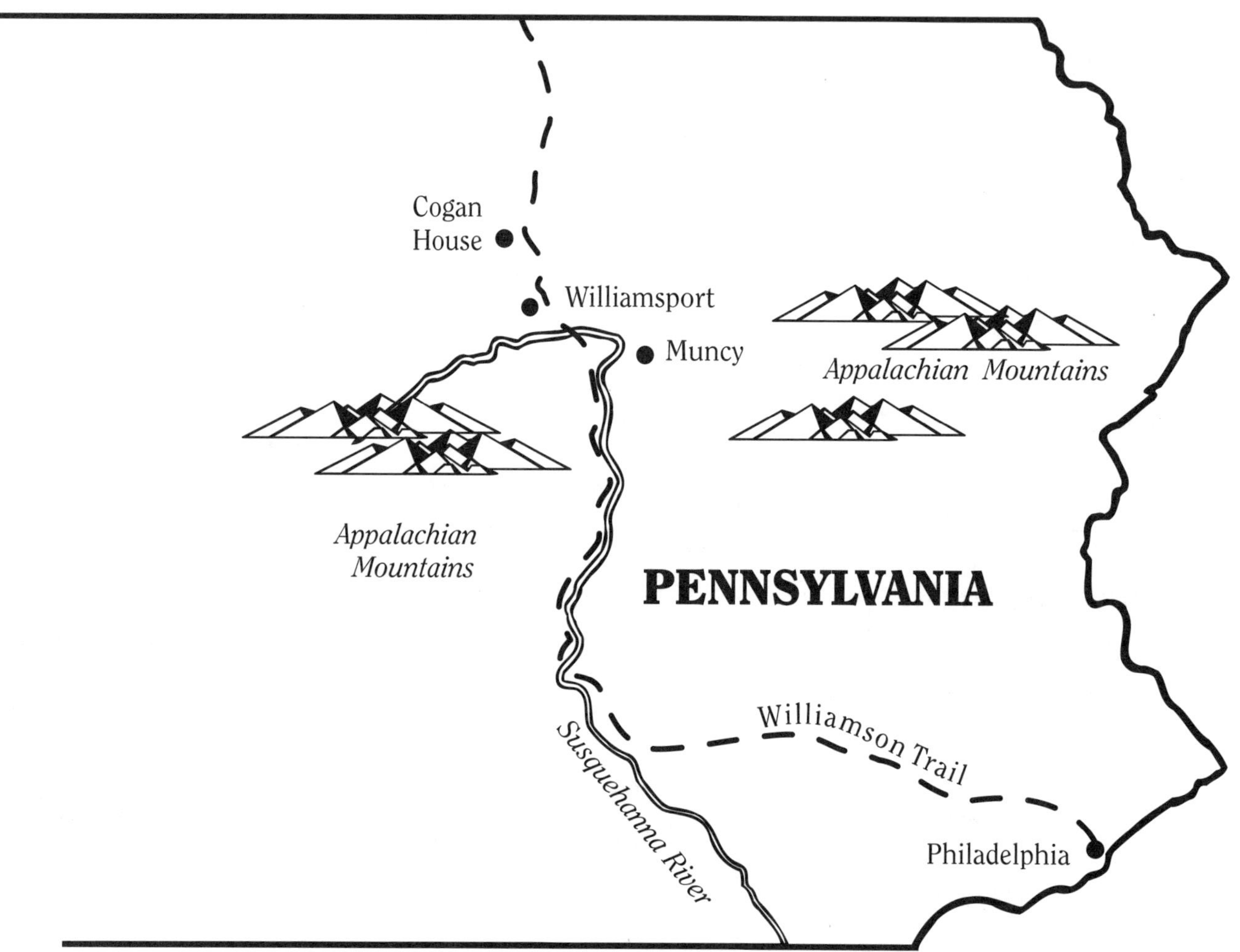
NEW YORK
Cogan
House
Williamsport
Muncy
Appalachian Mountains
Appalachian
Mountains
PENNSYLVANIA
Williamson Trail
Susquehanna River
Philadelphia
MARYLAND

MATERIALS LIST

Chapter 1

Lesson 1
- A pitcher of water
- A rock
- 5 letter envelopes for continent puzzle pieces
- A globe*
- *Heritage Studies 1 Student Notebook**
- *Heritage Studies 1 Student Textbook**
- Appendix, pages A2-A5: each continent shape cut apart into puzzle pieces*

Lesson 2
- A small sticker
- Maps and More 1, page M1
- A directional compass (optional)*
- A Bible
- A red construction-paper *N*
- Appendix, page A6: pattern for the *N**
- A yellow circle to represent the sun, hung on the west wall*

Lesson 3
- A long piece of cardboard with a curved or jagged edge
- A piece of blank paper
- A current calendar
- Maps and More 1, page M1
- The History TimeLine from the History Timeline Packet*
- The figure of the Indian groups (about 950) from the History TimeLine Packet*
- The figure of the Viking ship (1000) from the History TimeLine Packet*
- Appendix, page A6: Viking ship*
- Appendix, page A7: World map*

Lesson 4
- Maps and More 3, page M2
- A ruler
- Supplement, page S2: State map
- Supplement, page S3: Geographical map
- Supplement, page S4: Combined map

Supplemental Lesson
- Maps and More 4 and 5, page M3
- 10 cardboard tubes from rolls of paper towels*
- A marble
- A globe (optional)
- Supplement, page S5: the Aztec cities and causeways
- Supplement, page S6: the picture map, showing the pipeline and the water fountain

Chapter 2

Lesson 5
- A sturdy stepladder or alternative*
- A medium-sized cardboard box
- 2 to 3 items to place in the box, such as a toaster, a shoe, a lamp, or a plant
- Maps and More 1 and 6, pages M1 and M4
- A globe
- Several objects of various shapes: oval, cube, cone, and sphere
- A wire hanger
- A hole punch
- String

Lesson 6
- A piece of drawing paper
- Colored-paper shapes to represent furniture*
- A large piece of plain paper for a room map
- Colored pencils
- A ruler or yardstick
- Appendix, page A8: The New World map

Lesson 7
- A small piece of silk*
- Something made of gold
- Something made of porcelain (optional)*
- A variety of spices originating in Asia, such as pepper, ginger, nutmeg, cloves, and cinnamon*
- A wooden tongue depressor or craft stick*
- A globe
- Appendix, page A8: The New World map*
- Appendix, page A9: the Columbus ship, cut out and glued to a tongue depressor*
- Dolls, toy people, or stick puppets of your own creation*

Lesson 8
- Pictures or toys: wagon, airplane, ship*
- An hourglass or egg timer*

Lesson 9
- A calendar (optional)
- Examples of items Columbus found in the New World: corn, a sweet potato, a parrot (or picture of a parrot), small gold trinkets*
- The items collected for Lesson 7: porcelain, silk, spices, and gold
- The figure of Christopher Columbus (1492) from the History TimeLine Packet
- Maps and More 16, page M9
- Supplement, page S7: a rhyme
- Appendix, page A8: The New World Map

Supplemental Lesson
- Decorations for a variety of familiar holidays
- Maps and More 8, page M5
- A piece of art paper

Chapter 3

Lesson 10
- Maps and More 9, page M6
- The figures of the Indians (about 1200 and about 1400) from the History TimeLine Packet
- A sheet of paper

Lesson 11
- Maps and More 9 and 10, pages M6-M7
- Several modern tools*

Lesson 12
- Some dried meat*
- 12 to 15 relatively straight twigs about 12" long*
- String*
- A sheet of paper
- 3 or more toothpicks*
- Maps and More 9, page M6

Lesson 13
- Maps and More 9 and 12, pages M4 and M6

Lesson 14
- A completed Indian weaving*
- Two 12" square pieces of construction paper of different colors*
- Supplement, page S9: picture of the cotton boll
- A cotton boll or a piece of cotton wool (optional)*
- Several small pieces of cotton fabric*
- Maps and More 9, page M6
- A sheet of paper
- A piece of drawing paper

Supplemental Lesson
- Pictures or examples of a hammock, moccasins, a canoe, cotton cloth*
- Maps and More 16, page M9
- A sheet of paper

Chapter 4

Lesson 15
- A piece of cardboard or poster board
- A wooden stake or stick
- A felt-tip pen
- Maps and More 1 and 14, pages M1 and M8
- A welcome sign prepared by writing *Welcome to* on the cardboard and attaching it to the top of the wooden stake

Lesson 16
- Maps and More 15, page M8
- A toy sword*
- A toy tiara or paper crown*

Lesson 17
- The figure of Jamestown (1607) from the History TimeLine Packet
- A picture of the current president of the United States*
- A clean rag or sponge
- Cleanser
- A special treat of your choice

Lesson 18
- An ear of corn*
- A Bible
- A scrap of paper

Lesson 19
- Squash, such as yellow, acorn, or zucchini, or a picture of one of these*
- Beans, such as kidney, lima, navy, or string beans, or a picture of one of these*
- An ear of corn or a picture of corn*
- Plastic cups or egg carton sections*
- Enough soil to fill the cups or egg carton sections
- Some seeds*
- A piece of paper
- A piece of cotton clothing

Lesson 20
- Maps and More 16, page M9
- Two index cards with a *J* on one card and an *E* on the other card*
- A sheet of paper

Chapter 5

Lesson 21
- A newspaper
- 5 dolls or play people*
- Appendix, page A20: map of England and the New World*

Lesson 22
- Appendix, page A20: map of England and the New World*
- Appendix, page A21: a diagram of the ship*
- 8 craft sticks or tongue depressors*
- Selected area about 90' × 26'*

Lesson 23
- A sheet of parchment or similar paper

Lesson 24
- A small glass of water
- A half slice of bread
- 9 grains of dried corn*
- A Bible

Lesson 25
- Ingredients for Indian pudding*
- A 2-quart casserole dish, greased*
- A table knife
- Some food to eat on a knife
- The figure of the *Mayflower* (1620) from the History TimeLine Packet
- Maps and More 17, page M10
- Chart paper or a large sheet of paper

Chapter 6

Lesson 26
- Appendix, page A22: Building Graph*
- A highlighter pen
- A telephone book
- Maps and More 18, page M10

Lesson 27
- A $1\frac{1}{2}$" × 12" strip of brown construction paper*
- Four $1\frac{1}{4}$" × 8" strips of green construction paper*
- A brown paper bag or a sheet of tan construction paper*
- Maps and More 19, page M11
- Supplement, page S10: Making a Wigwam

Lesson 28
- A box or deep tray of soil or sand*
- A pair of tweezers (optional)
- A small, old make-up brush or paintbrush (optional)
- A plastic spoon
- A small toy, shell, or other "artifact"*
- An antique item, such as a kitchen gadget or a piece of jewelry*
- Maps and More 20, page M12

Lesson 29
- Maps and More 19, 22, and 24, pages M11 and M13

Lesson 30
- Appendix, page A23: Starting a Town

Chapter 7

Lesson 31
- The figure of Harvard College (1636) from the History TimeLine Packet
- A sheet of paper

Lesson 32
- A Bible
- A piece of paper

Lesson 33
- An $8\frac{1}{2}$" × 11" piece of stiff plastic or plastic wrap*
- A hole punch
- An $8\frac{1}{2}$" × 11" piece of cardboard*
- Maps and More 26, page M14
- An 18" length of string or ribbon*

Lesson 34
- Maps and More 27, page M14

Lesson 35
- A small piece of paper for each participating family member
- A sheet of paper, chart paper, or chalkboard
- An empty box
- Supplement, page S11: Children's Survey

Chapter 8

Lesson 36
- Some iron tools*
- Brightly colored cloth*
- Something made of animal fur (i.e., a collar, a hat, a coat)*
- Items for decision-making activity, such as a glass figurine, a small truck, a doll, a picture book, costume jewelry, a stuffed animal, money, and so on*

Lesson 37
- Moccasins (optional)*
- Two 4" × 11" pieces of brown paper (grocery sack or similar paper)*
- Items made of fur*
- Items made of leather*

Lesson 38
- The figure of Pierre Radisson (1652) from the History TimeLine Packet
- A 12" × 16" piece of poster board*
- Maps and More 16, page M9
- Appendix, page A25: mask (2 copies)*
- An old ruler or a paint paddle*
- Masking tape

Lesson 39
- 3 or 4 items that your child especially likes (may be food or nonfood)
- 1 or 2 items that your child does not care for

Lesson 40
- Approximately 40 hollow macaroni pieces (Rotini works best.)*
- Red, green, and blue food coloring*
- 4 bowls of water or rubbing alcohol
- Paper towels
- 4 spoons
- Heavy string or yarn, 24" long*

Chapter 9

Lesson 41
- Several toys*
- Several tools*
- Several items of clothing*
- Several food items*
- Scraps of felt (optional)*

Lesson 42
- A small paper bag or other container
- Small items to hide for a treasure hunt (stickers, pencils, packages of raisins, and so on)—enough for your child to find 3 or 4, as well as 1 of each item for you to show*
- Appendix, page A29: Mississippi River Map*

Lesson 43
- A chess set (optional)
- A sheet of paper

Lesson 44
- Maps and More 30, page M15
- Appendix, page A29: Mississippi River Map (used in Lesson 42)*
- Appendix, page A30: Indian sign language and canoes*
- The figure of La Salle (1682) from the History TimeLine Packet

Lesson 45
- Supplement, page S12: Map of Pennsylvania
- A sheet of handwriting paper with *What Makes Our Town or City Special?* written on it

Chapter 10

Lesson 46
- A Bible

Lesson 47
- A Bible

Lesson 48
- A Bible
- Maps and More 8, page M5
- A cassette player*
- *HERITAGE STUDIES Listening Cassette A**
- A pan
- A bag of dried beans*
- A small toy such as a block
- A sheet of paper with the following words written on it: *England, France, Spain, Atlantic Ocean*

Lesson 49
- A coin
- A sheet of paper with the words *IN GOD WE TRUST* on it

Chapter 11

Lesson 50
- Several camping items (a flashlight, matches, a sleeping bag, and so on)*
- Several miscellaneous items not needed for camping
- A large cardboard box in which you place the above items

Lesson 51
- A garden vegetable or fruit that contains seeds
- A prepackaged food, such as a can of vegetables
- A knife

Lesson 52
- A picture of a man dressed for construction or farm work*
- A picture of a man dressed in formal clothes*
- Maps and More 10 and 32, pages M7 and M16

Lesson 53
- A one-dollar bill
- A quarter
- Food, clothing, toy houses (or pictures of houses), toys, books, and other items that a child might want to buy
- A sheet of paper
- Blank stickers or Post-It Notes
- Play or real money*

Lesson 54
- Appendix, page A34: a spending chart
- Appendix, page A35: price tags for items (cut apart)
- An empty, well-rinsed plastic jug (milk or liquid detergent)*
- A chenille wire*
- Two buttons (optional)*
- Four small empty spools*
- Felt-tip pens*
- Construction paper (optional)
- A sheet of paper
- Various coins in the amount of 50¢
- A calculator (optional)

Chapter 12

Lesson 55
- A large piece of chart paper or butcher paper at least 4 feet long or a growth chart*
- A yardstick
- Tape or Plasti-Tak
- 1 or 2 books listing the meanings of first names*
- A piece of drawing paper

Lesson 56
- No new materials required for this lesson

Lesson 57
- Some dirty laundry
- A laundry basket
- A sheet of paper
- *If Everybody Did* by JoAnn Stover (BJUP) (optional)*

Lesson 58
- *Pulling Together* by Dawn Watkins (BJUP) (optional)*

Lesson 59
- An item that has been in your family for a long time*
- Maps and More 36, page M16

Lesson 60
- Maps and More 36, page M16
- 3 to 4 photographs of yourself at different ages, arranged in sequential order*
- Plasti-Tak or transparent tape
- Several pieces of art paper
- Photos of several important events in your child's life (optional)*
- Four sheets of construction paper prepared for a time line and taped together as shown in the lesson*

APPENDIX

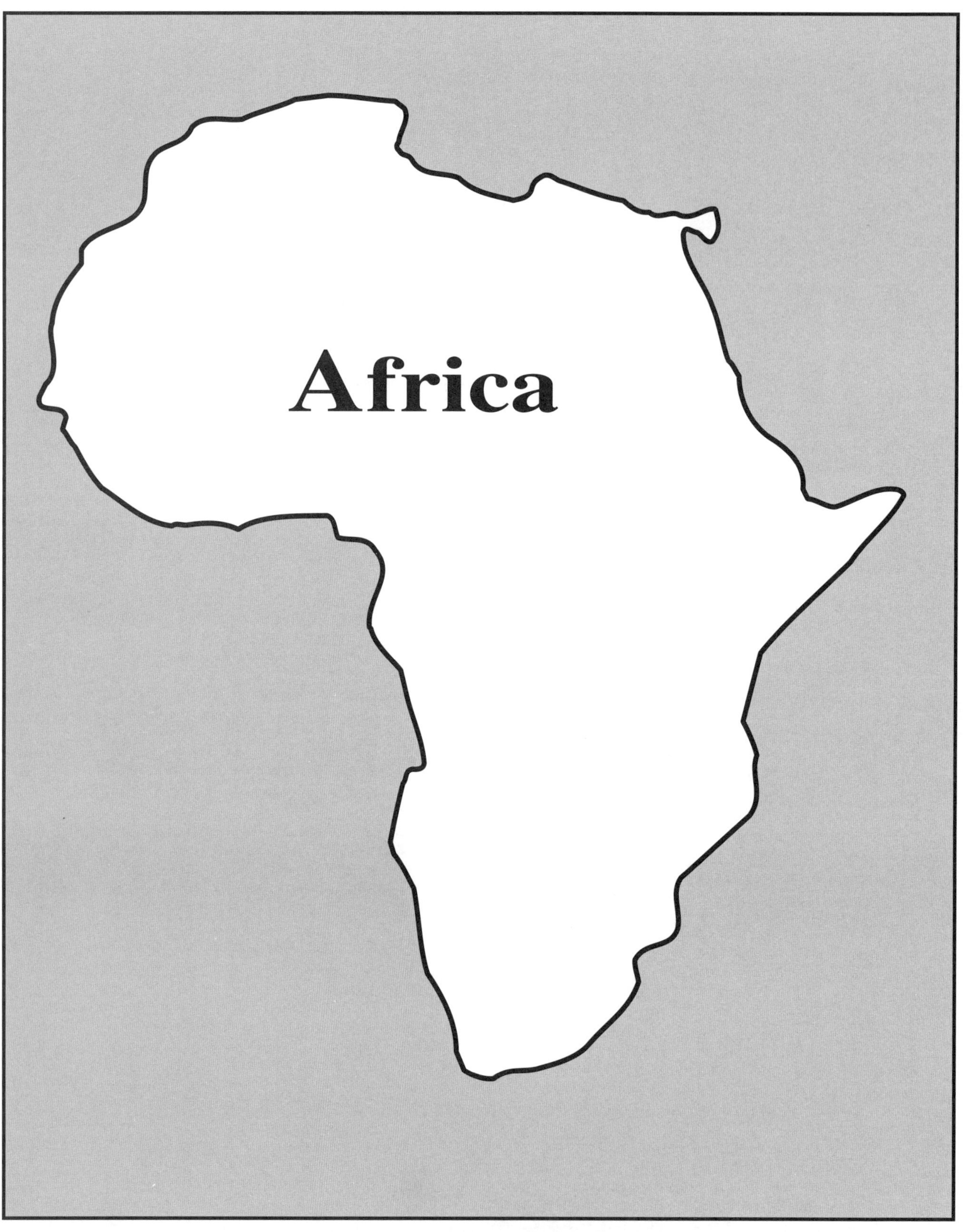
Africa

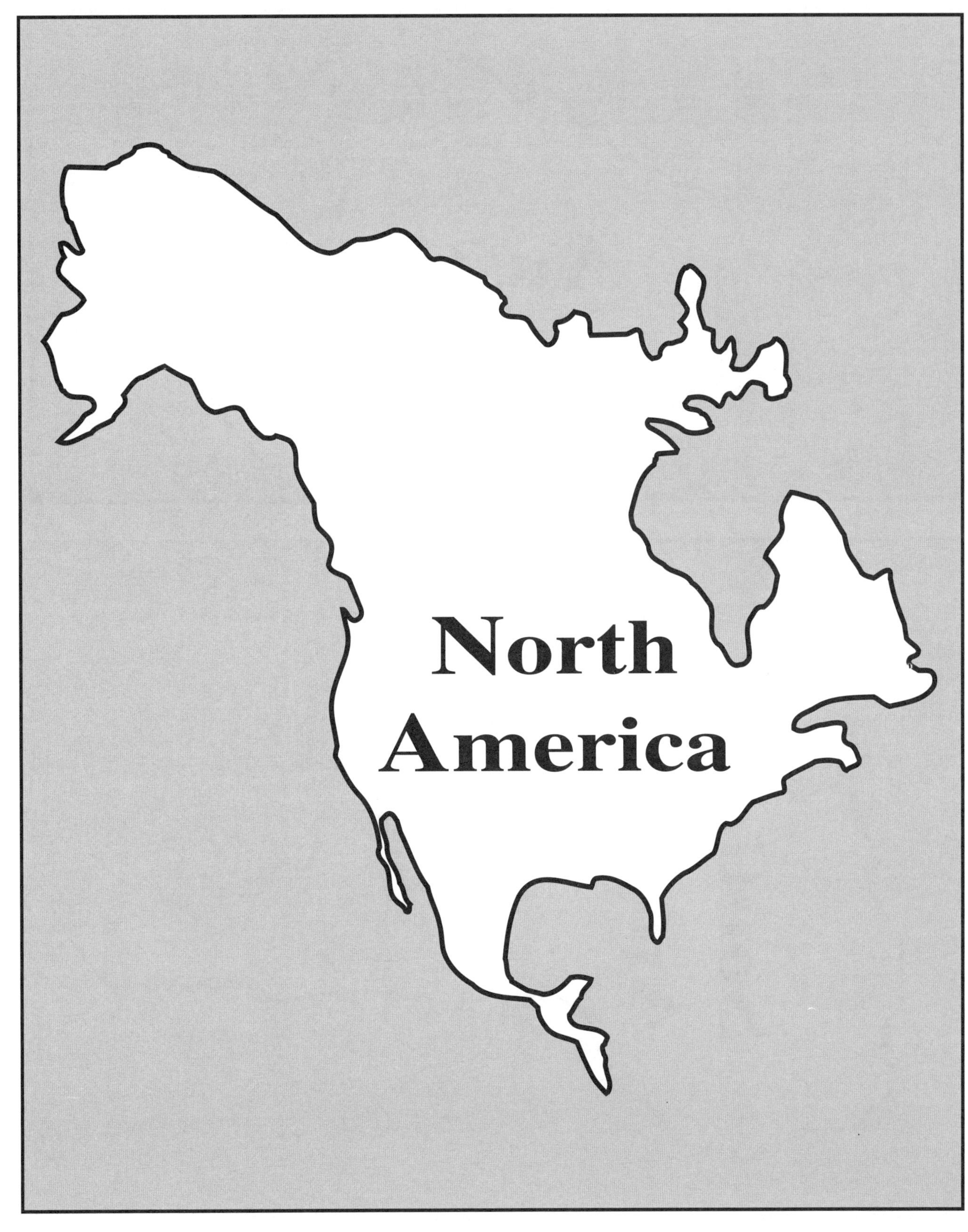
North America

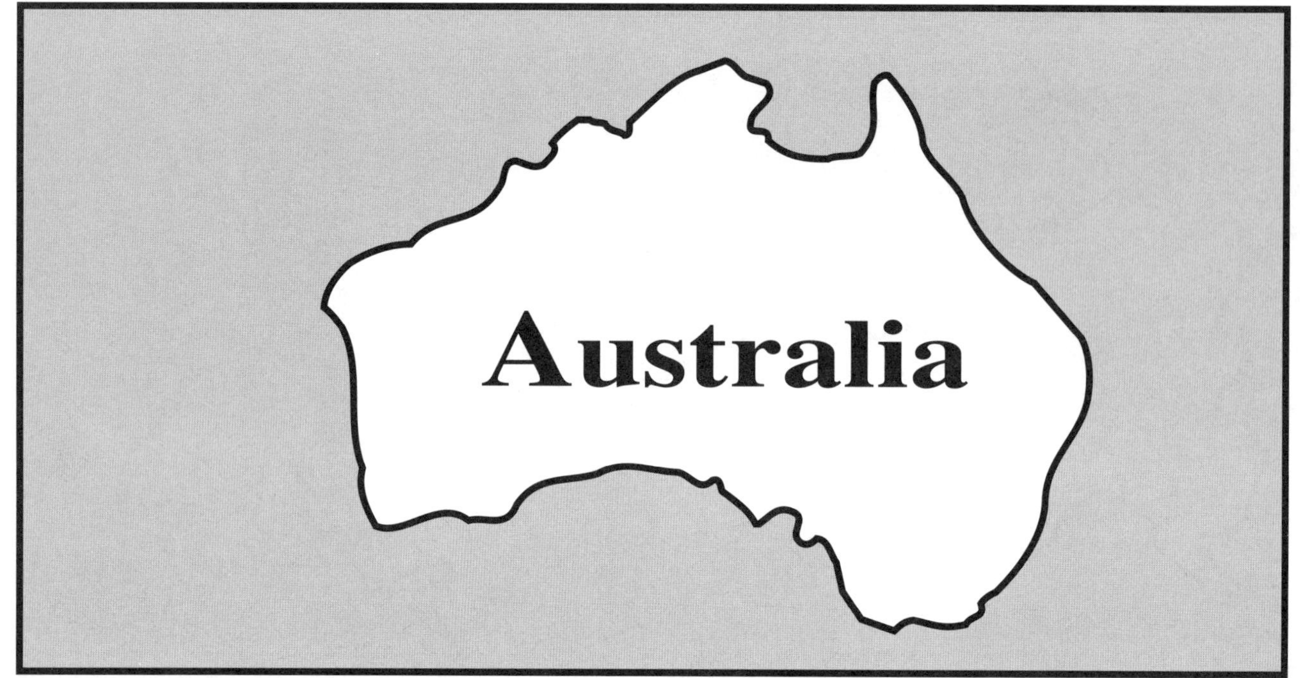

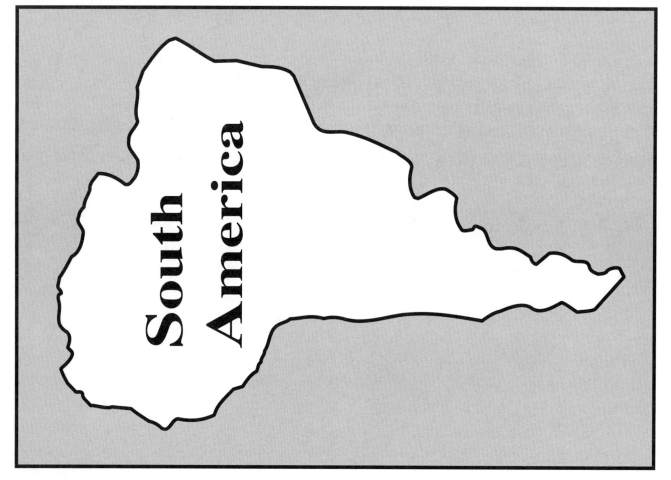

South America

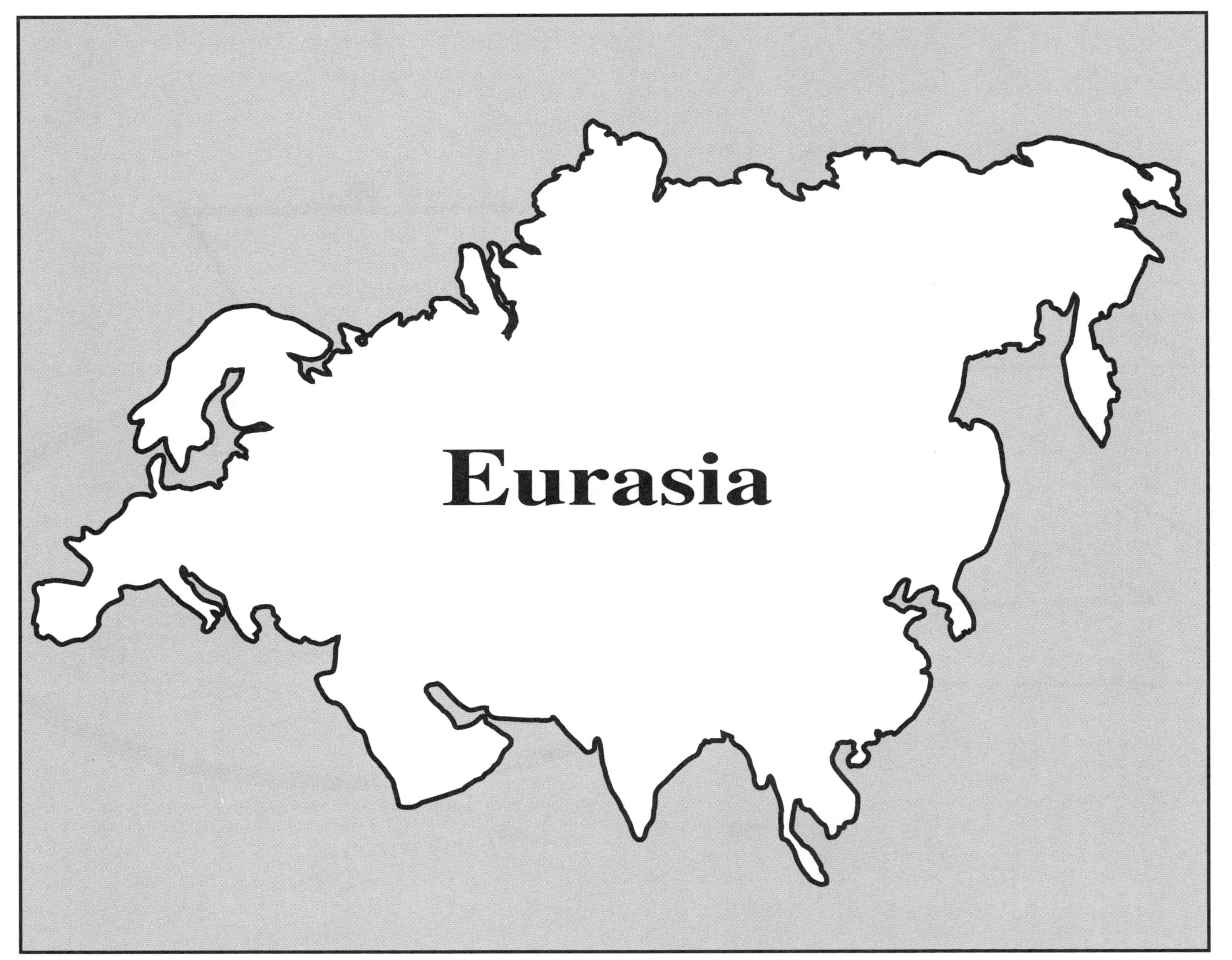
Eurasia

Use with Lesson 2.

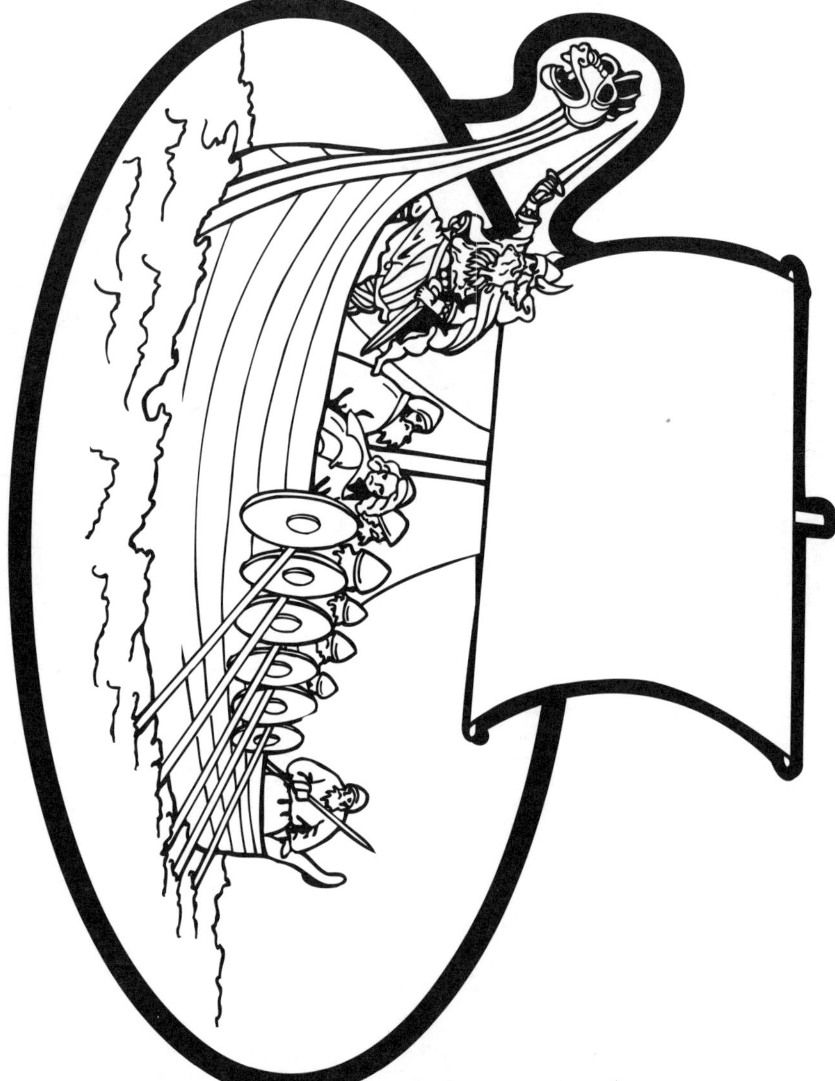

Use with Lesson 3.

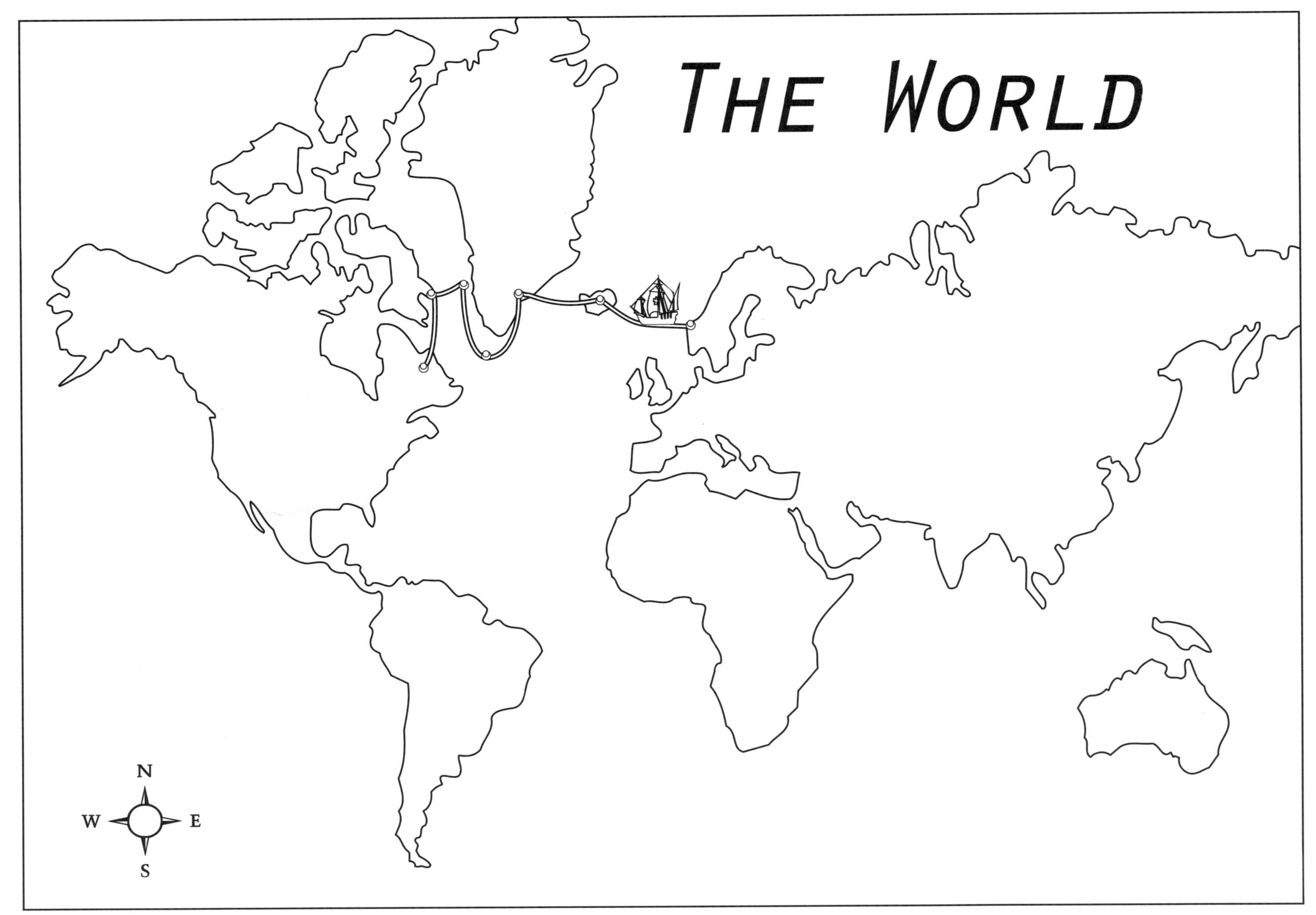
THE WORLD
N
W
E
S

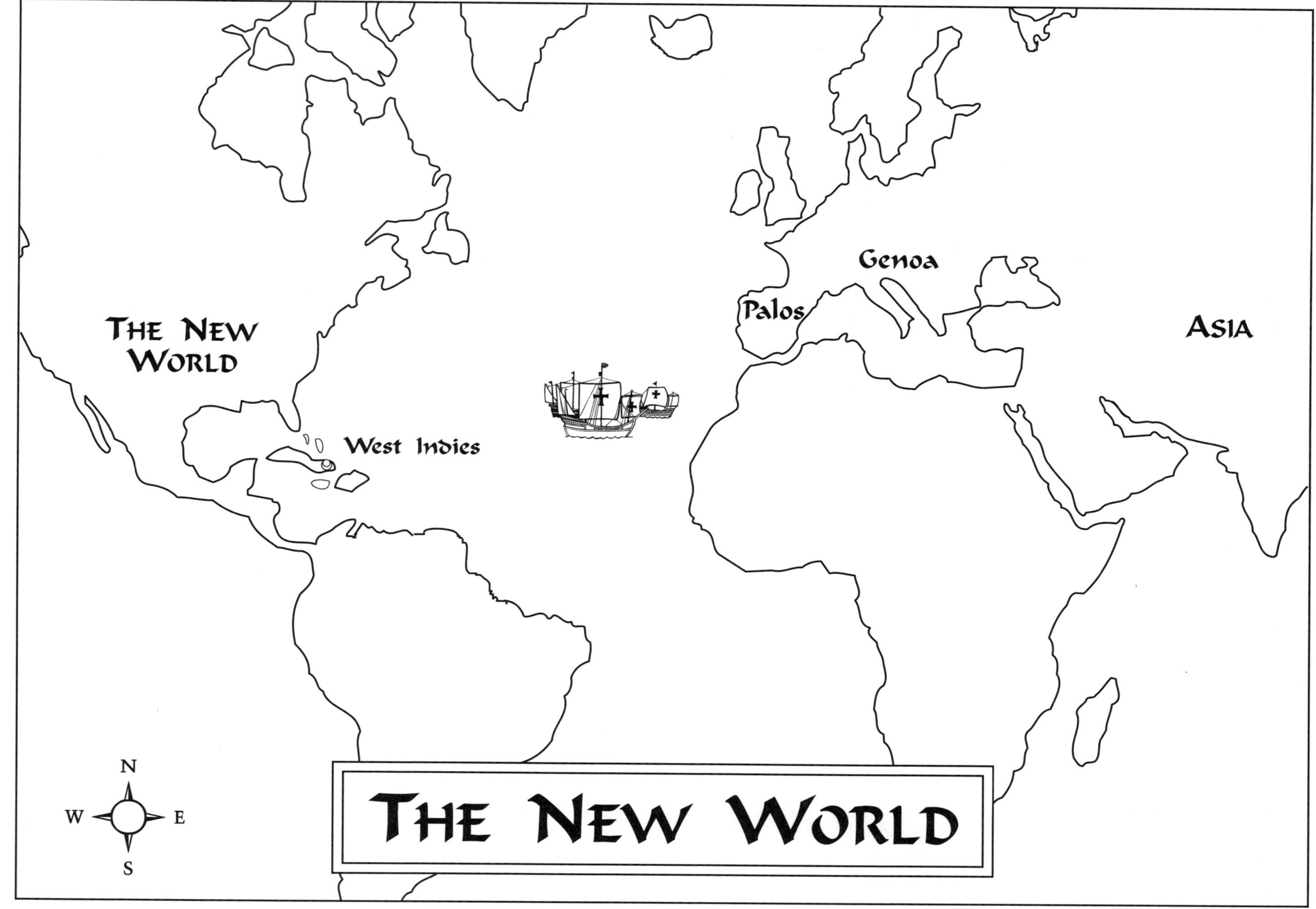
The New World
Genoa
Palos
Asia
West Indies
N
W
E
S
The New World

Setting Sail

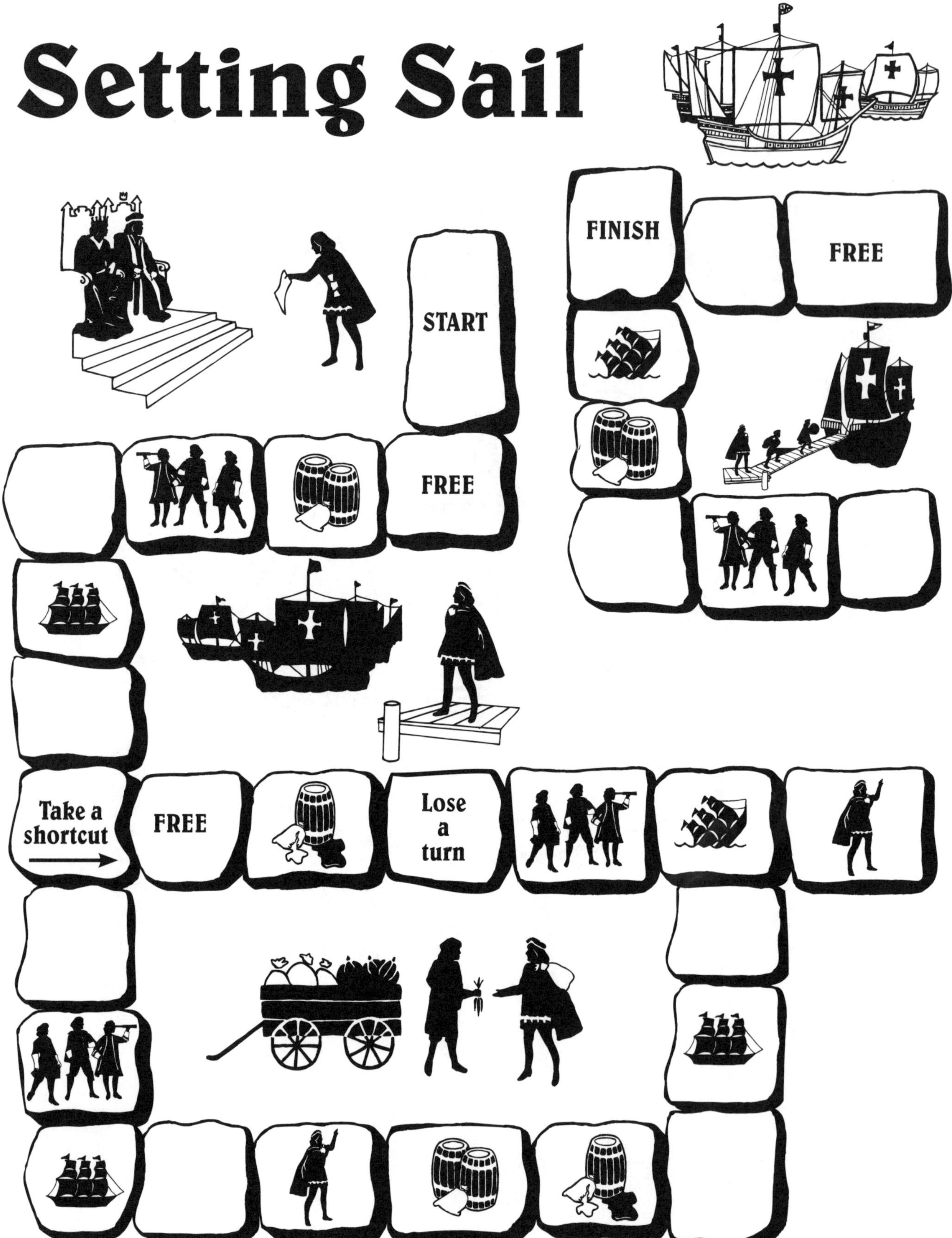

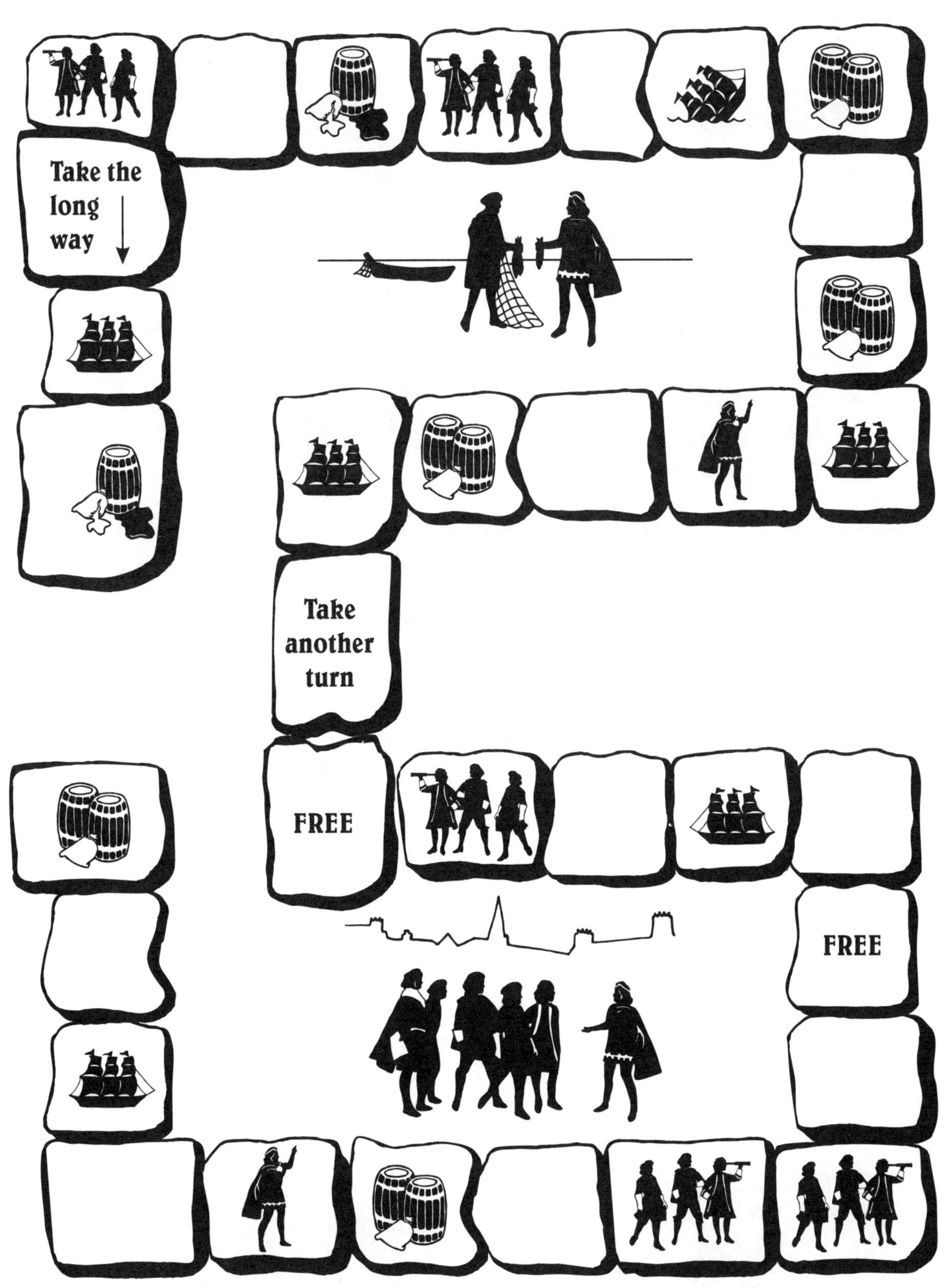

Take the long way
Take another turn
FREE
FREE

Make five copies of this page.

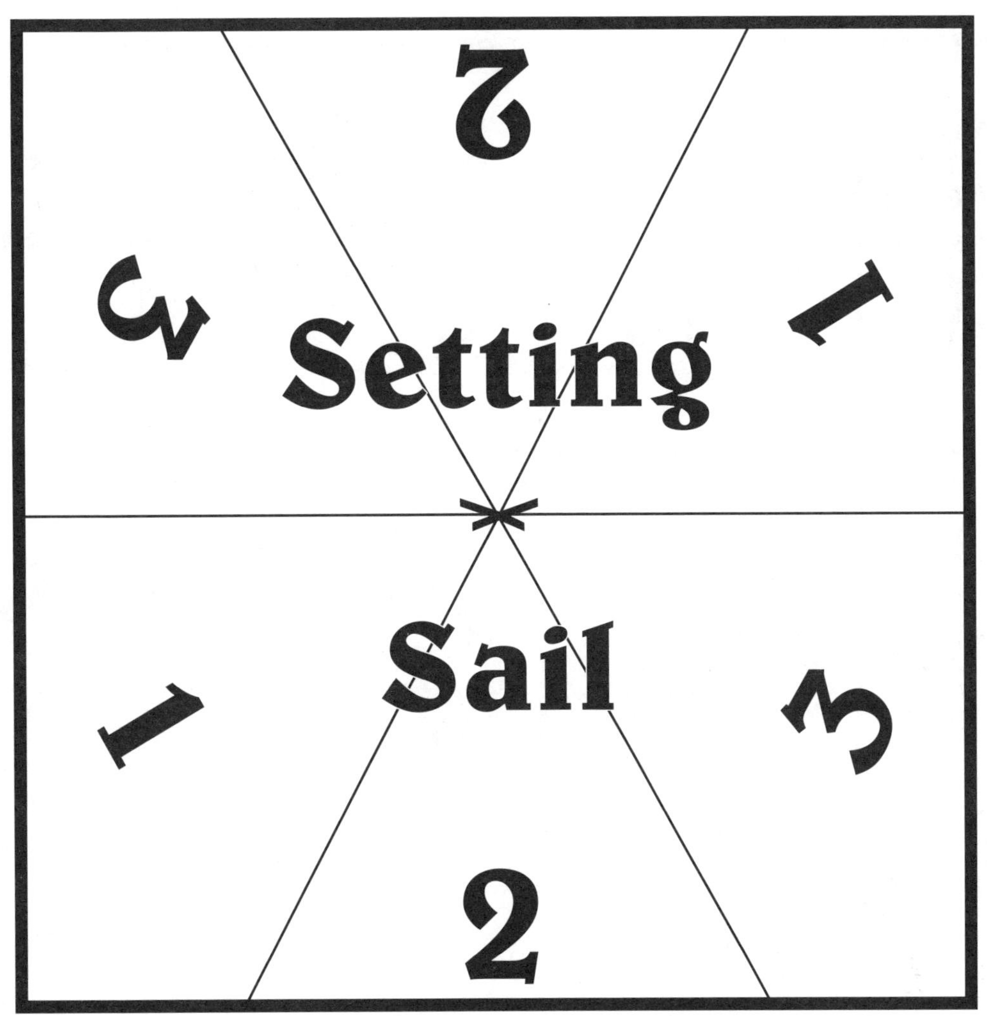

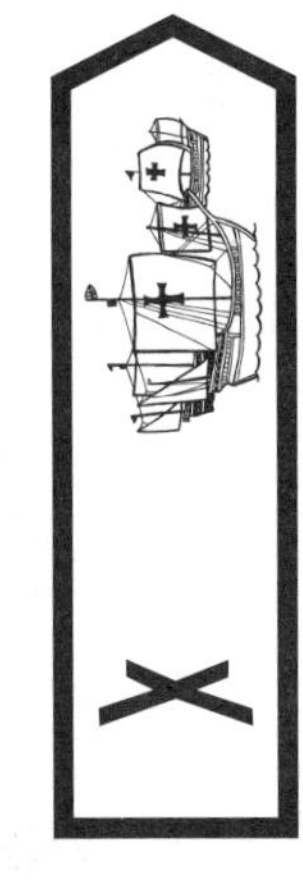

If you land on these squares, take a card.

Ships needed to cross the ocean

Sailors needed to sail the ships

Supplies needed for the long trip

If you land on these squares, put back a card.

Ship that got a leak

Sailor that turned back

Food that was spoiled

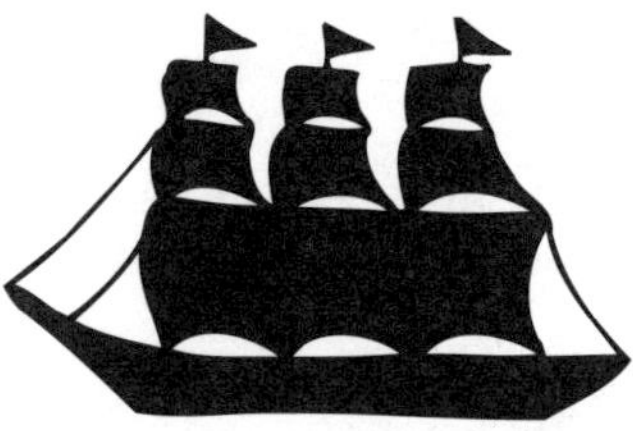

Journey to

JAMESTOWN

ATLANTIC

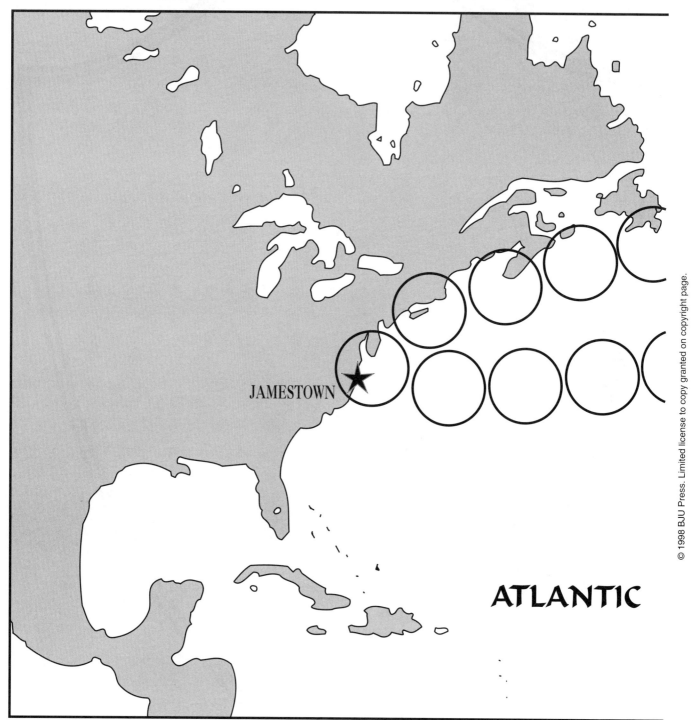

Jamestown

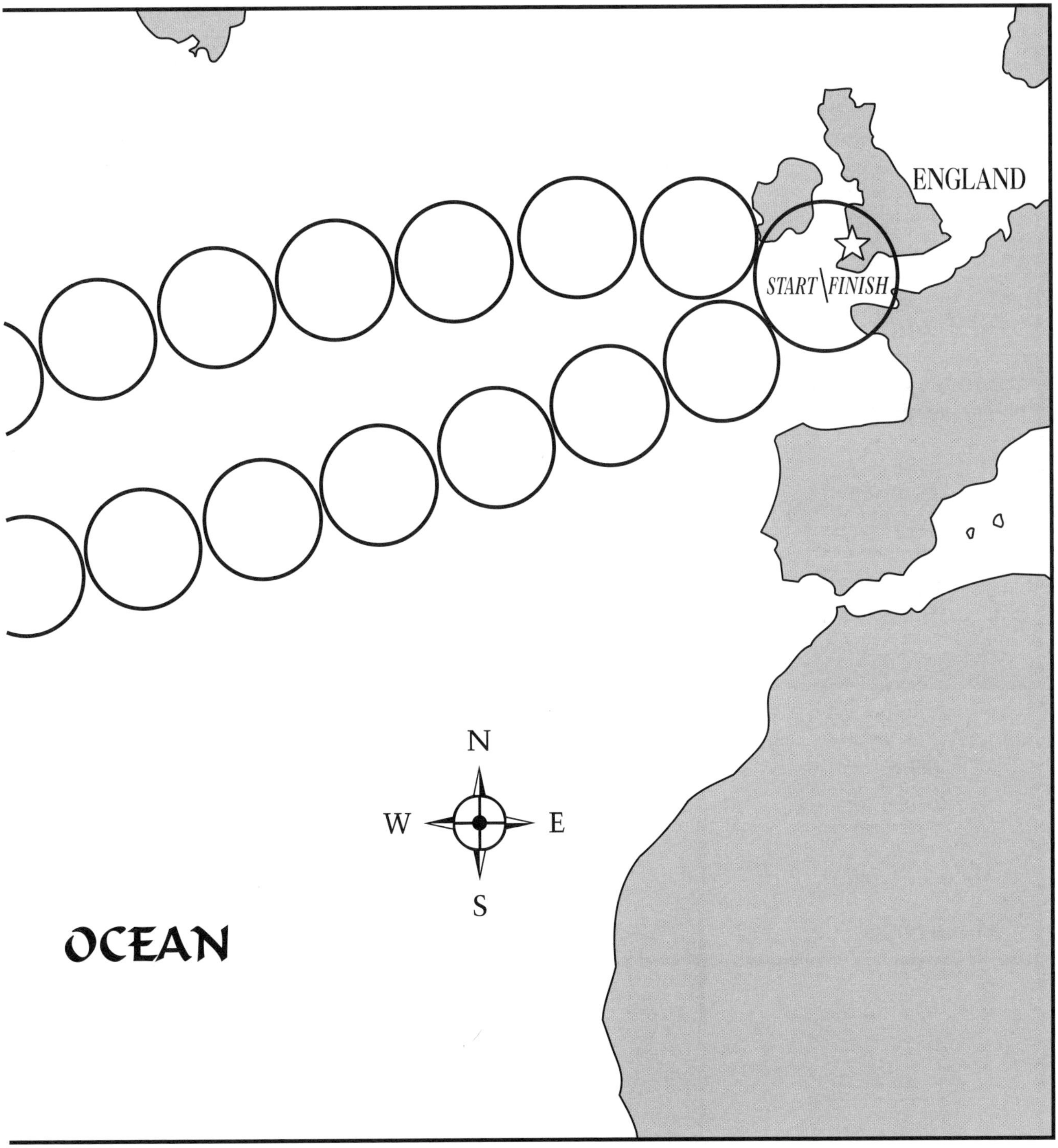

ENGLAND

START \ FINISH

N

W

E

S

OCEAN

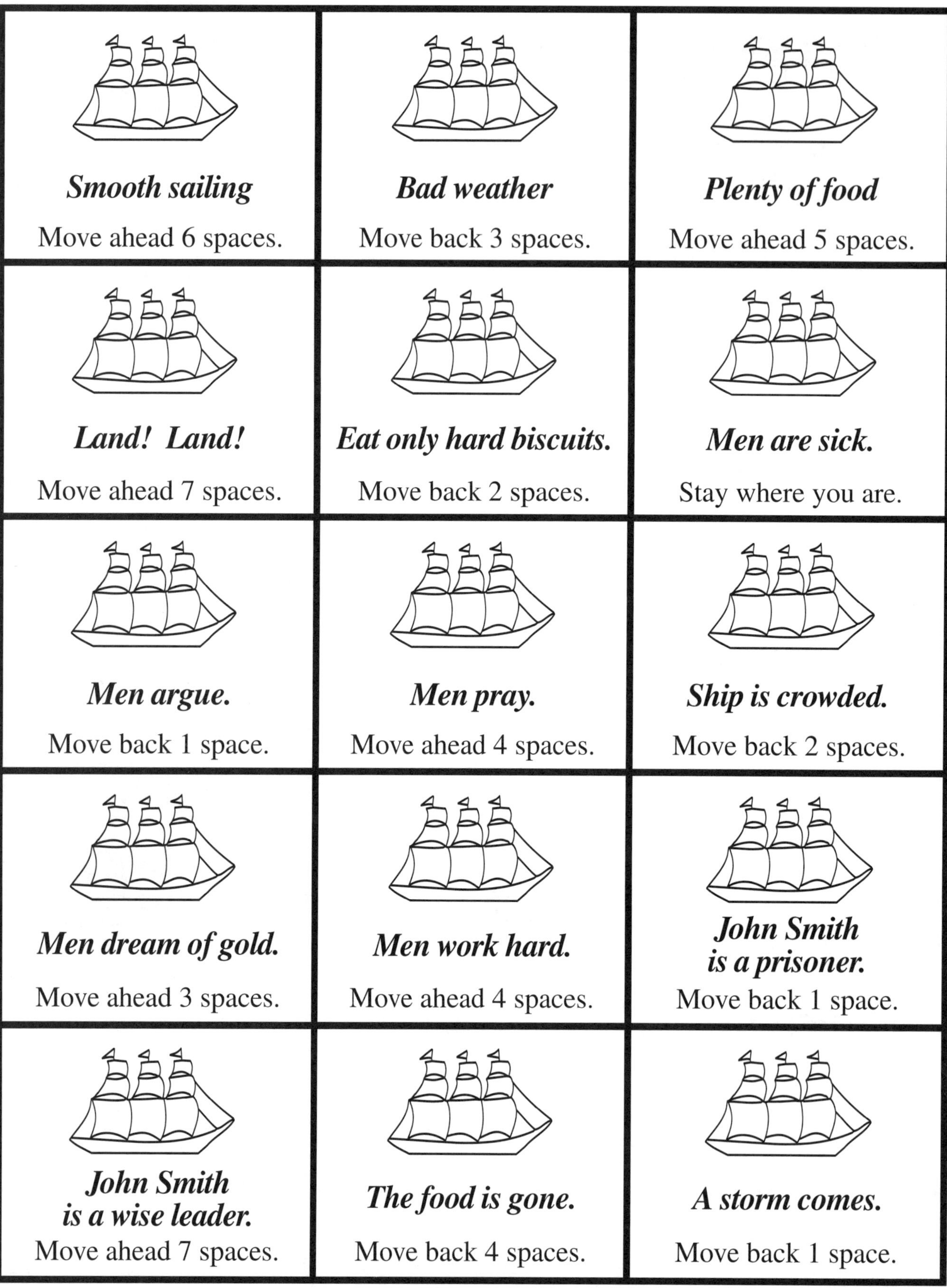

Smooth sailing
Move ahead 6 spaces.
Bad weather
Move back 3 spaces.
Plenty of food
Move ahead 5 spaces.
Land! Land!
Move ahead 7 spaces.
Eat only hard biscuits.
Move back 2 spaces.
Men are sick.
Stay where you are.
Men argue.
Move back 1 space.
Men pray.
Move ahead 4 spaces.
Ship is crowded.
Move back 2 spaces.
Men dream of gold.
Move ahead 3 spaces.
Men work hard.
Move ahead 4 spaces.
John Smith is a prisoner.
Move back 1 space.
John Smith is a wise leader.
Move ahead 7 spaces.
The food is gone.
Move back 4 spaces.
A storm comes.
Move back 1 space.

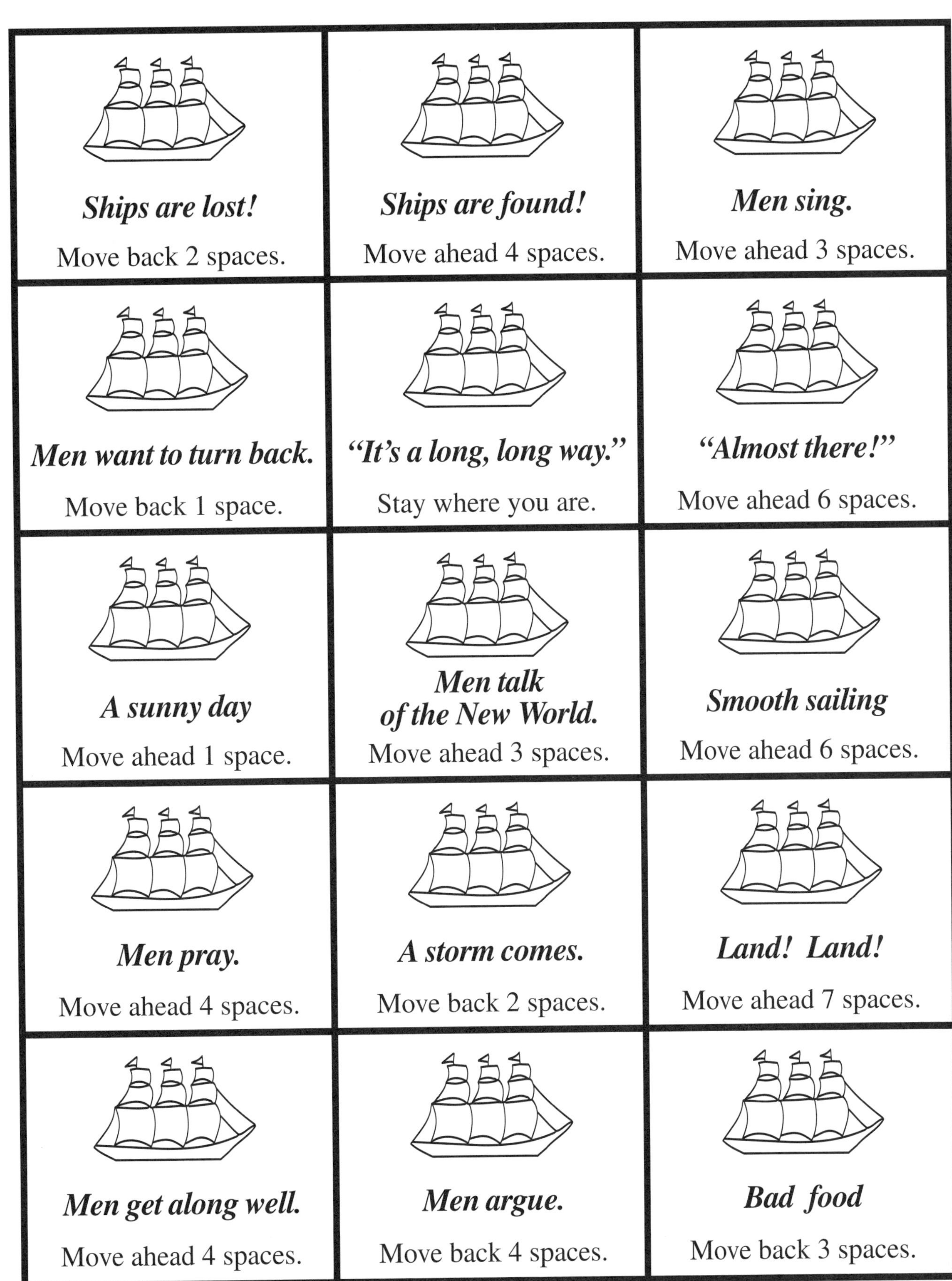
Ships are lost!
Move back 2 spaces.
Ships are found!
Move ahead 4 spaces.
Men sing.
Move ahead 3 spaces.
Men want to turn back.
Move back 1 space.
"It's a long, long way."
Stay where you are.
"Almost there!"
Move ahead 6 spaces.
A sunny day
Move ahead 1 space.
Men talk of the New World.
Move ahead 3 spaces.
Smooth sailing
Move ahead 6 spaces.
Men pray.
Move ahead 4 spaces.
A storm comes.
Move back 2 spaces.
Land! Land!
Move ahead 7 spaces.
Men get along well.
Move ahead 4 spaces.
Men argue.
Move back 4 spaces.
Bad food
Move back 3 spaces.

Use with Lesson 20.

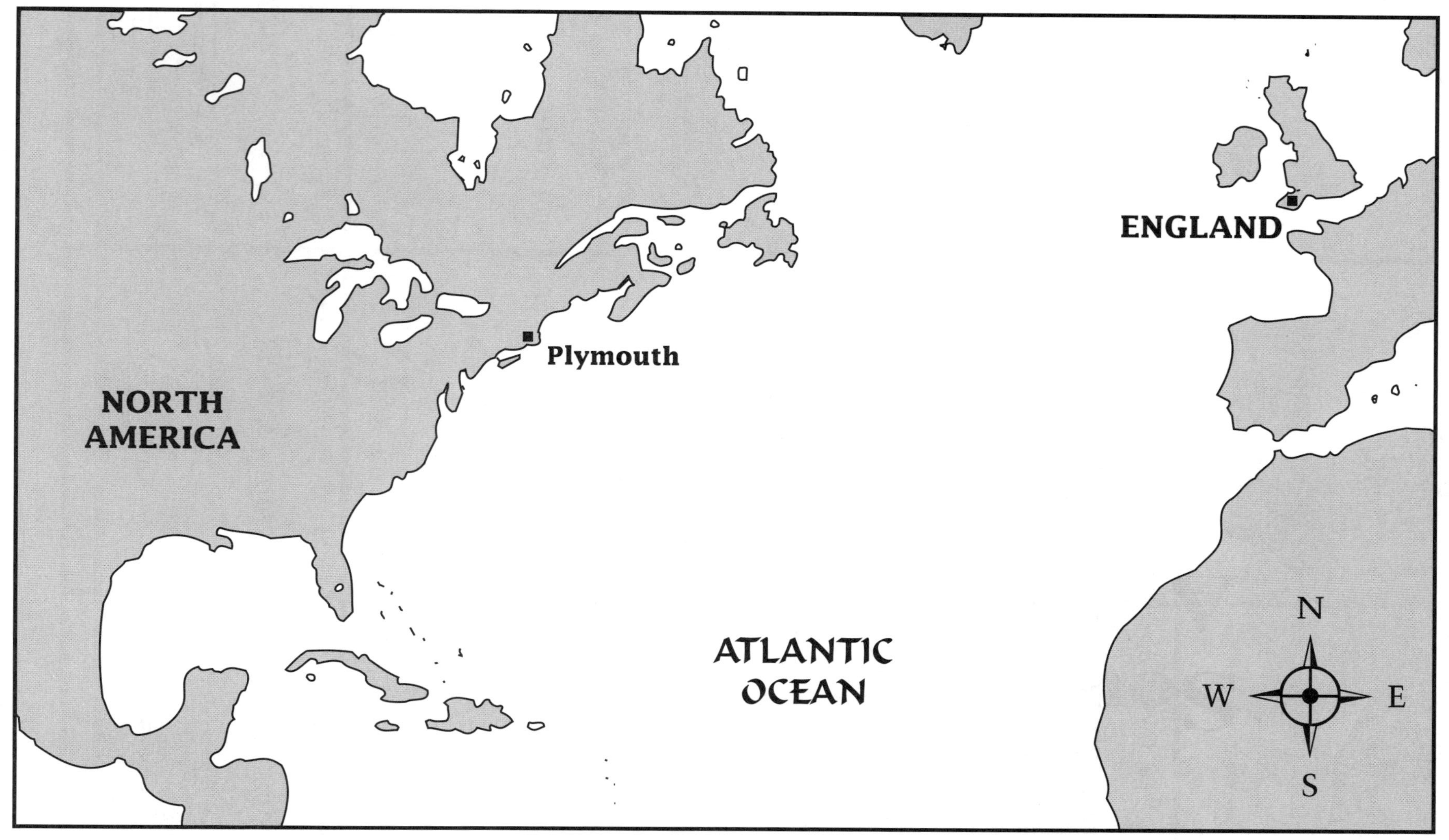
NORTH
AMERICA
Plymouth
ENGLAND
ATLANTIC
OCEAN
N
W
E
S

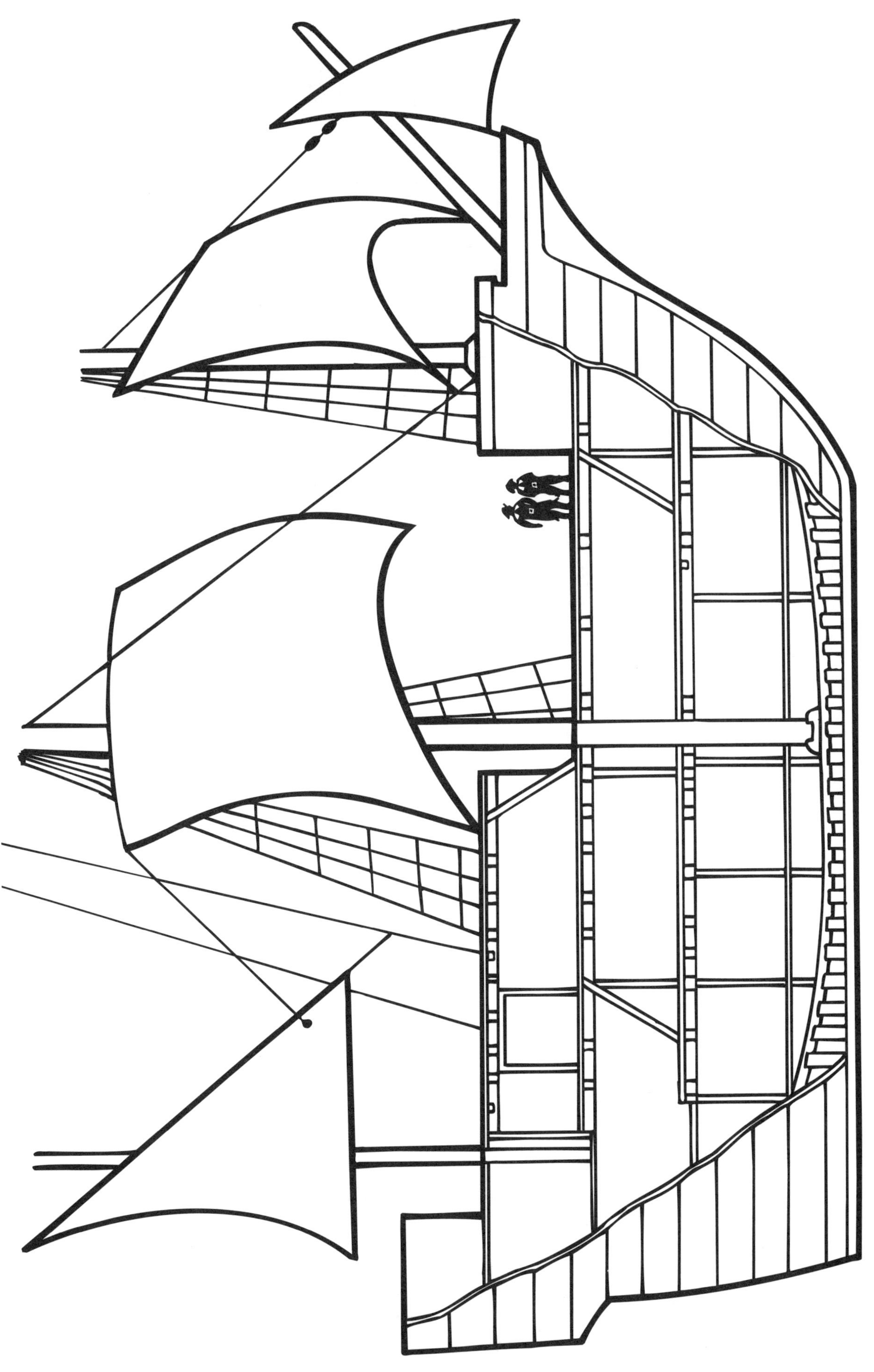

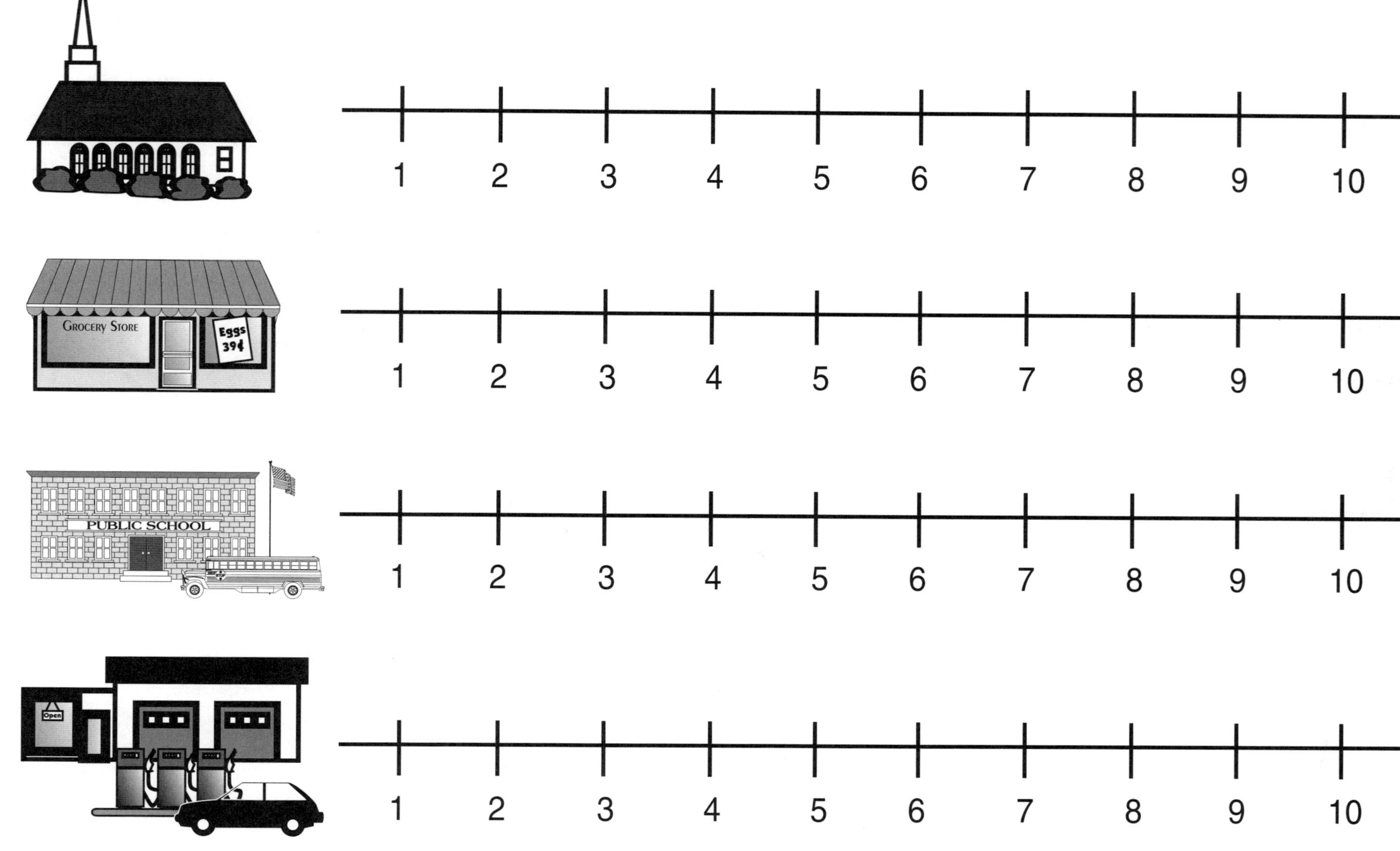

1 2 3 4 5 6 7 8 9 10
GROCERY STORE
Eggs 39¢
1 2 3 4 5 6 7 8 9 10
PUBLIC SCHOOL
1 2 3 4 5 6 7 8 9 10
Open
1 2 3 4 5 6 7 8 9 10

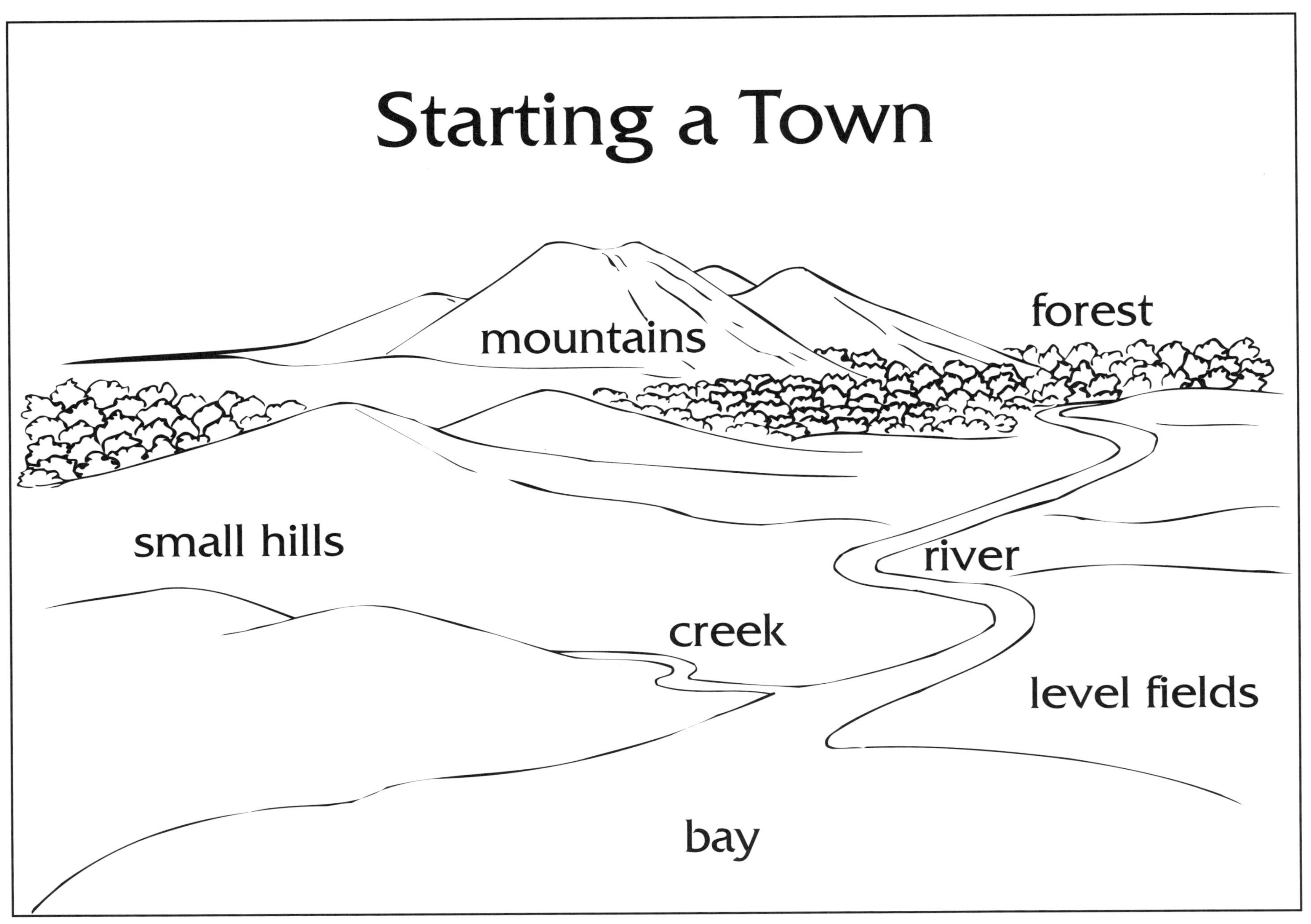
Starting a Town
mountains
forest
small hills
river
creek
level fields
bay

Voting on Rules

Rule 1

1	2	3	4	5	6	7	8	9	10	11
12	13	14	15	16	17	18	19	20	21	22

Rule 2

1	2	3	4	5	6	7	8	9	10	11
12	13	14	15	16	17	18	19	20	21	22

Rule 3

1	2	3	4	5	6	7	8	9	10	11
12	13	14	15	16	17	18	19	20	21	22

Make two copies of this page.

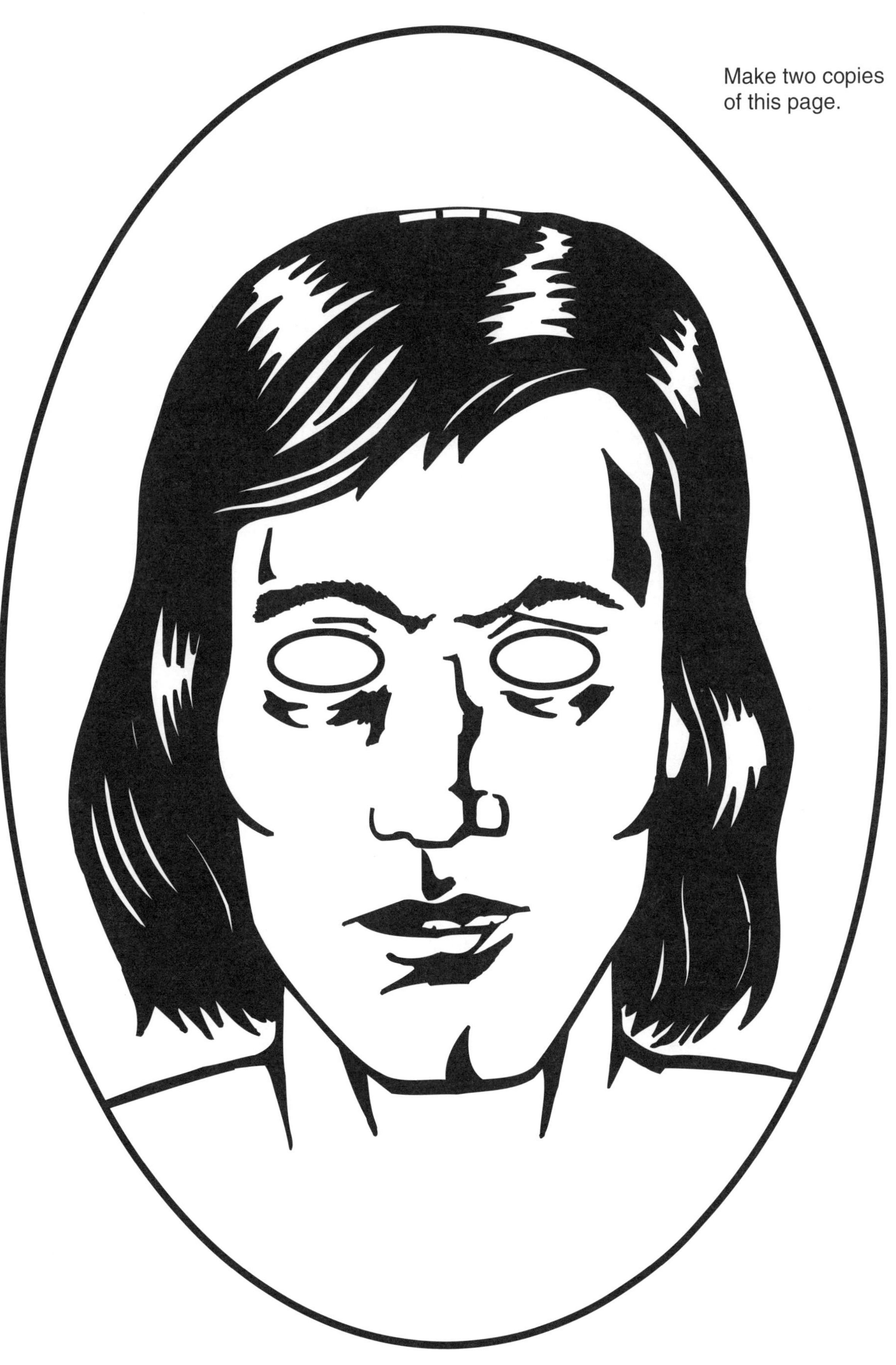

Let's Trade!

Let's trade!

Let's trade!

Your **hat** ____________________

For my ____________________.

Let's trade!

Let's trade!

Your **jar** ____________________

For my ____________________.

Let's trade!

Let's trade!

Your **blocks**____________________

For my ____________________.

Complete the sentence.

My wampum necklace has ______ white beads,

______ red beads, ______ blue beads,

______ green beads, and ______ black beads.

I would like to trade my wampum necklace for these things. (Mark two things with an *X*.)

- ❑ candy
- ❑ pencil
- ❑ stickers
- ❑ socks
- ❑ ring
- ❑ yo-yo

The Indians probably traded wampum for these things. (Mark five things with an *X*.)

- ❑ hammer
- ❑ blanket
- ❑ corn
- ❑ candles
- ❑ metal spoons
- ❑ wood and metal buckets
- ❑ moccasins
- ❑ mirrors
- ❑ brooms

My wampum necklace looks like this. (Draw a picture.)

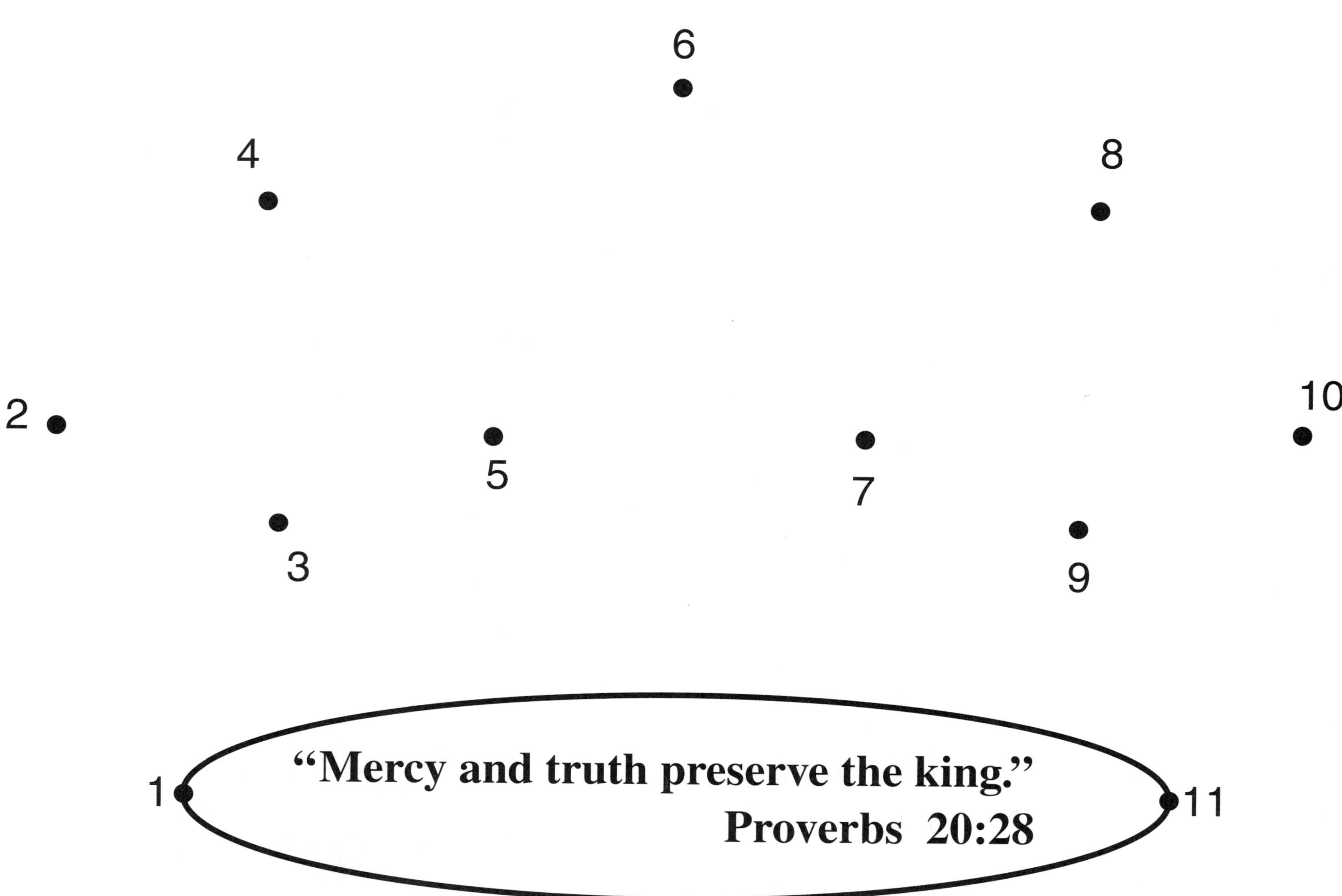
6
4
8
2
10
5
7
3
9
1
"Mercy and truth preserve the king."
Proverbs 20:28
11

Mississippi River

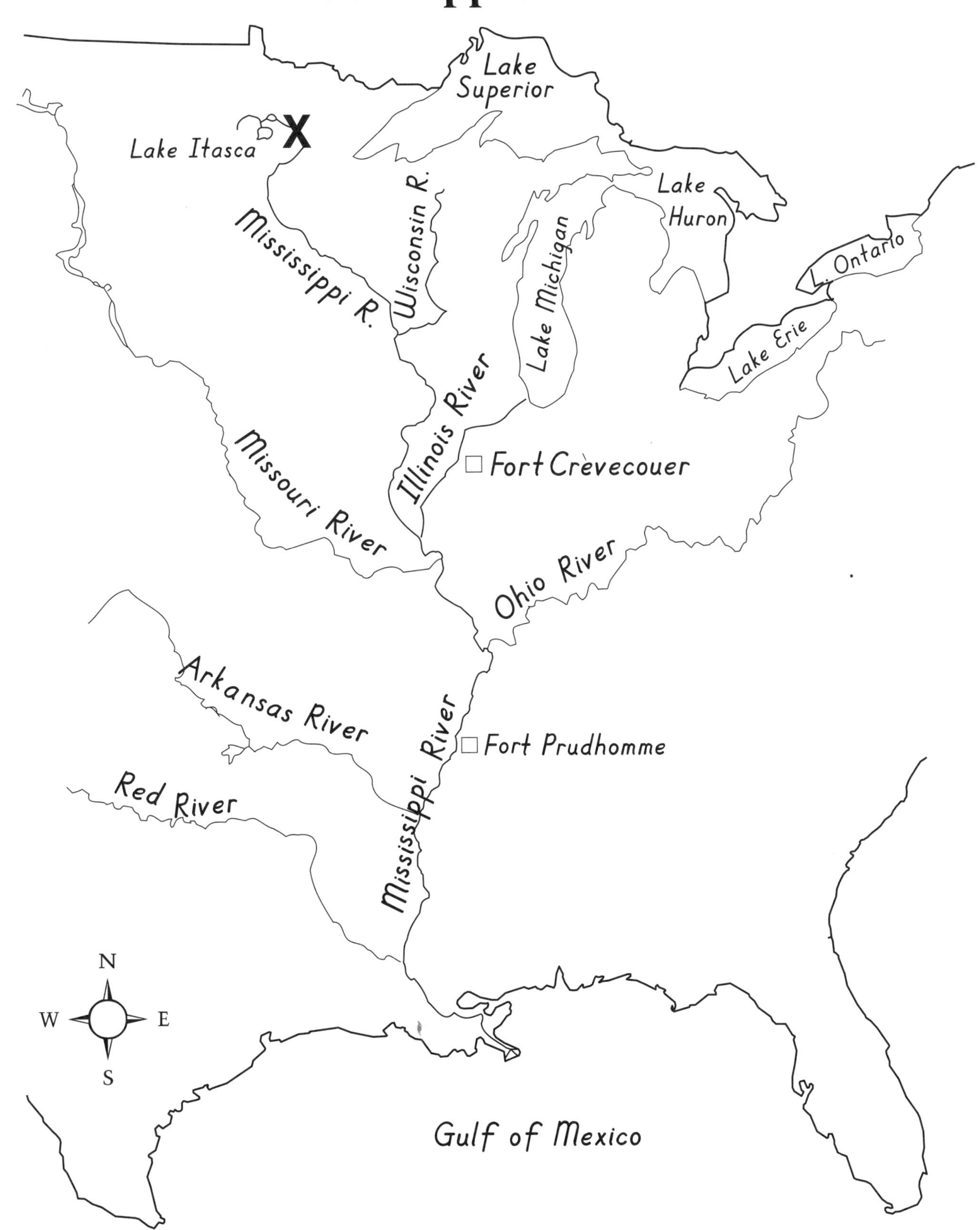
Lake Superior
Lake Itasca
X
Wisconsin R.
Mississippi R.
Lake Huron
Lake Michigan
L. Ontario
Lake Erie
Illinois River
Fort Crèvecouer
Missouri River
Ohio River
Arkansas River
Fort Prudhomme
Mississippi River
Red River
N
W
E
S
Gulf of Mexico

Indian Sign Language

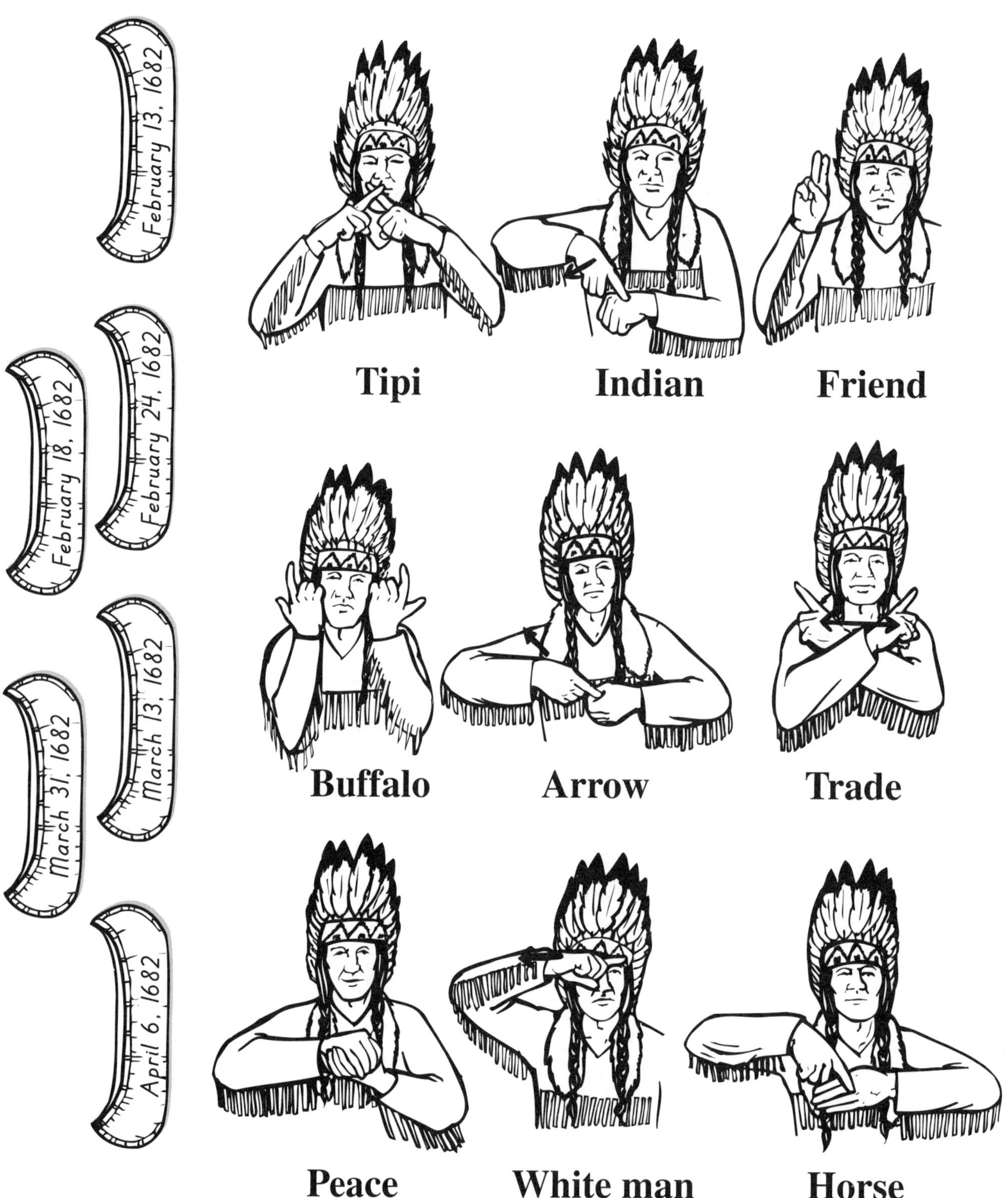

Psalm 23

1. The ______________ is my ______________________;

   I shall ________ want.

2. He maketh me to ____________ down in ________________

   ________________________: He leadeth me

   beside the __________________ ____________________.

3. He restoreth my __________: He leadeth me in the __________

   of ____________________________ for his name's sake.

4. Yea, though I walk through the valley of the shadow of death,
   I will fear no evil: for thou art with me; thy rod and thy staff
   they comfort me.

5. Thou preparest a table before me in the presence of mine
   enemies: thou anointest my head with oil; my cup runneth over.

6. Surely goodness and mercy shall follow me all the days of my life:
   and I will dwell in the house of the Lord for ever.

Who is in the story? ____________________

Where does this person live?	What food does this person eat?
What clothes does he wear?	Who gives him love?

Camping Out

"Billy," said Mother, "you need to finish your toast and get ready for the camping trip."

food **shelter** **clothing** **love**

"I can't wait to set up our new tent."

food **shelter** **clothing** **love**

"I can't forget to pack the marshmallows to roast over the fire."

food **shelter** **clothing** **love**

"Don't forget to pack an extra sweater too," Mother said. "It could get very cold tonight."

food **shelter** **clothing** **love**

"Oh, I'm not worried about getting cold. My friends and I will be having too much fun to get cold."

food **shelter** **clothing** **love**

Mother smiled. "Well, be sure to take your Bible too. You wouldn't want to leave God out of your camping trip."

food **shelter** **clothing** **love**

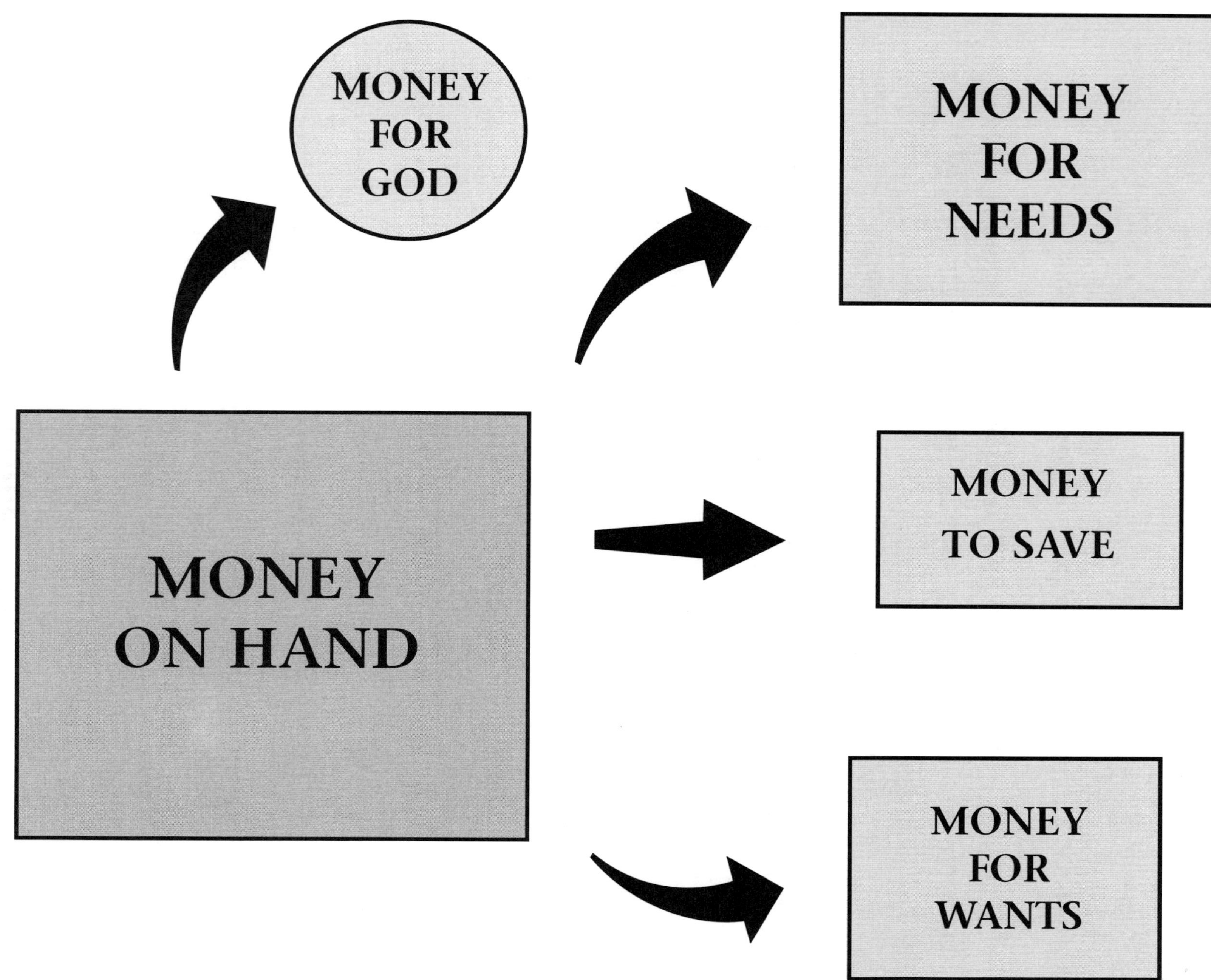
MONEY
ON HAND
MONEY
FOR
GOD
MONEY
FOR
NEEDS
MONEY
TO SAVE
MONEY
FOR
WANTS

5¢
6¢
5¢
4¢
2¢
3¢
7¢
4¢
10¢
5¢

Family Group Sheet

Husband

Wife

Children

1.

2.

3.

4.

5.

6.

7.

8.

Grandmother

Grandfather

Mother

Me

Father

Grandmother

Grandfather

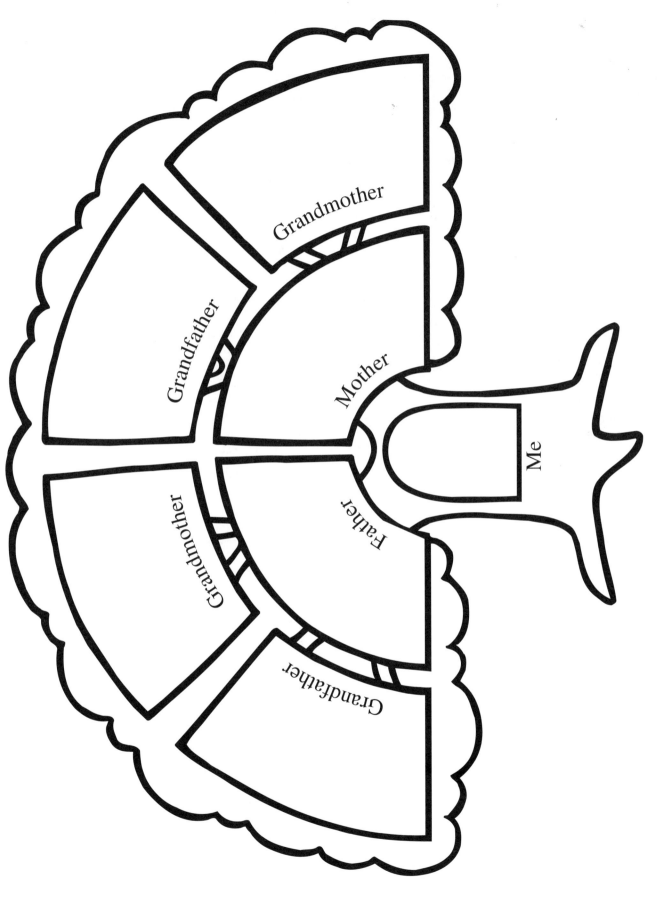

INDEX